IN THE COMPANY OF COPS
Jamie Newbold

Published by CopWorld Press
642 E. Main Street
Ashland, OR 97520
email: sales@copworldpress.com

Book design: Michael Campbell
Cover design: L. Redding

Cataloging In Publication Data is available from the publisher upon request.
ISBN: 978-1-946754-11-0

In the
COMPANY
of
COPS

W.E.C.A.N.

JAMIE
NEWBOLD

This book is dedicated to my retired police detective wife, Kim; my police officer son, Michael; and all the SDPD cops I worked with who put up with the stress and grind and hate and bullshit on The Job.

Contents

Tribute

TIM FAY AND JOHN TANGREDI passed during the nearly two years I spent on this book. Tim suffered from brain cancer and I was fortunate to have his Beach team and WECAN partner Cinda Jauregui get me in contact with him. Despite the crippling effects on Tim's mind and body, cancer did not stop him from perking up when I asked if he'd contribute to this work. His wife commented to him within earshot of the phone that any conversation with a former police officer could put a strain on him. "Nonsense," he replied, "I want to talk to Jamie." I was happy for him because he was enthusiastic about sharing his stories. He died three weeks later.

John was a different matter. I had little contact with him after he retired. I did bump into him at a party and learned that he was done with his San Diego life. He moved to New York and Florida after he retired. None of his old WECAN buddies had any further contact with him. He'd cut ties to all of us for a new life.

Tim and John were honest, determined, and smart cops. I salute these two extraordinary brothers-in-arms.

Introduction

This project began as a tribute to one of San Diego's most entertaining and admired police officers. An old Facebook post resurfaced from SDPD Detective Mo Parga. Mo had solicited stories about veteran officer RD Brown for another officer collecting them for some tome he was working on. I misread the post and cobbled together an eight-page memoir. When Mo straightened out my confusion, I wondered what to do with my work. I put in more time at a keyboard and watched eight pages balloon into twenty.

I decided the story needed a little more oomph to get any publication to print my stuff. I unloaded my memory banks and then asked, beseeched, begged and cajoled other SDPD officers to contribute. I collected stories about RD and the tellers of tales, too. Men and women who knew me contributed, some with reluctance, because they knew me too well. I had to convince them I meant no harm and worked without a vendetta. Others trusted I'd do what I said and gave me memories that were insightful and truthful accounts that I'd never have gathered without their efforts.

The typing and the recollections poured out in such volume that I had the revelation that this could be a book. This project was the book I always had in me.

As for Robert Dean "RD" Brown, every police department has one. The salty Vietnam veteran turned cop who grew into a legacy. RD was the hard-playing, hard-partying sportsman with broad shoulders and a powerful back to carry all the drama he'd engaged in over a thirty-plus year career. He was as whiplash a savage with his wit as he was smart-alecky with his biting jabs at just about everyone. RD was an equal-opportunity prankster. Anyone was a target for a smart-ass, well-timed barb from a guy that was both admired and intimidating all at the same time.

For years, cops would change-out their uniform nameplates donning bootleg RD Brown name tags for fun or practical jokes. I have no idea how many police contacts were recorded by the Department involving an RD Brown, but I know they were more than several men could have generated.

RD was a stocky six-footer with seeming casualness when it came to the maintenance of his physique. His challenge was to play as hard as he wanted in sports and in life. He engaged the world on his terms. His vices didn't weigh heavy on his daily decisions. One example was his strange balance when he worked out. More than once I shared the Western Division gym with RD, watched him put effort into a challenging session of bench presses and then rest with a cigarette between sets. He was shameless and a kidder at the same time. In another life I could picture him as both a demolition foreman and a high school football coach.

I found the matter of pinning down an exact description of RD's character to be tough. Many of the cops I know who knew RD only recalled him as an extremely macho man with a tough, jock charisma. In tighter circles, some fellow cops relate to moments where his facade was lowered, and he displayed a large heart for children in precarious situations. Any abusive parent connected to a crying or scared child needed to stay as small as possible to escape his wrath. RD loved young children. I likened him to a knight in shining armor when it came to the protection of a child in the throes of parental discord. RD was a cop's cop, but a father too.

I'm generally good at matching doppelgangers to people's profiles. Despite denials from non-believers, I always thought RD looked like a better-looking Dick Butkus, especially as he got older. RD had a quick-draw sense of humor, able to jab somebody with a stinger faster than anyone I'd ever seen. He matched the wit, timing and speed of a satirical Don Rickles. If a poor unsuspecting target, cop or civilian, provided any excuse in attire, mannerism or poor timing, RD's sharp zingers put him or her on the spot. He prodded people in good fun in public and never purposely tried to hurt anyone. He did remind guys like me that you could never beat him at his own game. Any attempts at one-upmanship released more mockery then most people could take. He was the kind of guy you respected because of his biting sense of humor tempered with a sense of fair-play and openness. Most cops would have been kindling in the acerbic fires of the master satirist.

Nobody ever wanted to be on RD's radar if he had dirt on them. He was especially rough on the guys with unchecked egos. Those guys got both barrels of his wit and were as likely to disappear in his presence as stand by and take the beat-down. Truly awful cops, or cops with smudged reputations, could expect an occasional earful, so most were mindful not to bring attention to themselves if RD was around. I've even seen ranking command-types, lieutenants and higher, actually make U-turns when they saw an unavoidable RD moving in their direction. The people he despised probably stayed clear. I listened to more than one revelation from RD about some guy responsible for a bonehead move or decision he could never outlive.

RD became my hero. A part of me wanted to emulate the late, great man. In order to achieve even a percentage of his character I'd have to spend two decades as a cop just to come close. I injected RD Brown levity into any encounter or confrontation whenever a smartass comment was warranted.

I'd hired onto the San Diego Police Department out of curiosity and because I needed a career. When I chose to be a cop I had only the vaguest of ideas about the job. I came from the generation that learned most of the stuff about the police from television. My parents brought me up to respect the police, so what I saw on television, I interpreted as mostly good. Whether I watched an old Western or a drama on the streets of a large metropolitan city the cops were mostly white males and all good guys. Oh sure, some were grizzled street veterans with gruff exteriors, but their blood all ran with the same desire to do right. If not for their department or some lick boot lieutenant, at least for the guest star victim of that evening's show.

The shows that stepped away from the time-honored plain clothes detective and put uniforms on the screen in the late 1960s were sanitized for family hours. *Adam 12* took viewers to boulevards of Los Angeles and portrayed two-dimensional images of patrol officers. The show rarely acknowledged the true hatred and violence that embodied the problems the LAPD struggled to come to terms with. Innovative dramas like *Police Story* that was created by Joseph Wambaugh took the audience into a world more closely resembling what true police officers of various ranks had to put up with. The writers dipped into characters with coarse personalities and borderline burnout disorders. Some of the openly heroic cops were characterized with personal and family problems, written as they existed in real life.

Both movies and television were incapable of encapsulating what fiction writers could in novel form. A cop's shift consisted of eight hours of mundane tedium, punctuated by sudden adrenaline surges that spun up the officers when they jumped into life-endangering action. The more stoic cops steeled themselves for violent confrontations and then unwound at the local cop-friendly bar.

Joseph Wambaugh's red-hot police novels and non-fiction tales got us closer, with less sensationalism and more realism derived from true experiences. They helped readers picture the characters and made them wonder what they would do if faced with the same dilemmas.

I took the police officer job because I had little else challenging to do. I was a blue-collar construction worker with a couple years of junior college, some street-smarts, and a great deal of energy. I took the written exam to be a cop two times before I put my head right and learned from my mistakes.

On the first test, my score was average. The numbers were high enough to pass and move me to the next level, but not above average enough to sell myself to the San Diego Police Department. The City of San Diego's rules required re-applicants to wait six months before they could take the written test again. I did my time working at an outdoor sign company to make a living. The second written test elevated my score to a decent middle of the pack rating. This time I went much further with a battery of physical, psychological, background and medical tests.

I breezed through most of it until I hit the medical. I got the shock of my life when diagnosed with an irregular heartbeat. I'd thought I was a top-notch physical specimen. There was no way anything was wrong with my heart. But there was, according to the Medical Liaison at the police department.

I worked for a Solana Beach, California based construction company called Ledford Stonewall. One of the partner-owners gave me permission to miss some work so I could get my heart examined. My income was bottom scale. I needed an EKG and was without the necessary cash or insurance to pay for it. I got over the hump by paying a stipend at the Mission Bay Free Clinic. The pro bono doctor sat with me in a private room to read the results.

I was a case of wavering nerves. Not only could my heart remove me from the SDPD depth chart, but I might be unhealthy and in mortal danger. My luck withstood though. I was given an explanation that jived with the medical term "arrhythmia." The test revealed that I had an extra heartbeat about every seven strokes. Da dum-da dum-da dum-DUM da-dum. The doc said it had no unhealthy impact on my circulatory system or my future health. I took his paper results back to Medical and awaited the green light to be hired.

Luck and timing are profoundly indifferent entities. The City's Medical garrison took their sweet time reviewing my status. The medical personnel funneled their decision to the police department's medical equivalent. They finally called with the proverbial good news/ bad news situation.

The City's sign-off on my heart exam was great news. I'd breached all the hurdles to hiring. I was ready to attend the police academy and be a cop. Except that my application period had just expired, and I'd have to go back through the whole process again.

I cursed the fates for a while. I'd already spent a year getting to this point and was sidelined again.

Police work was never a dream job for me. A high school friend of mine wanted it more than I did but he challenged me to cut my hair and make the effort. I applied alongside him for the same position somewhat ambivalently, but by the second series of application processes I was all in. I took the challenge fate had faced me with and went through the process, beginning to end, a third time. I had a chip on my shoulder and wanted a win.

I had the advantage of awareness now. I knew every aspect of the getting in processes. From the written test on I breezed past and got my job. I'd faced down the feeling of impending disappointment during the stressful wait time by concentrating on staying busy and out of trouble.

I wasn't born to be a cop, I made myself into one.

My new life started when I stepped into classroom orientation for day one of the San Diego Police Academy.

The stories included in this book are the ones I clearly recalled or put together from some of the book's contributors. My stories were either tattooed in place, or triggered by conversations with other officers, mostly retired. When I wrote the words, I moved back in time. The storytelling and word arrangement became cathartic. My concentration and mental energy were centered on the keyboard and written word. Hunting down more stories became like an addiction. I probably annoyed a few of my retired buddies. I tended to join groups of retirees who didn't know me well, always with paper and pencil nearby. There were often men and women who either wanted to forget, wanted no part of what I was doing, or just didn't give enough of a shit to contribute. Even my former work partners had some questions before they committed.

I had a reputation. I was either surly and over-aggressive, or part of the group of clowns that plagued the sergeants and lieutenants who we said wore their pants too tight. Some were wary and feared I bore a grudge against the department. I do not. I take responsibility for the acts I could control. My career was cut short due to injuries that I've never completely recovered from. I put my mind to work and treated my writing like an obsession. When I knuckled down, I created the *Forensic Comicologist*, a published book about owning a comic book business. There are pitfalls for anyone into collecting comic books. My book addresses the potential civil and criminal issues and how to fight back when confronted with them. That task, and the editorial lessons learned, taught me the basics that an author needs to get off the ground.

I like my first book. The written word became a tool for me to wield and it was mine. Writing put me in a zone where I could produce, not only a sequel, but the cop stories I always wanted to write. Those stores have resulted in a thousand pages of memories and stories.

I was an untested writer and an unknown. I had to chop the book into four parts to whittle the contents down to a workable size. *In the Company of Cops: W.E.C.A.N.* is the initial outcome.

CHAPTER 1:

ORIGIN

ROBERT DUVALL caught a round to the chest and slumped to the ground. Sean Penn held him in terror as his life drained away.

"Have some… somebody call my wife," gasped Duvall, prone on his back on the dirty hillside under the spotlight of a hovering police helicopter. Penn knelt beside his partner proving their relationship had bonded after all. He screamed into the crowd of officers and gangsters for someone to call an ambulance.

"I'm gonna rest my head a minute." Duvall was short of breath and stared into the bright light as he struggled to get his bearings. Penn opened Duvall's uniform shirt and revealed a pooling blood stain above his heart.

"…catch my breath… I'll be ready to roll in a minute."

"Stay calm," Penn pleaded. He fought back his tears and the panic of helplessness. "Stay calm," he almost demanded in absolute disbelief. How did this happen? The cops had everything under control, it seemed. The tendons in Penn's neck stood out against his taut skin, his pulse quickened as Duvall slowly slipped away.

Duvall's fate was out of his hands and the desperate Penn could only weep and howl in his emotional pain. Duvall's words were faint and reduced to wheezing and gurgle. The words on screen were no longer coherent. The audience watched a seminal death scene all police officers dread. The loud blades of the helicopter chopped at the air and drowned out some of the sounds on the ground. The light from above became the beacon for the angels to take Duvall home. Penn screamed at the sky.

This was the scene that made both men sympathetic characters in the movie, *Colors*. The CRASH cops had surrounded a gang party on the slope of an urban hillside. The gangsters were upset with the cops and one particularly inebriated individual triggered a rifle round hitting

Duvall's chest. He was the "good cop" that countered Penn's "bad cop" image. The underlying theme was LA's cool uniformed gang enforcement unit.

The Los Angeles Police Department's CRASH unit in the movie was modeled after the real deal in the LAPD that was designed to stem the tide of gangsterism. The San Diego Police Department had put together a similar unit, WECAN, or Walking Enforcement Campaign Against Narcotics.

L.A.'s CRASH stood for Community Research Against Street Hoodlums and those hoodlums were almost exclusively gang members. While San Diego's WECAN had narcotics in its title, its concurrent enforcement goal was to interdict the criminal activities of street gangs.

The working theory of both departments was, that if specially selected officers brushed shoulders with street gangs, those soldier gangsters would either disconnect from the gang life or find crimes harder to commit. The trained officers could solve crimes from the "inside" because they knew the players from their day-to-day contacts. Say "Hi" to them often enough and their bad antics reduce in number. Suddenly, the gangs are off-balance and less capable of lives of crime. They are no longer able to operate in the shadows or with anonymity.

While L.A. dealt with their gang problems, the gangs continued to gain ground thanks to their harness over crack cocaine, their primary source of power and wealth. This new, illegal fuel ran through the blood system of countless Americans and wreaked havoc. Each city had to enact measures to retain as much of their waning control as possible through law enforcement. City after city, town after town, sought to push-back against the swell of crack monsters and the well-organized gangsters pushing the vile addiction.

San Diego suffered, too. The same pressures and influences that overwhelmed minority populations in L.A. harmed San Diegans. San Diego's relatively tiny police department had few tools to cope with an unexpected rise in gang activities that ripped into the city with wanton abandon. The understaffed Gang Unit merited more personnel and resources that were not forthcoming.

In 1986 the San Diego Police Department's Chief William Kolender wondered if police officers could be inserted into gang territories to dialog with the residents and build new relations. The SDPD had to build a hybrid team that was not an army, but effective at neighborhood deployment, much like community relations officers with a strong sense of anti-crime and anti-gang enforcement. San Diego's community policing programs already in place said it could be done. The department had the talented officers to deal with drugs and gangs. Southeastern Division already had a team in place that targeted specific gangs and their sales of crack cocaine and PCP.

Drive-by shootings entered the American lexicon thanks to the role cars played in L.A.'s mobile society. Before that, drive-by shootings were gimmicks in 1930s gangster movies. Los Angeles street gangs took the concept of Al Capone and his cronies to new lows, even taking "Capone" as a moniker. High-powered weapons and quick getaways lit up L.A. like a warzone. The only way to stop the carnage was to detach officers from patrol duty and "load the bases" with uniformed cops in the midst of the violent street thugs who seemed on the verge of holding entire neighborhoods hostage with fear and intimidation. This untenable situation was met with an aggressive stance from L.A. police officers that became an undesired response to the residents of South-Central Los Angeles who saw the cops as a gang unto themselves.

The SDPD sought to build a more community friendly intervention tool. The SDPD envisioned something like CRASH, but on a more personal level. They wanted uniformed officers to park their cars and walk through specific neighborhoods like old-school cops. The people living on those troubled blocks would see and, hopefully, get friendly with the same cops walking the same beats every day. It was to be equal parts crime-fighting and public relations. Drive-by killings were on the rise. Those incidents would evaporate if the guy or woman standing next to the targets carried badges, guns and authority. And maybe, just maybe, the people who shared the blocks with bad people would share the things they saw with the police. Maybe they'd get to know the local force with regard and trust that any information they imparted to the police would help keep them safe later.

San Diego's leaders shared a fear that the city was coming dangerously close to being under siege by platoons of gang members. The new reality that gangs and police officers were equally armed and organized was too great a fear to ignore. Money would have to be found and spent to combat gangs. San Diegans always assumed that if crime problems were bad in San Diego, the same crime problems were significantly worse in Los Angeles. Crack had made San Diego begin to look like a mini-Los Angeles. L.A. had long been experiencing drive-by shootings and now San Diego had them too. Homicides were up in both cities. San Diego could no longer point fingers at L.A. as a singularly violent city.

The San Diego Mayor at the time, Maureen O'Connor, okayed funds from the city coffers. The new Chief, Bob Burgreen, utilized the funds and drafted a single lieutenant, George Saldamando, to build a force chosen from patrol officers everywhere in the city. The lieutenant was a veteran SDPD gang detective and knew what the goals of the team should be. The officers chosen would be taken from applicants first, and by reputation next. The money was in place to outfit the chosen officers with vehicles and equipment available only for them. Gear, instructions and new attitudes would infuse the initial twelve officer team. Eventually, the unit would expand to thirty-six officers chosen for their superior self-motivation, expertise with gangs, narcotics enforcement and hardwired people skills. Few washed out of the unit.

Lieutenant Saldamando began the development process to create the features and game play of the unit, soon to be known as the Walking Enforcement Campaign Against Narcotics or WECAN. A Departmental Announcement was circulated to all the divisions inviting applicants from uniformed patrol officers. The first twelve would wear their uniforms and remain independent of normal police radio activity. These twelve would spend their workdays developing intelligence, making contacts with the citizens living on the blocks, and targeting the gangsters for prosecution. Theirs was the template they'd create for the next groups to adapt to and alter if change was warranted.

The goal was to win back the streets fully engulfed in gang violence and drug dealing. The gangs left too many victims and frightened people in their wakes. It was time to show the residents who wanted to live in peace that the police were going to give them a chance to live safely. A press conference introduced WECAN to the city. The city and the department wanted everyone to know WECAN was the single largest attempt by the city to address the neighborhood plague of drugs and gangs. The city broadcast with pride its elite force of dedicated officers motivated to re-enter unsafe streets with a new philosophy that abhorred fear and fought the gangs at their street level. These embedded officers would be approachable to the citizens in rough neighborhoods.

WECAN officers were in place to hear the citizen voices that were stifled because of where they lived. Homeowners and renters alike would have access to police officers eagerly appreciative of their resistance to the gangs and to gain the tidbits of information they'd slip to us. The officers would be detached from the distraction of radio calls and give the public absolute attention. If the problem was within our scope of function, we'd handle it. If it was outside of our duties, we'd funnel the problems through the department to whatever unit needed to deal with it.

WECAN officers would be approachable cops who could take the time to answer complaints and respond with successful actions. For the cops manning the posts, this would be a new phase for their careers. I was accepted into the team with the second wave of twelve officers. I'd found a new home.

CHAPTER 2:

THE NEW ARRIVAL

San Diego's Southeastern Division housed the largest concentration of gangs. The patrol cops knew which streets and which players needed the most attention. One of their most violent neighborhoods was the streets around Lincoln High School. That area was a test bed for the fledgling WECAN operatives. Foot patrols would begin shortly with hand-picked officers who already knew the homes and the players.

Roger Barrett was a product of "F Troop," the denigrating moniker for the SDPD's Western Division. The division was considered a backwater place to work where the prospects of promotion were slim. Western was an amalgam of neighborhoods and terrains, from low-income hilltop residents to tony beach front homes. Western had a lateral valley that is developed almost beyond capacity with shopping centers, office buildings, hotels, condos and car lots. The less-than-mighty San Diego River flowed west from San Diego's back country through Mission Valley and into the Pacific Ocean. San Diego's gay community traced its roots to the community of Hillcrest spread along the south rim of the valley's walls. Some of the town's oldest and most historic buildings were clustered along quaint avenues that have spectacular views of San Diego's harbor. The hordes of apartments and inexpensive homes east of Mission Hills housed three generations of locals and transplants. This North Park community was a "demonstration model" of development gone awry and the ceaseless problems from high-density living. For some reason, some clever cop figured out that this odd conglomeration of a police division had a sucky reputation for advancement within the SDPD. The feeling was that, once you got planted there, you could rarely go "up" to get out.

Roger policed these streets with a low feeling of relegation to the limits of change or promotion for cops at F Troop. F Troop was the name of a long-ago television show about a wilderness fort in the Old West manned by a bunch of screw-ups. Their unfortunate designation as a military unit was F Troop, as in 4F which means not fit for military duty. There was an F Troop atmosphere about Western Division where I was currently serving. I witnessed and felt the sense among some of my fellow officers that only the lucky could get out and pursue great careers and advancement in the ranks. The rest of us just collected paychecks and occupied car seats.

Nobody knew when or why Western was codified as a lost command. There's no origin point when some disgruntled Western cop called out the division as a place for losers and slackers. The place was so named when I came on board, two years before Roger appeared. For us, it was always F Troop; a place to escape from for career enhancement.

Roger and I barely knew each other during our Western tenure, even though they overlapped. Neither of us knew why Western had become the repository for "bad boys and girls." Certain transfers ended up at Western because they'd crossed swords with someone at previous commands. Others just got there by a spin of the wheel of fortune and got zapped straight to the career neutering division after graduating the academy. All I realized was people who were unceremoniously drummed out of other divisions got sent to Western.

I was sent there not long after my successful transit from the academy into patrol. I'd impressed no one and earned no general regard from the division I was soon to leave and the same would be true for Western Division. I was only taking up space at that command in lieu of some other officer a sergeant or lieutenant would have preferred. I cooled my heels at F Troop until I saw the announcement inviting officers to join WECAN. Roger concurred that his existence felt like mine. He wanted out.

Just being assigned to F Troop seemed to be the inescapable, implacable enemy to all things related to career advancement. When the WECAN announcement was released, Roger decided the new assignment could help his career. He scrutinized the bulletin and liked the goals of hitting gangs and drug dealers head on. He was over the daily thrill of shagging too many radio calls. Roger had life experiences when he became a cop, experiences that were much like mine. We were both educated and construction workers who figured police work would be better fits for us. Construction jobs in San Diego could be temporary and typically hard on the body in later years. Police work was steady and looked a lot more physically doable over a lengthy career than pounding nails.

Roger filled out the required transfer application and sent it on to its next destination in Field Operations Management, the unit that managed transfer applications. When he got the job, he cleaned out his locker at F Troop and moved to the temporary trailers that WECAN was provided for its centralization. Initially, the new team went through a variety of training. Roger and the others went through everything from working alongside K-9 units to tactical weapons training. The command wanted them to be better trained then anyone in uniform, save for SWAT. Roger was now a better-trained specialist, one among twelve within the first WECAN wave.

Roger surveyed the eleven men and women around him on his first meeting with this new WECAN unit. Most he did not know. Bill "Woody" Woods, my former Ocean Beach, Beach Team partner, was in the group. Woody was one of the other cops from Western who took his shot and got out. Nobody outside WECAN yet knew how vibrant the job would be, but Woody was excited to be on the team from the get-go. His instincts proved correct when he put in for the transfer. Roger knew him and they were made a pair and sent right back to F Troop turf to work Ocean Beach on behalf of WECAN's Mission, to hit the drug dealers and gang members where they lived. I was still working OB on the Beach team with a new partner. I bumped into the WECAN duo and listened aptly as Woody recited all the fun and good work they were doing.

"It's not that much different from all the pro-active stuff we did on the Beach Team. They want us to be aggressive and go after the dealers in the beach area. We're supposed to go after the gangs, too." Woody had admitted what I already knew that the beach dealers were not the gangster types WECAN wanted to stop. I didn't yet know Roger very well. He'd always been on opposite shifts from mine, so we didn't know each other as friends.

I applied to WECAN early enough that my command allowed me to go down to the Southeastern Team for a one-week "ride-along." I would partner up with a current WECAN officer, be tested, and learn if I could mesh with the others. WECAN seemed unusually selective about their "recruits." I sensed that the few months of the unit's existence had allowed the boss to flesh out the type of cop he wanted. There'd be no more grand cattle calls for any volunteers. From now on, applicants would be scrutinized, even by other WECAN officers. Roger was selected to be my partner for that week. Roger took me through the streets he'd only just become familiar with. I was already familiar with the area because I'd dated a girl from that part of town in the nineteen-seventies. For both of us F Troopers accustomed to Western's general middle-class opulence, Southeast San Diego seemed poorer, disrupted by gangs, poverty and racial divides. I established myself at WECAN with the unwitting help of one neighborhood Crip named Robert Hayes.

The first three days of WECAN were uneventful. Most of our adventures amounted to walking the streets around Lincoln High School, a hotbed of gang nastiness. It was on one of those streets that Roger had to explain the facts of life to me about this part of town.

Each house on one block had one wire hanging from the power and phone lines to that dwelling. I saw the thin strings of black spaghetti wire dangle lifeless as though they'd been professionally cut by someone and left there as a piece of urban art. Roger explained that he'd been on that street the day the cuts happened. The local cable television company had a guy on a cherry-picker snipping the wires to two different homes. Roger didn't need to ask why. This hard-hit, black and Hispanic neighborhood was filled with cable subscribers down on their luck. Once they missed a payment or two, they got their subscriptions cut-off, literally. Others were banned from service because they'd been caught pirating cable television. The process of cancellation by wire snips enveloped the entire block. The scene of all those dangling wires was, to me, like an indignity left behind to remind residents they were tarnished for being poor cable bill cheats.

I sat through my fourth WECAN line-up with Roger. A flyer was passed around about a wanted Crip gang member named Hayes. He was wanted for some felony drug charge and was considered important enough to warrant a wanted poster. Once in the field, I saw a guy, a rather large black man in his mid-twenties. The poster was a generic black and white photo with little to provide in the way of distinguishing characteristics. These kinds of posters are handed out constantly or pinned to walls all over every police station across the land. The likelihood of a sighting is as remote as viewing the star Alpha Centauri.

We were on the road less than fifteen minutes from the barn, another way of referring to the station, when I saw a guy who pinged my recognition skills. I told Roger I thought it was the guy from the wanted flyer. He looked doubtful, and then made the U-turn to find out. We stopped ahead of him and halted his advance. The man was dressed in an inordinate amount of blue, a heinous color for a red Piru gang zone. His choice of color could grant him a day of execution in this Piru stronghold. Pirus were the Blood set and archenemies of the Crips.

Roger flanked the guy in case of trouble, while I asked the man his name. He was a little nervous, but not the way a gang member usually gets nervous around cops. Being stopped by the police was a norm in his world. Roger and I were both veterans of the police job. Confronting a guy who might not relish the challenge of two cops meant we'd be better off if we stayed frosty to help him relax. After all, there was s no rush. If we took our time, then the chore might get done with less drama.

The man was poised as though he expected the question when I asked for ID. He tugged a wallet out of his pants pocket and produced his school identification card from seven years prior. The photo was a younger version of a man named Hayes. Roger's face tightened up. I think he thought this couldn't be happening. I looked Hayes in the eyes and asked his date of birth. He didn't flinch when it matched the information I'd seen earlier. I guess he knew that walking the streets would get him in trouble. I had the right guy!

I knew it. Roger begrudgingly accepted it and Hayes grew nervous knowing it. The whole time we detained Hayes he looked around like he expected something bad to happen to him, but not necessarily from us. Something else worried him. We hooked him up for the warrant. I was curious about why he was so easy to spot. He came clean that he knew he was wanted and wasn't bothered about being arrested. He explained that he'd been in that neighborhood since last night. He'd met a woman that brought him home to her place for a late-night tryst. There was plenty of boom-booming and too much Courvoisier. The cognac left him in dire straits in the morning and he woke too late to get his promised ride home.

He needed to get home to his turf. He was a gang member in enemy territory. Being a Crip stranded in Blood territory was more worrisome than getting picked up by the po-po. He caught the safest ride in town. Jail was better than dead, which he could well have been if the Bloods saw him. All that blue was an affront to their egos and a challenge to a turf war. I got my position with WECAN soon afterwards. Barrett never admitted he'd said anything about me to his boss. I don't know if they vetted me behind my back, but I assume that when I pulled the Hayes flyer off the wall with some sensationalism and said. "I got him," I might have gotten some notice.

There was an interim before they picked me up. Woody and Roger were paired up and assigned fledgling WECAN walking duty to assess the potential gang problem in Ocean Beach. I was back in OB after the WECAN tour. I bumped into those guys on duty one day and asked them how the unit treated them. Roger spoke first. "Sometimes we work Southeast," he said "and help that team out. Sometimes we work the Heights or go up to Northern to cover the WECAN team working those beaches."

Woody added, "We're all treated really well like we're special, or something. You've seen what we've been doing. You should put in, for sure." I was burned out on the Beach Team and way done with F Troop. I'd seen the light in that one week with Roger. I put in for the transfer and got picked-up in the second wave. I found out later that prospective members of the second wave were voted on by the members of the first twelve. Our names were written on the chalkboard and each name was given a thumbs-up, or a resounding no. I got the "up" thumb, but

I never bugged Woody or Roger about their decision. I assumed they stood up for me.

With the introduction of the second wave of twelve, the unit was growing out of its own skin. WECAN had money and a mandate that few officers will ever enjoy. However, our workstation in the beginning left a lot to be desired.

I was a stranger among a cadre of cops that were seemingly bonded, either through trial by fire, or friendships spanning their department time. Outside of Roger and Woody I knew none of the other team members. I'd been a uniformed patrol officer and then a beach cop with six years of street work under my belt. That's considered long enough to reach "veteran" status. I was expected to have my act together by five years, as are most cops. The assumption was that I'd do the WECAN job because I was ready.

The two teams were all crammed into rental trailers restructured to the specs of a police divisional facility. The first wave had shared quarters with the officers and investigators at Southeastern Division. Our lieutenant was promised we'd earn our own office space. He pushed for us to be someplace other than Southeastern Division's already cramped building. His bosses found some locker room openings at Traffic Division, which was conveniently three blocks from the home I shared with my wife of three years.

The trailers were shared with Traffic Division and showed signs of withered décor and structural failure. Eastern Division was right next door to Traffic and those officers were getting a brand-new building built for them. We had to be careful where we stepped because some of the trailer's flooring sank and holes formed under the thin indoor-outdoor carpeting. Traffic cops and WECAN cops were all clustered together, albeit temporarily, until the department rearranged rooms at Headquarters for a more permanent solution. Our spirits were high. The first wave loved their job and their enthusiasm was infectious. I only lived a mile away and enjoyed my bicycle commute.

When I transferred to Western, the division building was a series of cramped, thinly walled office trailers sewn together to make a temporary substation. The temporary compound placed the Division in assembled trailer offices next to San Diego County's Animal Control, the dog pound in another parlance. The mournful barking and meowing of frightened and stressed animals kept the neighborhood up at night. This mixed-use neighborhood was affectionately named "Dog Patch" by the locals. Western waited patiently as the construction began almost right after I got the transfer from downtown. The work progressed slowly there because the location chosen was over a drainage culvert hastily filled in with topsoil. The inescapable ground moisture would cause humidity problems for years to come.

Western officers watched a permanent facility across the street grow from a foundation into an impenetrable brick building. I was much happier at F Troop when moving day came and the innards of our trailer got moved into the new construction. I wasn't so happy when the silly workers left several lockers outside in the parking lot adjacent to the new locker room. Somehow, somebody miscalculated and had more old lockers to replace than new ones. More new lockers were on order. I came back to work from days off to discover that my old locker sat outside, and my duty gun exposed to the elements. I had a devil of a time rubbing the rust off the gun.

My move to WECAN put me right back into a cramped, shoulder-to-shoulder trailer office just like I'd shared at Traffic Division in another part of town. I'd gone full circle, from F Troop's trailers to F Troops' new building, then on to WECAN's trailers. This relocation program was all part of a decentralization effort to move more cops out of one spot and spread them throughout the city. The modular office and lockers on wheels were interconnected with aluminum siding and fake paneling. The trailer buildings were all sided with plywood and had thin roofs. Luckily, there was heat and air conditioning. The trailers were narrow with skinny hallways and lacked arm-width space when all troops were aboard.

CHAPTER 3:

BUILDING BLOCKS

WECAN operated out of a semi-quiet city fund apart from the Police Department's budget. That meant we had money for our bosses to play with. Linda Dederman was brought onto the unit as a civilian exchequer to spend the money assigned only to us under the auspices of the city's Fiscal Management department. They were the ones who floated the money to us at the mayor's request. Linda saw the money and felt it odd that the flow of cash to WECAN didn't seem to get contested like budgets for other departments did. Linda's job included processing purchase orders for WECAN. She noted that some of the orders were tagged with grant money numbers while others were not.

Tales abounded about a ranking officer in WECAN's chain of command writing these mysterious grants, in all probability though, it was a non-sworn employee assigned to Management Analysis. A woman named Donna Warlick probably wrote many of the grants. The money had to come from somewhere and WECAN's budget was a guarded secret. Clearly, for the time being, the city shone WECAN in a positive light and rained money down on us to get the job done.

Linda's focus was on getting WECAN cops the tools they needed to do the best work we could. Linda was clear in what her role was. This did not make her popular with Fiscal Management or some of the assistant police chiefs. She hammered at them constantly about the money as these other city functionaries tried to spend it out from underneath WECAN. Linda stayed focused and corralled the grant money that WECAN was promised. Fiscal management often shuffled the money to satisfy the Chiefs and WECAN, covering the accountability of the grants. Ultimately, whoever had the SDPD Chief's ear probably got the money.

Linda loved the WECAN job. She had no desire to promote or move to a different position. She was always clear and focused on her twenty-three-year mission to take care of whatever unit she was attached to. She was the person cops could trust to honestly tell her what they needed to make their jobs better. She knew she could make that happen. WECAN was an opportunity to prove to the administration that, if you gave cops what they needed, they would be happier. If they had the right equipment, Linda felt they would take better care of it and return it. Her office proved that with WECAN. Ninety percent of all WECAN-issued equipment was returned in working order when WECAN was later subsumed into another unit. Unfortunately, the administration didn't see things Linda's way and ninety percent of the equipment was redistributed to Patrol at that time.

One of the four video cameras Linda purchased for WECAN did disappear. Somehow, it turned up later at a police lieutenant's mother's house. Go figure.

In every project Linda was assigned to over her career, she kept the WECAN model in mind. She always tried to give the cops the gear they needed to get the job done to their satisfaction. When all was said and done, she was content that she'd done all she could within her limited power base.

Linda recalled Nancy MacPherson, a civilian involved with the SDPD's Neighborhood Policing, as part of a federal program to fund city governments working to take their streets back from thugs. Nancy had a connection through the International Association of Chiefs of Police and our police chief wanted to be a part of it. Nancy worked as a Special Assistant to the Chief to start the Neighborhood Policing effort in San Diego. For a time, WECAN and Neighborhood Policing received separate grant monies to do the same job on the same streets. Nancy often rode with a WECAN supervisor to see the results of the federal grant money being spent. All any WECAN officers knew was that our unit was better funded and taken better care of than any other division in the city.

The results were that the WECAN Unit was awarded commendations for the increases in arrests of drug dealers, drug users and gang members. Lieutenant Saldamando was delighted with the force he helped marshal into being. He celebrated the unit's first year with a

huge meeting down at Qualcomm Stadium, home of the then San Diego
Chargers. SWAT was called in for some ad hoc training that concluded
with them facing us in the massive parking lot. Our team faced the
accumulation of dozens of SWAT officers. We got an impromptu mob
and riot control challenge to test our training with SWAT as the aggressors. When that nonsense ended and SWAT got their jollies shouting
"WECAN't" at us, the lieutenant turned us all around in his direction
to face a speech.

Lt. Saldamando turned out to be full of surprises when he pronounced
us as elite and celebrated by the bosses above him for meeting the street
challenge head on and seemingly making differences. We made massive
drug seizures, abnormally large for uniformed officers. We also ramped
up the number of community meetings attended by officers in uniform.
We were everywhere in those communities we were built to police. For
a time, violent crime was so far down that when a drive-by shooting
occurred we took it personally. How dare they destroy the peace we'd
been so successful at bringing to troubled neighborhoods. Gang-related
stabbings and shootings were, often as not, solved because WECAN knew
all the players in each of the worst gang neighborhoods. Patrol officers,
Gang and Narcotics detectives, and WECAN cast a net over the City of
San Diego and kicked the bad guys in the proverbial teeth. The lieutenant held a sheaf of papers. He serenaded us with rewards in the form of
commendations for our work. One-by-one we were handed our own
certificate of accomplishment. The first wave officers received straight-
up Department Commendations. Those are top of the food chain accli-
mations for the work done. We second wave guys were handed notes of
lesser esteem, since we were not part of the initial experiment. Although
the division between the forces seemed a little chintzy, the LT's act of
unity brought us all together. That brother-sisterhood dynamic was the
essence of the team.

CHAPTER 4:

GETTING ACQUAINTED

The Southeastern WECAN team's first home was at that division's substation. Everybody on the WECAN team came from there and felt at home. The beach unit, which consisted of four cops to cover Ocean Beach, Mission Beach and Pacific Beach, were squeezed into the Traffic trailer locker rooms with the rest of us. Roger and Woody had been teamed up briefly for O.B. before that concept was deemed non-productive and erased from the board. The last division, Central, got along with the other folks at SDPD's headquarters facility downtown. The newness of that building hadn't quite worn off. The place was beautiful and roomy. Seven floors above ground and two for parking below, the tower even included a rooftop helicopter pad that was later determined unusable because the architectural firm's building designers failed to design an emergency drain for fuel spills. Room was eventually provided at the main building to centralize the teams under one roof. Any of the teams could be temporarily diverted to any other spot in the city if needed. We literally had the run of the town and all the time to do what was needed.

I began the job with a stint with Woody, replacing Roger when he was deployed elsewhere. Woody was one of my former Beach Team partners (Woody is the kind of guy with a big body and a big heart you expect with that nickname). Remarkably, his reposting back to O.B. working WECAN seemed wondrous. We were friends when we worked together in the past and now we were partners again.

Bill and I had spent months together on the Beach Team and shared some after-work time drinking and jawing about our pre-cop histories. I confessed to him that I was a comic book nerd from my earliest years. The heroes in those four-color pages inspired me to mold their core values into my own. In our society, there were no such options as capes and cowls. I'd grown up not focused on my career or my future roles in the work force and in life. I'd been bullied and had suffered loss from petty thieves. Somewhere inside me burned the desire to make right what was wrong around me. The justice that I sought to deliver could only be manifested in the uniform or suit of a law enforcer. For someone of my background and means, and above average intelligence, three years of junior college and a good heart, service as a police officer intrigued me. WECAN was the outfit where I could do some real crime-fighting.

Woody was more practical about this venture. He was a cop through-and-through, but the transfer to WECAN was a pragmatic move to heighten his chances of advancement. Western Division, with its F Troop Lost Command image, was no place to promote from, yet here we were, back at Western. As planned, though, F Troop had no hold over either of us now.

Ocean Beach had no gangs resembling those evil organizations in the southern and eastern parts of the city. Bill and I hadn't worked together in about a year. Our heads were not in the same places they'd been in before. We needed some time to reacquaint and get past the changes in each of us we'd experienced in that year of separation. We got along fine, but I feared my ego was not in tune with his. I was more headstrong and reckless, plus a little more jaded from a longer F Troop sentence, while Woody was practical and thoughtful. The chemistry wasn't the same after a year apart.

Our WECAN objective was to walk the troublesome War Zone blocks of Ocean Beach. Walking O.B. for crime wasn't the same as walking gang-infested neighborhoods. The criminals in the beach area were of a different make-up and didn't hover in clusters. We two O.B. cops knew that roaming the streets in a police car would be more productive. We'd spot the bad guys and snap them up much quicker. The WECAN mission didn't carry the same vibe in the beach. When we did park the car and walk, the foot patrol seemed silly since it was so out of character for us. The thugs were either mobile or indoors. Lumps of bad people didn't exist on street corners. I saw the looks beat cops gave us when they drove by. We looked like two dweebs standing on street corners looking for trouble with our thumbs up our asses. The assignment allowed us to wear Beach Team garb, which made little real sense. Those Class B shirts and knee length shorts were for the sand. Woody and I stood on the corner of Voltaire and Abbot Streets in front of Pat's Liquor, looking like ducks in the desert, with exposed white legs and high-top white sneakers. We'd shift back to pants soon enough.

O.B. still retained its own hard-working beach team. The officers in that unit were as aggressive as the rest of us who'd served in our pasts. O.B. beach teamers have a legacy of enforcement rivaling any good narcotics unit. Woody and I felt redundant in the beach and knew we were probably needed elsewhere. The beach version of WECAN ran its course until the lieutenant absorbed the northern division pair and Woody and me into the larger teams that were comprised of Eastern, Central and Southeastern Divisions.

For edification, Central encompassed the downtown area and the low-income neighborhoods south to the border with National City and Southeastern Division. Eastern Division was a broad dimension of rich, middle class and dirt-poor streets. The lowest-income blocks were occupied by gangs of every hue that included a United Nations of Southeast Asian teenagers turned to crime and violence to cope with the hated Black and Hispanic gangs. The Oriental Killer Boys, et al, were facets Eastern WECAN had to add to their list of targets.

The closest Woody and I ever came to an actual gang in the beach was the small numbers of white supremacist skateboard punks that are ubiquitous along San Diego's beach fronts. They were more bullies than thugs organized for profit. Their kind tended to turn and disappear when familiar cops drive up on them.

When separated, Woody went to Eastern and I went to Central. I was truly leaving my comfort zone behind when I moved out of the trailers and onto the third floor of the relatively new headquarters building. Central Division was housed there as well. The cops there had to regulate the Crips who frightened neighborhoods, and the *vatos* who ruled independent of the Black gangs and went back two or more generations.

The HQ building was all modern glass and metal with ninety-degree angles and walls trimmed with dull blue paint. The old San Diego Police

Department station had been an architectural thing of practical beauty forty years prior. That building's time had passed, and the new police HQ would carry the San Diego Police Department into the future where more cops would be needed.

Our lockers were built within the building that was only three years old. The place had seven floors, each themed in a different, subdued color. The muted palette included avocado, puce, mauve and an aqua best described as navy grey with a touch of tidy bowl blue. The elevators tended to stop functioning, so you never knew which ones were operational. I was fortunate the first afternoon at my new assignment to get on a working elevator and make it all the way to my avocado-colored floor. I would get stuck with a partner I barely knew and had never worked with, and I was tired of always working with new partners.

Cops who love to work with partners want to work with the same partner. Partners are like family. Good partners can finish each other's sentences. Bad partners squabble or pray for separation every day they are stuck in the same patrol car. Life is disrupted when partnerships change. Imagine if Joe Friday of Dragnet was forced to work with a new partner. How odd would it have been if the guys of *Adam 12* television fame were separated? Cops who work two officer units, bond in pairs.

Manny Rivera and I were graduates of the 98th Police Academy, but in different sections. We never schooled together and had not worked together after the Academy. Manny was the Central Team partner I'd be assigned to, or I was the partner he got stuck with. Manny turned out to be a gregarious guy and partner. He was straight out of the Brooklyn in New York, was Puerto Rican to the bone and my age. He was swarthy, taller than me by an inch and maintained a thick cop 'stache'. I still remember walking into the Central locker room to get my new life oriented. Manny was already getting dressed. He looked at his new partner; I'm sure, with a little trepidation. I figured we'd have to work at being partners. I wondered if I'd even fit in at Central WECAN with its team of cops I'd never seen before. Central was full of hard chargers. F Troop was filled with some aggressive officers who often felt that their hands were tied, or cops who were content to stay in place and not rock the boat. The rough streets of Central's Logan and Sherman

Heights in one of the city's oldest and roughest neighborhoods made no allowances for lazy officers.

In typical pseudo-Hollywood fashion, Manny greeted me with a formal handshake and a hearty "Babe!" The 'A' sound drawn out to make a "Baaaabe" callout. I was instantly at ease but got distracted when I noticed that the Mylar-constructed, man-height mirror inside the locker room appeared to be a favorite target for guys with angry fists. Now it looked like a two hundred-and thirty-dollar slab of pop-art. Manny's off-hand greeting had disarmed my apprehension. I knew right there he would be one good partner.

"Hi, Manny," I greeted back to him as we shook hands for the icebreaker in the locker room. I still had to find one for myself among the myriad lockers occupied by Central cops. I wasn't sure they'd be pleased to squeeze in another body.

"Dude! Are you ready to rock?" Manny asked in true Ozzy Osborne fashion. The toothy grin under his Pancho Villa mustache signaled that he knew I was on his turf, but he was making me feel at home.

What followed was the scintillating, getting-to-know-you conversation that would begin a thirty-plus year friendship. Manny was hysterical when he mocked the West Coast Californian with his SoCal surfer dialect. It never ceased to crack me up. He'd say something like, "Dude, how's it going? Did you surf some tasty waves?" adopting the stereotypical virtues of some of my beach brethren.

At first, WECAN appeared to me to be on a budget. I hadn't seen anything special since my earlier arrival at the trailers. So far, the only thing that looked new was the police car assigned to Manny. His previous partner had been promoted to detectives. WECAN officers got to use their assigned police cars, bought and paid and for, brand new just for us. Then, money from somewhere began to buy us all kinds of frills. If we wanted cameras, we got cameras, all kinds of brand-new cameras. We became the only field units in the department with brand new, state of the art video cameras and Polaroid Land cameras.

The ranking officers over us wanted the teams to be public, walk the streets, knock on doors, talk to people and ask them where the bad guys were. Of course, that pipe dream only lasted in WECAN's infancy. The walking aspect of our duties suited the framework of the program, but it suffered from a redundant malaise. When Manny and I were paired up, he'd already been in the unit for four months. He and his former partner had begun a pattern that stationed them in the faces of mostly black gangsters. These Crips and their pervasive drug sales invited violence. The city saw nightly news about black gangsters hammering away at civilized society as they broke up neighborhoods, friends, families and even schools with fights for street control. The residents who bordered the fringes of downtown were notorious for anti-police rigidity that stemmed from generations of racial tensions and economic repression. The gangsters of the day were the sons of families who lived in the margins. Some families were broken apart by choices made for them, while others were comprised of criminals that gave rise to a new group of bad guys.

Manny's WECAN assignment began at the troubled intersection of 32nd and Market Streets and enveloped a couple of blocks in each direction. When I got to Central, Manny already had a work pattern for a typical day. He and his former partner, Wayne Starr, would park their marked unit at about 32nd and Island. From there, they pocketed several Field Interview pads. FI forms came in booklets resembling ticket books that were also pre-printed with fill-in boxes to plug in information. Anybody under suspicion could find themselves in front of a police officer "volunteering" their identity, to be recorded on the pad and later transferred into a computer by the crime analysis unit. We began the hours-long walk around the neighborhood from there. Starr's promotion to detective was an almost assured move up from WECAN. Now it was my turn to follow in his path.

This portion of the neighborhood, Logan Heights, was chosen because of the strong presence of West Coast Crips. These blocks were notorious for pot, heroin and the more dangerous crack sales. The community that surrounded 32nd and Market raised many of these gangsters but did little to turn their lives around. The elementary school built in the center of Logan Heights bordered 32nd and was considered an island of safety for the children when they were at school. Their lives were worrisome for the teachers and administrators when the kids left campus after school. The streets they lived on were perilous. WECAN was to be the visible deterrent to gang control. My job was to enter this cauldron and make the place less fearsome for me and for the good people who existed as uncomfortable neighbors to the men, and a few women, who preyed upon the weak and the frightened.

The only way to know what gang oppression felt like was to be within their zones of control. Our only way to grasp the fear of the people there was to talk to them, but most of them wouldn't talk to us. WECAN's extraordinary role was to open dialog with the few who knew that they needed our help and would engage in conversation. The foot patrols in confined areas meant that we saw the same people every day, almost like we lived there part time. Other residents braved concealed contacts with WECAN officers under the cover of a brush-pass and a mumbled piece of gang gossip. It comprised a great risk to speak to us, but Manny had already broken the ice on 32nd Street. People who saw him, especially fellow Spanish speakers, were comfortable enough to feed us tidbits of information. If we asked the right questions, they gave us the answers.

WECAN's pilot experiment lost some of its deterrence when the gang members got used to us. They dealt drugs as usual, up to, and until, we strolled into their midst. We'd see them but were in no position to do more than FI them once again. Our daily protocol was to fill out those triplicate information cards and give the bangers the impression we intended to interview them to death. A daily ritual for us was to walk the block and talk to a few wary citizens. The public was wary of the "Blue." The people that lived there had no place to hide from random violence angry black gangsters were prone to deliver. The Crips would not hesi-tate to render their brand of injustice on anyone friendly with the police, so our meet-ups with the locals had to be discreet. Some good people did get used to us and made small talk. If we incidentally met them out of sight of anyone, they might share a scrap of enlightenment. Rarely were we able to gain the intel we needed to hear. The most crucial ques-tions were aimed at, "who normally holds the dope?" "Where are their weapons hidden?" "Where are their stashes concealed?" The odds were not steeped in our favor. Conversely, we weren't troubled by the lack of community disclosure. The way the good citizens turned their backs away from the bad ones told us these people had uneasy détentes with their gangster neighbors. WECAN was designed to work around the iffy cooperation in the hood.

Yeah, interviewing gang members everyday got old and Manny had been at it for months. The Heights area was new to me, but wasted effort was not. I could tell when we were wasted talent, and frankly, we got bored. Manny and I spent so much time walking three short blocks that we got the notion that foot work wasn't getting enough gain for the unit's goals. The neighborhood was one of San Diego's oldest. Old mansions built in the 19th Century were either converted to fire-trap apartments, or destroyed so developers could build modern, fire-trap apartments.

In the latter half of the 20th Century, homes built in the Craftsman and Victorian styles were preserved wherever the owners and historical societies could stop developers. All the other single-family plots of land suffered the neglect of an aging, poor neighborhood, or got scooped up so that another narrow, twelve-unit apartment building. Sadly, this almost Soviet-style of sameness designed each buildings to every other apartment building, could squeeze a few more low-incomers into already crowded city blocks. In this pressure-cooker it was difficult for hard-charging drug officers to play the role of constantly happy, glad-handing, community cops. That was the work of lazy, non-confrontational types of cops. We were meat-eaters and wanted more action.

CHAPTER 5:

ACCLIMATION

WECAN's leader's had access to large coin. A fleet of new Fords were painted SDPD white, decaled as SDPD, outfitted with prisoner cages, light bars and handed out to each WECAN duo as their service vehicle. They weren't take-home patrol cars, so we picked them up at work. The command urged us to stay in the assigned areas we patrolled and not explore too much by car. Our task was to mother-hen assigned city blocks for the express purpose of being gadflies to gang members and to be law enforcement bridges to law-abiding folks. While it seemed unlikely that we'd ground ourselves, the command wanted otherwise. Their solution was to furnish us with large panel vans that resembled commercial bread trucks to be used as mobile offices for the teams. They were part of our expansive budget that also furnished each two-man unit with new Ford four-doors. The vans were new, too. Paint them with red, yellow and blue balls and they'd match the old Weber Bread vans.

The vans were outfitted with worktables, laminated cabinets, station-to-station radios and all the staples a rolling office could need. I'm certain passing patrol officers took some offense at our level of comfort. To them, we must have appeared as pampered Department favorites. I can just see some offended cops thinking ill of the WECAN cops with all our shiny toys. I tell you a cop handling a police report in the discomfort of his police car would not feel kind to cops seeming to lounge around in a mobile office furnished with a refrigerator.

Our instructions were to park the vans in high crime target neighborhoods and staff them when we had reports to write. The big vehicles' presence was thought to generate a fat deterrent to crime. The theory was that vans moved into place and the bad people hunkered down or split. Otherwise, we would prowl the streets around the vans for trouble. We strove to keep the driving of our police cruisers to a minimum so the residents could get used to us being approachable. I think most of the teams were comfortable with that arrangement at first. We knew we were blind sitting ducks if the worst elements took potshots at us seated in the vans. The vans weren't designed with side windows which limited our three-hundred-and-sixty-degree sight range. All we had to look out through were the front and back windows, and the windows mounted into the back doors were little better than portholes. The vans were cool, though, just not in the way the command planned.

The blind spots were a true tactical problem at 22nd and J, the heart of one particularly nasty street gang. I believe it was the Sherman Heights street gang that held sway over this part of the Heights. I can barely recall the lines of demarcation anymore. One gang's east-west streets drifted into another gang's north-south streets. All I know is that one elementary school administration had some leverage over our command and "asked" for specific WECAN attention. The bread vans were ordered in place during school hours with at least one pair of officers pulling foot duty in circles around the blocks within sight of the van.

Cops couldn't sit without a view of oncoming danger in a tough neighborhood. With our orders in place, we had little choice. We reasoned we'd give it the effort and make a few arrests on the side. Because of the potential for some random gun attack by nefarious gangster snipers, one of us would write up whatever paperwork we had in the comfort of the van while the other stood guard outside. Two days of this show was enough. Manny and I were joined by fellow Central Team members John Tangredi and his partner Chuck Davis. With what amounted to a swarm of cops, we made a statement, especially after Roger joined us as well. No Sherman gang members were within sight. They were on the streets the first few days, but after the van roosted on 22nd Street the bad guys melted away.

Long and Boyd were supposed to deal with the Shermans from morning to afternoon. Maybe they'd forced some of those thugs to move elsewhere to hangout. We never saw the Long and Grano duo, and didn't share information. I don't want to say we figured they got special treatment from our Command, but they were stubbornly absent when they could have supplemented our cause.

If the gangsters moved out when we moved in, they'd shuffle right back onto the block when we left. We were burning out at this spot, too.

The police vans became useful, moving platforms for justice just like the police cars. Instead of driving through a trouble spot like 30th Street and Imperial Avenue, the Crips' most visible loitering spot, with highly identifiable cop cars, the vans were huge white affairs that looked a lot like city maintenance trucks. Everyone ignores maintenance trucks including the bad guys. We could load the vans full of officers and drive right up to a group of drug-dealer West Coasters. We'd leap out of the van and surround the bangers before they even knew who we were. They got caught armed and carrying dope without a chance to dump any of it. They'd get wise soon enough, but the initial barrage of 'bread truck cops' stunned the bad men.

The vans provided us with versatility that the patrol cars did not. We could group the entire Central Team into the van and take it on a joyride to specific destinations. I thought the act of parking this nondescript vehicle dead-center in a new gang hot spot looked awesome when six or seven cops jumped out and shocked the hell out of the embedded players. The van didn't fit the police profile that normally warned people the cops were in their midst.

The quintet of Tangredi, Davis, Rivera, Barrett and I headed north on Fwy163 in the van for a run to East San Diego to assist the Eastern WECAN team. Barrett took shotgun while I drove. I had the van in the fast lane when Barrett told me to slow down. I looked over at him and asked, "What's up?"

"I think the woman in the Volvo station wagon next to us is smoking a joint. Get parallel with her."

I got the van lined up with the driver's window. The van had SAN DIEGO POLICE DEPARTMENT decaling on all four sides. The letters are only three inches tall against a massive all-white canvas. Our markings were not demonstrative. Barrett stared through the window.

"Yeah, she's smoking a joint. What a bitch. Shit, there's a baby seat in back!" I squeezed in a glance and caught the telltale pinched fingers to

the puckered lips. Barrett slid open the passenger van door and exposed
his full uniform. Then, he grabbed the microphone and switched the
selection dial to Public Address. The guys in the rear of the van hustled
forward to look over Barrett's shoulders to see her for themselves. We
were in a hurry to cover the Eastern WECAN people and had no time
to stop her on a busy freeway for a small-time ticket. Since there was
no child in the kid-seat, she'd get a scare, but no ticket.

"Hey. Way to go mother of the year!" He had the volume turned up.
Her window was up, but the deafening reverb caught her attention.
I saw her look at us, specifically the uniformed cop talking to her.
She freaked out when her eyes widened at the sight of the police. The
joint dropped into her lap. She managed to slap her nether regions
to put out the burning cherry. We sped up and laughed all the way
to Interstate 8. The gangsters, in almost every instance, were rocked
by a barrel full of cops disguised as a huge white elephant that just
happened to stop next to them.

The commercial intersection of 30th Street and Imperial Avenue was
the heart of West Coast Crip turf. Even before the Crips sprouted their
colors there, gangs defiantly felt at home running dope and committing
other crimes with that intersection as their safe place. The intersection
had a decades-long reputation with its denizens easily triggered into
confrontations with the police. Just before I arrived at Central after post
academy phase-training, the Department had ended a walking program
encompassing that stretch of Imperial. Two officers, Al Massey and Ted
Kasinak, would become living legends for the actions they withstood
patrolling that area.

I met them both when I worked Central C Squad years earlier. I
listened to others spread stories about the two officers as though they'd
survived a war. Everything centered on their months-long campaign to
put officers in the faces of the Crips and drug sellers. These guys were
patrol officers familiar with the neighborhood and the players. Their
function was to force the bad people to exercise restraint on turf they
felt they owned. The Crips did what they wanted to do and weren't used

to direct action by cops not likely to get sidetracked by radio calls. I heard stories about Ted and Al putting out more cover calls and Eleven Ninety-Nines, the code that meant officers' lives were in danger, than anyone in the history of the Department. These two men knew the players and treated them with respect. The thugs and gangsters still took them on and forced the violent confrontations.

The Crips either had to grow passive in the presence of two seasoned cops or confront them to try and force them out. Too often, the local baddies chose to fight. The storytellers recalled in conversation with me, that Massey and Kasinak got so up to their eyeballs in confrontations at 30th and Imperial Avenue that they literally called for cover every work night. Massey was a combat veteran from the Vietnam War. Ted was a SWAT officer with a decoration for valor for when he volunteered to drive a dump truck into the line of fire to stop Brenda Spencer, one of the first school shooters, from killing more than the two poor souls she'd already extinguished.

I never asked either man about those walking days until I later partnered with Kasinak. Al was too intimidating for a rookie grunt like me to brace for stories. Ted was easy going. We were paired up for a while on C Squad. Since we were partners, I asked him about the 30th and Imperial Avenue days. He wasn't a talker about himself. The one time I asked the question he smiled and simply uttered, "Those were some days."

After working those blocks later, I didn't need to hear Ted's and Al's stories, I lived them.

My Central Patrol buddy from our rookie days, Cam Hansen, and his partner stopped to interrogate a couple of Crips in the parking lot at Mullen's Liquor Store one evening. Mullen's was the hotspot for thugs for booze, cigarettes and the prime spot to hang out at that intersection. The gang members formed up at Mullen's every day and night for their nefarious activities. In a place like Mullen's parking lot, nothing good came from any group loitering there at night. If it was the Crips in place, any liquor buyers were better off getting their drink-on someplace else.

Cam and his partner rolled their patrol cruiser into the darkened lot. The group they wanted to talk too stood at the south end of the lot with their backs to the west wall. The air was cool and a few of the Crips wore hoodies. Too many bad things can be hidden in hoodies. The two officers used flanking positioning to keep the Crips in check during the chat.

Cam was a big guy and a tempting target for a guy with a weapon and a grudge. His partner stood to one side and faced the three guys from their flank. That way, he could watch them and Cam's back at the same time. Towering Cam faced them with his FI pad and jotted down information. Suddenly, a spear-like object zipped past Cam and smacked into the wall in back of him. All five individuals were surprised and ducked a little. Cam's partner had his gun out, but no target to threaten. Everyone stared-off over the rooftops for the source of the projectile. Cam bent down and looked it over. It was a metal-tipped, feathered arrow.

Cam had trouble digesting the nature of the weapon. Had somebody shot an arrow at him? He was the closest to its trajectory. His partner was already calling for help. He had a difficult time dispensing radio information because he didn't believe it himself. This spot was tough enough with occasional drive-by shootings and constant fighting. But an arrow?

There was no resolution for the seeming attack. Cam and his partner scooted the Crips along and joined other officers as they poked around for man with a bow.

Our big WECAN vans attracted flies. Whenever we were parked in the Heights with the doors open, flies filled it up. The buzzing irritants started out a bit annoying until they flew at us like dive bombers. Roger was done with a police report and got bored as he sat deep inside the vehicle. He explored the many drawers built into the van and found a bag of rubber bands. He was tired of the flies and chose to take them out with his unique skills.

Roger took a comfortable seat and started firing the rubber bands at the stationary flies. The one's that were flying would put us in the lines of fire. Roger fired off a couple and nailed one. With a couple of more shots his body count rose to two. Four of us watched with rapt focus. By the time we were due back on patrol he'd racked up seven kills. That day, his moniker was born. He became, *Mosca*, Spanish for Fly. I wanted a cool moniker too. I'd once been the acting sergeant for months. The best the boys could give me was *Cabeza*, which was Spanish for head. I tended to be the decision maker when we plotted a course of action. I wasn't keen on that label and it left our unit lexicon shortly after it began.

There were dramatic news reports of gangsters shooting at cops in their cars in L.A. Our natural wariness and a touch of paranoia led to us parking the vans. We went back to our cars for mobility. We were not going to be easy prey for some cowardly drive-by attack. The vans ended up back at the police station to be redeployed when we wanted to attack targets with greater numbers, or set-up house in the middle of a temporary hotbed of gang actions.

To be mobile in cars meant we'd surprise people, move quickly and randomly. That way, we'd set no patterns like the ones that hampered our ability to surprise anyone while on foot. Something else we couldn't do on foot was traffic stops. A lot of the gangsters, those making good drug money, had cars. We reasoned that the gangsters at the head of some of the most egregious problems in the Heights had purchased the cars with drug proceeds. The dealers moved drugs with cars, so we stopped the cars. Slowly we took the "Walking" out of WECAN.

What the public saw less of in Central WECAN's area were cops on foot walking past their homes each day. We tired of shaking down the same guys daily and learned that Eastern and Southeastern Teams had responded in kind. My Central Team was supposed to operate in specific areas where black gangs were rolling out drug sales near schools. We stood around them at peak drug sales periods in the day and their activities slowed to a trickle. WECAN began to turn into babysitters with little impact. The Crips and associated problem people moved on down the street, so we were obliged to follow. This was the maddening success we brought. We shut down one small group each day we worked for the few hours we haunted them. We accomplished much and nothing at the same time. I left officers back at F Troop who'd take this assignment in a heartbeat. Get paid to hike and tan. You bet!

We wanted action. We saw the bigger picture and our goal was to "take ›em off the streets."

CHAPTER 6:

CRIPPN' IT

Manny and I toiled daily with the same contacts on 32nd Street. We knew who they were, where they lived, who their families were and what they did all day, which was mostly getting high and then doing nothing. The dope sales were small time to begin with. If they were doing real crime it was rarely in front of the walking team.

I knew the Martin Luther King Jr. Elementary School appreciated their guardian angels. We were there when school let out and hovered over the kids that walked home. Parents were relieved their children were under observation for about a block in any direction. The Crips displayed no outward threat. The kids were more likely to succumb to offers of drugs when we weren't around. Our presence did minimize unpredictable drive-bys and other random shootings between gangsters. Frankly, Manny and I knew this weak Band-aid approach couldn't last. The Crips needed more than escorts.

"What's your name, Dennis?" I asked one with the preordained knowledge of a cop resigned to repetition. I thought, once again, "unto the breach," as we parked the car and walked over to a group in blue and baggie clothes before I asked the question. Despite the air of relaxed routine, we never took our eyes off the hands of our opponents. That clothing may have been gang chic, but weapons as large as a rifle could be concealed under all that cotton.

"Shit, you already know my name. Why you hassling me?" Dennis made eye contact with Manny. Manny often drew the regard a white officer was less likely to receive. If I wanted to be front and center, I could take command with my presence and a voice timber likely to get attention. But why rock the boat? Manny hesitated for a second. I took that as a sign and stepped into the gangster's line of sight.

"You are a gang member. I am a gang cop. You do the math. Now what's your name and DOB?"

Exasperated, Dennis muttered, "Motherfucker" under his breath. "This is police harassment. You can't fuck with me like this."

"I can now. That's why we're here." I pointed to a nifty pin fastened to my left shirt pocket below my badge. The pin was a custom job for all WECAN officers to show unit identity. A lot of bad people squinted to read it and asked what it meant.

Dennis was one of those targets we wanted off the streets. He squinted at the badge and read it. "Walking Enforcement Campaign Against Narcotics" he said out loud. "Y'all is supposed to be walking. How come I see you cops in cars, too? They don't leave me be, neither."

"That's Patrol. You have two kinds of cops to deal with now. Just think, if you didn't bang and scare the shit out of people, none of this would be necessary." The levity was lost on the man. He was truly a villain with nothing but malice in his heart and he wasn't even the worst example. There were guys in the Hood adorned in blue that were beyond "borderline psychopath." Their unpredictable menace was the reason WECAN existed.

Dennis and his cronies got to read the pin throughout each of WECAN's target neighborhoods. They slowly realized we were not patrol cops whizzing by to some other destination. Dennis and his mates *were* our destination. He would look forlorn from this point forward each time we jammed him up. He could be as pissed as he wanted to. He and the others were not used to cops that didn't go away. Manny and his first partner had set the tone months prior. The Crips and other various and sundry bad people were already frustrated by the time I arrived and took my seat next to Manny. Yet, few would not work up to antagonism. Most got angry, even perilously so, but SDPD had confidence the right cops in pairs could deter most attacks. Hell, hundreds of FIs later the gangsters saw no percentage in fights with police. Southeastern WECAN officer Joe Howie got into a fight with one of the Crips on 32nd on the Central Team's turf. Joe's opponent was one of two brothers from the 32nd and J St. block across from MLK Elementary. This was before my arrival and I understood from Manny that the Crip gave Howie quite a struggle. Both men were matched in size, but Howie dropped the man into a patch of parkway plants before he went down with the guy. Fortunately, Joe got the upper hand and made the arrest.

The Crip raised a fuss and fought hard. That might have been the last Crip-Cop fight WECAN suffered through. Manny introduced me to that Crip months later. He was out of jail and back on the corner of 32nd and J. Manny cautioned me about the man. He didn't think the guy was mentally squared away. The best approach was low-key and guarded.

Neither of us could converse with the guy. He was all grunts and mumbles, never making eye contact. I spotted one nickel in each ear and naturally asked what that was all about. "I got earaches," he said.

I looked at Manny for some clarification. Maybe this was some street lingo I was unaccustomed to. Manny cocked his head sideways to peer at the nickels from an askew angle. "They help with the ears?"

"Supposed to. My auntie told me to do this whenever I got sore ears. She said it makes it go away."

"Is it working?" I asked, incredulous that a thug and possible killer stuck nickels in his ears like a witchdoctor was his family practitioner.

"I dunno." This was one of the strangest ice breakers I'd engaged in, but the guy loosened up. I figured ignorance met old wife's tale, but the dialog gave Manny the opening to ask if we could search him for dope. The Crip didn't bristle and didn't tighten up his muscles. He looked Manny in the orbs for the first time and muttered, "I got nothing to hide."

I took that as a positive sign and approached him from behind. He raised his arms in subjugation, so I checked his pockets on down. His pants were low-rider, so concealed weapons wouldn't have been possible in his waistband. The man was clean. There was no dope and no danger. He was docile enough. Perhaps Joe had taught him a lesson. Maybe two cops were what it took to keep the peace. He wasn't high, had smoked a little pot maybe, but that was not a jail able offense.

Manny kept the patter going with, "How long do you keep those nickels in your ears?"

"Ain't gonna take them out until my mom or my auntie tells me to."

"Alright, we're done here," I concluded. "Good luck with the ears." The Crip broke off eye contact and stared off into the distance again. Some of our contacts with these guys were even shorter than this. The gangsters often played it deadpan with the cops. WECAN officers could squeeze out a little more of the Crip's character only because we bugged them every day, instead of the usual stare-downs through sunglasses from patrol officers. Sometimes, the Crips seemed confused when we walked around them. If we stopped, they walked. If we walked, they stopped. If we did both, they would bounce off each other as they tried to decide what to do.

Manny and I erased the players north of Market from our thoughts. We crossed with the traffic light and headed south to J Street. The action was less plentiful, but the residents, some friendly, most apprehensive or disdainful of the police, got the show WECAN intended. Our "good friend" Desmond, sometimes pimp, sometimes dealer, all-time gang-ster, should have bailed. Instead, he stood his ground on the corner of J and 32nd. The woman he was with had the good sense to split in her stilettos and rejoin the other hookers two blocks south.

"Why you always messin' wit me?" Desmond said. He looked frus-trated. Maybe the exiting woman was his main street-walker earner or maybe some "piece" he hooked for the day. Who knows? The Crips are not monogamous and those who are pimps run their girls both day and night.

"Why Desmond, what else should I do?" I asked innocently.

"Don't you have to go write tickets or do radio stuff. Why you jackin' me up. Why ain't you lookin' for robbers and rapists and such?"

I took on the role of the talker while Manny kept an eye on the scene for any other crew members. "My job is to be with you and your buddies. I don't know where the bank robbers, murderers and rapists are, but I know where you are. So, here I am."

"You be fuckin' wit me every damn day, Officer" he said as he leaned in to read my nametag for the fifteenth time. "Newbold. Don't 'chu got nothing better to do?"

"Hell, no Desmond. You are my nothing better to do." I replied in my most chipper voice. Desmond's hands were in his pockets. He hadn't been patted down and there's always the chance his fingers tickled the handle of a knife or gun. But Manny was right behind him to get the drop if he suspected the guy was truly armed. Our focus was always on Crips' hands and on our immediate surroundings. At least one Crip had a reputation for the ambush of a cop he'd when he shot the Central patrol officer through the open window of his cruiser. That officer survived. The Crip went on to pimp girls in the beach area after he got out of prison.

We took no chances as we loitered near them when they sat to kill a forty-ounce bottle of beer. We walked behind them when they grouped together. If they split up, we stayed with one or the other. We never split ourselves up. There was safety in our numbers. We wanted 32nd around MLK Elementary to be devoid of Crips. The deck was always stacked against us because many of them lived right there. All we could do was take a chunk of the day out of their criminal activities. Also, they slung dope to repeat customers. When the Crips were off the set, then the customers would go elsewhere.

The customers would return when we left. The cycle frustrated us. This action reminded me of a prostitution detail back at F Troop. We'd babysit the B-girls, or prostitutes, on the strip to interrupt their business. Night in and night out some Western beach cops walked behind the girls, FI'd them, or drove ridiculously slow in traffic to frustrate them and their potential johns. The only way to break the chain of events was to take the Crips off the board.

For them to get out of real trouble all they had to do was move a few blocks in any direction and we'd lose our hold over their behavior. The five of us assigned to walk around that territory were properly tired of our nursemaid roles to a bunch of hardened criminals. We wanted action. We wanted to show the Crips our teeth, so we began a short series of tactical plans to lessen our frustration.

The first action we took was to set up surveillance on the dope-dealing Crips who, so far, had seemed immune from foot patrols. Few of those FIs produced dope or other evidence of their crimes. We needed to put them into jail for our authority to have real value.

There was a favorite spot the Crips frequented daily. They chose a front yard to a small house on 32nd just above Market. They were there every day and rarely reacted to our snooping around. Southeastern WECAN shared the streets with Neighborhood Crips and the Blood sets down there. They made arrests through plots and subterfuge. Central needed to get into that game, too.

The surest way for a team that didn't have a mandate to work CIs, or confidential informants, into our plans was to hide and catch the dealers in the act. We found true luck there in the form of a huge commercial lot that sat across the street from 32nd and Market. The facility and vehicle lot were ringed with tall cinderblock walls. Manny and I scouted the place when the facility was open. It turned out to be run by a security guard company friendly to cops. After one request for a padlock key, we gained entry into the large acreage whenever we pleased. The wall to the west was less than forty feet from the small front yard that the Crips had taken over.

I never met the residents and they never showed themselves. It seemed clear that the residents were not going to get involved or were complicit with what was going on.

I could see over the wall by standing on the hood of our car. I didn't need binoculars to peer through the concertina wire at the men across the street and our proximity set us up nicely for courtroom testimony later. Our plan was to watch the dealers from the lot while two arrest teams sat planted nearby. On our first up to bat, we saw a car pulling up across the street. We could see the driver through the passenger window. One of the Crips got off the low block retaining wall and leaned in through the driver's side. The buyer cast some cash his way and a palmed baggie of pot dropped from seller to buyer's hand. We let that one go, so we could get the lay of the operation.

The next buyer's car approached slowly before parking on the opposite side of the street. This time, the dealer needed to re-supply. The guy removed trash from one of the brick openings at the top of the low front yard wall as his gaze darted about for signs of trouble. Manny and I watched him pull out a clear plastic liter bag of marijuana. He removed a few nickel or five-dollar-bags and then stuffed the rest back into the wall. One of his cronies dumped camouflaging trash back into the hole. The deal we needed to see in order to take action was complete when the dealer worked through the passenger window. We'd seen enough. We radioed one of the other cars to go after the buyer, while another car sped up to the Crips, three of them, and froze the scene until we got there.

The gate into the large lot we occupied was on the other side of the block. Our entry and exit were out of visual range for the Crips. Five of us in three cars exited the east gate out of sight of the Crip dealers and sped westbound. Roger Barrett, the solo officer, chased down the previous buyer and took him prisoner. Three Crips were all seated next to each other on the wall right next to the stash. Three of us took stances for defense just in case. We didn't know what the Crips had around them, but they'd already been patted down for weapons. Manny took point position over the dope hidey-hole. All the dealers had for the moment was a lot of cash in the hands of one player. One gangster had a couple of baggies of pot. I had the three guys scoot over. Once they slid down the wall a few feet Manny reached down and plucked the stash from the brick wall's concealment.

Manny seized the Crips' cash and counted out fifty nickel bags of dope. Anything over three bags was considered possession for sale and that was a felony. For a Crip gangster, any gangster, the District Attorney could attach his gang membership to his charges. The DA wanted his kind off the streets. This little pot bust could cost him years in custody. Roger returned with the buyer in his back seat. Roger seized the bag of dope at the site of the traffic stop. The buyer freely admitted to buying it from "the guy on 32nd Street." He didn't plan on being returned to face that Crip and his buddies. He wisely sought other places to buy pot after that day.

For now, we had a Crip for dope sales, possession of dope for sales, and the now-confiscated moolah from actual sales of dope. We couldn't make a case on his two homies, so we did what we always did. We FI'd them to death and then sent them walking. The arrest was tight and perfectly set up for court. Our seller would be convicted and go to jail.

The buyer got off with a citation for the pot. We'd repeat this operation in a week.

We had similar success the next time, but we wanted more. Picking these guys off for pot sales was like eating withered French fries instead of fresh baked potatoes. We were smart and trained. We were supposed to be more talented than this. We brainstormed some other options and realized that the elementary school was the ignored ace-in-the-hole.

We only ran the operation a couple of times before the Crips wised up and moved on anyway. We sought big picture circumstances to spider web more Crips for solid dope arrests.

We had a handle on these 32nd Street Crips. We knew who they were and where to strike at them. The Heights was a big place for them to roam around in. The combined efforts of WECAN, patrol and investigations could curtail some of their activity, but not remove them as a problem. We were seeded in and around 32nd St. because that was the place they currently plagued.

The most interested party was MLK Jr. Elementary School. The staff and students at King had been terrified for years. The school occupied grounds the Crips considered theirs. The school had suffered indignities from the chaotic violence that comes from rival gangs attacking the turf. Vandalism and thefts at the school were commonplace. The school had been tagged by Crips for so long that the school district painted the buildings soft hues of blue to deter the Crips from defacing their sacred color.

There was recent legislation passed in San Diego designed to curtail the savage actions of gang members. Illicit drug sales within a thousand feet of a school could get the arrested enhanced time in prison. That meant our favorite neighborhood baddies could get busted and see real time in custody. We'd already pitted a few of the brothers on 32nd. We reasoned we could do more damage to them if we had the proper backing to set them up for federal prosecution.

We WECAN officers were not SDPD detectives. That level of policing was considered a promotion. Detectives worked with higher degrees of latitude. Narcotics detectives could use confidential informants and had funds to earmark for undercover work. WECAN did not. As uniformed cops, about the best we could expect was to think of some cool operation and then suggest it up the chain for somebody to initiate. No, this was our time and our project. We'd do our own proactive narcotics and gang detective work without the undercover guys involvement and call our own shots. We'd do this from within.

To accomplish that, we needed a pipeline into the Feds to work with us. The Feds could take the prosecution of gang members who dealt drugs near a school to higher levels. Luckily, WECAN got a lot of positive attention from the communities, the department and the press. Our command was eager to do many things for us, including letting us meet with a federal prosecutor.

The United States Attorney's Office in San Diego is a lofty place. Uniformed cops aren't meant to access such resources, let alone partner up and run a drug sting operation. We did. Wheels were greased and a couple of us from the Central Team got an appointment with one of the federal prosecutors. His office was enticed into cooperation when we provided a synopsis of our intentions. He was sensitive to the plan because we challenged his Office to live up to its mandate. They wanted to hammer the street gangs that plied their drug trades around the very schools they had just enacted laws for. Well, we had the plan and it was simple.

We already knew who the street characters were, and they were truly bad guys with prison records and histories of violence. We'd already tested our plan to remove them from the chessboard with a few surgical arrests. The guys we pulled down were all within one thousand feet of King Elementary. We offered them up to the federal prosecutor on a silver platter. We had a plan to nail them again for the same things we got them for just weeks prior. The plan was simple. We'd recruit a triad of rookie SDPD cops to make drug buys from a specific list of O.G., or original gangster, Crips. These were the older, proven-dangerous men on the block. All this would be done out in the open, near the school, and with all cops as witnesses. Our unshakable feeling was our arrests would become airtight prosecutable cases.

Our meeting with the federal attorney went almost as planned. He listened to our proposal and thought it over. We complemented our plan by promising that all resources would be in-house. No federal money would be spent, and no other federal resources would be utilized. We'd do all the work and his office would get the glory in court. We just wanted the Crips to feel us cutting into their freedom. He gave us his blessing.

"I like your plan," commented the attorney. "My office respects what you're doing and will prosecute the cases. It would help if you caught them selling crack, as well." Uh oh. We wanted that, too, but so far, we hadn't pulled any crack off of our Crips. We told the attorney we would do our best and left it at that.

CHAPTER 7:

THE FEDS

We knew what we wanted to pull off this operation. First up, was to ask our Command to locate three young, black police officers. Our previous observations were that it was always black men that rolled up or walked to the Crip dealers. For whatever reason, that was their customer base on 32nd. If we could give them black men to sell to, they probably would. Our command found three black patrol officers from our Department to work for us. Street Narcotics would furnish a control officer slaved to us to govern the buy money and any equipment they contributed to us. That included one of their vans with a periscope mounted in the center. We could sit at the viewing scope that was disguised as a vent, raise the glass eye through the ceiling, and watch in all directions. We would set the van up as a remote command post and park where the occupants could monitor the buys.

We put the operation into motion and watched with confidence as our undercover buyers waited until they were signaled. All three undercover operatives were in cool cars, ordinary pastel colored fords purchased by the department for undercover work, or in seized vehicles loaned out to us.

Law enforcement seized cars from drug dealers as ill-gotten booty. These asset forfeitures granted the vehicles to various police agencies as property for their department's use. Some agencies loaned their seized cars to other departments. The system worked really well for cops who needed particular models of cars. For instance, if a drug unit wanted to pull off an undercover coup at a race car track, nothing blended in and set the drug dealers at ease more than a 1970 Chevelle with a 350 small block in the hands of a "buyer" who actually borrowed the car from the DEA.

We'd send in our undercover car team when our more desired Crip targets shambled onto the block and took up their usual post on 32nd and within a hundred yards of the school. Kevin, our undercover cop, or UC was in a moss-colored 1986 Mustang with a four-banger engine. Nobody on the block would have pegged him in that rolling shanty as a cop. The buyers arrived like clockwork as they rolled up next to the Crips we knew. We chose the cop buyers from the same neighborhoods or relied on Crip greed, to avoid danger. Each Crip made a sale to one of our buyers. No arrests were made for the moment. We'd get as many of them to sell as possible and nail them another day. This process is the essence of a tactic labeled "buy-walk," buy dope now and arrest later. We'd get as many of the unsuspecting gangsters to sell dope to our crew as we could and then hand a neat, prosecutable package to the attorney. We had all the seized dope efficiently identified. Any seller we didn't know would be contacted out in the open by one of our chase cars as though it was business as usual. We would FI them as usual, but with more depth to the intent.

We ran the operation for two days. That was all it took to roll up eight dope-dealing street thugs. We now had a who's who of bangers on a short list to prison. We felt pretty much like "top cops" for the moment.

The next meeting was set up with the same federal attorney. We had a Street Narcotics detective with us as sort of a liaison in case we needed his investigatory weight behind us. There was another federal attorney who accompanied the one that set this operation in motion. The primary attorney had the files of the arrests delivered to his office days prior. He'd reviewed everything and started the meeting with warm greetings. Then, he sank the floor right out from underneath us when he confessed that when the program was green-lit, he thought we were going to pull down hardened, armed street soldiers that moved kilos of people-destroying crack cocaine. All he saw laid out before him were a bunch of pot dealers who wore blue Pendleton shirts and gang rags. Our first meeting was the genesis for the arrests of the Crips we arrested selling marijuana in front of a school. When the attorney expected more dramatic offerings, our pride was deflated. We gave them the plan. We fed them the post-project data, and that wasn't enough. We home-brewed amber lager and the feds wanted honey mead.

I had the lead on this project from its inception. This was a big deal for me and encompassed a lot of firsts including first work with federal law enforcement, first spy van use, and my first gang sweep as the planner. The attorney sounded like he wanted to scrap the whole project. The SDPD side of the table all protested. I sat up straight and asked how to retain his interest in this gambit. He took a moment to contemplate then counseled us about delivering a "product" at the federal level. He wanted more and bigger. Never mind that the suspects were the exact people he wanted. He pronounced it would take more than a quick one-time for each of the future prisoners. Without the malignant scent of crack on their persons, we just didn't have the glamorous arrests the government wanted to spend prosecution time and money on.

We pushed back and responded with how our efforts checked all the boxes. When the parents and families of the kids at King Elementary saw the police attack at the roots of drug sales, there was a momentary restoration of their faith in the system. How could this go unrewarded? None of the men we'd bagged selling dope had ever done federal prison time. If we scooped up a handful of diehard gangsters and sent them into federal court, we would make the strong impression WECAN strived to achieve.

The two attorneys debated with each other. They'd projected our response before we ever walked into the meeting. Our main attorney was just testing our resolve. They'd already decided to counter our concerns with a response. To keep the operation active and placate us, we'd have to do it all over again.

This head-banging moment was brought to you by the good people at the Federal Prosecutor's Office. The SDPD side had lost a few breaths. The attorney was firm that we'd have to do it all over again. If we ran the identical program and got the same crew again, his office would take the cases. Our Command would not be happy, but what choice did we have? If we caught them for what we had on them now, they would see the District Attorney in court. They would get convicted for certain. The penalty for sales near the school enhanced the crime to a federal felony. The prosecutor said that this time they would shoot for several years apiece. Those that plead out would start at three-to-five years in prison. The attorney wasn't shy when he admitted that they'd parole out after the first year. If a Crip took them to trial and lost, as expected, he'd do the full stretch in custody. Crack would have netted twice that amount of incarceration. "It's just pot, gentlemen." We sucked it up and told the Feds we'd be back.

We reassembled the buyers, the WECAN cops, the Narcotics van, the narcotics detective and the buy money. The ever-present Crips knew nothing. They were on the set as always, no smarter from our previous actions. We gathered together the same undercover buyers and equipment and did it again. This time, we stretched the operation out to several days over a two-week period. We projected two weeks in order to get our previous targets the necessary second time. These bangers tended to not keep bankers' hours. To get them all again would mean we'd have to cover a succession of afternoons since none of them seemed to be up before lunch.

To get this project rolling, we'd stayed clear of the 32nd Street group. After we'd left them alone for a couple of weeks, we lulled them into false senses of security which fit right into our plan. We knew that they knew a beef for pot was a ticket. A beef for sales of pot was local jail time. In their minds, nobody ever did prison for marijuana. They didn't sense that their vulnerability to state or federal jail time was tied to their choices to be in street gangs and to sell too close to schools.

The streetwise Crips never "saw" their true fate until WECAN delivered the news with the long-awaited arrests.

CHAPTER 8:
SHOTS FIRED!

Some of the Crips' family homes were spread out around the blocks near 32nd and J. Historically, Central Division cops had chased and fought some of those families for decades. There were still plenty of veteran officers around the department who remembered names similar to those of the thugs we'd taken off the streets. Those were the names that belonged to older brothers, fathers, uncles and even grandfathers. The gang infestation was embedded and could not be removed permanently. Crippin' was for life.

After our initial big scheme to pinch the group, others took their places, but south of Market. They still sold dope across from the school. Their imprisoned brethren warned them away from the house above Market and to not sell when school was in session. The Crips who replaced the others got FI'd daily and were caught up in our reset. Four of us planned to wait until dark to pick up a couple more arrests if players we still needed to find, showed up.

Manny and I used the darkness to stand in the schoolyard and watch the action at 32nd and J Streets. John Tangredi and Chuck Davis were the chase car team, parked two blocks away and ready to pounce on our say-so. We parked in front of the closed elementary school and gained entry through a gate left open by the custodial crew who were cleaning the rooms. The pair of us had no backlighting to give our positions away as we walked east onto the decomposed granite play yard. We were close enough to see and not be seen by one Crip who stood under a streetlight on the corner across the street from the yard's tall chain-link fence. The Crip, one of the Duckett clan, was a target we'd not been able to nail the first go-round. The Duckett brothers were particularly hard-nosed and fought cops as easily as they'd scratch an itch. One of the Ducketts, an oddball we called, "Fuck-It Duckett," got his nickname from his responses to police officer stops: "Fuck-it, you're not taking me to jail," meant the fight was on.

Time passed and so did a few cars. Nobody slowed and we began to doubt that Duckett carried. We gave it a few more minutes and still no cars took quick detours to score. Finally, we decided to see what Duckett would do if John and Chuck rolled up. We knew the guy was easily provoked. John and Chuck wouldn't give him a chance to plant his feet when they confronted him. I called them in.

They parked their car close by, but out of sight of Duckett. The two officers closed in on foot and surprised him. Manny and I watched them get the drop, hoping he'd throw down some dope. Instead, he calmly faced them, giving us the impression that he didn't hold. The Tangredi, Davis team would be reduced to yet another FI.

The conversation between cops and crook was abruptly interrupted by a fast-moving sedan racing by on 32nd. Without warning, a shot came from the car and the zing of a bullet raced past the three men who all hit the ground. Manny and I saw and heard the shot but none of us were able to see the car's rear license plate. John and Chuck popped back up as Manny and I ran out of the school to our car. It didn't matter, the car was a ghost.

John Tangredi was a tightly-wired guy. He bristled easily and was a little high-strung. His upside as a WECAN member was his dope and street savvy. Tangredi had been SWAT but had to give up his pins to be on WECAN. Chuck Davis, a monolith of a man hovered over John and acted as his anchor since he was generally taciturn when dealing with the bad guys. His silence sometimes intimidated detainees who felt more at ease if he said anything to them. John and Chuck were courageous men without being foolish. Neither officer put themselves at risk unless they'd calculated the odds. This drive-by threw all that reasoning out the window and amped both men up. They would have chased the offensive car on foot and shot downrange at it if they'd recovered their composure faster from the initial surprise.

John and Chuck kicked Duckett free. Manny and I rounded the bend and hooked up with them. We were all breathless. What do we do? All four of us were certain that was a shot from a drive-by. Duckett sure acted like it was. But we hadn't put it out over the radio. John and Chuck were wired after the massive adrenaline dump. We just weren't certain what had just happened. I mean, who drives by on cops? The car was dark and had four wheels. After that, we had nothing factual to call in for cops to look for. We just decided to put out over the radio that it happened, and no one was hurt. Central Patrol would become edgy because the incident happened in their area. Maybe they'd be targeted next. The dispatcher had little to say and just notified her frequency to "keep your heads on swivels."

The four of us were in uniforms, the tans of the day, so it was likely the shooter knew John and Chuck were the police. Maybe the lack of a police car sent a different message to the shooter. The event was never solved.

CHAPTER 9:

MORE CRIPPIN'

When Central WECAN went mobile we targeted the blocks and intersections controlled by Hispanic gangs, mostly Mexican or Mexican Americans. The black gangs seemed to generate more violence which caught more news time than Hispanic and Asian gangs. The crack epidemic bled the inner neighborhoods of America's cities nearly to death. The battles over crack turf impacted black youth, more than the other cultures that were less likely to move crack in San Diego. We moved against Hispanic crack dealers when we found them, but they were not always San Diego street gangs. They were Mexican nationals on our side of the border, legally or not.

We caught flak from the bosses above because those Hispanic gang zones were not on our "to do" list. When our felony arrest statistics rose dramatically, the flak from upstairs subsided. Those gangs weren't often caught slinging crack, so they stayed out of the local press limelight. They committed every other crime available to man except cattle rustling and matched the crime quotas of the black gangs. Hispanics shared the same streets with the African Americans. I dealt with both sets of gangs with equal determination. If the Hispanic dealers were caught with crack as their market, we could only speculate how they got involved. Perhaps the Crips in Central Division's area supplied them. The Crips didn't care who sold dope on their streets, if they got a cut, or wholesaled the dope in the first place.

There was a seeming lack of public interaction between black and Hispanic gangs. You'd think the gangs lived apart from each other, but they shared the same blocks for the most part. I saw the dichotomy as two great armies with bad intent somehow living together. The uneasy peace the two ethnic groups of villains operated with was a testimonial to how much they didn't want turf wars based upon race. The few skirmishes I was privy to were usually one-on-one indiscretions settled with a knife blade or a gunshot. Besides, these people were not strangers to each other. They grew up together, went to the same schools, if they went at all, and lived next to each other. They understood they were not natural enemies. Zip codes were more likely to incite wars than skin colors.

We continually ramped down the WECAN walking assignment and spread ourselves throughout the Heights. We did get out and walk gangland in neighborhoods and on blocks we rarely traveled. The impact was gradual until we figured out who the players were. Suddenly we weren't there on foot, but arrests went up. We added more subterfuge and surveillance to our bags of tricks. When we returned to walk the same turf, the bad guys moved on. Gangsters grew more wary. We were hit-and-miss and unpredictable. The bad guys didn't know when to sell drugs or shoot each other because our unpredictability lessened their impulsive moves on their rivals. If a gangster was "hot" he'd generally make himself scarce. When he disappeared, we'd pressure snitches for the bad guy's hideouts. We'd borrow a little manpower and hit them there. Our tactics began to make a difference.

The snitches were all around us. Logan Heights' mean streets were uncivilized. Prostitutes were from the neighborhood. They might have been moved off to hotels by their "daddies," but they were still from these streets. And they talked to the police if there was a slim chance cooperation would make the police go away. I had leverage over a few of the street-walkers in the Heights. A prostitute might "dime off" someone she knew was wanted if she was high and didn't want to get handcuffed and run down to jail. These addicted women rarely hesitated to turn in people close to them if it meant freedom to feed their habits. Heroin, crack and the other pharmaceuticals are stronger than a conscience. In some cases, we hooked the women up for show to get them out of the neighborhood so everything looked legit. We'd drop them off where they asked, for their safety. The unselfish act was a deterrent to them for hooking on the block in front of children. The Heights up and down 32nd street was one messed up place right out of some L.A. based TV show. The other two WECAN Teams adopted similar practices at the same time. Sometimes, we would link-up and really stick it to a gang-infested block in each other's turfs.

We also got to know the players. We were with them every one of our workdays. We knew the gangsters' habits, their families and friends and how to match them to crimes. These are the aspects of intelligence collection that street cops are keen to develop. Drive-bys were rare. Thugs must have weighed the probability of getting caught against more caution than many of us had witnessed in the past. The Teams were making impact. The gangs hadn't gained a sense of Nirvana. They worried about the mysterious police tactics that didn't stop and warn them to get off the street. We stayed and shared the street with them.

WECAN was formed to tackle black gang territories and impede, make arrests and stop their violence above everything else. The Central Team, my team, targeted streets, intersections and school zones picked for us to hit. Early on, we walked those hoods, then we drove them. If violence crept back, we put the Walking back into WECAN, or parked a vehicle on the block and began anew.

The West Coast Crips home base was traditionally the intersection of Imperial Ave. and 30th Street. Anchored by two corner markets that sold booze to the gangsters all the time, the gangsters in blue had a ready-made location they could flank to sell dope and do bad-gang stuff. At some point, the lull in gang action at that intersection ended, followed by a flare up of fired shots. Gang-on-gang violence occurred when a player, or players, trod on another gang's turf. The crack epidemic brought gangsters to war over sales territory. Crack brought gang members to war over money and respect.

Gangsters killed because it's what gangsters do. The reasons could be as simple as a mad-dog glare while at school. Or, a Crip saw a Blood on Crip turf and didn't question why. He got a gun and went after the enemy. Those were issues of respect. Thrill-killers popped up and shot at the other colors for no better reason than seasoning a new player.

To counter the madness, our command stationed the mobile head-quarters next to Mullen's. This was the time where we set up the surveillance from the furniture store. The massive motorhome-style office re-birthed a lull in gang violence. We literally sat out front on lawn chairs and watched gang members try to act cool or dry up and disappear. Of course, they'd reappear blocks down, but this cat-and-mouse game was new to them. Whatever it meant to them the violence decreased again. WECAN had the money and resources to do what we wanted, where we intended to, for short periods of time. These daily acts may have been nothing more than Band Aid approaches, but the Band Aids covered big plots of gang territory.

The Central Team, less spread out than the Eastern and Southeastern Teams, worked in equally tough zones. The Heights produced high-value gang targets but encompassed less land. That compressed area was easier to cover. All the team members were pulling down increasing numbers of non-gang arrests, as well. The people we popped were also junkies and drug dealers not directly related to street gangs. Non-gang drug addicts, prostitutes, parolees, and probationers fell into our nets. This included gang members who used the drugs they sold. Some got hooked while others liked to get high before they pulled off crimes. WECAN watched and waited.

The users became instrumental to our cause. Under interrogation, they had tendencies to lie. When that failed to deter us, they changed tactics and tried to "Please, officer" their way out of jail.

Their pleas could quickly turn into offers of information we cared about. Sharing was caring. We waited until the crap they spewed out sounded like the truth rather than general bullshit. Inevitably they cut to the good stuff and spit out the location of a drug dealer.

Giving up dealers was easy for street people right up to the point where a gang member was involved. Their reluctance was born of wisely earned fear. We occasionally parleyed with these street people. We didn't push somebody who was just a small-timer to give up gang knowledge. The frightened, down-turned eyes explained that there was a line they wouldn't cross if it meant their likely endangerment. We were not detectives. We did not have the backing of our police department to work snitches beyond minor league street contacts. We were not allowed to set up and pay informants, although some of us found that an occasional shekel tossed their way could help our cause. Pushing street people to give up gangsters wasn't worth terrifying them.

What we got were sources who sent us to the same kinds of houses and apartments narcotics detectives got paid to take down. We began to relish these opportunities because they fascinated us. The dope places provided great spectacle and pounds of dope, guns and money seizures. Slowly, we tripped into the same work that comprised the job description of the narcotics detectives.

CHAPTER 10:

PROS

The Street Narcotics detectives work undercover. I've seen clean-cut investigators join narcotics and turn into bikers in every aspect except one, the fact that they were cops. I've watched beards grow, hair get braided and ears get pierced. Some detectives went steps further and made up fake scabs over the veins in their arms to mimic needle track marks. I only prayed that when stuck in a van with them on a raid, they'd all bathed.

Narc detectives work from pre-operation plans and contacts. They are trained and equipped to hit hard and fast, even if the plan was spur of the moment. WECAN always went into action in the now. The detectives worked deliberately, WECAN worked fast. The detectives worked from offices, while we were mobile and quick to engage. We could get a tip from say, a prostitute trading info for freedom from an under the influence pinch, and then follow up on the tip the next moment. The prostitutes were great sources for drug tips. Most were women and junkies, and almost had to contend with pimps. The pimps could be Crip or Blood gangsters, or they could be street criminals with no gang affiliation. The working women had to contend with violence and fear from every direction. Their prime directive was to work and make their bosses money. Goal number two was to beat back their daily, if not hourly, drug cravings. The failure to make money meant punishment or drug sickness. The women had every motivation to turn secret drug locations over to the police and stay in the game. WECAN had the time to work the information.

The places with dope for sale activity could be one of several places a junkie B-girl copped her dope. If the woman was high, she could go down, or get arrested for that offense. We preferred their insight over their incarceration. Most of the tips were accurate. The street ladies knew WECAN would be out the next day with all the time in the world to find them and hold them accountable for lies.

A hooker's reasons for giving it up were to stay out of jail and continue to get high. Not infrequently, the pimp behind the street "girl" was a man with the same pressures and habits. The place she gave up could be just one of several she bought from. At any given time, one place might be empty while another had dope. She may have given up the empty one, gambling we wouldn't know any better. Or, she was pissed at a place that was "up," because they cheated her. There's no complaint department at a dope house. Frankly, the junkies don't think too far into the future. The hooker spills a location because that was the only thing in her head, besides the draining euphoria from her last fix or puff.

"Hey, my dear. Why don't you hold up and talk to us?" John Tangredi asked. He and Chuck saw one of the regulars in front of a church on 32nd. She wore a worn minidress that accentuated long, thin legs in six-inch stilettos. No doubt the church pastor noticed a soul that needed saving, since the time was three o'clock in the afternoon. God would not interface with a hooker unless it was on her terms. Her pimp was somewhere around, just in case the preacher made a move. The cops were another story. Pimps boogey at the sight of cops. If John and Chuck were lucky, the pimp was nowhere around to cause this woman trouble later.

"I'm not carrying any drugs, Officer Tangredi," she said as she opened her purse and exposed only the vitals, lipstick, cheap perfume, hair spray, condoms, and a tampon. Her cash was smartly tucked into her underwear. She also knew John from the myriad times he and Chuck had intercepted her on 32nd as she trolled for the johns there.

"I know you aren't carrying, Tanya. Have you got a new dope place for us?"

"I gave you one last week. I don't like telling you stuff. I'm gonna get in trouble. Can't you leave me alone?"

Chuck Davis wore a stoic look and stood next to Tanya. The man's face was blank, but even without expression he broadcast the Jail is open' look. Tanya tried not to look up at Chuck for fear his eyes would lock onto hers and her veneer would crack.

"Tanya, I don't want to arrest you. I'm not threatening to arrest you. Last week was last week. I'm sure you know we took the place down. We want a new one. Look, some dope house must have pissed you off. Give it to us. You'll still get to buy from some other place. We'll take down the asshole you don't like and were all happy, *capiche*?"

"Huh?"

"Do you understand?" John momentarily forgot that his Italian jargon was as alien as the Queen's English to the dregs of the heights.

Tanya blew out some air and said, "There's a place off of Franklin, right around the corner from here."

"Who and what, Tanya?"

"Huh?"

"Who are they and what are they slinging?"

"Are you sure I have to do this? I don't even want to be seen here seen with you guys now." Her head swiveled as she looked for threats, certain her pimp was watching. Pimps are scary men for the ladies of the night. Movies don't exaggerate their retribution and their deadliness. "Act like you're still searching my purse, so I don't look like we're just talking, she said. The place on Franklin is for real. Mexicans. They sell black and white from a window off the alley." She said. The term "black and white" refers to black as the color of heroin, although the drug is really a dark chocolate brown. White relates to the crystalline form of powdered cocaine. Users of crack deal with another form of cocaine, but rarely buy it in combination with heroin. Crack will range from white to a light, tannish hue.

"How do we find it?" John asked.

"The place is a house in the back of another house. The gate has spray paint on it, some gang shit. And, a trash can is in front of the gate sometimes. When they don't have no dope, the can is off to the side."

"Are they up now?"

"Should be. One of the girls asked me to go with her. That alley is scary at night." John looked past Tanya at the immobile Chuck Davis. Chuck lowered an eyebrow like he was doubtful they'd find the place. John tilted his head to one side and gave a slight shrug. The old saying, "You pays your money and you take your chances," signified the decision was made to let her go while they tried their luck finding the location. There was always the outside chance Tanya would burn the two cops by getting word to the dopers. That's why WECAN generally worked its ploys with more than just a couple of cops. We prepared for every contingency to cover our backsides. "Bye, Tanya. It might be time for you to work another part of town," John warned.

WECAN cops, like other cops, were living lie detector machines. We could tell truth from fiction with most sources. Their "tells" gave them up quick, furtive movement with down-cast eyes, sudden twitches, or other nervous tics when junkies test lies to see if they can sell them. Even the best liars fouled up when we already knew the answers. We knew when a dope location sounded right and when it didn't. For instance, we had a junkie get a pass after he told us of a place on Clay Street that slung *chiva* out a side window. *Chiva* was a Mexican street term for the lowest quality, reddish-brown resin extracted from poppies. We were in marked cars, so gliding past a place to spot-check the action just alerted the ne'er-do-wells that cops were in the mix. Unfortunately, our source failed to mention that a watcher was posted on the porch to this ramshackle rental house. I made eye-contact with him purely by chance and that was enough for the occupants to shut down for the day. They were gone when we snuck back an hour later.

When the vibe was wrong and we hadn't kicked the source free, all we had to do was explain that we'd take them to the location for clarification. The zesty truth that had eluded us escaped their mouths pretty quickly after that. Nothing encouraged a junkie's cooperation more than putting them in the back seat as we slowly passed dealers and gangsters who stood on their tippy toes to get a view of the huddled body behind our cage.

CHAPTER 11:
DOPERS

For every street corner dealer, there seemed to be an equal number moving their inventories from fixed dwellings. They work from houses and apartments where they could lock themselves in behind bars, doors and walls and turn them into fortresses. Their standings in the community as transitory, criminal drug peddlers, didn't guarantee them protection against thieves and robbers. There'd always be a worse predator than the ones selling dope. The windows would be sealed, save for one fashioned into a take-out window with a tiny opening. The thieves were restricted to hand-to-hand contact to pass money through the portal, designed to keep them outside and the dealers safe inside. Everyone in the game was aware of the riches within, especially the hungry junkies. All dope houses ran the risk of being invaded by dope-rip thugs or police raids.

Just to clarify a point, the Crips were notorious criminals, but a specific incident surprised even the cops. There was a neighborhood backroom card game in Southeast that ran late into the evening. The locals were gambling the night away without the knowledge of the police and placed a lot of cash on the tables. There were guys to watch the action and offer some level of protection, but no outdoor impediments to a raid. That raid did come and not from the police. Masked Crips poured into the room with guns drawn and attempted a rash take-down effort to freeze everybody in place. The plan was ill-thought. Perhaps someone on the inside gave the Crips the half-assed plan. Actions went awry almost from the beginning as guns were drawn by some of the victims. The Crips tried to scoop up cash as they realized they might be in over their heads. The sight of guns drawn down on them was enough to scatter the robbers as they raced panic-stricken for two exits. Witnesses gave some descriptions as a bunch of amped-up, frightened thugs tore out into the night with perhaps a few gunshots aimed loosely in their direction. People knew who they were. They'd been preying on their own turf for years. The brash attack shocked everybody. The Crips held nothing sacred.

Many dope places operated with little inventory on site. If there was a rip-off or seizure, they didn't lose a lot of product. The example of the Crips gambling room attack had been repeated many times by other raiders and the dope houses were prime targets. The houses or apartments were all organized and run by somebody responsible for groups of dope dens. For the handlers, they were charged with drop-off replacement dope and removal of excess cash. Since it was a cash business, robbers knew they wouldn't get stuck with checks and credit card slips.

Most of the dope sold in this fashion was powdered cocaine and heroin. The dope houses set up traditions ages ago in the drug subculture. The safety is in the fort. Neither the bad guys nor the cops could get in fast enough to prevent either a repulse by the dealers inside, or destruction of the evidence, the toilet being the quick and efficient destroyer.

Some junkies would buy both coke and *chiva* at the window. The combination of the two created a longer-lasting concoction, slang worded "speedball." A lot of our house busts were for both cocaine and heroin. The combo of the two gave the user a quick cocaine rush followed by a longer heroin high that lasted up to eight to ten hours. Neither drug alone could furnish that length of action in a person's physiology. The problem for the junkie was the drug might cost twice as much as one dose of either. Crack was available if you knew which home was moving it.

The coke user was only there to score coke. The heroin user was there to buy the skag, a street word for both. The heroin user was the one feeding a biological addiction four to six times a day. The speedball's effects may have extended the high long enough to reduce the numerous, daily times needed to get the dope. Four to six times a day is the daily dosage for heroin addicts. Speedballing can reduce that time to fewer trips to the dope connection. With the number of junkies countywide that headed to Logan Heights to score so many times a day, we could pick them off and trail the origin back to a dope house. This routine seemed almost assembly-line simple. One dope spot went down through our manipulations while another surfaced elsewhere.

The dopers didn't bank dope. They bought one, maybe two doses at a time. If they bought more, they'd want to use it all at once and probably kill themselves. If able to resist the desire to consume everything they scored, they could sell a little to a user farther away from the source. That dealer made a little more when he or she raised the price. That way the user-dealer saved their buyer the price and hassle of a ride to the source.

WECAN's visibility attracted a lot of attention. Attorneys for the prosecutorial side all wanted to ride with us to see what the fuss was all about. We were in court all the time on preliminary hearings with lock-tight reports and testimonies. Thirty-six officers swept through gangland and rolled up a lot of in-custodies. I can attest to a busy life at court. Our workdays were consumed with "tagging and bagging" the detestable gangsters of the Heights for crimes destined to be reviewed by prosecutors. There would be no winging it on reports. The facts would be in depth, articulate and meet the rules of the laws of arrest.

When I saw a dude caught in my headlights handing a foil bindle to another dude at Chicano Park, my report would reflect Bad Guy #1 was in my line of sight when I turned the street corner next to La Central Market. Bad Guy #2 froze in place at the sight of the police car as his right hand proffered a couple of U.S. bills to Bad Guy #1. Both Dudes were popped on the spot. Dude #1 moved a foil bindle of "lovely" or PCP to Dude #2 for cash money. Bad Guy #1 is quickly arrested before he bolts and is charged with the sales of a controlled substance: Bad Guy #2 got nailed for simple possession, but it's still a felony.

PCP scared the hell out of everybody, and the courts were none too pleased with the sellers and the users. There'd be no "opium crisis" sentiment for PCP abusers. Many in today's society feel great leniency towards opiate users who got trapped by the overeager pharmaceutical world and its vast dispersal of painkillers. PCP users will likely never see kindness from the general public.

Defense attorneys wanted to know what this aggressive army was doing hammering away at their clients. They'd seen little previous precedent for this level of gang and dope enforcement in San Diego. Many defense attorneys became preoccupied with strategies to beat us in court, but few did. Some investigators within the department were standoffish. They complained that we got underfoot when we invaded their territory so often that we had to find ways to work together. The investigators from each division got stuck processing our arrests. We seemed to have doubled their workload overnight, which probably would have irritated me to no end if I was in their shoes.

San Diego County and law enforcement from the State level on down accessed the same relatively new county computer filing system set up to round-file police target locations to keep officers from interfering with each other when seeking search warrants. Whichever law enforcement agency or specific officer set their target raid in the system first had priority, as in, first come, first served. WECAN used to ignore the sign-up file until a near-feud with Street Narcotics forced us to keep the list in mind. The computer system built to alert police agencies about upcoming targets was called the NIN File. Nobody can recall decades later what NIN stood for.

CHAPTER 12:

INTERESTED PARTIES

Street Narcotics Detective Max fumed the day his team hit a house and found Central WECAN inside collecting dope and prisoners. He yelled "Did you check the NIN File? You're not supposed to be here. This is Street Narcotics territory." Five of us looked at him nonplussed. His team looked everywhere but at him.

"Sorry, Max. This is the first I heard about any file." I had no defense. He was right. We learned about the file and practiced proper boundaries. But then, one of Tangredi and Davis's snitches gave up a location during our shift. The day was late, so either Tangredi or Davis listed the location in the NIN File. They consulted with the rest of us and it was decided none of us wanted to go home late that evening.

We gathered forces to hit the target the next day. It was a tiny cubicle like an ancient granny-flat the size of two sheds. Five of us had perimeter control before the three chosen knocked on the door. The only problem was that the door was already open because the place was filled with narcotics detectives. Detective Max got there first, after disregarding the NIN file he'd yelled at us about ignoring mere days before.

"What the fuck, Max? Really? This how you want to play it?" I was pissed. This time, a couple of his fellow detectives cleared the room for a smoke break. They'd already found the dope, the money and two Mexican nationals.

Nobody wanted an in-house fight. We were wrong the first time. But this was just Max slinging the dog shit, the "big dog" teaching the "little dog" a lesson. Max's team kept their opinions to themselves, so I couldn't get a feel for their level of support of WECAN or their frustration with Max.

I shared our Street Narcotics encounter with some of the folks from the other two WECAN teams. So far, those officers had remained immune from the touchy subject of *internecine* rivalry.

I hated being the odd man out. Meanwhile, Street Narcotics received newly minted detectives. Some of those came up through WECAN. WECAN now had brothers and sisters in the right place. Street Narcotics became our allies.

San Diego's City Attorney's Office was wholly unprepared for the increase in their workload. WECAN savaged their prosecutors with bunches of drug arrest cases overnight. The individual attorneys were not all on board with the heavier work that filled up courtroom dockets with dozens of weekly preliminary hearings, the process that occurs to assure there's enough probable to move forward with prosecution. Some of the more curious prosecutors got our cases and wisely asked their origins. We explained, there was a new sheriff in town, so to speak. WECAN was going to take the streets back from drugs and gangs. At least, that was the cowboy imagery we imagined. The attorneys with attitudes seemed perturbed about the increase in junkies and dopers we wrangled through the legal system. Some of the prosecutors either hated dope cases or thought too much was being done about nothing. Those attorneys who wanted other legal challenges moved up, or out.

The prosecution side of the courtroom wasn't the only one affected. Defense attorneys, especially those who had their own practices, saw increases in the defendant count. San Diego County had a legal outfit called Public Defenders. Public Defenders are essentially employees of a public agency whose mission is to represent indigent defendants. A lot of the people we arrested were penniless or below the scale set for middle income boundaries. Court-Appointed Lawyers are private practice attorneys contracted to provide representation to indigent defendants. The influx of arrests of Mexicans illegally in San Diego provided Public defenders with an army of indigent clients.

Court-Appointed Lawyers, a private law firm, subbed-in for cases where the Public Defender didn't have the capacity to take on additional cases or where a potential conflict of interest existed for the Office of Public Defenders. Sometimes, the term Court-Appointed Lawyer is used to refer to both Public Defenders and private practice attorneys. WECAN got introduced to a variety of defense attorneys because of the constancy of court appearances over our arrests. One attorney, Inge

Brauer, received the overflow of our undocumented alien arrests. I faced off with her in court over my dope house pinches on a regular basis.

Brauer showed more spunk than some of the attorneys playing from the Public Defender bullpen. She made representation of undocumented Mexicans her cause. I picked up on comments that claimed Brauer thought WECAN railroaded alien dope dealers and singled them out because they were illegals and Mexicans. There was no unofficial stage for a Brauer-type and a WECAN officer to sit and work out their differences. Inge could only talk to me through the auspices of court. On the stage in front of a judge, Brauer would pry and attack, but she could only read my thoughts in the form of answers to her questions:

"How did you come across my client?"

"My team got a tip that drugs were being sold by illegal aliens in a house. The defendant was caught inside a place where heroin and cocaine were being sold."

"Who gave you permission to enter?"

"The Defendant. My partner spoke to him in Spanish and asked if we could come inside and search for drugs. He said yes and we performed our duties."

"Did you admonish him or explain he wasn't obligated to let you in?"

"No to both questions. He wasn't under arrest, so the Miranda warning didn't yet matter."

"You mentioned your tip referred to illegal aliens. Did you specifically target people crossing the border without papers?"

"No."

"You have a propensity for arresting undocumented persons, based upon prior cases involving you and your team. Are you told to pick them out for arrests?"

"No."

"Then how do you come to be in court again with more undocumented people from Mexico?"

"WECAN is designed to stop anyone from selling dope. We make a lot of those arrests. It seems the world of dealing heroin and cocaine in San Diego is inhabited by Mexicans from across the border. We go where the dope is. We don't target people from a foreign nation."

Brauer expected, and got, the WECAN official line. I booked hundreds of people. So many, in fact, that there became an unofficial testimonial template. I testified to each case as though many were written in the same pamphlet on police officer testimony for drug and gang enforcement. Brauer and I bandied back and forth over probable cause and the laws of arrest. Brauer was a worthy adversary, much better educated than me. Unlike me, she had the words of her clients and nothing more to argue against us. I was in those drug dens and she was not.

Brauer was not a fan of WECAN as her client list grew and we were the constant names on the arrest reports. Every case I had with a Brauer client that went to a preliminary hearing was bound over for court by the sitting judge. All those cases skipped trial when Brauer's clients took deals from the prosecution. I doubt if the punishment was severe. More than likely, Brauer got her clients off with local time and deportation, and that was a joke. There was nothing I despised more than the succubi that poured drugs into our neighborhoods and lived off the poison's effects. The only way it could get worse was if the deportees reappeared in the same communities.

Manny and I nailed a dope dealer from Mexico soon after my transfer to Central. He was a conspicuous corner dealer at 25th and Imperial and intersection that was a hotbed of drug activity. Our guy caught a glimpse of our car as we crept up on him in traffic. Rather than run, blend in with the crowd of Hispanics around him, or toss his stash somewhere, he dropped the baggie on the ground. Pounce! We got him with no need to establish more probable cause to set up the arrest. He practically handed the arrest to us. He'd conveniently tossed away fourteen tiny balloons of heroin. We pinched him on the spot for the dope. Heroin users were hooked for life. They bought the dope they needed for the moment or for the day if they had the cash. Nobody does fourteen balloons of dope in a day and lives, so the court would see our justification for popping him for possession for sale.

The man was in Brauer's hands. True to form, he lost at prelim and went into the system after a plea deal. Deportation would follow jail. He was back at the intersection of 25th and Imperial two months later.

He'd gotten a free ride back to Mexico and had time to visit his family before returning to work in the U.S.

Central WECAN brought the greatest number of Mexican nationals to prelim. Those dealers infested Logan and Sherman Heights. Brauer's offices were in their neighborhood. She may very well have displayed her shingle in the Heights turf to collect a greater number of cross-border customers. She sure stink-eyed WECAN officers when we were in court testifying on behalf of the law.

CHAPTER 13:

ACLU

Like I said, everybody wanted to know about WECAN. The attorneys from the other side weren't granted access to us at work. Their only quality time with WECAN was on the opposite side in court. A few were friendly to police officers, even social. Others were not and never intended to be social with cops. The police were simply impediments to successful court defenses. But then, a curious request was granted. An attorney from the ACLU got permission to meet us. Strictly speaking, defense attorneys, even civil rights attorneys, don't mix with uniformed cops. Oil and water don't mix. We tried to put the genie of evil back in the bottle. The ACLU tried to redefine the genie and the bottle.

The ACLU attorney, Karen, was a petite, middle-aged white woman with notches on her belt for her lifetime fight for people's rights. Suddenly, her office was inundated with complaints about WECAN. Few of the complaints came from community leaders, but had originated from African American sources in the areas WECAN worked. Our bosses received an inquiry from her office to set up a meet. The local ACLU wasn't so sure the police needed to be investigated by their office. They wanted to bridge the gulf between us with a request for an ordinary event, a ride-along. Our command was eager to please them and shut the inquiry down at the same time. Our department trusted our professionalism and decorum. As far as they were concerned, we had nothing to hide. The ride-along request was briefly mulled over and then granted. Manny and I were the pair chosen to escort Karen around the hood.

We met Karen in our supervisor's office. She attended her first police line-up. WECAN line-ups are dull affairs. We listened to a few bulletins and talk a little shop. Department announcements geared towards the troops were read aloud by the line-up supervisor and then posted.

"To All Hands: Department Announcement dated Four dash Thirty dash Twenty Eighteen supersedes Department Announcement dated Twelve dash One dash Twenty Seventeen. This new announcement voids the previous announcement instructing sworn personnel to disregard the previous instructions about the Sign-In roster for pool cars. The prior instruction instructed sworn employees to sign the Sign-In Form with their full names. Due to the inability of the Department to audit illegible names, employees are hereby commanded to sign their names and then print their names. A 'Print Name Here' box has been added to a new version of the Sign-In Form. Divisional commanders are instructed to destroy the previous version of the Sign-In Forms. Implementation of the new forms begins immediately. Disregard all previous Department Announcements referring to the Sign-In lists." It wasn't easy to ignore such scintillating verbiage, but somehow, we always managed.

Karen got to sit through one of these stimulating reads. The rest of the line-up was short. Patrol line-ups require the troops to verbally participate. WECAN's were quick because we only had six or seven members at each division. Patrol could mass up to fifteen, even twenty cops, at line-up. Line-ups began twenty minutes before shift pay cut-in. The idea was to get the secretarial crap out of the way so we could enter the field on the hour our pay started and replace the incoming officers from the prior shift. In twenty years, that daily twenty minutes added up. Battles were fought between the Police Officers Association and the city to compensate cops for that dead time. We never won our side of the dispute and the city continued to get away with paycheck theft.

The patrol sergeants were ordered to go around the room and spotlight each officer and ask them if they had any contributions. Most cops saw this wasted twenty minutes they didn't get paid for as a necessary evil.

Karen knew hers was an incursion into "enemy territory" but wanted it to be a benign one. She spoke up and talked about her background. As expected, her education and life's experiences were tremendously different from my WECAN brothers and sisters. She shared that she wasn't a rabid anti-police liberal and that she wasn't so concerned about police officers that she distrusted all of us. She worked from the angle that the police should be monitored for their behavior with greater scrutiny than San Diego's Police Department. Citizen complaints were motivators in her mind for that oversight.

WECAN's superiors stored citizen complaints. They could be made public upon request. The ACLU recorded their SDPD complaints and occasionally sought out SDPD complaint records.

Karen was intrigued by a specialized police unit that produced so many arrests but gathered few complaints. In fact, the only complaints came from the relatives of gang members WECAN officers had arrested. She thought our record was extraordinary.

Lieutenant Saldamando stepped into the line-up room as Karen spoke and laid out the results of our effectiveness and proof that hand-picked officers for specific jobs can do the task without bias. The fact that we did not appeal to the "feel good" press by painting fences or standing for photo ops, irked some. The fact that we had good relations with the public in downtrodden neighborhoods was a surprise to her.

Manny had distaste for liberal attorneys and was no fan of the ACLU. He had no interest in putting on a show for Karen or even conversing with her. The toothpick gritted between his teeth would likely shred within the first hour she was with us. I wanted to convince Karen that WECAN's social commitment was not an act. We talked to the regular people within our midst when they had something to say. We didn't choose the time and places to brace citizens for conversation. They made the advances and we listened. A lot of their questions centered on why we police officers did what we did. Rather than blow smoke, we explained how our department and our unit worked.

"Officer, I don't understand why you stopped that young man. He was just crossing the street from what I could see," was a question that Karen heard.

"I know the guy. He's a Crip and he's on probation for selling dope," I explained.

"But he wasn't doing nothing when you stopped him. Is that allowed?"

"His probation allows us to stop him at any time without a warrant or even a reason. But that could go on all day with any probationer. This guy is a gang member with some history of violence. He deals crack and is bound to get into trouble again, probably even hurt somebody or get hurt. He shouldn't even be on this block because this is where he gets into that trouble. Because he's a gangster and we're gang cops, it's what we're told to do. We bug 'em until they get tired of it and take off for some other place. If we get it right, we can slow down the violence and drug-dealing on this block." I looked at the man, a black guy about ten years older than me. I could read his thoughts, intuiting he was mulling over my words. I added, "Do you live on this block?"

"I live a block away. I go this way to get to Bruno's. I see all these young guys out here and I know they're up to no good. But I don't think it's right the police harassing them all the time, either."

"I get that. We're not looking to jam up black guys for being black. But the gangsters are a whole other issue and it goes beyond skin color. This community may not all be behind us on the gang problem, but I figure enough people want us around though. That's why we're here, to reduce the BS and ease some minds." I gave Karen the exact same speech when she asked Manny and I about our mandate to reduce the gang and drug problems.

Manny and I borrowed our sergeant's cage-less car for the ride-along. Although, I do have a habit of cracking wise with liberals, placing her in the back of our regular cage patrol car wasn't going to gain us any points. We cruised Karen around Logan Heights and showed her the gangster hot spots. As usual, 30th and Imperial, 32nd and J, Chicano Park, 400 S. Evans, 25th and Imperial, and all the rest were cooperatively occupied by the denizens we anticipated.

We stopped for some FIs and allowed Karen to speak with the men we braced. She wanted to hear from these men about the circumstances that lead them and others like them to complain about the police. She didn't divulge her position as an attorney. She watched our various interactions. If they addressed her directly, she was free to chat with them. At each stop there was some back and forth conversation between me and Karen. I'm the talker and Manny's the wary, silent type. Karen suggested that the street life seemed to doom too many men of color.

At least one Crip we talked to thought Karen was a police lieutenant. Karen tried to ask him questions about being a gang member.

"Why are you in a gang?" is not a question I would lead with when talking to Crips, but Karen did.

The guy responded, mumbling, "I'm not in a gang, Lieutenant." Karen looked perplexed. She witnessed Manny and I approach him and use his first name in a streetwise greeting. She wasn't naïve. The guy was dressed in Crip blue from head to toe.

"I'm sorry, I'm not a police officer. I'm with the ACLU. I was under the impression you were a Crip gang member." Karen would have been attacked by this man and his friends if she made that statement and wasn't with us. No real lieutenant, in plain clothes, would contact hostile gangsters alone.

The Crip lined his eyes up with Karen's and warned, "You don't need to be in my face, Lieutenant. I ain't been doing nothin." Her representation of the ACLU didn't register with him. I guessed this encounter was a first for him. I doubt if he even paid attention to the ACLU. I've met few Crips who politicized their gang membership. The only regard the gangsters had for attorneys was the ones that got them back onto the streets after arrests.

I bailed Karen out from the Crip's focus and told the man to chill. "The lady's an attorney, man, from the ACLU. I wouldn't piss her off if I were you. You might need her one day." A couple of street people we talked to sussed out that Karen was a sort of social worker. They snapped at a perceived opportunity, thinking she was the "free hand-out" kind of social clinician. She corrected them and outed herself as an attorney with the ACLU. They had no idea what she was talking about. They just wanted money.

One or two of our pedestrian stops figured out who she was, what she wanted to know and why she was with the police. They looked over at Manny and me to see if this was legit. When one of us nodded, at least one inquirer, Tremont, got on his soapbox and blasted the police for this kind of daily harassment. Karen gave Tremont her full attention to his snappy repartee. She wanted the honesty and nastiness out in the open. Her street experience at this level was nil. She got the raw emotions she'd only witnessed at organized rallies or in office meetings in the past. Tremont raised his voice and took advantage of this rare moment to ramble on in a tirade against the unfairness of the police. Manny told him to get wise and lower it a notch. Tremont stepped back and "tsked" us through gritted teeth. With a dismissal of his hand, he turned and stormed off.

Karen didn't anticipate this kind of outburst. She'd been at countless venues where people yelled in groups, or in meetings, where the audience was riled at the police and wanted to vent. She told us that the heat comes off the audience in their vehemence. She's the lucky one, she gets to advocate for their complaints and become the "good guy."

Karen watched Manny and I remain cool and speak with measured control. There's no extra pay for bullying needlessly. We'll attack if challenged but getting yelled at by a Crip because he gets stopped by the police is just whining to me. He's the bad guy. Suck it up. I didn't put that into so many words. His frustration and loud words are not uncommon to cops in the Heights. I wanted Karen to see what it takes to work the job. She got the necessary earful, while Manny and I remained loose in stance and guarded her in case the man crossed the line. Karen came to understand more about the roles cops and bad guys play on the streets.

Our conversations about our actions within WECAN's mandate led Karen to consider how important it was to get out in uniform and select out the worst villains we could find for these street-side chats. She saw the upside to two cops watching their own backs so they could talk to people who were often dangerous to the point of being killers. She also gauged the line between contact and forceful detention. I told her that line blurs on the streets and is often the crux between what she just witnessed and what her office investigates. I also reminded her that these contacts can get raw fast and it takes "two to tango" and that there's two sides to each story. I commented that the worst people can be mental cases who could pop off with little provocation or warning. A lone WECAN officer is as vulnerable as any officer working anywhere. SDPD has a roll call of fallen officers felled because they were alone in the field. WECAN's partner teams were designed to reduce those fearful incidents.

I knew a fifteen-year-old Hispanic kid, named Hernando who I'd been watching ever since Manny and I took him home to his parents. We'd found him wandering past houses on G Street with that telltale PCP gaze. He wasn't so stoned he couldn't answer questions accurately. Like, "What's your name?"

"Hernando."

"You get stoned, Hernando?" I could smell the ether from his breath. "Where do you live, Hernando?" He either smoked a fraction of a dose of lovely, or he was coming down. I needed to get him off the street and home to his folks. "Where do you live?"

"Why?"

"To get you home to your parents."

"Oh, Yeah."

"Sooo, your address?" I wasn't penetrating the haze completely.

"Clay Street. I don't know the numbers. I can take you there."

Fifteen and he didn't know his address. This kid stood no chance of staying out of a gang. We took him home and met his mother at the door. She spoke English. "Ma'am, Hernando is on drugs." She tightened her face into worry.

"*Drogas*?" I didn't need Manny's Spanish to translate.

"*Si, senora. Mas drogas.*"

Manny edged in front of me and broke the conversation down to simple phrases in a blend of English and Spanish I couldn't follow but she did. I did catch "*mi esposo.*" So, there was a father, I thought. Hernando stood with us with a goofy look on his face. His mother, Esmeralda, just stared at him like it was the first time she'd seen her boy turn into something she didn't understand. We left him with her and parted ways.

I told Karen we intended to check up on this kid, Hernando, this evening and gave her the back story. Manny would translate if Karen wanted to ask them questions. This was a different kind of police contact, the humanitarian side. The kid was on the verge of joining the Logan Heights Red Steps gang. The Red Steps had been around for a couple of generations. They took their name from an old apartment building a block away from the kid's house. If Hernando joined the gang, his folks would lose their son.

We took Karen to meet the family and check up on the boy. Mom was at home, but the dad was at work. The boy was in his bedroom and came out at mom's behest. Karen saw a tiny house for a family of five. The teen lived with his younger brother and sister in the same cramped bedroom, the beds all touched each other so that the kids had to crawl over each other to extricate themselves from the room.

Manny explained to mom why we were here. This was a visit out of concern, not to create fear. I could see the look of concern in her eyes. The mere mention of Hernando made her eyes well up with tears almost immediately. She didn't fear us. We weren't there to arrest the kid or scare anybody. She feared for her boy. She knew in her heart she was losing him to other influences. She was more comfortable conversing in Spanish when she was upset. She told Manny her husband works so hard and spends little time with his family. He cares deeply for Hernando. But both parents were unaccustomed to raising kids in this environment. Life was different in Mexico. I didn't ask if they were in this country illegally. I didn't care and that wasn't the focus here. Manny walked her through the possibility of school counseling for her boy. He warned her, the path Hernando was on would not include school. His new friends would see to that.

Karen just listened while I asked the boy if he was doing okay. He mumbled single word responses, clearly waiting for this moment to end. I could see Hernando was too far away from what happened in his own home. The boy already developed that distant, standoffish look about him that young gangsters perfect. They adopt the slouch and the off camera look that broadcasts "I'm not involved and not listening." I wanted Karen to see what kind of cops we were and to respect our workload. Karen saw all this and caught the vibe that we were more than two dimensional uniforms.

We said our goodbyes and left. Weeks later, Manny and I cruised through Chicano Park and I spotted the boy. He walked with the stiffened, odd gait I'd seen many times before. We stopped him and smelled the strong ether smell of PCP. He was Shermed-out, which refers to a

Sherman cigarette that had been dipped in PCP. He'd clearly fallen into the gang trap. His family was losing him to the neighborhood influences we tried to deflect.

We had an ongoing cherry spot for drug sales near the kid's house. A snitch had told us it was either the automobile electric repair shop on the block, or the auto repair yard a block down, or the Fruiteria Market across from the auto yard. Whichever one it was, it was supplying bindles of cocaine to buyers on this stretch of Logan Avenue. Once we tripped across that problem, Central WECAN initiated plans to nail the street dealers. The plan was similar to others we'd implemented, spy on the dealers from a hiding place and take down the seller and the buyer. Hell, arrest everybody.

The action on Logan was not gang related. At least, organically, the activity originated from Mexican nationals in the U.S. illegally. Behind the scenes it was likely to be the Mexican gang *La Familia,* with connections across the border. Mexican nationals hovered on the block in small numbers and sold bindles of powdered cocaine with an eye out for *la policia.*

Central WECAN members set up out of sight in chase cars while at least one stood off with binoculars and watched the dealers go at it. This time, we had Karen with us. I wanted to dispel any suspicion that we set these people up and fudged our arrests. She stood next to Manny and watched me survey the dealers for any distinct sign of drug activity. She even got to see the bustle through my binoculars.

The two targets today were a couple of Hispanics of about twenty who stood on the south side of Logan scrutinizing every vehicle that drove by. That was standard dealer behavior, so all we had to do was wait. Soon enough, I watched a car slow down in front of the two guys. I pointed them out to Karen so she could watch some of what was happening. I took the binoculars back while Manny watched for signs our outpost was burned by witnesses who were friendly to the dealers. One of the dealers looked in through the passenger window and spoke to the driver. The other guy looked around for the cops. Satisfied we were not around he walked back into a dirt lot adjacent to the sidewalk. I watched him kneel in the cobblestone-strewn dirt patch and select a particular rock. He picked up a tiny paper bindle and walked back to the car. The first guy backed off to resume his lookout position while guy number two handed the bindle to the driver through the same window. He received currency in exchange and backed away from the now-moving car.

The chase team listened in on Nalemars frequency for my message calling out the direction the buyer was headed. Nalemars was a station-to-station frequency with no monitoring dispatcher. One team took off after the vehicle while another stood by to roll up on the dealers to keep them from disappearing. Once the chase car stopped the buyer and produced the purchased bindle of powdered cocaine, the game was afoot. Despite its prevalence, powdered cocaine was very limited on the streets and there weren't many street spots dealing the stuff. Crack and pot were more likely to be purchased on the streets than powdered coke. Bindles of cocaine were more prevalent from the dope houses. We let another buyer into our web to see if the other guy would do a hand-to-hand. It would be much easier to nail both in court if they both handed-off and took cash.

A second buy took place. The buyer stopped in his car a block from the chase team after the purchase and was quickly arrested. By now, I had both dealers partaking in the hand-to-hand transaction. We packed Karen into our sergeant's car and crossed over the short Sampson Street Bridge to Logan Avenue. The chase car still held its two prisoners when it joined our other team and drove up to the sellers to freeze them in place.

Karen, Manny and I parked behind the other cars and sauntered up to make our victory arrival. We had everything in place, bad guys, badder guys, cash and some coke. All we needed was the stash. The dirt lot looked a lot bigger when I stood in it. The number of rocks seemed greater and all looked alike. Karen was expecting me to go right to the stash since I told her it existed. I was now a little unsure. Man, there were a lot of similar stones. Meanwhile, our prisoners were stone-faced. They spoke to each other in quiet tones. I didn't care if they talked to each other. These guys never talk to the police under any circumstances. We either had them on our observations and evidence or we didn't have them at all.

In nature, there are no naturally occurring right angles. Organic life abhors right angles. But in Logan Heights, inorganic right angles were grounds for suspicion. So here I was looking at a lot full of round stones trying to pick out the right one. I didn't want Karen thinking I was on a fishing expedition. I stood there and looked at the forty or fifty stones that covered the patch of dirt where the stash had to be. Everything was naturally positioned in haphazard manner. Then I spotted the suspicious right angle. Two stones out of two thousand, but only one pair stood in an L shape to each other. The position of the stones was certainly an anomaly and that made me skeptical. Karen watched me deliberately walk over to the two stones. I knelt and picked them up. Voila! A baggie of coke bindles lay hidden under one of the stones. WECAN scored and the ACLU witness saw how good we were at our job!

I did not turn the ACLU into admirers. But Karen saw us put on a good face and not try to song-and-dance her with fluff and a muted program. Lieutenant Saladamando, the orchestrator of this event, got a meet with us. One of the local television news stations wanted to film us at our job. The LT promised Karen she could be in the spotlight on this recording. The press and the LT assumed we could take them through a "typical Heights drug house" just on a whim. Luckily for the press and or Karen, we always had some spot worth a look-see.

We'd taken the place down a week prior. We got a little dope and scored when I shoved a sheet of corrugate aluminum roofing aside and exposed a pile of cash in the backyard. The two nationals went to Border Patrol after jail, so they weren't back in the country yet. The place was abandoned and had no power. The only running water had pooled in the living room from a busted pipe. The camera crew was content for the recorded broadcast. Karen was tickled to be on camera and even spoke a few words about her connection to us. Man, our LT was happy. We managed to stagecraft an ACLU attorney on local news with good things to say about our unit. I couldn't make this stuff up, people.

Karen thanked us for the ride-along and added a heart-felt comment that WECAN could teach others about professionalism. We thanked her back for the comment and properly invited her back anytime. These platitudes would go far with our Command. I suspected she was dumped on us by our boss, maybe to screw with us. We turned vinegar into wine. Karen even sent a letter to our boss thanking him for her opportunity to observe his cops in action. Not to depreciate the value of comments such as those from a lofty civil rights institution, but the good feelings never last long. Now it was time to go kick some ass.

CHAPTER 14:
THE CHERRY PATCH

Sergeant Chuck O'Donnell was the Central WECAN sergeant for the time being. He was the type of leader best suited for his office desk. He was the overseer for our daily walking assignments and made it clear we were to stay put. So, that meant the 32nd Street corridor with forays to 30th and Imperial, only.

Manny and the rest of us were sick of the routine. Arrests trumped FIs and we were hungry for that real action. O'Donnell had other ideas. He had a plan to split up Manny and I for a bit and team us with other officers. Manny got one of the Southeast guys and I got Tim Fay from Eastern WECAN. Poor Manny was stuck back on 32nd with a fresh pad of FIs and the same stale crew of Crips.

Tim was a "by the book" cop with an impression of the world through black and white lenses. When he and I drew 30th and Imperial, the towering Tim drove us to the intersection and we "planted our flag." Tim, by the way, was 6'7" and required a specially designed car interior just to fit. His car came with a prisoner cage that was set back so the driver's seat could roll back further. Tim took up so much space up front that no prisoner's legs could fit behind him. That limited the number of bodies that could be pushed together in the back.

The intersection known to us as "Crip Central" was always busy with gangsters, hangers-on, pedestrian traffic, business customers and vehicles. The West Coast Crips challenged anyone that set up shop to do Crip-style business with "leave or get wasted." Any street violence there would likely come from those confrontations. Our job was to be the nuisances to shut the Crips down which logically was supposed to put a halt to their presence. Tim and I had a full day to walk no more than a block in any of four directions. That limited distance meant we couldn't follow the lazy Crips who only had to walk an additional half block to skip out on our attention.

We hung there with the foot patrol for about three hours. The day was warm and sunny, and everybody was out on the streets. And blue-clad homies marched around corners and down each block. Two white guys, Mutt and Jeff in tandem, dressed in tans, stood out against the royal blue backdrop.

Tim and I felt useless. Nobody committed any crimes in front of us. Our sharp eyes would have picked out any hand-to-hand transactions despite the dozens of brush-passes going on around us. The Crips showed no signs of distress over their crumbling business, or over two hawk-eyed cops with their vision trained on them. Day turned to dusk, and Tim and I headed down the avenue to get tacos. We ate at the food stand until we got an angry transmission from Sgt. O'Donnell to return to 30th. I told Tim that our sergeant was not the right guy for this job.

We drove the four blocks and saw the sergeant bunkered in his supervisor car in the corner parking lot of Mullen's Liquor. He was not the type to stand out to make an impression on the locals. He waited for us to approach him, so he didn't have to leave the safety or convenience of his car. "I told you guys to stay put. That's your job," he said. "No wandering off, Jamie. You keep pushing the envelope and that's why you and Manny are split up for the day. You need to set your asses down here until we send you somewhere else."

I noted that he said "we." He meant that his boss, the lieutenant had ordered him to get out of the office and make sure Newbold and the others were doing as ordered. Those forays into Chicano Park and elsewhere were not yet on our menu and were still considered *verboten*. I also noted O'Donnell never looked up at Tim or even referred to his presence. He then split in a huff. Tim's attitude was, "That's rough, Bud. Eastern has it so much easier with Sgt. Wray. He leads from the front and works like one of us. We have none of this bullshit." We stood there in the growing darkness until it turned pitch black and ten o'clock in the evening rolled around. Tim dropped me and my gear off at HQ and then headed back to his duty station at Eastern.

The sergeant had more words with me after shift. I got the distinct impression he would angle for my transfer from the unit if I didn't fall in line.

Manny and I returned to our pairing the next day. O'Donnell ignored us. We took a little outing with John and Chuck after line-up and discussed my confrontation. So far, I was the only officer to get chewed out. There was clearly bad chemistry between me and the sergeant. That might mean I was also in the lieutenant's sights. My partners consoled me with the feeling that we were all bored with the orders and all in it together. Our solution was to pay lip service at the beginning of the shift and then scoot around for greener pastures.

The conditional edict from above was a disappointing resignation. We were to stay put, babysit felons, make FI's and stay away from other parts of the Heights.

The restriction disappeared the night after my squad and I went to the Camel's Breath Inn for cocktails after work. For some inexplicable reason O'Donnell showed up. He was already lit when he tried to pigeonhole me into a conversation. I was wary but who knew what might come out of a one-on-one with my adversary. First, he told me to stop rocking the boat. Meaning, stop agitating for more action in the Heights. Then, he confessed that the lieutenant pressured him to get out of the office and be more of a hands-on supervisor. I had the sense all along that the LT was pissing all over O'Donnell. But he brought it on himself. The sergeants on the other two Teams loved to join their squads and the teams had no problems with that.

Our somewhat uncomfortable connection in the bar fizzled when O'Donnell turned surly and threatened to, "kick me off the squad if I didn't fall in line." The statement didn't bother me so much as the grip on my left arm as he emphasized his point with a little physical pressure. I held a bottle of beer in my left hand. I brought my right arm up and shoved him back against a table.

I warned him to never touch me again. Others around us turned to see what the commotion was about. Those more than a few feet away couldn't hear us over the bar music. O'Donnell was tipsy and unfocused. I'm not even sure he comprehended what just happened. He wobbled his way back to vertical and said, "Your days are numbered, Newbold." One of the guys in our group knew that now was the time to get O'Donnell out of the bar.

"Sergeant, I think you've had too much to drink. You need to go home. Let's get you a cab," one of them said.

"No. I don't need a cab." He was in no shape to drive but the unfortunate code of the bar, and of cops who drank together, was to let their compatriots make their own choices. We cops knew when even our consumption limits were met, but O'Donnell wasn't there yet as far as he was concerned.

The next day was a workday. I made a phone call to the Police Officer's Association and asked to speak to a police representative. I spoke with Don Fasching in person and gave him a heads-up that I might require an advisor should O'Donnell go after me. Don was an old training officer of mine and a sharp guy. He suggested I document everything and send him a copy if my world went to shit.

I saw O'Donnell at line-up the next day. Not a word was spoken between us. O'Donnell held line-up humbly then disappeared. He never approached me about the bar incident. I never bothered to talk to him again unless I had to. Surprisingly, he was aced out of his position by a new sergeant. Sergeant Sleeper was another desk jockey, but I knew him from F Troop, and he was a likable, if not hard-charging boss. Unfortunately, his mantra was similar to O'Donnell's. "Don't make any waves and don't get in trouble." Yeah, right!

The 2500 block of Logan Avenue was a perfect "cherry patch" during my tenure on WECAN. We made all kinds of arrests and logged in a lot of hours figuring out where the dope was hidden. Fellow WECAN member Vickie Burnham was with me one day when we got word the bindle sellers had moved around the block to 26th Street. Apparently, we'd have to chop off their business at the knees one block at a time. The pizza place next to an alley on 26th slipped word to the PD that coke sales were suddenly going on in front of the business. We figured the sellers felt our pressure but didn't want to relocate too far from their normal action. Vickie and I planned a little outing where we would scope out the location in darkness and figure out how things worked there.

We'd be on foot for this venture. The car was a nice, warm crutch on what passed for a cold evening in San Diego but was contrary to subterfuge. Our car would stay in the dark a block away and gather little notice from our targets. We took advantage of the quiet alley in front of the pizza shop and the dealers at the south end of the alley. We used uneven fence lines and a utility pole as slight cover. That would be good enough to avoid the bad guys' eyes as they flitted about on constant watch for predators who would take them down if given half a chance. The cops were less of a threat to them. The dealers worked from the opposite alley entrance, with the pizza place right at their backs. Because it was dark, we didn't need much concealment when we advanced a bit closer.

We approached from the west end of the alleyway behind 2500 Logan. We had a pair of "binos" and set ourselves up in perfect blackness about thirty yards from our targets. We were perfectly hidden. The only risk came from anything with a motor that happened to drive through our alley at an inconvenient moment. For that reason, we hugged the walls. The dealers obliged us with their usual tactics, hide the dope until a buyer arrived, grab the product and make the exchange. There was no need for conversation. The buyer sped off and the dealer returned to his nonchalance. This time, the bindles were stashed behind a city sign affixed to a wooden power pole.

We had no chase car. This was a purely spontaneous approach. Vicki and I were after the dope and the dealer. The buyers were the bait. The hiding place was the hook. We cooled our heels until the next car approached. The hidden dope spot was easy enough to locate, even from thirty yards away. We watched just long enough to identify the location. One deal was all we needed.

Vickie and I were not going to get into a foot chase. We needed an unbreakable line of sight, so we couldn't go back for our car. How do we approach on foot without being seen, was the question. The answer came when a southbound truck entered our alley. He moved slowly. I thought somebody was looking for us. I tugged my gun out of my holster. Vicky had her eyes on the truck and on me. She copied my motion and pulled her gun out, too. We stayed glued to the wall until the truck passed. It turned out to be just a random passerby. However, he provided us with an unexpected opportunity and we just trotted in behind him. His lights blinded the targets to our approach. When the truck turned onto 26th, we materialized out of nowhere and grabbed two of them. We were on them so fast they didn't have time to consider escape. We had the dope and pulled more bindles of coke from behind a flyer nailed to the pole. Two of the dealers reached behind the flyer, so two went for sales and possession of cocaine for sales. Another slam-dunk. The guy had about eighty dollars cash in his pants pocket. Vicky added the cash to the bindles of coke and stashed the various confiscations into an envelope. Safe in our glove box, she'd impound the booty at HQ as evidence. Our prisoner would join the milieu of the family of crime in the legal system.

All these arrests padded our impressive stats. All three WECAN teams amassed arrest numbers not seen before in such a short time by our department. The bosses were suitably amazed. WECAN loved doing this stuff! We were having a great time. This kind of action was what the job was all about to me. Admittedly, we all felt elite, even spoiled, that we got to do what we did for a living. This would never get old. Not every arrest guaranteed satisfaction though. The doors of justice seemed to revolve the villains into jail and return them to the streets too soon.

Manny and I were paired up as usual when we set up on Sampson and Logan to pull down a few more coke dealers before we called it a night. We set up across the freeway from the targets. We occupied the usual surveillance locale and went on the hunt for drug crime. Our chase team was John and Chuck. They parked half a block away and out of sight of the action. When we radioed the description of the first drive-up buyer, they pulled off our first arrest in no time. They held the guy in custody as they reset the car for another run.

The next buyer was in an older pick-up truck. He turned onto Sampson from Logan and pulled to the curb and was immediately set upon by the Mexican peddler. The deal was done through the driver's window. Manny notified the other pair to get the truck while we nailed the lone dealer.

The buyer started forward just as the Tangredi and Davis duo stopped him. He didn't get more than twenty-five feet. We drove up and caught the dealer as he slinked away. Manny warned the guy in Spanish not to flee when he tensed up. Neither of us was likely to chase a "rabbit" on foot if we could help it. The cocky dealer carried more coke bindles that he made no effort to hide.

I walked over to the truck and asked John for the buyer's information. The name on the driver's license seemed familiar. I looked in the cab and stared at the face of the seated man. No recollection registered. I looked at the name again. Man, this guy's name is so familiar. I asked him to step out. He pointed to a collapsible wheelchair on the passenger side and then at his legs. "I'm in a wheelchair," he said. I told him he'd have to come out and asked if he needed help. "Just give me a sec," he responded unhappily.

He was none too happy about the bust. I told him it was for the cocaine as he reached over and grabbed the wheelchair. I swung it over his lap and dropped it on the ground. I told him to leave the drugs on the seat, assuming he had them close by. Without a word, he removed the pocketed coke, three bindles, and left them on the truck's seat. He had his own unique way of extrication from his truck. He hung out a bit while he held onto the door and frame. When he lined up with the wheeled seat, he dropped neatly into it and then pivoted one-hundred-and-eighty degrees to face us.

I collected the dope and formally placed him under arrest. He looked forlorn, probably weighing the experience of going to jail without being able to walk. He'd go downtown with us, his wheelchair, too. Our partners took the seller.

I finally figured out that our prisoner, Scott, went to high school with me. I asked him if I looked familiar, but he said I did not. I told him I knew him from high school, and he screwed on a quizzical look. I described the three years we were in the same graduation class and watched a tinge of embarrassment cross his face. Scott deflated right in front of me. Any pretense of pride shattered because it dawned on him that we knew the same people. He didn't know me in school, but he sure knew me now.

I didn't want to be in this position. I had no great contact with school with Scott. I held no grudges for the guy and slowly felt bad for him. So far, he was just a forlorn joe with bad luck.

Scott bought drugs to escape his debilitated life. He was paralyzed from the waist down from a terrible fall he took on a construction job. He broke his back and felt like life restrained him from natural joy. He got that from coke, booze and anything else that dulled his consciousness for a while. I felt bad for him. I also felt like a heel putting him through this ordeal. Admittedly, it was my job. The dealer was the true villain. Scott was just a poor *schlub* caught in the trap. We needed Scott to be under arrest to seal the arrest on the dealer. The courts wouldn't buy the arrest if we let the buyer go. Scott knew that and didn't whine about his circumstances. I had to put my job in front of my feelings. The department made no allowances for "grey-area" thoughts or actions in these situations. There'd be no field catch and release.

The four of us WECAN officers delivered the two prisoners to HQ and began the report process. Scott and I had a little time to talk. Jail didn't scare him that much. Scott's concern was his fate after jail. I commiserated as much as I could. I salved over his dilemma to try and anticipate his fears. The suggestion of probation and drug rehab was addressed. Realistically, he had a good reason to want to bathe in chemical escapes. Who was I to disagree with a broken man? Scott did go to jail and I never heard from him again. I see him at our high school reunions. He doesn't recognize me, and I go out of my way to avoid him. No ghosts from the past for me.

CHAPTER 15:

BNE

Like I said earlier, a lot of people came out of the woodwork during WECAN's tenure. WECAN met with ATF agents, Federal Marshalls, Border Patrol and a litany of alphabet soup organizations. One I'd never heard of was the Bureau of Narcotics Enforcement or BNE for short. The BNE was a State of California police agency tasked with working the state's drug problems. The state organization was from as far back as 1927, disbanded years later, and partnered up later with the State Department of Justice. I'd still never heard of it until the night Manny and I encountered a white gentleman in a mid-sized compact blocking an alley in a black neighborhood.

We'd been in a scrum earlier that evening down off of Oceanview across the street from a park famous for PCP sales and use. Manny and I prowled the north side by car to spot any Logan *Treinta* gangster action. Manny was the passenger this evening as I rolled down the quiet nighttime avenue. Suddenly, Manny's spotlight skirted over the face of a guy yards away that stunned him. "Shit! That's the guy that beat up one of the Central patrol guys a few months ago."

I tapped the brakes to slow, but Manny told me to keep going and turn at the intersection. "What am I doing?" I asked, perplexed.

"Go into the alley. There. There." Manny's mood was elevated as I turned and then turned again into the west alley of Oceanview. "Stop the car. There. There!"

"What's this all about? I take it you know the guy. Is he wanted?"

"That's the dude who nearly killed a Central cop, like six months ago, dude. Ray had a female trainee and they stopped to FI that dude for training. The guy grabbed the trainee and pulled her gun out of her holster. Ray had to fight him and nearly got shot."

"What happened?" I asked as I glided the patrol car to a stop.

"Ray was on his own. The trainee was too scared to fight back as the guy took her gun. Ray got pistol-whipped when the guy couldn't figure out how to release the safety. Thank God the trainee had done that much. Ray rolled around with the guy as he screamed at the girl to call for cover. Sirens were close just as Ray got to his gun. The bad guy, this asshole, dropped the gun and gave up."

I got the picture.

"Let's go have a word with him," I suggested. My get even implication was silently shared between us. Manny kept a pile of FI cards in his gear bag. He pulled out one on that guy and quietly ran him for warrants. Meanwhile, we walked cautiously to an un-gated fence-line that led to a walkway between apartment buildings. From there, it was a straight-shot to Oceanview. The darkness enveloped us and gave me a concealed clump of bushes to hide in. I saw the guy across the street. He hadn't been wary enough to split when we lit him up. Maybe he was expecting somebody. Manny shared that he was drug-tested the night of the fight and PCP was added to the charges.

We stood in near silence as Communications told us he had a warrant for that arrest. He'd never appeared in court and was in the system as a wanted felon. Manny cleared the radio just as our man, Ernesto Diaz, crossed the street in our direction. Nothing need be said between us. Manny and I set the trap.

Diaz chose the pathway that led straight to us. How convenient. He made it past the first apartment and straight into my arms as I stepped out from behind a plant. Manny moved in behind him just as I plowed a fist into his stomach. There'd be no surprise combat with this fool. Manny wrapped his right arm around the guy's neck for the intended chokehold. He was bent over from the blow, so his lowered stature made it easy on Manny to gain leverage around his throat. Diaz went limp and then Manny let him roll sideways to the ground.

Nothing of import was spoken between the two of us. With an almost uncanny mental link, we both know we'd blown out any sense of vengeance on Ray's behalf and any other cop this jerk had menaced. We'd never see this chap again after we took him to jail. Fuck him. He was lucky we weren't dirty cops. His death would have been a mystery.

The white guy mentioned earlier sat in a white Chevy four-door, was alone and dressed in casual attire. There was a badge clipped to his belt. I recognized him immediately as a former F Troop cop. We shook hands and answered each other's rapid-fire questions. Manny didn't know him so proper introductions were made. Manny meet Ken and all that. Of course, I assumed he was a detective on our department. I hadn't seen him in years and figured he'd advanced. Ted was his name and he explained that he was working a snitch in the area and looking for her when she failed to make their meet. The Heights at night could be precarious. I wondered if Ted felt safe out here alone. He did not. He admitted that the sight of a police car was welcome. His badge was not SDPD issue. What the hell was that? "I'm with the BNE now, Jamie," Ted said.

I wanted to know about his mysterious organization. He laughed a little at our ignorance. He said they were a small agency for such a large state. The BNE was sort of a redundant law department, considering it was squeezed in between a state chock full of municipal cops and the big-time federal guys. He offered that the BNE wanted a piece of the asset seizure funds every other law agency got from drug arrests. His department was so small they only had three agents in San Diego and a boss, the Special Agent in Charge or SAIC. The way he described the job, with lots of seized cash to spend, the BNE sounded like a pampered organization.

I asked the million-dollar question about space for some more San Diego cops. He placated me and acknowledged that the drug business was good for the BNE. He said they were currently hiring. He admitted that when he worked SDPD he wasn't much of a drug cop. The job popped up on his radar and it sounded better than shagging radio calls at the Lost Command. Nobody else applied worth a damn, partly because few knew what the BNE was. He took the shot and now he was happy. He suggested I check it out. Manny was thinking about our conversation, as well. I got the BNE information from my buddy and we parted ways.

Manny and I discussed our job, our prospects of prevailing in the future and what that future might look like. From the former

SDPD-turned-BNE agent point of view, our futures might look much better with his people. I made a phone call a couple of days later for an appointment with the BNE SAIC. Manny and I both attended. Our intent was to check out the job opening situation. The SAIC was more than happy to talk to us.

We showed up at the SAIC's office, on-duty and in uniform for the appointment we made. The SAIC was a polite, older man with a beautiful corner office in a high-rise near the Karl Strauss Brewery restaurant on Columbia. He greeted us with firm handshakes and a big smile. We sat facing his big desk and told him we considered switching jobs. He kept his smile, but I could tell it was now a bit forced. He agreed there was a job opening, three in fact. We told him one of his agents helped to get us here. He already knew.

When we mentioned that the BNE was a mystery to us he laughed. "Yeah, I get that a lot," he said.

He reminisced about hiring the former SDPD officer. Back then, they had to work to find people. He then apologized when he disclosed that was true once, not anymore. So far, he told us, the state had over 3,000 applicants for three positions. The organization looked to expand for all the free drug money out there to be seized. The BNE was no longer hidden. They now had the pick of the litter and two uniforms from San Diego were not priorities. Dope cops were a dime a dozen. He apologized and that was that.

CHAPTER 16:

FBI

The pair of us were disappointed by the SAIC's disappointing news. We both knew we were ready for BNE work. We had massive street experience, knew the dope business, were cool under pressure and worked well individually or in a team setting. But we weren't investigators. Police detectives were the worker pool law enforcement agencies like the BNE were more willing to draw from. I don't know which one of us was more dejected. We drove around and stewed over a blown opportunity. I told Manny we should pick up some take-out and go back to HQ to drown our sorrows in spicy Thai food.

The nine-to-fivers at the headquarters building don't wait long after the clock strikes five to clear the building. We took the meals up to the seventh-floor cafeteria and sat in silence. The food was a little too spicy and I tossed out a portion. Manny surrendered to the burning in his throat and dumped the rest of his food in the trash. We walked on back to the elevators and saw the civilian cleaning crew going about their chores. The cleaners were contracted by the city and a couple of them were regular sights on the seven floors of HQ.

The two women, Maria and Esmeralda, were Mexicans who'd achieved the status to work in the United States. I always looked forward to seeing them on the night shift, especially Maria. She was a little older than me and spoke no English, but she was pretty and smiled when she saw us. There was an occasional male worker who conveniently ducked into rooms when he saw us talking to the girls.

There was a little flirting when Manny broke the language barrier. I was married so nothing serious grew from the nightly encounters. Maria was pretty. Manny spoke to both women and broke the ice. If they were nervous around men in uniform the trepidation melted away. I'd found out early on that Manny was feeding Maria stories about a crush

I supposedly had on her. She'd told him I was cute, and she appreciated the complimentary male attention. This evening's meeting was different.

Maria was morose and looked uncertain, like something bothered her. She didn't smile at me as usual and looked down at the floor. Manny saw what I saw and asked her if something was wrong. She suddenly spouted off a lengthy sentence in Spanish. Thanks to junior high Spanish class and Manny's attempts to teach me street Spanish, I picked up a few words here and there. One of the words closely mimics its English counterpart, *teniente*, Lieutenant.

Maria cried softly as she tugged on Manny's sleeve as we followed her into one of the offices, away from prying eyes. I walked along while her workmate continued her job. Manny held a conversation with Maria. The rapid lingo had to be translated. She was really broken up, even scared. I waited patiently for the story while I kept my concerned eyes on her, to reassure her I was as considerate as Manny. Finally, Manny turned to me and detailed a problem neither of us ever saw coming. Apparently, I wasn't the only one fond of Maria. One of our lieutenants also had the eye on her, but in a more salacious light.

The lieutenant was in the building late the night before. Maria was with her small crew but separated herself to clean the gang detectives' office by herself. The lieutenant caught sight of her and followed her in without making a sound. Maria had a vacuum plugged in and pressed down on the armature to operate the machine. Suddenly, she sensed a presence behind her and a brush of clothing against her back. She was alarmed as she reflexively turned around only to be shocked at the sight of a police lieutenant. She was confused until he gently nudged her into a wall. She was boxed in. He wore a silly grin, but his eyes were focused, humorless. Maria was challenged by this unwanted advance as so many women have experienced in life. She was mortified. A policeman was in her space and cooed that he found her attractive. Her "Uh Oh," revelation was made grimmer because this policeman was a boss in the building. Bosses in Mexico have power over people like her. She didn't know what to do. The lieutenant put a hand on her shoulder to complete the closure of that insulating eighteen inches of personal space. When she didn't resist, Maria thought he took that as a sign that she wouldn't resist.

Manny and I knew who he was. He was Hispanic and spoke the language like a native. He was also nowhere near the embodiment of chivalry. He was a player and she was that evening's plaything. Maria cried softly as Manny finished the story for my benefit. Maria was convinced the lieutenant would not stop as he pinned her to the wall and tried to kiss her. She didn't know how to fight back against a boss. She was afraid for her job. All the scary thoughts that went through her head evaporated when the door to the office noisily opened and a pile of gang detectives poured in. The interruption was inconvenient for the lieutenant who quickly let go and slinked into the chamber of a cubicle. Maria fled out the door to find the other cleaners. The guy that usually accompanied them volunteered to take her job for the night.

Manny asked her what she wanted to do about the uncomfortable encounter. We knew she'd choose to do nothing. Our best intentions could backfire and jeopardize her job. Manny and I conferred about our roles in a potential fix for this awful conundrum. I suggested that Manny tell her we would stand up for her if there was trouble. We'd keep the attack out of the department pipeline, but add John, Chuck and Roger to the roster of men with knowledge. The decision on retribution was hers to make. We'd back her up.

A week passed before I saw Maria again. She was friendly and smiled, but the flirtatious back-and-forth was nonexistent. The lieutenant robbed all of us of something that was friendly and genuine. Maria trusted us, but there was now a gulf between us. She was no longer on that staff a month later. Her partners were still there. They told Manny she quit to go to work for a family in town. The lieutenant never knew what we knew about his predatory advances.

Anytime I saw a G-ride, or gangster style car, with a white male occupant in the Heights at night, I reasoned that the occupants were either junkies or cops. Nobody in any other walk of life fit that combination where I worked.

One night, Manny and I were parked across the street from the recreation center. This time there'd be no Ernesto Diaz to filter out and attack for his past crimes. The rec itself was a hotbed of PCP sales. The gym was open at night, so a lot of people milled about for basketball inside and PCP sales outside. The Logan 30th Street gangsters were fond of the high they got from the angel dust and made tidy profits through its sales. These guys brazenly loitered around the gym doors, ignoring the adults and children gathered for games and recreation center fun. We'd talked to rec directors in the past, just to see how they felt about the punk bangers who dealt poison in the heart of the park. Each director ignored the problem due to the reality of gang threats and violence if they took public action or were seen to be in cahoots with the police. The rec employees and their bosses kept an uneasy peace by avoiding confrontations. This creaky détente meant the gangsters operated side-by-side with minimal imposition on the regular people. The dealers dealt to buyers on foot and those who drove into the parking lot adjacent to the gym entrance. The good people in the park did their best to ignore them.

Manny and I had time to kill. We drove into the lot to see if we recognized any of the 30th Street guys slinging dope. Nothing was happening at this end of the park. Rather than continue a search for trouble from another angle, we parked on the street to knock out some paperwork from earlier arrests. A parked WECAN car near the park was a great deterrent. The gangster-dealers would step off if they saw us haunting their sales turf.

Our heads were always on swivels when we parked anywhere in the Heights. The neighborhood was home turf to some of the worst, most violent men in the county and not just gang members. When a pastel, government-type car pulled up behind us, Manny caught it in his rearview mirror. We both watched the suspicious car get closer to us before it stopped. The single white occupant stepped out, dressed in a suit but no tie. It was clearly a government car with the cop-like air about the occupant. What was it this time? Manny and I alighted and faced him from either side of our car. Manny gave him a "Whassup?"

He slowly stepped out and asked to speak with us. This guy did not belong in this part of town. Cop or not, we figured he was lost and a little frightened. He held up a small, shiny badge and pointed to it identifying himself as an FBI agent. Really? Here? Now? I didn't know what to make of this strange encounter. There had to be some weird angle here. We remained taut when we introduced ourselves. The agent explained that he was assigned to the FBI's San Diego Narcotics Bureau and could sure use a little help. This encounter seemed to be going in a direction even stranger than the bump-into with the BNE.

Special Agent Chuck was an interesting guy. Unlike other agents and the portrayal of FBI agents on television, Chuck was cool with us. He'd been assigned to the San Diego's FBI Narcotics office less than a year prior and found himself working informants just like every other narcotics unit in the county. I worked at the municipal level with various county drug units. I'd met and worked with numerous city and county cops, the multi-departmental Narcotics Task Force, the state's BNE, even the DEA, but now the FBI was doing drugs? Everybody wanted those arrest stats and those seized assets.

The FBI wanted the American public to see that they functioned at the city level. Crack was big, so the FBI was on it. Gangs were big-time crime targets, so the FBI was on them. There was public outcry insisting to know what the FBI was doing about gangs and crime. The Soviets were turning themselves inside-out and the Mafia was just another gang, from a San Diego cop's point of view. The FBI was pressured to search inward for grand domestic plagues. Homegrown gangsters of the street variety needed to be on the federal radar.

I'd attended illuminating Gang Schools throughout the state that told tales of the power and the wealth of California street gangs. One gang expert brought a slideshow to his class that displayed several L.A.-based businesses. One opulent and massive car dealership flashed onto the screen. The instructor left the picture on the screen for several seconds before he shocked some of us with its ownership. An L.A. Crip crew owned the successful dealership behind a screen of legitimate souls. That seemed Mafia-big to us. Gangs were the ordinary American's daily concern. Considering the heavy poundage in forces the FBI could muster up, Chuck was reassurance that the FBI had agents pounding the pavement in inner city neighborhoods to worry the unchecked street gangs and narcotics sellers.

Agent Chuck worked with a confidential informant responsible for the location and set-up for big time FBI dope scores. Whatever Agent Chuck's CI generated that paid off in seizures of drugs and money, a percentage was eventually paid back to the CI. We weren't in the loop to know or meet the CI, which was probably wise.

Agent Chuck didn't know Manny, or me. He just happened to stumble across two trained cops working specific dope targets in the area the CI labored in for Agent Chuck. Agent Chuck explained how the CI came through with all kinds of dope spots, but only the big ones would be worked by the FBI. Smaller fish were ignored, which meant the CI would do the work and get nothing for it. Agent Chuck devised a means to fix that blank spot if he could get someone to work the smaller tips, say cops who patrolled the same streets and looked for the same targets. He got two hungry WECAN officers. What a great coincidence and a coup for Agent Chuck. He liked us and thought the karmic moment of our first meeting boded well. He was not naïve and reasoned he could only trust us to a point. He was less concerned we'd fail him than he was about us learning his CI's name and somehow fouling up that secret. We knew how the system worked. He compartmentalized what we were allowed to know.

We discussed how his plan would be implemented, so we could take down some dope dealers we didn't know existed. In the first CI-tipped place Agent Chuck fed to us, the CI found two Mexican nationals dealing from a tiny rental house on Julian Avenue. The place had old iron bars on every window and a wrought iron security gate over the only doorway into the place. This circa 1920, ground-level duplex was a miniature fortress perfect for the people who fronted the dealers.

Like so many dope pads run by illegal aliens, the two guys in this place were worried enough about American police officers to let four of us inside the day we knocked on the door. In Mexico, I assume a refusal would see men like these get strung up by the cops.

Once the occupiers unlocked the security door, we let ourselves in and looked around. This place was a wreck. There was no power and no running water. The living room ceiling had a massive hole like somebody once fell through it. I thought the place was abandoned and these two *pollitos*, translated as baby chicks in English and slang for poor, rural Mexican border crossers, were trespassers. The thought could have been true. But possession, ownership and legal tenancy are convoluted concepts in the poor sections of the Heights.

So far, Agent Chuck's CI seemed to be on the right track with this place. We hadn't seen any action and the two occupants were tight mouthed after we filtered through the trashed house. There wasn't even any furniture. The place looked more like a job site than a place where these two guys lived. There weren't any chairs for us to stand on. Luckily, we had tall Chuck Davis. He could reach through the hole in the ceiling and feel around the edges for any contraband. We had the two souls sit on the floor. Neither said a word after they let us in and agreed to the search. Chuck reached up into the hole and walked his fingers around the perimeter. Within seconds, he pulled down a full baggie of tiny red toy balloons. Each was knotted up and filled with cheap Mexican tar heroin.

This was quite a score. I estimated about fifty balloons. We reasoned that the short drug dealers tossed the booty up into the ceiling when we worried them at the door. Theoretically, somebody connected to them, or a little piggy-back assist, would retrieve the contraband after we left empty-handed. Obviously, the handlers were excited about the money coming out of this place.

This was amount of heroin was more than the usual amount we found at other dope houses. The bosses didn't seem to feel the police were a threat. The large quantity of dope and small amount of cash implied that the dope delivery hoodlum had made a recent drop. The discovery was pure luck for us. Half that amount of heroin was the average, or even less. We found about a hundred dollars in cash to feed back to Agent Chuck and arrested our two guys.

I called FBI Agent Chuck from the station and thanked him for turning us onto his CI's knowledge. I impounded the money at our station and made a copy of the impound slip for FBI Agent Chuck. We scheduled a meet for the next day out in the field. Agent Chuck wanted to retain an aloofness from the ranks of the other SDPD employees and facilities. He didn't work undercover often, but he needed to be unidentifiable to most everyone not FBI. Our meets were always in the Heights, or over the phone.

Agent Chuck never introduced us to the CI, even though the trust factor was no longer an issue. He kept the person a secret, a secret that ramped up our dope dealer arrests and drug seizures. The smaller, yet frequent cash back from Agent Chuck kept the CI in his stable. The payout to Agent Chuck's CI from this first project netted the guy a few hundred bucks. He was happy, which made FBI Agent Chuck happy. He made Central WECAN cops happy. In exchange for signing on with this friendly FBI man, Chuck allowed us access to the FBI Headquarters' Fingerprint Lab and introduced us to the lab tech he felt was most cooperative, a woman named Cathie.

Back then, our department had limited world range for fingerprint identification. The FBI had everybody in its data banks. Our system couldn't reach Federal prints, military, Federal prisons, organized crime and the like. I found more opportunity with the fingerprinted deportees. We finally had leverage over the countless border-crossers who returned through the fences to sell dope in the Heights once again. No one was in any rush from non-citizen action groups to fight for the rights of these assholes. The FBI had all that access and more. Because of the types of gangsters roaming around in the roughest neighborhoods, Federal identification was a huge help to us. Plus, we were the only uniforms on SDPD to have this arrangement.

Our team's relationship with the FBI got tighter, thanks to Agent Chuck. Cathie worked in the Fingerprint Lab at the FBI's downtown headquarters. Fingerprint samples handed over to Cathie by the Central WECAN team turned misdemeanor prisoners we'd booked, into felons after they'd been identified through the FBI lab. Our lieutenant wrote a letter of commendation to the FBI Agent in Charge for allowing Cathie to work with us. Once we identified the jokers we'd booked under false names, we went out into the field and booked them anew for the major warrants they'd hidden from us.

Cathie was a treat. Her tenure in the lab went back ten years. All that time in the FBI and she'd never met city cops, until now. She spent a lot of time in her lab with her federal male and female co-workers. Cathie liked where she was at and felt her coworkers and superiors regarded her well. But, seeing a couple of us in uniforms in her office seemed to thrill her to no end. She loved cops but everybody in her office wore suits and didn't slather her with a kudo or a thank you. She couldn't get enough of us and we couldn't get enough of what she could do for us with her fingerprint lab. With us around, she felt like she was contributing to people eternally grateful for her job skills and acumen. We were. WECAN and the FBI lab had real symbiosis. We wanted our department to have the worldly ability to track and download the identity of bad people through fingerprints. The limitations of the city, county and state of California meant we couldn't identify people we arrested like the FBI could..

The most prolific dope house dope sellers were the Mexican nationals working from rental homes and apartments. If we had an illegal alien who we suspected of being a greater threat than appeared on the surface, we could run his prints through the FBI. If he'd been expelled from our country, the expulsion data would be in the Federal databanks. We tagged a man from a dope house on Kearny Street. We had no arrestable crime, so we took our chances and kept him on ice at HQ to run his prints through Cathie. The estimated time in the hopper was ninety minutes. The FBI's database was enormous and takes time for Cathie's computer to regurgitate a match. And it did.

Cathie called us through Police Communications. Our prisoner was in the federal system as a three-time illegal border-crosser. His status had no impact on city cops like us. But it was the hook to formally detain him. Border Patrol would take him. The Feds then had the option to charge him as an undesirable and kick him across the border again or penalize him with Federal prison time. At least Manny and I got to see how effective those FBI print runs could be. The FBI's fingerprint data banks also came in handy with the usual rabble of street people.

In one case we detained a black man for a traffic infraction with no identification. We stopped him for riding his bicycle in traffic like he owned the road. The man had to be in his forties. He was polite and calm. His lack of a surly attitude warned us that the guy hoped to lull us into complacency. He treated us with deference and seemed calm. This guy was a pro at covering up his true self.

The other drivers were furious at this carefree idiot, so our traffic stop served a purpose. He had nothing to identify himself. He was friendly enough. He said his name was Bill Jackson and told us he was new in town and looking for a place to live. We believed nothing that he told us. His verbal identification sounded like a dodge to avoid letting his true self come to light. We needed corroborative identification to write him a ticket. Since he couldn't produce that and our radio inquiries yielded no trace of the name, we took him downtown.

Once we returned to HQ, we had him remove his jacket. I saw a shoulder tattoo that looked like a mushroom cloud. Manny knew what it was, the raised fist of a Black Panther. Since we had no proof of his existence, we fingerprinted him, or at least tried. He knew the game better than we did. He purposefully wiggled his fingers just enough to obscure his prints. We didn't notice at first. When we caught on, we made him do it again under threat of arrest for obstruction of justice. The next sets were clean.

The investigation into his identity was on a Sunday. Our SDPD fingerprint analyst said the guy didn't exist under the name he claimed was his. SDPD officers would not get print records from people convicted of federal crimes. There was a time when Black Panthers were pursued without abatement by the Feds. If this guy was more than a sympathetic supporter of the organization once touted as terrorists, then he might be in the federal system.

The FBI office was closed. We'd reached a dead end even though we knew in our bones this guy was hiding his true self for a reason important to him. A wasted ticket for the unsafe riding of a bicycle without a license offense was ludicrous. His name and story were bogus, and we had no other reason to hold him. We had to let him go.

Not all good deeds go unpunished. The SAIC, the supreme-being in charge at the San Diego FBI, was unaware of the brotherly relationship between the FBI and Central WECAN. He subsequently warned the Fingerprint Lab to cease providing us with information derived from the prints we submitted. We only found out about it when Cathie sheepishly called us and said the party was over. I asked her what happened. She said the FBI doesn't spend their money on our municipal needs. The stereotypical portrayal of snooty FBI agents emerged.

The next day was Monday. We adjusted our hours to work morning and get to the FBI when they opened. We ran the prints up to Cathie. She got permission just this one more time because the Black Panthers were not forgotten by the Feds. Hours later, she produced a match, the fellow's true name, as suspected, had a federal felony warrant attached to it for evading the law, whatever that meant. He was in the wind, now. We'd never see him again.

When WECAN held a party for itself, we invited Cathie to attend. She was grateful and pulled me aside later to tell me she'd never been invited to an FBI party, unless the office staff held its own get together.

CHAPTER 17:

AGENT CHUCK

One of FBI Agent Chuck's feeds to us via his CI was an apartment building on Martin Street in the Stockton part of the Heights. The CI described the two-floor apartment building as a base for marijuana sales on a grand level, conducting business as though the police department didn't matter. They were moving pounds instead of ounces. We set up a surveillance project a block over to study the place for a future warrant. Nobody burned us when we parked and snuck through a courtyard to a house that faced the Martin Street apartments. The lush, overgrown silkwood tree in the front yard hung so low we could stand in the center and be completely hidden from view. In less than an hour, we watched a transaction at the front door of one of the apartments. The chase team caught the buyer and recovered the dope, which sealed the fate of those dealers.

I went to court to have a judge sign the search warrant and arranged with SWAT to make the forced entry. The CI had forewarned us this group was dangerous. On the day of the warrant service we planted our people around the complex before SWAT made entry. Unfortunately, the SWAT officer making the entry wasn't quite paying attention. He slammed a door with the heavy steel doorknocker but hit the neighbor's door by mistake. I yelled at him to step over one to the right and hit that door. By that time, the dealers inside were alerted. The neighbors whose door was hit were not home. The city would financially work out the fix for the mistake with the building manager if the manager even gave a shit.

SWAT hit the correct door and knocked it down. Two of the three occupants simultaneously jumped out the rear living room window. Our guys were below on a dirt incline next to a cinderblock wall three feet from the rear wall of the apartment building. A female jumper dropped right into an officer's arms. He'd staged just to cover that possibility. The male jumper was not so lucky and hit the block wall, fracturing a leg. He'd be carted off by ambulance with a police guard. The sole resident was trapped between the failed exits and a storm of cops. The frightened man couldn't calm down. I cuffed him and took him into a back room to stifle his panic. He hyperventilated to the point I thought paramedics needed to be check him out. "Hey guys, you gotta come back here," I yelled. SWAT had cleared the rooms and mentioned there was some pot in one of them. My prisoner calmed a bit even though one of the rooms contained a crowd and kilos of bagged marijuana stacked like pillows against one of the walls.

The other WECAN guys filtered in to see the bounty we'd just taken. I estimated forty-five pounds, which wasn't a major haul for the Narcotics investigators, but was a huge haul for us. I grabbed the guy that I'd cuffed and stood him up. "Here. This is a copy of the search warrant. You've hereby been served."

Agent Chuck's CI paid off again. There were enough kilos of pot stored in this place to make both the CI and FBI Agent Chuck happy. In exchange, the CI fed back information about another apartment in the same building selling more dope. This place seemed to be a haven for drugs. I doubt if the owners cared if we knocked all the front doors down, but the place couldn't get enough SDPD attention. The ensuing "Flight of the Dealers" would not go unnoticed.

Roger Barrett took the lead on drug apartment part two, also on the second floor but almost all WECAN officers shared the effort and the glory equally. WECAN officers Long and Grano had split off from the rest of the pack and were given carte blanche to operate without supervision. Unfortunately, they were part of the Central Team and several of us resented them. They chose their own hours, so they got to work daytime hours with weekends off. The remaining thirty-four WECAN cops worked afternoons through evenings and rarely had weekends with their families. Only John Tangredi had any sort of friendship with one of the day guys, but even John agreed that their rosy independence was a result of intense ass-kissing.

WECAN officers were a tight knit group and could work interchangeably. Each WECAN officer was both a leader and a follower. We were trained and treated like Special Forces. There were no unbalanced skills or lopsided leadership roles. We had sergeants for that. If I ran an assignment, I knew any one of my teammates could step in and replace me. Unfortunately, because we worked swing shift, we couldn't gather a force in the mornings when search warrants are often less hazardous. This next hit would be in the more perilous afternoon when the bad guys tended to be more alert.

Rather than go through the necessary labor to seek a search warrant, Roger opted to knock and talk our way in. He picked a day not long after we hit the drug apartment part one. We didn't need SWAT for this one. We just walked up the stairs and knocked on the door. The single occupant was an undocumented Mexican male with some English skills. When Roger told him we'd heard that dope was sold there the guy seemed surprised and reassured us it wasn't true. Roger asked if we could come in and search and the guy gave us a hurried, "Sure, sure."

Roger was a pretty gruff character. He was strictly back-country San Diego County with an inclination to get in the faces of clowns who wasted his time. The cretins we dealt with every day were a blur of skin colors and attitudes to Roger. Most street people wanted their face time with Roger to be brief.

The two-bedroom apartment we entered was sparsely furnished. Uh, oh, that was a sign. There wasn't even a chair for the occupant to sit on, let alone much else in the form of creature comforts. We corralled him into one of the bedrooms and the search began in earnest. We assumed the exploration would be quick since there was virtually nothing to search. Yet, we came up empty. There was simply no place to conceal contraband and all the known hiding spots we typically uncovered weren't there.

The detained Mexican national was glib and a bit too talkative. He must have known we weren't going to find contraband and smiled like he was in charge, not us. Usually the drug den operators confine their confidence to themselves. This guy broadcast his with ear-to-ear grins that baffled us. He was either very clever or had no fear of the police in his apartment. I voted for the former.

Roger was a talented carpenter. He could have killed time during the search and built a chair if asked to. He wandered around studying the walls, the doors and even the framework. At one point he examined a door jamb, walked forward a step, and then turned back to the same jamb. He noticed a fine saw mark across one side of the jamb. The kerf of a saw blade was barely noticeable. Roger's trained eye counted an identical cut about eighteen inches lower. With his right hand, Roger grabbed the jamb between the two cuts and pulled. The wooden door edifice pulled cleanly with just a little effort. He let go of his discovery, almost in disbelief as the portion of door frame snapped back into place. He called me over and said, "Watch."

This time he pulled back with a firmer grasp and held the board. We both looked inside and saw cut spaces in the door frame with gaps filled with heroin and cocaine. Springs were fastened to the segment of jamb to tug it back into place. Velcro strips held the piece of wood in place. Roger told another team member to cuff the new prisoner.

The soon-to-be prisoner had other ideas. He got to his feet and jumped through the open window knocking out the window screen. Shit! Not Again! None of us had thought to cover the back window after we gained entry thinking we had it under control. We left one guy behind and ran down and around to the drop zone. When we turned the corner, it was clear that things didn't work out so well for the jumper. When he took the swan dive, he went out head-first. His hands were cuffed behind him so he couldn't break his fall. The guy hit face first into gravel ground cover. Luckily, the embankment was high enough to make it only a short drop. He was conscious and in decent shape for a guy who looked like he'd been pepper box-blasted to the face. There'd be no ambulance for this one. He'd survive with inexplicable adult acne scars. For some reason, Roger had a set of Delta pilot wings in his car. He pinned them on our suspect and thanked him for flying Delta on his way to jail.

The dope in the door frame was a considerable amount of heroin wrapped in toy balloons, and paper bindles of powdered cocaine, the usual popular combo for the speedball contingent. Since this was the third jumper from the same apartment building in as many days, the press sniffed around. Presumably, somebody in the suspect building thought we were sadist cops, rogues who had gone too far. This person contacted the San Diego Union-Tribune newspaper and talked to a reporter about the bloodthirsty cops. The press figured out who we were and that we belonged to WECAN. A small accusatory blurb in a column in the newspaper's local section claimed that witnesses saw drug cops throw people out windows on Martin Street. However, there were so many cops and witnesses to the first event, the department seemed to ignore it. Nobody else who read the paper responded either. The notice was a shocker and should have at least opened some eyes normally suspicious of cops, but nothing happened. We never heard a word from anyone. I don't think anyone at the department even read the article. So much for the U-T's credibility.

We gave the numbers on the swan-diver bust to FBI Agent Chuck after the dust settled. His CI was going gangbusters for all of us. All good things would come to an end way too soon. Agent Chuck called us to meet him in the field. We figured it would be another tip. Agent Chuck had some bad news. He got a transfer to the Chicago office. He explained he'd had his transfer in for months. In his FBI world Chicago was the big leagues, a place to get noticed and promoted, San Diego, not so much. His exit was in a week. His CI was already assigned to someone else. He chatted the agent up on our behalf and provided our contact information. We never heard from him. I suspected the SAIC kept Agent Chuck on a shorter leash after the bust-up with the Fingerprint Lab. Agent Chuck's replacement probably reasoned that getting tangled up with us might not be in his best interest.

CHAPTER 18:

A DAY BEGINS

Manny kept a photo spread of his family taped or held in place with magnets to the inside walls of his locker. One afternoon as I got suited up into my uniform, I happened to look over at his open locker at his photo spread. I saw pictures of him with his beautiful family. Then I saw a photo of half a body laid out over some train tracks, squeezed in between pictures of his little girls. Below those I saw a scene of a man shot dead. There were all kinds of death photos interspersed with family pictures. "Nice, Manny. You keep your gore photos pinned up with your family," I commented drolly.

"They're just souvenirs of my time in the Heights, man." Many of us keep souvenirs as mementos of our lives as cops, sort of a "gallows-humor" approach to the harder parts of our existence. I looked over a few of the grisly photos. The Heights, without a doubt, tends to showcase more grotesque photo ops than any other place in town. The dead are everywhere down there. The locals, the transients and the damned, chew each other up and spit out broken corpses weekly, if not daily. Manny shut the locker door and accompanied me to line-up. We'd be off to the mean, meaner, and meanest streets for our ten-hour shift.

A friend and former F Troop partner, Don Simpkins, kept binders with photos of dozens of the dead. He collected them like Indians collected scalps two centuries past. I thumbed through two of the binders as a challenge. I'd seen the dead in the worst reposes, but Don's books were a test of one's stomach. One showed the aftermath of a collision between a train and a hobo, another the graphic mess from a corpse that exploded from the pressure of internal gasses, and a picture of just how far a human neck can stretch when the body had been hung from a tree. This death probably masked a story of pain great enough to induce the man, maybe a veteran himself, to tie the rope to the branch of a tree planted at Fort Rosecrans National Cemetery where gravesites mark the deaths of thousands of Americans all the way back to the Spanish-American War. These grotesque pictures of death were just another aspect of our lives as a cops.

I knew a handful of San Diego officers with death photos. Each cop had his or her own reason to keep them. One former Homicide detective found the death disturbing and often too grotesque to manage. Richard Carlson painted the dead as he saw them. He even presented an art gallery with his renditions and put on a display open to the public. Rich felt a catharsis when he dealt with the horror of murder and graphic death in his artistic manner.

A typical line-up for the three WECAN Teams was at our respective divisional facilities. Friday line-ups were required for all of us at a large meeting room in the Headquarters building which was also Central WECAN's HQ. The large meetings were an entertaining affair. All thirty-six officers and their sergeants had chances to schmooze with each other. The meetings included specific training best given to all of us at once. Sometimes, the training came from outside experts. City attorneys and district attorneys were frequent guests. Some of our instruction came from within. One example was a former prison specialist turned SDPD cop. He kept abreast of the activities that inmates shared within prison walls. Prisoners relentlessly looked for ways to defeat cops. The officer brought photos and film of "yard birds" who practiced disarming other prisoners who held mock guns. These deadly skills were designed to use against cops encountered on the streets after their release. These future ex-cons trained to disarm police officers and kill them with their own guns.

The prison expert emphasized the importance of body condition, gun retention practice, and body position when interacting with ex-cons fresh out of prison. Former convicts were a large percentage of our street adversaries. I didn't know about all the others, but I trained hard not to be a victim.

On a more positive note, members of the WECAN teams gathered frequent accolades from inside and outside the department. Friday line-ups were great times to reinforce the high morale of the unit. Police brass were often on hand to heap commendations and praise on the teams. The feeling among my peers was that we were the department's flagship unit.

We listened to a lecture and a warning about handling shotguns at a subsequent Friday line-up. Each marked police car is outfitted with one shotgun. The double-aught rounds are stored separately by each officer. We discussed the loud whumping sound we'd heard outside the walls of the building the week before. One of the patrol officers assigned to Central Division ineptly jacked a round into his shotgun's receiver and pulled the trigger. Fortunately, he held it pointed up into a safety container downstairs in the parking garage. The pole-mounted canister was designed to catch accidental discharges. The SDPD-assigned Remington 810 makes one helluva boom. Because of that officer's failure to perform a five-point safety check, all had to suffer through more retraining.

After we cleared line-up Manny and I chose to eat a little something before our workday began. Manny introduced several of us to a mom-and-pop barbecue place like no other I'd eaten at in San Diego. He loved Henry's Barbecue. The first time I saw the place, a tiny hovel on Broadway crammed in between two tall buildings, I thought it was joke. The kitchen was too small, and seating was limited to a short bench next to the only window. The grill, stove and smoker combo looked like a cast-iron machine from the 19th Century, blackened with years of burnt grease and smoke. Manny saw past the décor and told me to get the ham sandwich on a burger bun. He placed the order for both of us and made sure I watched, "You're gonna want to watch this, Bro."

The cook grilled thin slices of ham he cut himself. The buns laid facedown next to the meat. He tossed a couple of thick slices of cheddar cheese on the same grill. When it was time, he scooped everything off the grill and stacked the food together off to the side. Manny nudged me to watch the cook lift the top bun off. The man, side-by-side with his equally elderly wife, produced a ladle from below the grill. He literally poured homemade barbecue sauce all over the structure of the sandwich and then slammed the burger bun on top to try and hold it all together.

The same chemistry went into the beef and chicken recipes. There were no sides, no salads, no chips not even a pickle. The greasy snack was pure meat-lover joy under a shroud of melted cheese and tangy BBQ deliciousness. The incredible ham, beef and chicken sandwich choices were the juiciest in town. Covered in cheese and sauce they were also the messiest. We couldn't eat them sitting down, our uniforms would never survive. Instead, we ate bent forward over the patrol car, leaving splashes of yellow and red on the hood. Sometimes we even had to get the car washed after a meal!

We ate this meal on the upper parking lot at HQ. We needed to be close to our lockers if the sandwiches exploded over our uniforms, Manny taught me that. Tangredi and Davis met us with their own snack choices. We'd already laid out our snacks across the hood of our car. The two newcomers set their bags of food on top of our car as well. "Where'd you guys go?" I asked looking at the fat burritos in their hands.

"The Green Fly," John replied. "You guys went to Henry's I see." John smirked at the red and yellow mess that was once a white police car's hood.

"Yep," Manny spoke with a full mouth, as another blob of barbecue sauce, mustard and cheese landed on the car.

John remarked, "Man, those things are messy, but they sure are good. We'd have gone there too, but Chuck wanted Mexican." Chuck just smiled in front of his burrito number one. Number two was warming on the hood of our car in the mid-day sun. Also, the cooling engine left residual heat turning the hood into a hot plate. Chuck possibly had the largest appetite in the entire unit. Southeast WECAN had Kevin Ammon and Tyrone Crosby, two of the largest guys in the teams, but Chuck could match them for pounds consumed and not show an ounce of weight gain. No matter what he consumed he, remained flat-bellied and flat-butted. Tall and square-shouldered he reminded me of a human door with appendages.

"Chuck, you keep going like that and you might actually grow a butt," I joked. John and Manny laughed. "As it is now, it looks like you're suffering from GTA." GTA stood for Grand Theft Ass. Somehow, up until then, we'd all deftly avoided stains of rainbow colors on our uniforms. I made a misstep and a chunk of greasy deliciousness landed on my shirt. "Damn it!" I spat out testily. But with a little bit of spit rub I was suitable for the field. As usual, the Latin gentleman remained spotless. His rakish smile set ladies hearts aflame. Tightly poured into his uniform, he always looked like he'd place "First in Show." Manny was right about Henry's barbeque. I'd die for one more shot at one of those "Arby's on steroids" sandwiches.

Alas, Henry's went the way of all things downtown San Diego as the millennial-oriented developers and short-sighted city fathers knocked the building down for gentrified places called shoppes, topped with condo towers.

Manny's heritage as Puerto Rican American gifted him with Spanish-speaking skills but his *latino* language skills didn't mean he could instantly communicate with all Spanish speakers. His first years on the job forced him to interpret street lingo also spoken in Spanish. New York Puerto Rican is dissimilar from Mexican Spanish. They are both different from the street Spanish slang spoken by gangsters and criminals in San Diego. Whether Manny understood everything spoken in front of him or not, the average street character treated him with respect. His Latin heritage spoke volumes to the street people. Manny was an easy-going fellow, prone to issuing vocal terror if provoked by the bad guys. His Latin temper flattened out a lot of supposed bad asses in the field. "Look, you rat bastard *maricon*. I told you to back off and shut up." Seething between clenched teeth, Manny wouldn't have to touch a guy to get him to do what Manny said. "I'm gonna knock your teeth out of your head if you don't quiet down and show respect. *Puto!*"

Manny and I believed in respect being granted both ways. We showed respect to our criminal counterparts and expected earned deference in return. This is the way of the streets. Sometimes the most concerning confrontation with a gang member could be stopped immediately when their disrespect is challenged. I've gone toe-to-toe with six-foot plus monsters ready to kick my ass. But, when challenged with, "Did I show you disrespect?" my opponent would take measure of the situation and reduce his volatile demeanor with a simple, "No."

"Then why are you disrespecting me?" The opponent would be perplexed long enough for me to lay down what respect means as pertains to the legal reason I was talking to him in the first place. Suddenly, logic or levity washed over them and the situations deflated. The three 'R's of the Heights: Rock cocaine, Rip-offs and Respect.

During my time on WECAN, San Diego Police Officers wore tan uniforms. Our administration did not believe in anything militant for police attire. The police chiefs theorized we appeared less of a threat. We didn't even have shoulder patches for the first one hundred years of the department's existence. We looked like custodians. An uptick of police injuries and death in the 1980s generated officer safety investigations. The outcome, pronounced from upon high, was that San Diego's cops needed a uniform change. Popular theory, garnered from other departments carrying darker uniforms, suggested that San Diego police officers would suffer less if we wore darker, more authoritative uniforms. San Diego went to dark blue in the 1990s.

I thought the darker blues were more authoritative when we were wrapped in our black leather gun belts. We looked more official, and with the color-matched shoulder patches we dressed up "to mean business." The only accessory missing were the old leather straps cops wore generations back.

The Sam Browne belt is wide, usually leather, and supported by a narrower strap passing diagonally over the right shoulder. For cops like me the shoulder element would have taken the strain off my lower back. That was never a permitted aspect of SDPD's uniform code while I was on the department. In hindsight, my poor back wishes it was standard uniform wear. Either way, the change from tan to deep blue, which looks almost black, enhanced the way I felt when I put on the uniform. The dark attire adorned with all the police accoutrements commanded respect. Respect goes a long way when a WECAN officer is face-to-face with hardcore thugs willing to mete out death to anyone standing in their way.

CHAPTER 19:
THE HEIGHTS

In many parts of the roughest neighborhoods the dealers worked from rental homes and apartments. These houses were incorporated into blocks of similar, nondescript dwellings. The only time they stood out against the backdrop of an ordinary row of homes was when the junkies were seen coming and going all day and all night. The poor neighbors had no strong voice to prevent these set-ups from opening and thriving. The residents were often frightened, but smart enough to ignore these places as best they could to avoid trouble. The theory behind WECAN was we could turn some of those people into sources of information. So far, the results were less than hoped for. But most of the WECAN officers managed to wheedle information out of people, good and bad. The Heights had a hundred years of trouble and resistance. WECAN regarded the neighborhoods as challenges we'd meet the best we could.

Central WECAN concentrated its efforts within three neighboring areas, Logan Heights, Sherman Heights and Stockton. Collectively, we verbally lumped the three communities into "The Heights," casting aside any individual identities the map books granted them. The streets east of the Heights were Stockton. The blocks north of Sherman Heights were Grant Hill and Golden Hill. All were considered the Heights when police officers talked about everything below downtown. Any police officer who worked Central in any capacity would always tell you, he or she either worked downtown or the Heights. Central Division also included Balboa Park, the emerald jewel of San Diego and home to our world-class zoo.

Some of the original buildings from the 1915 Pan-Pacific Exposition were still standing in the park. One of the buildings built long after the Expo was the Moorish-influenced Natural History Museum. This imposing chunk of San Diego history was built with chambers on multiple floors. The top floor gazes out over all of San Diego's Central Division neighborhoods.

The scenic park was a couple miles from the teeming streets of Logan heights. The park's gorgeous scenery was a place for a cop to roll through and let the park's beauty provide a psychological respite from the havoc two miles away as the crow or the vulture flies. I took that winding tour one night when I worked alone while Manny took the day off. Chuck and John were tied up for the rest of the shift with a prisoner. My shift was coming to an end and I wanted to kill the remaining time on the clock. The park was so serene at night I found that a pass through the serenity and beauty chilled me out. Of course, that couldn't last.

My radio chirped: "Five-Twenty-One John, Four-Five-Nine alarm at the Natural History Museum, One-Seven-Eight-Eight El Prado. Unit to cover?" I was in the park! I volunteered and made a U-turn to zip to the museum. The museum had suffered a burglary a few months prior. Somebody got in and stole samples of gold on display. Worries were that the thieves would return for other precious metals and gemstones. I got there just as the Central Division patrol unit arrived. 521 John was a single-officer unit. The two of us were met by a park employee with a key to the door.

521 John and I walked the perimeter first, to look for signs of forced entry. The park employee waited yards away from the building and out of sight of its windows. 521 and I were all that was available for the building wide search. Dispatch said she would send the next available unit as soon as one cleared. 521 and I had our flashlights out and flashed them through the three floors of windows. Maybe we'd be rewarded with a moon-faced burglar caught in the beams of our flashlights. That was just about any cop's wet dream; to catch the thief right in the act.

Another police unit showed up. We collected a plan together and headed inside to begin the more laborious room-to-room search. So far, there'd been no signs of a break in.

The interior was compartmentalized into dozens of rooms only to be remodeled in recent years to open the center into a massive atrium. Attendees can stand in the middle of the museum, ringed by walkways finished with balustrades. The open ceiling reaches the roof generating a spectacular hollow sound when many voices speak. We walked the lowest-to-highest floors until everything below the roof was secured. There were still no signs of entry. A low stairway on the third floor led to a small, steel portal leading out onto the roof. My cover officers followed me up to the roof door. The door was half the size of a man. The only way any person could climb through it was to hunch over and step backwards through the metal portal. I figured I'd go first.

The moonless night was on the other side of the doorway. One of my cover officers was behind me as I turned to walk backwards. He had his gun out in case of danger and faced my back. I couldn't peer over my shoulder to see what was behind me until I was all the way through. He couldn't point his flashlight forward into the darkness without blinding me. I pulled my gun and held it down until I pivoted with my light in my other hand. All I heard was silence through the gloom.

I brought my flashlight up to torso height and had my gun extended. I would not be caught by a thief without a strong defense. Suddenly, I was met with a frightening screech and the menacing sound of giant wings flapping in panic. "AGGHHHHH!" My mouth was as wide as a scream would open it! I have no idea what was going on behind me, but I can bet I had two guns pointed my direction. Ahead of me I saw an angry winged predator with a six-foot wingspan!

My cover officers receded through the doorway they'd just stepped through in near panic. "What the Hell?" one shouted. I backed up to the wall and shone my light on more startled, winged monsters. The job of a police officer is to remain unnerved in times of crisis. I forced myself to regain composure and reason out the sight confronting me. What I finally registered was a giant cage full of large vultures somehow living on the roof of an antique building in a park in the middle of urban San Diego. In fact, there were multiple cages filled with a dozen scavenger birds of prey. All of them screeched and bounced around and flapped their wings about. The cacophony in such close quarters was deafening. The night air was filled with avian windmills shooting feathers out in all directions. My heart raced. I tried to calm down and make sense of these winged beasts. Why the hell were they up there? The park employee heard the screams and shouts from downstairs and rushed up to us. By then, the other officers and I had replaced stunned reactions with curious ones.

The park employee explained that the museum ornithologist kept the vultures as pets. He'd feed them meat on the bone from carcasses and then use clean bones for his museum purposes. What a great, symbiotic relationship. I kidded the employee when I asked if the ornithologist ever cleaned off the bones of wayward museum goers who ended up in my circumstances. He gave a dry chuckle and attended to the birds.

The officers and I walked around the massive wood and chicken-wire cages to look over the amazing birds. This was a treat, to see them this close and not be their dinner. We let Dispatch know we were secure with no signs of entry and no crime. "We're Code Four with vultures," took some explaining over the Tactical frequency, or Tac for short.

When I told friends and acquaintances about my life in the Heights as a WECAN officer they almost always asked if the Heights were as bad as they heard. They pictured Logan and Sherman as a vast ghetto filled with the poor who exist in sub-standard conditions in homes that looked like shanties out of 1930s gangster movies. They imagined rundown and tawdry row houses fronted with stoops filled daily with human predators waiting for their next unsuspecting victims.

Few grasped the historical significance of the large number of build-ings that survived the wrecking ball. They had no idea that San Diego's earlier wealthy had palaces built for them on stately properties a carriage ride away from the hustle and bustle of busy, commercial downtown.

Some of the less cared for venerable structures wore more than one hundred and twenty years of paint. More than a few underwent reha-bilitation and were preserved through the Save Our Heritage Organiza-tion. I had a keen eye towards the treasures beneath the old paint and rotted fasciae.

I loved to explore the once-stately majestic relics in the Sherman and Logan neighborhoods when we entered these buildings in search for drugs and the evildoers rooted inside. To many mansions had been remodeled into low-income apartments, or simply replaced with slapped-together apartment buildings to accommodate post-World War II San Diegans. Some of the less cared for venerable structures were beaten down into abandoned relics long past any developer's dreams of a reconstructed former glory. Working class people found the mansions they once envied renovated as affordable apartments. Many of the beautiful artifices were still adorned with ornate cupolas, Victorian archways and actual two-inch by four-inch two-by-fours. These castles of the bygone era were the homes of San Diego's earliest elite and wealthy.

The big houses were built on the slopes and along avenues that overlooked the bay and the sea. The workers' homes were built at the foot of the hillside near the blue-collar jobs that sprung up around the fishing industry, shipbuilders and the Navy.

Sherman Heights was one of the earliest neighborhoods in town and surrounded downtown San Diego. Matthew Sherman purchased one hundred and sixty acres for speculation just south and east of downtown in the 19th Century. He subdivided his property allowing others to build garish Queen Anne and Victorian folk-and-stick homes as castles to advertise their wealth. As San Diego developed and grew, transportation allowed the wealthiest to move beyond the narrow boundaries of the mid-19th century homes. Cable cars and automobiles encouraged the wealthy of Sherman Heights to live farther away. Their exodus created vacancies filled by people of lesser means. Working class people found the mansions they once envied renovated as affordable apartments.

New homes were built for the newer gentry moving onto the Heights. Craftsman-style bungalows, Spanish-revival one-story houses, and neo-Classical cottages lined the streets. Prairie-style apartment buildings were built on property that once showcased beautiful last-Century mansions on tree-lined thoroughfares. An increase in population demands saw more historical residences get knocked down in the name of progress, progress being narrow, eight-unit apartment buildings all crushed together in parallel.

Everything built was squeezed in between streets and alleys. As the reduction of free space continued and dwellings were barely separated from each other, property crimes increased. Nobody knew their neighbors anymore, not like it was decades before. A transitory population occupied thousands of tiny hovels. People walking the neighborhoods were often strangers to the residents who were also strangers to each other. Criminals figured out how to burglarize shoddily built houses and apartments. Crime was on the rise. Normally utilitarian alleyways became arteries of crime with thieves who traversed them to stay out of sight.

By the 1930s, once-grandiose homes overflowed with foreign and domestic workers, the poor and the destitute. Sherman Heights began to resemble a slum. White, middle, and upper class, families moved away as Sherman Height's population grew into a packed enclave of Hispanic and African American families. Other larger homes were gutted and turned into low-income rentals. Those who could afford to purchase in Sherman Heights might have seen their dreams dissolved as their inheritors turned their precious investments into more rentals.

Back then, there was little city control over the impact of such grossly saturated rentals. This debacle would have a negative impact on property values and the people living there. The area screamed for a moratorium on living density. By the beginning of the 1940s, parts of Sherman Heights were inhabited by German, Irish and Japanese Americans. World War II saw the Japanese Americans forcibly resettled into camps. The whites left too, for new neighborhoods further away from downtown and somewhat segregated.

Sherman Heights and neighboring Logan Heights gained reputations as rough places to live. Newly created freeways cut painful swathes through Logan and Sherman Heights and destroyed cohesive neighborhoods. Neighbors became strangers and families were split apart. Interstate 5 separated both neighborhoods from centralized downtown furthering the rift between San Diego's leaders and the disenfranchised communities across the freeway.

Logan Heights' history was not unlike the Sherman neighborhoods. Many prominent business leaders, well-paid professionals and their families lived within this shore-front community. "The soil was fertile; a sightly location and accessibility to the business district by horse and buggy" made 19th Century Logan Heights a perfect place to raise families said the San Diego Union newspaper of the day. I'd like to have seen the Heights of a hundred years ago. Only the history-minded or architecturally inclined who live in the Heights now can appreciate the beauty that once was.

Future development would come to the Heights in time, but crushing poverty, an indifferent City of San Diego, the fear of gangs and drug dealers discouraged little positive change. The neighborhood activists rarely took on drug dealers and gang members. There were men and women from the neighborhood who tried to institute change from within. They lived within socially vibrant neighborhoods but were frustrated by political negligence and insufficient public funding to create meaningful change. The activists knew the players on all sides; many had come up from these same mean streets. Some were progressive and coaxed gang members into better ways of life. Others were militant and would not bridge the gulf between their politics and cooperation with the police. All understood they had no control over the foreign drug dealers that infested block after block.

WECAN provided a direction, a link to people who saw us as more than cops. We didn't live there, but daily contact with the residents and the appearance of a handful of officers in line-of-sight action seemed to embolden people to openly speak to us. I found many of the elderly residents were comfortable when we chatted about neighborhood problems in general, instead of hiding behind locked doors and shuttered windows when we passed by on foot. Manny had already built a rapport with some of the people on 32nd Street. Now it was my turn to hear their thoughts and concerns. "How do you get along with the guys who hang out across the street?" I asked an elderly black man seated on his front porch and facing the elementary school across the boulevard.

"Oh they don't bother me."

"But they're out there dealing drugs all day and all night. Doesn't that scare you?"

"I know some of them boys. If I pay them no never mind, they don't bother me. I hear them shoutin' and jibber-jabbin' all the time. I'd like them to shut up at night, but I'm not going out there in the dark to talk to them. One of them lives behind me with his mom, Cecile. If'n I have to, I'll go talk to her."

"What about calling the police for help?"

"Officer, what'r you going to do after you run them off? They be right back after you leave. They be knowing I'm here and you ain't. You know how it is." Sadly, the story was the same all over. WECAN couldn't touch that concern with all the cops and all the tools at its fingertips.

I was aware that I'd be just another white cop trying to dialogue with the people possibly jaded by Officer Friendlies such as me in the past who also meant well but accomplished less than advertised.

The gangs showed little respect for the foundations of their community. They occupied the same places as their non-gang peers, but it was hard to tell who was in control. Community leaders could only warn and shame them into respect for the good people who lived amongst them. Community activists existed in uneasy alliances with the gangs. The non-gang drug dealers, the transient exploiters, had no connection to the communities they peddled in.

I saw the microcosm of the Heights as a sample of segregation for poverty, for being black or brown, or for maintaining solidarity with the community they were raised in. Thousands of Spanish-speakers inhabited the Heights because it had been familiar ground for generations of families and travelers. I'd met the struggling, blue collar workers and restaurant employees, maids and security guards who lived with their gangster and drug dealing neighbors. I'd asked some of them how they managed against nearly insurmountable odds. The humbling answer was their choices were few. Even worse, they sadly admitted that some of the problem gangsters were their own kids. So many were disconnected from their teenagers and could do little to cancel the influence of their kids' dangerous peers.

WECAN in the Heights meant walks through the homes, complexes and businesses. No territory or building was to remain an unknown quantity to WECAN officers on their turf. I had to deal with one large apartment complex on Franklin because of one apartment that was occupied by a round-file of 30th Street gangsters. I had no idea why the manager even rented to these guys. Almost every other unit housed Hispanic families with blue collar, or no-collar husbands and wives. The place was an enclave of happy kids and tantalizing cooking smells coming from multiple kitchens. Then you had these assholes who strained the patience of everyone tasked with trying to ignore them. A problem of this nature was usually for patrol officers to manage, but since the sonsabitches were thugs, WECAN made it ours.

The matter was simple. We needed to bag these guys acting their worst, which seemed to be every night when they sat in their cars in the parking lot, got drunk and high, and snubbed their neighbors' complaints. Word got to us through our LT who knew somebody in the complex. "Their lease is expired, but they won't leave. See if there's anything you do can about those guys."

Our first step was to identify the men involved. We wouldn't put the apartment complex manager in the middle with awkward attempts to enlist his aid. Besides, we didn't know about any potential alliances. Pacts with the police were more dangerous than doing nothing at all. We used computers to track down the names of the culprits. Their rides gave up more info through their license plates. At least one guy was on probation. Two others had crime histories and one was an absconder from a traffic ticket. That warrant was our ticket in.

Manny, Chuck, John and I became a quartet within Central WECAN. We schemed on a specific evening to appear out of nowhere on top of a group of Logan gangsters often gathered in the parking lot of this one complex. We rode in pairs and parked our cars in two spots to try and disguise that the cops were staging for a sweep. The locals that watched the police like hawks knew one parked police car in the Heights could mean anything; a call to keep the peace, a family squabble, or just a police officer writing a routine theft report. Two marked units parked together in a dark alley brought on a whole other connotation.

John and Chuck met us half a click down the alley where we stashed our marked units. On a Friday night, the fellows should already be rocking. They didn't disappoint. Two cars with stereos at full volume parked askew in the private parking lot. Too bad. If they'd been on the street, we'd already have their cars ready for impound for grossly expired registrations and outstanding parking tickets. One of their guys boogied to his car as soon as we appeared. He wasn't so lucky. His low-slung Chevy also had outstanding parking tickets, enough of them for us to tow his car. He bristled at the uniforms materializing around him while he entertained his *vato* brothers. "Why you hassling us? We just barely got here. We didn't do nothing."

Chuck recognized the one guy from stops in that car around Chicano Park. He was closest to him as the man's anger spilled out. "I've dealt with you before. I treated you right then, so you should ramp down the attitude and take this warning. We're here because of the gang problem. This has nothing to do with anything else. Logan *Treinta* has our full and undivided attention. This place with you in it has our attention."

Manny had a conversation with the others at the same time and suggested they should leave this place for good. "You *cabrones* will have us here too often. You see that *pendejo* with my partner and the other cop? That will be you soon if you don't move on. Soon." The threat was not a warning but a promise. We would make life hard on them. They already knew who we were from other WECAN days and nights. The sight of the "wanted" Chevy stuck in place for a tow truck by our direction began to sink in. There wasn't even a peep out of the rest of the bangers. We identified them, probably not for the last time and then let them melt away into the darkness. The Chevy owner scraped together some property from his car under my careful observation. They were all gone by morning.

Many of the Hispanic residents did not trust the police. We didn't want to be the other bullies they had to contend with. Their fears were valid when one considered that cops had chased them around for generations. WECAN was asked to approach the people of the Heights with greater communication, perhaps even some compassion through simple daily contact. For the suffering of a handful, the larger group got to take a breath for once.

A lot of the people who lived in the two-story complex kept to themselves whenever the police showed up. More than a few might have been concerned we were there for drug or gang issues and then suddenly pulled someone out of their home for immigration status. Nothing could be further from our minds. I knew a lot of the souls watching us at that very moment were here illegally. I didn't care. I know Manny, John and Chuck shared my lack of interest. Only the reliably troublesome gangsters who might be there illegally needed to fear deportation from us. Maybe, some of the folks who'd finally stepped out onto their porches to study us grasped that we were tasked to do the very enforcement they'd been hoping for, for months. I did catch the eye of one Latin gentleman on the second floor. He was still garbed in chef's attire and dirty from a day's kitchen work. None of the bad guys saw the interchange between the two of us. I winked at the cook and managed a slight smile only for him. He approved and signaled back with a very slight twitch of the thumb into a brief, thumbs up sign. His endorsement was justification enough for our cause.

WECAN took baby steps to build community bridges while still providing gang and narcotics deterrence. The culture's fear of the police was rigid down there, though. The Hispanic people feared us as extensions of *La Migra*. WECAN was inundated with Mexican nationals who ran amok in the Heights. Some were members of San Diego street gangs and others, drug dealers connected to ghostly, organized dealers on both sides of the border. We hauled quite a few of the bad ones over to Border Patrol for shipment back to Mexico. They kept returning illegally because the gain here was significantly greater than in their country. Here resided the money and the better life. We had no interest in the deportation and separation of undocumented people. We'd let someone else take on that task. We'd undo any good done so far if we yanked the people who cause no problems and sent them south.

The African American population was about the only other dominant culture in the Heights. There were few Asian people in comparison. The whites lived above the Heights in the quaint, older neighborhoods above Broadway that had been renovated into an almost bohemian, middle class atmosphere. Many black people shared the same disconnect and distrust of the police. There was no way to know how many Logan Heights families supported the police until we could talk to them all. The great task of gaining support from people traditionally suspicious of the police was daunting. Their complaints mirrored those of many urban, minority-dominant cities nationwide. Manny, Chuck, John, Roger and I only had to contend with the people of the Heights.

The WECAN philosophy showed signs of success in the Heights. Residents got used to our presence. They saw we didn't rush in and rush out. We rolled up and stayed awhile. The locals saw our impact on the gangs. San Diego PD repainted its fleet of police cars in black and white. WECAN wasn't in the budget for the new paint. We weren't disappointed. The all-white WECAN mobiles stuck out and signified that the drug and gang cops were on the block.

I theorized our effectiveness could only go so far. There were not enough of us and we were effective at making arrests. Our arrest rates increased, but our exposure on the streets decreased. Each arrest and the processes that followed took us off the streets. We altered the purpose of the unit and its visibility to be felony cops. The people who needed us didn't get us as often as they liked. That was the trade-off. We scoured their streets and removed their problem people, but we also removed ourselves.

The four of us let the clock run up to seven o'clock and then made a meet in front of La Central market just to irritate the Red Steps gangsters. As usual we got stuck again on the nightly debate about where to eat. "I'm up for Chuey's" Manny suggested. The turned-down corners of John and Chuck's mouths displayed their opinions. I wasn't in the mood for Mexican, although Chuey's, not far from Chicano Park, was great food. Chuey's was no taco stand, but a full-blown restaurant with a sports bar atmosphere.

"If I'm going to do Mexican, I'd rather go to the Green Fly," John tried to interject. Chuck looked on blankly. He almost always followed John's lead. Legions of Central cops loved the Green Fly, technically called *Las Quatros Milpas*, which doesn't translate into the Green Fly. The Green Fly was an older name for the spot, and it stuck with cops.

"Forget that, John. Look at the time. The line will be half an hour long to get seated and I don't want to get it to go and eat off the car again this week," I admonished.

"Alright, then. What about Vesuvio's?" Manny knew if we couldn't agree on anyplace at once we'd always agree with Vesuvio's downtown.

"I'm good with that. The price is right." Nobody could argue with my little add-on as a motivator to go to the little pizza and pasta joint on Broadway.

John didn't mull over the request for long. "Yeah, that works." Off we went.

Vesuvio's was notorious or legendary, depending on if you are a boss or a trooper, for its special rates for police officers. Department policy restricted cops from eateries that gave discounts to law enforcement. The department saw the action as currying favor from police. In theory, the officers could be compromised in a quid pro quo scenario. The restaurant curried the favor and could hold that favor over an officer. No cop should be beholden to anyone in the line of duty. The owner of Vesuvio's had a business smack dead-center in a part of downtown inhabited by less-desirable people. We ate there and he had no problems for a while. Cops can relish the most off-beat eating places. In the six years Manny'd eaten there, he'd never been called out or called upon to do any favors for Vesuvio's. They just respected cops and helped us out with lower-priced food.

The Department's policy had two sides to its enforcement. If cops ate there for half-price, nothing happened. Nobody spoke about the nature of the prices we paid, so nobody upstairs had to know. Not every meal was guaranteed to be discounted. Vesuvio's went through cashiers monthly and the new ones were not always hip. We kept the status quo and never asked for the price reduction. If the cashier didn't provide, we didn't ask. If we got the discount, we'd keep the knowledge quiet and tip heavier after the meal. One Central patrolman almost blew the sweet deal one night for dinner when he didn't get the discount. Other cops present had to shut him up when he demanded the price get reduced. Unfortunately for him, and us, there was a uniformed Central Patrol lieutenant seated inside and he listened to everything that officer had to say: "I eat here all the time. What happened to fifty percent off?"

Central cops had instructed the owner of Vesuvio's to charge full price to sergeants and above. That way, they'd never catch on and we'd never get burned. Officer Loud-Mouth said just enough stupid stuff to warrant a conversation with the lieutenant. He instructed the staff to refrain from future discounts. Officer Loud-Mouth wasn't the only patrol officer to consume a meal. Two other officers had seen the LT and tried to warn their big mouth squad mate. He was clueless to begin with, so any hopes he'd back-down before the flames were fanned were hopeless.

Our trip to Vesuvio's was two weeks after the LT sent out an announcement that reminded cops to refrain from restaurants that provided discounts. Vesuvio's told him they would not stop, so he added that the pizza joint was off-limits to us. We enjoyed large plates of pasta with deep ladles of sauce at half price. We really hated to lose this dining place. We'd have settled on full price despite the owner's benevolent nature, just to plop down in front of a plate of Vesuvio's mountainous pasta dishes. I was addicted to their mountainous plates of mostaccioli. The lieutenant wouldn't differentiate between his patrol officers and WECAN cops. We ate when his shift was over. Conundrum solved.

"Let's go try our luck in Sherman after this. We can scope out and swoop on the Shermans off that alley behind 2500 Broadway," Chuck said. Chuck and John had veered over there in the past few weeks. The Hispanic Sherman street gang was not a primary group on our radar, but my two friends thought they should be permanent projects. We'd pulled off some effective arrests in Logan Heights. The Shermans should get some attention, too.

CHAPTER 20:
UNDERSTANDING THE TURF

Somewhere along the way the children and grandchildren of settled Sherman and Logan Heights families formed street gangs and challenged the police for control of those neighborhoods. Where once homogenous city blocks of people lived and gathered, Logan and Sherman were divided into camps by competing criminal gangs. Places once defined by prosperity and a sense of community were subjugated by gang rivals signaling their existence and menace with hand-signs and graffiti. Sherman and Logan Heights devolved into sub-ordinary "inner-city" neighborhoods, inner-city being synonymous with ghetto in places where leaders did what they could to revive them.

I must have worked a hundred drug houses in low income neighborhoods the years I worked narcotics and gangs. These places were generally set in motion to move individual amounts of heroin and cocaine directly to the junkie consumers. Marijuana was moved with great alacrity. The drug was bulky and had a much larger customer base. Almost nobody in the Heights complained about pot sales.

To a degree, the types of drugs available were divided up by ethnicity and location. In Logan Heights, for instance, crack cocaine tended to be in the hands of African Americans controlled by black street gangs. There were others who popped up, but not without the approval of those gangs. No matter who prepped and sold crack, the cocaine suppliers originated with the cartels south of the border. Crack was such a strong mover I rarely encountered an indoor location selling it. The street action was extraordinarily profitable. It was drive, walk, or crawl up to your street corner dealer, then buy and go.

The actual fixed locations my team worked almost always fit the same pattern: A no-frills home in a low-income part of a large neighborhood. Windows might exist, or they could be boarded up. At least one window had a small opening that was either cut or broken. The opening provided a secure spot to hand the drugs through, providing a modicum of safety for the drug dealer inside. If the air outside was chilly, cardboard was taped over the gap to keep the cold out. Look for the hole, the cardboard and the tape and we generally had a dope house. The interior by the way was almost always sparsely furnished, if at all. It was proof the place was rented for one specific reason. The occupants were almost always a pair of undocumented Mexican nationals. I guess the bosses found the employment of a third *narcotraficante* to be unnecessary and redundant. Dope house or not, somebody was the bean counter who watched the bottom line.

Their employer brought them into the U.S. to work and set them up as a temporary crew to move heroin and cocaine. At some point, another staff might take over if the place wasn't shut down. The crew in the house was there for only one reason, hence the lack of furnishings. They worked twenty-four-hours a day until their dope supply was gone. Dependent on the action and the supplier's set-up, the crew might get resupplied to keep that spot open.

One odd clue proved the sellers' origins. Their toilet paper was never flushed. A small wastebasket always sat next to the toilet and rarely contained anything other than soiled toilet paper. Many of the "salesmen" came from poorer parts of Mexico without efficient flushing systems and toilet paper clogged the plumbing.

The dominant Hispanic gang sets just south of downtown San Diego were comprised of three or four neighborhood claimants all within a two-mile radius. Each of the sub-gangs was a member of the much larger Logan Heights Gang. Nobody claimed such a wide swath of territory that there'd be spite from others who lived there and wanted more neighborly representation. Each gang had some drug sales claim to fame. Under one banner there were virtually no gang clashes within the Logan Heights membership. Persistent gang clashes originated between rival gangs, those to the east of Freeway 15 and north into

Sherman Heights' territory. The scrolls of graffiti tagged upon walls neighborhood-wide told the tale of who was pissed at whom and who challenged another gang for turf or reputation.

If, for instance, a Logan Red Steps *vato* who tagged with the moniker Flacco had a beef with a Sherman *Varrio* member Omar, spray painted challenges would show up on Sherman's turf. Both Sherman and Omar's neighborhood tags might be crossed out by Flacco and his buddies. Whatever the beef was, if a violent response was called for, the police had all the documentation they needed to go after Flacco or Omar.

The Logan Heights gangs had strong ties to the Mexican Mafia and identified with the Southern or *sureno* sect of that prison gang. Logan Heights' alliance with one of the large, cross-border Mexican drug cartels empowered the gang to work outside of San Diego. Its fearsome reputation provided soldiers for the drug cartels working on both sides of the border.

The dynamic duo of Manny and me needed to get back to certain basics. We assured ourselves and our boss that gangs were still our main business. We explained that at every turn, the gangs acted benign when we rolled up on them. The dope house tips were always in our faces and tantalized us with grand seizures of dope, guns, money and dealers. How could we resist the constant string of detours? One tip promised a dope apartment with actual gang members who moved heroin. Despite the street gang's cartel connections to the dope that travelled from dwelling to user, rare was the occasion where we encountered an actual documented gang member at the scene, unless he was a strung-out junkie the sellers were afraid to interact with. If the dealers in the house decided to get rid of an unconscious gangster they'd risk the reactions of ten more extremely vindictive gangster brothers.

The tipster was an addict with a warrant for absconding from court over his previous 11550 arrest. 11550 was a California Health and Safety Code for being under the influence of a narcotic. Once convicted of the offence, the conviction carried a mandatory jail sentence of ninety days. He knew he couldn't talk his way out of jail but gave up a place on 30th Street freely out of spite. He blamed his addiction on the pushers and took only partial credit for his pain. The place on 30th was particularly odious to him because of the people who ran the place. He called them gangsters and thieves. "What do you mean gangsters? Are you talking real gang members, or what?" He'd piqued my curiosity. Coincidentally, the target was on Sherman turf and we wanted an excuse to hit a place there.

"Yeah, they're gang members. I don't know what gang, but the guy at the window flashed his tattoos and warned us that costs had gone up. They go up at that place all the time. I think these guys are there to steal from us." He didn't even stall when I asked for the address. He told us they deal through a broken window in the kitchen and suggested we be careful.

"Have you seen any guns?"

"Nah. I ain't seen nothing like that. They almost always have no shirts on to show off their tats. They're both covered in pics of guns, though, and naked women." We knew those designs represented recklessness, their real families, their gang families, fearlessness and strength. We drove him to HQ for the booking process and then left him at jail.

The early evening meant dinner first. Then, we made the trip to 30th to scope out the dwelling. Both of us were more interested in the action than food. We popped into Adalberto's; a prime example of Southern California's fast-food taco stands with grilled, stringy beef cooked to an almost crispy delight. They were the best tacos at three in the morning. I could never understand why such Hispanic food establishments hadn't been exported across the country in large numbers. Every out-of-stater I'd ever met said they couldn't get Mexican food like this. New York had knishes, Milwaukee had cheese curds and San Diego had real tacos.

After the filling taco interlude, we hurried across the Heights to our target. We made a pass by the apartment building and saw the broken window on the north, ground-level side of the apartment. The building was two units over two units. Ours was at the front of the place. There were no fences to protect the property. Drug buyers could approach in the shadows and the darkness from different angles that disguised their destination. We slipped our car in a parallel parking spot with two trucks. The higher profile work vehicles would conceal the light bar from a distance.

Manny went to the door while I covered the cracked kitchen glass. There wasn't much left to the window but some shards with sharp edges framing the open portal. The guy who answered the door was tatted down with the art the addict described to us. The other guy had the same artistic additions that I could see through the window. I moved closer to the open window and signaled with my gun to hold still. He was in the middle of cooking hot carrots with peppers in a pan on the stovetop.

The two of us were inside together almost immediately. Manny kept an eye on the guys in the kitchen while I performed a permissive search. The carrots continued to simmer in the tepid water and their own juices. I had initial success. We'd recently discovered a lot of dope in the drapes of some of the places we explored. The drapes in the living room had drawstrings. These guys had conveniently tied a baggie of balloons to one drawstring. I showed the catch to Manny and hooked up the guy closest to me. In Spanish, Manny ordered the other guy under arrest as well.

The lean *Latino* man stared at Manny. I could see his muscles tense up across his shirtless torso. I don't know if Manny saw the warning signs as he moved around behind him to get his hands. The guy said not one word as he twirled around to his right and grabbed Manny's holstered gun. Manny reacted to the threat with rapid awareness, but the guy struck surprisingly quickly and took the gun part way out and fought to free the gun.

I pushed my prisoner to the ground and snarled at him to stay still. The tiny kitchen barely had room for three people let alone all four of us in a battle. Manny gritted his teeth and hissed at the guy as he broke the pistol free of the holster. Manny gripped the barrel and shoulder struck the attacker to knock him off balance. The man brought the gun up with sheer determination so that the barrel was at chest height. Manny used his other hand to push the man's arm to the side and away from him. The fight was furious. I couldn't get an angle to shoot the guy. Instead, I pulled my baton and bounced it off his head. The blow stunned him long enough to loosen his grip. Manny had one arm around him and managed to release the slide over the barrel. The gun dropped to the floor in two pieces, making the gun inoperable. The fighter didn't stop. He saw an opportunity to hurt Manny when he held him in a head-lock and pulled him toward the sharp glass in the window. I aimed the baton at him again just as the two battlers twisted around. Manny caught the blow to his right arm. He grunted in pain and dropped out of the headlock. I saw what I'd done and was horrified. I'd crippled my partner and couldn't stop this would-be killer. Worse yet, Manny's gun was in shambles and he was in pain. The bad man wouldn't stop. He knew Manny couldn't put up more resistance.

I was next to the stove and yelled, "Shit!" The pan of carrots was within reach and perfect for a knee-jerk reaction. I grabbed the pot by the handle and slung the liquid contents at the aggressor. He caught the contents full in the face and screamed with hurt. His pal wiggled around to see what we'd done to him. Manny was back on his feet with his sore arm cradled by the other.

The wounded man's eyes swelled up almost instantly. He mewled in panic and pressed his hands to his eyes. I know how the juice of the pepper stings the eyes. The basic chemistry is the same as our issued pepper spray. The incapacitation was quick and debilitating. Both pris-oners were in our control. I provided relief to the aching eyes with cool water from the kitchen tap. The water diluted the chemical in the peppers and flushed it out. I had him handcuffed before I sat him in a chair. The water in the pan was only luke-warm, so there'd be no burns to the skin.

Manny put his gun together while he gave me mad looks. "Dude, I think you broke my arm."

"I'm sorry, Manny. The guy was gonna cut you on that glass. I just reacted fast. How's does it feel?"

"Hurts like hell, man. it might not be broken, but it hurts like hell."

"You want me to call another unit and take you to the hospital?"

"No. let's see how the evening goes." Fortunately, the arm was contused but no bone was cracked. The asshole I'd doused with spicy peeper water went to jail. Ordinarily, if he was stung with our pepper spray, Depart-ment policy dictated he get driven to an emergency room for an exam. Since the stuff I hit him with wasn't a weapon, just weaponized stew, we babysat the bastard at HQ until we were certain the jail would take him without a medical evaluation. My confidence in my baton diminished. I gained new respect for "better police science through chemistry."

Neither prisoner was related to the Sherman gang. Both men were illegals from Mexico embedded to make money for some entity further up the food chain than the street corner Sherman thugs.

CHAPTER 21:
TWO ARMIES

Within the same boundaries of the LH gangs, the West Coast Crips shared turf. The Crips and the Hispanic gangs rarely interacted publicly. The impression was they worked independently to move drugs but didn't go to war even though they shared the same streets. Nobody wanted a race war. On the face of it, law enforcement saw the gangs as entrenched criminal forces who worked the same turf with barely any outward acknowledgement of each other. Often as not, the boys that knew each other in school became the older teens and men that populated the street gangs in the same neighborhoods. The general rule seemed to be that one gang didn't socialize with another gang, but they might do business together.

However, the Crips were in a constant, simmering state of war with other black gangs. Their notorious archenemies, the Bloods, shared borders with Crips who made the boundaries more like hot zones for cross-border interdiction on both sides. Tagging was a constant action with the black gangs, just like their Hispanic counterparts. Wars declared, and open feuds were given broadcast time on walls of neighborhood turfs in spray paint. For San Diego lower income and ethnic neighborhoods, the ancient dividing line between Crips and Bloods was roughly drawn along Freeway 805 with Crips to the west and north and Bloods to the east and south.

My WECAN days were a jumble of street gang education. I enforced law and watched the daily habits of gangsters for years. I was constantly amazed at the seamless partitioning of two ethnic cultures of crime. The blacks and Hispanics fought skirmishes all around them for turf and wealth, but not with each other. The source of the wealth was overwhelmingly tied to illicit drug sales. The brokered détente was dependent upon the gangs not competing over the wealth brought on by specific drugs, yet they all sold narcotics on the same shared streets. What I remember from those days was the lessons on movement of drugs through the gangs.

The Hispanic and black street gangs from the same neighborhoods all sold marijuana. They did not share the same streets to do it. An LH gangster might sell pot from a park at 30th and Oceanview while less than a mile away, still in the same "hood," a black Crip would sell dime bags at the intersection of 32nd and Market. Differences in sales choices arose with harder drugs. Heroin was almost always moved by Hispanics and not black dealers. I couldn't always prove the Hispanic dealers were connected to San Diego street gangs. A lot of the Hispanics I busted for *chiva* sales were tatted up, but from gangs south of the U.S. border.

La Eme, the Mexican Mafia, supplied foot soldiers and was in a unique position to wield immense influence from American prisons. The cartels moved the product to the United States. *La Eme* ran the dealers who fed the junkies.

Some sort of arrangement by the gangs to move heroin had to include cartel sources from Central and South America. The same was true for powdered cocaine. The sales within the boundaries of Central WECAN were heavily in the hands of Mexican nationals. Not many sellers were identifiable San Diego gang members, although most of the action took place with their knowledge. Quite a few of the men we stopped bore tattoos that appeared to be from other countries. The Logan gang members, prone to expose themselves in order to sell drugs on the streets, usually moved *mota* or marijuana, and "lovely" or Sherm. Sherman Cigarettellos were most often the choice for the dealers when they needed a smokable cigarette to dip in liquid PCP. The 101mm unfiltered smokes were wrapped in dark brown and sold in box packs. The dealers tended to cut them up into segments for sales purposes. Any of the Hispanic drug sales hotspots were almost certainly separate from black gangs. Black gangs were rarely caught moving quantities of heroin or powdered cocaine. Again, *La Eme* had the power over the turf.

The breakdown for cocaine considered the difference between powdered and "rock," San Diego slang for crack cocaine. Each form seemed to have a different clientele. I arrested umpteen Hispanic dealers who moved bindles of powder. The sellers were undocumented Mexicans, as often as American citizens. Once again, the coke sales were sheltered under the auspices of *La Eme* and cartel operations possibly using street gangs as soldiers, even field commanders.

Crack use was not a thing within the Hispanic gang culture in Central Division. With all the busts I made, I found it odd when some Hispanic banger was a crack addict. The sales of crack were dominated by black gangs, but there was no racial divide among the users. African American users made up a disproportionate number of crack users who ended up in the hands of the police in San Diego. They were overrepresented until time caught up to every other culture and skin color. Whatever the makeup of the addict, the dominant street-level dealers were black. The sellers in the Heights that I chased-off, busted, or spied on were black street gangs. Each gang set moved crack in black and Hispanic neighborhoods. As the flavor of some of those neighborhoods gained more diversity, Asian street gangs added to the mix in certain neighborhoods, but the local black bangers were still the ones moving crack.

Some places were unusually shared by crack dealers who didn't fit the mold. One of those spots was the intersection at 25th and Imperial. The junkies and addicts there were thick as fleas on a dirty pooch any afternoon of the week. They were jostled around by dealers trying to cage them for a quick drug sale buck. The times I worked that crap hole I would constantly be surprised by some little Mexican crawlers I caught selling something on the corner. Probable cause was generated when I put two-and-two together and connected the dots to legally search the guys. However, those dots that joined the results on a police report had to stand up in court. Somehow Hispanics got dispensation to move crack on black gang turf. Maybe 25th was too far east for the Crips, or some weird alliance set up an annex with Mexican nationals to do the Crips bidding. More than likely, whoever had the supply had had an unwritten truce with the Crips. I don't think the Crips maintained a color code when it came to making money. The yards of street surrounding 25th and Imperial were one big shooting gallery for drug sales. If the dealers wanted to slough off some of the work onto a shill, the strategy was to throw off the police. If the shill got nailed by the cops, the Crip remained untouched.

Crack was demonstrably more public than the dealers who moved other drugs. I saw occasional guys sell pot right out in public, ancient history in the 21st Century, but that was still a big deal for the times. Crack was just as public and finding crack dealers took as much skill as the bet that a dropped a penny would land on a flat side. The crack monsters followed the dealers in droves. Imagine how times have changed. Marijuana is legal. Now imagine if crack was sold semi-legally on the streets now. That's how prolific crack sales were at 25th and Imperial back in my WECAN days. Marijuana is a life choice. Crack removes that ability to make the choice. Users are hooked and the way back to normalcy is a hard road to follow.

To get the drug sold, the dealers had to stake out territory the buyers would go to. WECAN and Central Patrol followed the crowd of junkies to the usual suspects who sold rock at the usual places.

At the dawn of the crack epidemic, the users were enormous in quantity. WECAN was formed during the crack revolution, when America and the law figured out how universal and awful the problem was. I looked for it daily on the job. I was amazed that our society would ever successfully beat back the increased throngs of deteriorated people-turned-crack addicts.

When crack was sold out in public, the users huddled around the source. The drug was so compelling and so short-lived that the buyers had a constant hunger. Crack was most addictive when smoked, which was the common ingestion choice by all the addicts I ever met. The euphoria comes on quick, a minute or less. The crash after use comes within a couple of hours. The withdrawal from crack can psychologically drive the user back for more. If they are cut off, say from spent time off the streets for jail or rehab, the withdrawal could last for weeks, if not months. The poor slobs so attuned to the stuff that they can't escape it roamed the streets looking for the means to get more dope.

I saw crack from a personal standpoint almost at its inception. I had a friend of mine slide down that well of destruction from crack. One of our mutual friends gossiped within a group that Malcolm was using. I was a new cop and didn't yet appreciate what crack's devastation meant. Soon enough, Malcolm got my phone number from somebody and called me, something he'd never done. Whoever gave him my number was unaware of Malcolm's ulterior motive. He asked me for money. Malcolm lied to everyone he knew, while he tried to borrow money from new sources. I was not yet savvy about junkies' manipulations.

Malcolm gave me a quick greeting and then got to the point, "Can I borrow fifty dollars?" He gave me some patent excuse about getting laid off at work and needing to make rent. He labeled me a "really good guy," the kind of guy that wouldn't turn down a friend in a tough spot. I didn't buy it. I dodged his request and feigned poverty. I figured he'd realize I wasn't the guy he could manipulate. He didn't even bother to lay out his case or beg. He simply hung up, presumably to try the next victim on his list.

By far, the dubious legend of crack cocaine, mirrored in movies and on television crime dramas, was the picture of young black males clumped together in a tightly knit corner operation to sell crack in full view of everyone. Even the cops could be present and crack business would continue.

Typically, street sellers maintained a stash away from their persons, but hidden close by. If not, one guy controlled the dope. Another guy might handle the cash after taking it from the guy who made the sale. There are spotters for trouble with their own host of red alert callouts. Cops remind each other that crack sellers are probably under the watchful eye of a partner with a gun. When crack was at its peak, the gangsters and their lookouts adopted the term "Five-o" as their warning code about police on the scene. Somebody must have been a Hawaii Five-O television show fan because the gangsters I talked to claimed that's where the appropriation came from. For them, it represented mostly white cops because the lead cops, "were as white as white cops can be."

The crack heads were desperate people. Although I rarely ever heard of a junkie who tried to rip off a crack dealer, rival gangs would target their crack-dealer opponents. The moves they made were more about revenge over a personal slight, than attempts to raid a rival for their business. Crack's violence and addiction ripped neighborhoods apart in Central Division.

The more homogenous neighborhoods of East San Diego suffered from all kinds of gang problems not existent in the less ethnically diverse places further south. East SD was saturated with old, small homes, blocks of cheap apartments and gangsters from more diverse racial strata that were non-existent in the Heights in large numbers. Central Division rarely had to deal with Asian gangs, white bikers and meth heads.

Crips and Bloods roosted closer in neighborhoods outside of Central and Southeastern Division. Families who attempted to live outside of the gang neighborhoods in Central and Southeastern Divisions ended up raising their kids against the same gang influences they tried to escape.

Hispanic gangs expanded and claimed new turf they shared with burgeoning Asian gangs. The Southeast Asian people who escaped Vietnam and adjoining countries in the 1970s were now rooted in lands often strange to them. The neighborhoods they moved to were more affordable than other parts of town. Their low incomes and lack of affordable housing almost guaranteed that their housing choices stuck them in the middle of gang-contested and congested areas. There were racial overtones with black and Hispanic teens who didn't like the Southeast Asian kids and resented their presence. To the established gangs, these new faces were a threat that made them adversaries. The Asian kids had no response until they banded together to fight off the locals that hated the color of their skin and ridiculed their poor English. Parts of poorer San Diego symbolized the new power groups when a stretch of University Avenue became known as Little Saigon.

The former post-War community of Linda Vista, LV, just north of Freeway 8 and above the deep river depression called Mission Valley, was somewhat undesirable. The houses were hastily constructed for military workers and their families and considered shoddy by 1960s standards. Middle class whites moved out for the haughty three-bedroom homes of better suburbia and Asian ex-patriots moved in. In a rare example of clever wordsmithing, LV became known as "Little Vietnam."

The children of the new Americans, born on U.S. soil, had trouble when they tried to fit in. They were ostracized and threatened by the

Hispanic and black gangs. Then all sides acclimated to the new normal. Now, the Asian gangs had to battle with a new problem, each other. Laotians fought the Vietnamese. Cambodians hated the Laotians and all three fought over their home grounds that had the least amount of property value in the county.

Their parents tried to find their places in this new world. They often didn't relate to the external and internal threat of gang problems. Many couldn't identify with their kids. The kids spoke English while many of the ex-pat Vietnamese, Cambodian and Laotian parents struggled with this new language. The communication gap created a recruiting ground for children unified to fight back on the streets they lived on.

The parents didn't want the attention of the authorities and kept to themselves and their fellow countrymen. The kids saw the gap between them and their relatives. They had no fear of the police when they saw the imbedded gangs behave with no regard for the law and its consequences. The upsurge of Asian street gangs meant they were pushed together into the blocks of streets likened to pressure-cookers. There were, and still are, too many people who struggled to survive in neighborhoods too confining for the numbers of people there.

The culture of the implants from Southeast Asia was radically different from what most San Diegans were used to. Their alien-ness within Linda Vista set of waves of criticism about the way they lived and behaved. The teens were tough fits in schools that had never coped with so many new tongues. The culture they brought with them sometimes defied the norms of the community.

I remember working that part of town and getting a radio call to the Tecolote Golf Course in the winding canyon below LV. The course manager told Dispatch that a group of about twenty Vietnamese armed with rifles and spears surrounded a group of golfers at the far end of the greens. My partner and I drove into the golf course from the main entrance and rolled in between the course holes to reach this group. We were the first of three cars to arrive. I saw exactly what I couldn't believe was happening. Twenty Asian men and boys had surrounded a frightened group of golfers at the 12th Hole. I saw the weapons, a couple of bb rifles and a bunch of pointed sticks. The Asians stood in a semi-circle but weren't displaying the weapons as threats. They seemed more determined to stand their ground because they'd discovered that part of the canyon was great for hunting rabbits.

The course manager rolled up in a golf cart and filled us in. One of the newly arrived officers found an English-speaker and broke ground with him. I learned that the manger simply tried to do his job and kick the hunters off the property. The Asian men were the fathers and the young teens were their sons. They'd refused to leave because they weren't familiar with the concept of a golf course. The way they saw things, they got to the grassy plain ahead of the golfers and that gave them the right to hunt first. They had no idea the course was private property. Our liaison officer spent a length of time in explanation. The men were perplexed. Their boys were nervous. Cops from back home were interpreted differently than cops here.

A peaceful accord was reached. The hunters could move back up into the ravines to hunt as long as they didn't have firearms. None of us were going to argue that killing wild animals in the canyon could be illegal. Twenty hungry soles were certainly arranging to feed a lot more people above the canyon's rim. The manager made sure we warned the group the golf course was off-limits.

When I worked the area of East San Diego, it seemed new black gangs sprung up overnight and took turf for their own to move crack. Their customer base, those we saw out in the open, was no longer largely Afri-can American. The neighborhoods were filled with repeat crack-head business. These were areas replete with low, and middle-income white residents not often counted among the legions of crack users. Crack had certainly found many of those white locals. The police were inun-dated with radio calls for relief from this epidemic within a community that had no social response to the behemoth that had landed on the residential streets. The disease had spread from the greatly ignored inner-city streets.

I couldn't stand ESD. If I thought the Heights were a challenge, then the crowded avenues between University Avenue and El Cajon

Boulevard made me cringe. This area south of Mission Valley was rich with old San Diego money, but the further south a traveler toured, the more the blocks resembled each other with identical houses and cheap apartments. South of those blocks the apartments began to look less cared for. Many of those two-story templates bore brass plaques sunk into the concrete entries, bearing the name of the contractor. Go east and there'd be block after block of Ray Huffman buildings. Go west and it was the same thing. Hundreds of original homes gave up their lives to be covered in apartments with the same design and lay-out. I called them American-Ugly. I lived in a couple of those complexes before and during my tenure with the SDPD and could appreciate how badly people wanted to move out if fortunes improved their lots in life. They were truly Soviet style living quarters. If I met Ray Huffman on the street, I would have found a reason to arrest him. Maybe for felony bad architecture.

The Eastern WECAN Team found the place to be so busy that arrests were as common as breaths of air. They had so much activity that the other two teams would periodically go up to help them out.

CHAPTER 22:
METH

In the neighborhoods I worked during my WECAN tenure I rarely dealt with crystal meth amphetamine. The meth population was normally considered a white people problem. Meth, like crack and heroin, was a pandemic drug. A poison that just happens to be a drug filtered through white populations in this country. Unlike crack, there were no groups selling meth on the street corners in San Diego. The drug found its way into the hands of its customers with fewer theatrics than crack.

Mexico was a producer of meth and its precursors with tasty names like red phosphorus, acetone, anhydrous ammonia and ephedrine. Tweak, as we called it, found its roosts in the lower income enclaves of mostly white, middle class neighborhoods. The nightmare of meth crept up in my part of town and San Diego's beaches when I was a young kid. The substance was pushed by bikers and chronic users for the cash its sales could bring. The rampage of meth through suburbia created an urban fiasco of theft that still reigns today. Tweakers don't serve the same gods as heroin. Although both are prolific thieves, meth-heads are extraordinarily versatile when choosing what they will steal. They take everything. The mindset of a tweaker was quite shallow. If something was not nailed down, they took it. To this day, nothing is safe, not potted plants, not trash cans, not broken toys and absolutely nothing made of metal. If a cheap bicycle is locked to a bicycle rack in a shopping center, everything, including the lock, is gone and can be blamed on the tweakers.

A meth dealer could be nothing more than a tweaker on a bicycle going over to some other tweaker's house to buy or sell a few grams. Only a trained eye would know the crime was being committed. By the time I'd been on WECAN awhile, Law Enforcement seminars taught officers that the bikers who traditionally ran meth on the streets were being muscled out by Mexican-bred and sold crystal meth. The biker gangs still sponsored meth labs that were now in competition with weekend labs run by Mexican nationals and residents. They'd constantly set up labs on Fridays out on farmlands and orchards, anywhere they could run an illicit lab near sources of water and remain hidden from view for the three, or so days it took to make. The harebrained chemists would be done by Monday. The waste leftovers from their "cooks" were chemical pollutants that would kill the vegetation and poison the soil.

Inherently, the types of people attracted to the drug lived in ESD for the cheap rent. Meth brought along a problem of violence that ran arm-in-arm with the crack fiends and heroin addicts in ESD. Meth made users angry and paranoid. More drug trouble was the last thing the compressed residents in ESD needed. I entered way too many homes and saw too much street use not to be concerned that ESD was always on the verge of being a lost locality. There were a lot of immigrant families who tried to raise their children in a part of town that may have seemed only slightly less dangerous than some of the places they came from. I met plenty of Asian, African, Central and South American parents urged by community leaders to speak up for help to squash the scourges of drugs and gangs.

I thought Central Division was overwhelming. ESD had greater square footage and such diversity that it was a challenge to shift focus from one gang set to another. The numbers of bangers staggered the mind. The area was so overbuilt it was hard to tell one target from another. The Eastern WECAN team should have doubled in size.

Meth was a commodity amongst users. If you wanted a drug that causes euphoric physical and psychological changes, that provided a heightened sense of pleasure, energy and confidence, then meth was your thing. You could get similar buzzes from cocaine, but the expense was a killer. Meth appealed to a crowd initially targeted by bikers in California. The buyers and users were mostly white. The pushers knew quickly enough who their customers were and hammered away at them with each new generation.

I worked meth in Ocean Beach and witnessed the tragedy for myself before I shifted to WECAN. The stuff seemed almost a normal part of the daily lives of normal people. If you needed to get up early and get some work done you could drop a little crystal in your coffee. Feeling frisky after being up for two days, smoke a rail and wake your nearly comatose date for another round of hide the salami. If you're really conditioned to steal stuff all night to get meth money, use the needle and shoot the stuff. After all, the drug isn't like heroin. There are no physical withdrawal symptoms like heroin, so you won't get sick without it. Just get used to the alienation of your family, the loss of a job and the maniacal frenzy your brain will constantly go through until the part of your brain that recognizes the people loved is burnt out from your soul. Meth literally destroys parts of the human mind, the parts that govern conscience. What's left is a person with no soul as we know it, an almost two-dimensional being with no aptitude for society's restrictions.

I was sick of tweakers from my O.B. days and the superficiality of their behavior. If you ever wanted to see a fully developed human fake being like the rest of us, study a tweaker. Those users are dirty, subhuman wastes of skin and bones with barely anything resembling a conscience. Rockstar Lemmy Kilmister of Motorhead was once quoted as saying, "If we move in next door to you, your lawn dies." Motorhead portrayed the mystique of a dirty group of street toughs who could give a fuck-all about their booze, drug and hygiene habits. Take away the charm and talent of a Motorhead band member, think of someone who'd steal anything they could, become paranoid, and possibly schizophrenic and you have a tweaker.

I took a class in sociology while I was a police officer. My goal was to advance my career through education. I took one class to see if I could handle school and work, but court attendance made that venture nearly impossible. One task for this class was to do a paper on some societal aspect from an expert's point-of-view. I chose the County Mental Health facility since I'd spent so much time there with detainees. I had an in with the staff as a cop and got an appointment with a charge nurse.

The forty-five-minute interview started with the two of us as we mused over some of our best stories about the mental cases we'd dealt with. Eventually, I took notes as she got more mundane about the facility's operations. I thought I knew the answers to my questions, me being a CMH devotee and such, only to learn more than I thought would. The nurse laid out the custodial make-up of most of the building's patients. She shocked me when she said that roughly seventy-five percent of the temporary patients accepted from police detentions were meth users. Seventy-five percent!

CMH was an emergency placement institution for law enforcement and the occasional voluntary walk-ins. The ones that volunteered off the street were almost always in the care of a doctor for mental impairment to begin with. If they felt an "episode" coming on and the doctor was not available, CMH would accept them for up to seventy-two hours. The rest of the committals were brought in off the streets by cops. If accepted, they would be institutionalized for a seventy-two-hour observation and then released or shunted off elsewhere. The seventy-five percent who shifted from police custody over to CMH staffers were people with severe drug habits, with meth being the most prominent. The reason they were in custody was their behavior. Their psychotic, violent and incoherent actions were attributed to the drug. The nurse fleshed out the CMH and meth aspect of things for me. "You guys bring them in rattled, incoherent or angry, because they haven't slept in three or four days. Meth keeps them up and the lack of sleep builds psychosis." The less REM, rapid eye movement, the deeper part of sleep these patients received, the deeper their mental instability. Meth burned out their mental faculties.

If Logan Heights had one redemptive quality, it was the lack of a true meth problem. The crack, heroin and PCP were enough.

Sometimes, the corrupted world of the Heights got to be too much. We chose those moments near the end of shift to get out of our heads for a spell. The four of us plus Roger, who was now on the team, loved a pie place down south in National City. We headed there a little earlier than normal and enjoyed coffee and a fine desert. We failed to exhaust enough time to head back to the barn and were stuck back in the heights for another ninety minutes. This was a typical Wednesday night when even the denizens around Main Street, transvestite hooker central, were absent. Roger suggested we park over on one end of main where all the closed warehouses were, and he'd show us a trick. "Okay, just stand there and watch," he said as he got back into his car and drove down the block a short distance. Once he made the U-turn, he sped back on Main. He was eyeball-to-eyeball with the four of us when he appeared to hit the brakes. Suddenly, the car was thrown into a screeching, one-hundred-and-eighty-degree turn. Smoke, sound and fury spread out from the car's tires.

The car's motor stopped. The hurl into a gravity-well had caused the engine to stall. He restarted the car and rolled to the curb. We were all astounded and wanted to take our turns. Roger provided the instructions for what is termed a parking brake turn. In cooler parlance, the move is also coined a "bat-turn" as in Batman. The secret, if there was one, was to gun the car forward and then stomp on the emergency brake while the steering wheel is yanked to the left or to the right. If all goes according to plan, the driver can slam the car's transmission into Reverse and keep the momentum moving in the same direction it was headed in Drive. We all took turns at safe speeds until we were confident that we had the skills. The big LTDs were not up to the task and kept stalling. We appropriated more speed until I had the confidence to go into the turn at forty MPH. I made the U-ey on a dime and in a space a little longer than the length of the car. I loved the fun!

Roger had another trick up his sleeve with the Fords. The brakes for that model were designed with unbalanced brake power. Roger taught us that the rear-wheel held seventy percent of the stopping power in one wheel and thirty percent in the other. Roger got back in his car and started the engine. He left the car in Park and pushed down on the brake pedal about six times. He explained that the chore pumped up the brakes to maximum capacity and warned us to step back. "This place is gonna be a stinking smoke screen in a few seconds," he howled.

He kept his left foot on the brake and then slowly applied pressure to the gas pedal. One rear wheel began to rotate. The other held fast. As the engine revved, the whirling wheel spun and hummed against the asphalt. The other wheel was held in place by the brake. Slowly, the hum created a cloud of noxious grey smoke from the burnt tire rubber. The cloud enveloped his car and sent a plume down the avenue. "Geez!

He's turned the car into a rolling smoke bomb," Chuck said out loud. We were all amazed at the auto buffoonery we could learn from Roger.

"The technique is called torque-loading. Our cars are heavy, which makes it easier to pop smoke. Other cars may not work so well," Roger told us. We each took turns, although John spun one turn of the wheel and then deferred to the rest of us for our jollies. Don't do this with your car. Your engine mounts may suffer from the torque.

CHAPTER 23:
LOGAN HEIGHTS AND PCP

There's a lot of information and shared, written experiences about street drugs. All those stories and documentaries flood the internet with fiction and non-fiction. I like to tell my own stories and reference the drugs in the context of the tales I can resurrect from drug busts. I have a thousand drug stories. WECAN was the genesis for more than half of the best stories. I have to tell you though my PCP tales are my favorites. So far, I've written some words about heroin, cocaine base and cocaine hydrochloride, some pot and the drug I hate the most, methamphetamine. I can't stand the people who use meth. They *are the worst*. But PCP is the weirdest of the drug culture's chemical escapes. PCP has the unique distinction of appealing to a narrow market of people who have absolutely no awareness under its influence.

PCP was developed in the 1950s as an intravenous anesthetic, but due to the serious neurotoxic side effects, its development for human medical use was discontinued. PCP was more suitable to veterinarians as a horse tranquilizer. When I worked street drugs in WECAN, PCP was one of our targets. PCP was the drug sought after in low income neighborhoods, but only by a select few. Angel dust as it was often referred too appealed to an oddly eclectic few. There seemed to be fewer racial boundaries for this one drug. We caught handfuls of buyers, but not the mountain of customers with crack or heroin. People of all walks of life got caught in the crosshairs of cops and got busted. White middle class, suburban Mexican Americans, housewives from the beach, teachers from San Ysidro near the border and black gang members from the wrong side of the 805 Freeway comprised some of the customers. PCP is one freaky drug and the buyers were freaky people who got a one-of-a-kind escapist thrill from the high.

The sales were controlled by Hispanic gangs, even sold by gang members. We discovered PCP would be sold on Logan Heights' turf, but to an oddly diverse customer base including other gangs. The problem of PCP was squarely in Central's arena. The officers who worked Central Patrol knew all the hotspots for PCP sales. Those of us new to WECAN and new to Central learned fast. The sales locales never changed, and the crush was up to us to figure out how to slow down its use.

Memorial Recreation Center and the surrounding park were the first targets my team worked. When time permitted, the Central WECAN guys would scope out the dealers from hiding places or hit the guys outside the gym so fast they hadn't had enough warning to ditch the drugs or run away. The gym bordered a public school. I found the correlation a shame since most of the guys we bagged with PCP for sale were once students there. Beat patrol officers knew crime surrounded that gym and that the arena inside was the only safe oasis in the entire park. Central cops and WECAN could "knock the dealers' heads together" any day of the week and the little bastards would be back again within a couple of days.

The high the users sought couldn't be described with much detail when they were sober. They liked the uncanny, disconnect from reality. The drug provided an odd shield from its disassociation from reality with distorted sights, sounds and their base sense of self. Pain's impact was virtually eliminated, and the users felt a sense of detached power. I could see why kids were such easy targets. The Heights were filled with young teens easily manipulated by gangsters who could take their cash and recruit at the same time.

My first lessons on the cultural diversity of the users came from observations of the buyers who'd slink into the park to buy PCP. Unlike crack on the street, the dealers who sold PCP were not surrounded by blank-eyed addicts. These were people looking for a little vacation from their present states of mind. There was no addiction to PCP. Casual users just liked the thrill and detachment the angel dust provided and swore there were no addictive qualities.

John, Chuck and Manny were all familiar with PCP. The three men spent much of their careers to this point policing the same streets I joined them on. PCP was so common in the Heights I found the notion that any Central Division officer had missed an encounter with the drug highly unlikely.

The most powerful aspect of the drug was the wariness it created among cops. The police academy instructed recruits on all the drugs, but PCP was the one that came with a slideshow of the damage and injuries that users' incoherent wrath wrought. We were all shown the same pictures, mostly from Los Angeles area police departments, everything bad in San Diego seems to start there and be more dramatic. Broken restraints included snapped handcuff chains, chewed up car seats, police car doors nearly knocked off their hinges from the inside. The bruised and battered officers warned all law enforcement that anyone on that substance could rage like a beast and destroy you if not controlled.

Back to that school opposite the rec entrance, Manny and the others knew from experience that the school buildings were perfect places to spy on those dealers. There was even a classroom key floating around our unit that gained us access to one of the rooms overlooking the gym parking lot. The school was happy to hide some cops in one of their school rooms if it meant we'd clobber the drug problem next door. The team would take up a lookout point in the classroom with the best window observation point and watch the late afternoon, or early evening action.

The set up was a classroom with back windows that overlooked the rec center parking lot. The doors to the gymnasium were also in view. Every cop knew that the Logan gangsters sat on the low wall around the gym and waited for buyers to make a loop through the parking lot in their cars and conduct the transaction through the car windows. Very few customers parked and made deals on foot. Some of the locals, mostly Hispanic teens, would enter the park on foot or on bicycles and make their deals. The business was all done as quickly and quietly as could be. There was never any delay or negotiation over price. A bindle of lovely, marijuana laced with crystallized PCP, set a user back about twenty-five dollars.

We pulled off a lot of stakeout busts, meaning that we got both buyers and sellers. PCP attracted a variety of users. Whoever was cooking up PCP was close and connected to the Logan gangs. The customer base ranged from a guy headed to work at a bakery, to Bloods willing to cross over into Crip territory for a dose. PCP didn't get stocked at the local Drug Mart. The chemistry to produce the one-time medicine often originated in Los Angeles labs. San Diego had a healthy market, but the big money for retail was two hours north. Down here in San Diego, the center of the action was held by the Logan gangs. PCP sales never seemed to stretch beyond their turf.

Our plan was the tried and true model of spot the bad guys and swoop in after a few sales were made. Somebody in a chase car took off the buyers. As an extra back door, we planted a chase car beyond the gym in the park if we had the extra manpower. That car cut off any escape towards Oceanview Boulevard, the direction everyone went when they fled the police. It pays to know the turf. The park might have been Logan territory, but we owned the night and the escape routes.

We'd only gotten started on the operation when I was gob smacked by the types of people who used the stuff. Any misconception that PCP was for "problem people from other parts of town" was dispelled working the Heights. We got the drop on one guy who was headed to work at an elementary school in another part of town. He taught first grade. We held on to another guy who was the janitor at a church across the freeway from Chicano Park. The sellers were young Logan Heights' gangsters. A couple of the teens went to the very school we hid in to spy on them. Some of these guys were often high from either toying with their product or from their skin contact with the drug. The chemicals in PCP would get absorbed into the hands and fingers. They'd suffer from a contact high that left them stupefied and much easier to catch in the act. What the hell would drive any soul to use this shit?

One urban myth that surfaced was the use among black gang members of something called "shamrock." Supposedly, they manufactured the ultimate thrill when they sprinkled crumbles of rock cocaine on bindles filled with lovely. This became shamrock in at least name only. I never saw it myself. One locale might have sold lovely. Another setup might sell Sherms elsewhere. Lovely was the choice of the Skyline Piru gangsters, a San Diego Blood set the Southeast Team had to play with that drove into the Memorial Rec Center parking lot under our very noses.

We studied a young Blood when he drove onto the gymnasium lot. He dressed without the customary gang set red. He was careful not to flash any Blood colors that would be seen by Crips to avoid being set upon with violence. He rolled into the parking lot outside the Rec Center's indoor basketball court. Our chase team was ready when we watched the hand-to-hand from the rear window of our classroom warren. The chase car waited until the driver was out of sight of the gym and took the guy down. Manny and I were the guys in the classroom. When the chase car had their guy and gave the "All Clear," we left the school and drove nonchalantly into the same parking lot. There wasn't going to be any attempt to wait for other buyers. We weren't certain enough that locals hadn't spotted the chase car, so we took down the seller before he hinked up and ran.

The buyer was arrested, and a single foil bindle of PCP was seized. The seller wasn't in sight when we got the drop on him. We peered into the doorway of the gym and saw the little Logan shit was inside with a couple of buddies watching a basketball game. Manny and I walked in under everybody's noses and simply lifted him up like a chair and walked him outside. We didn't even interrupt the game. We handcuffed him outside. We also held onto his two companions to figure out who they were and what their roles were. The audience inside must have been numb to the experience. Nobody missed a beat as the game continued unabated. How jaded these honest people must have become. This scenario was new to me but not to them.

Our prisoner carried buy money and four more foil bindles. They each reeked of that ether smell so strong in PCP. Neither Manny nor I risked getting contact highs since we didn't have gloves on. The two companions were FI'd as Logan 30th Street gangsters and set free. They were all junior high school age.

The players and coaches in the gym barely paid any outward attention to us. They were all wary of repercussions if they supported the police.

The gangster-dealers feared no repercussions. They didn't even know what the word meant. The maintenance of a tenuous peace between the bad and the good required the good people to recognize certain boundaries of behavior. The gangsters had some marginal version of respect for the people who ran the Rec Center. The peace would all end if any one gangster felt those people snitched on him.

The chase car returned with the buyer. He was nervous for two reasons. He was under arrest and he was in was in Crip territory. He knew the risks when he removed any sign of red before he cautiously headed into unfriendly land to get drugs. I asked him why he'd take the chance to score in a part of town where his enemies existed to kill him. He freely spoke about mixing crack with PCP, which he called shamrock, and the high so intense that he wanted it all the time.

One of the chase car's officers, John, donned gloves and opened the foil wrapper. The bindle contained marijuana that had been soaked with liquid PCP. The PCP turned to a crystalline powder when it dried. Shamrock provided the user with a different, heightened sense of unreality. Just imagine a stone-cold street gang member high on that chemical cocktail. His gang set was notorious for crack sales. He admitted that he'd ingest the drug blend and then chill on his couch at home. Nobody in his gang minded if he smoked up some of the crack supply.

Sherms could be made on demand which appealed to a lot of customers. The cigs might be wet when purchased, so the buyer would deal with the inhaled high and whatever seeped into his skin when he held it to his lips to puff. This one drug did not have a large female following. PCP drove people mad, made them irrational, violent and completely stupefied. The effects of PCP didn't seem to appeal to most ladies. PCP did appeal to a lot of teenagers. We always seemed to catch younger gangsters who sold and used PCP in this form. Their ages ranged from fourteen to late teens. These boys-to-men were already hardened gangbangers. They feared only the older guys in their gang and no one else. The consequences of their criminal actions never fazed them. They would either run, or resist. The more violence-prone thugs would fight, stab or kill anyone in their way. PCP was a great drug if a user wanted to stifle their sense of responsibility.

There's a scene in the movie, *Apocalypse Now*, where American soldiers are stuck guarding some bridge at the last outpost on a Vietnamese river. Martin Sheen's character is shocked by the state of these trained fighters. The soldiers were penned inside a bunker dug into the riverbank soil and covered with sandbags against enemy fire. They all appeared to be dazed or stoned as rifle shells zinged past the men who remained above ground to return fire. An enemy soldier or guerilla shouted taunts as he fired large rounds that exploded all around the soldiers. Martin Sheen tried to urge the men into action, but nobody seemed motivated or even frightened. Finally, one Army man told Sheen not to worry, that 'Roach' will take care of him.

There in the darkness was a guy with a grenade launcher and a blank stare with wide-open eyes. He looked as though he slept that way until called up to do his job. The astonished Sheen watched in horror as Roach appeared to be headed up top to certain death. Roach was not fazed and barely acknowledged the hazard above. With exquisite calm, Roach loaded a shell into the gun's breach, his ears perked for the origin of the noise coming from the annoying Vietnamese shooter. After a handful of seconds, Roach tilted the barrel up a few degrees and pulled the trigger. The distinctive bloop sound of the exiting round detonated in the brush with an explosion and a scream. Roach paid no attention to the sounds of the aftermath. He dipped back into the bunker to sit and continue to stare at the muddy wall in front of him. That look, that stare into the void, was very much the gaze of a dusted user. They could function, but on a wavelength outside of the normal band.

The four of us counted Chicano Park as part of our territory to patrol. Some of our arrests already went through the court system and got the attention of one of the judges, Judge Stall. She, too, was curious about this formation of officers doing God's work in the Heights. She was fascinated with the idea that a neighborhood heritage such as Chicano Park, long feared as a haven for gangster-killers, had a police unit drawing back the covers to reveal names and send them into her courtroom.

Central Patrol dealt with Chicano Park from its inception as a people's park in 1969. The Coronado Bay Bridge was new and left a huge footprint on the San Diego side of the bay. Several businesses and homes had to be demolished to make way for progress. The park rose after a grassroots battle with the city and State of California in 1969 over the parcel of land. Locals wanted a public park, the government wanted something not public friendly. Local activists protested and the government saw wisdom in backing down.

Chicano Park lies under a couple of freeway overpasses. The park backers painted murals on the bridge supports displaying American Indian and Mexican cultural heritages. Unfortunately, LHG Red Steps namesake and origin point is an old apartment complex three blocks away. With the formation of Chicano Park, the gangsters found an environment more to their liking.

There was a time in the late 1970s when the park was a consistent danger to the police. Sunday nights became the magnet for Heights car clubs to parade back and forth on the streets surrounding the park. The show-stopper low-riders and hot rods gave way to gang melees and fights. Officers and the public got hurt. The department got a handle on the Sunday night pageants and quelled most of the problems. The low-riders scaled back in numbers as the car guys moved elsewhere. The police action could not sustain itself because cops were constantly pulled in many directions. Now it was up to Patrol and WECAN to stifle the thugs who stayed or had returned.

One lieutenant, new to the unit, was Bill Becker. He had no qualms about WECAN at the park. The unit had merit and brought reduced crime when it descended on this center of Latin culture. He'd been around the department a long time and was quite aware of the LH Red Steps gang control over the park. They weren't getting enough attention from the police. Let WECAN insert itself and make a difference. We warned him that a few of the strident activists would howl at an increased police presence. Lieutenant Becker told us he'd deal with any backlash. The family joy and community get-togethers at the park were overshadowed by a vicious street gang organization. WECAN was the weapon the police department would wield to pushback. We would make arrests and identify the Red Steps that had flown under the radar so far. Any intelligence we gathered would travel over to the Gang Unit to collate and add data to what they knew or needed to know.

The Logan Red Steps used the local bodega, La Central Market, as an ad hoc home base. Chicano Park became an auxiliary target for us against the initial wishes of our command. We knew that the unwritten agreement between WECAN's bosses and the park activists was for the police to retain a low profile there. The problem was more pronounced than we were prepared for. Like Memorial Park and its rec center, Chicano Park was dominated by a gang that thought it was in complete control. We would not ignore a hardened street gang in charge of a San Diego jewel. The activists may have lulled themselves into believing the gangsters could be controlled or occupy the park alongside the people who wanted no problems as though they existed in two parallel worlds.

The gangsters and the community were all from the same streets. There were no secrets between each other. The kid that grew up on Sampson Street with his neighbors was the same kid as a Red Step. The people he knew from Logan Heights learned to be cautious of him and his gang. The kid-turned-gangster was part of a syndicate that gained respect through fear and intimidation. The good people of the Heights that loved the park for its open space and family-friendly development knew a dark force was in control. That kid may have been the son of a father or a mother who enjoyed the park. But his primary loyalty was no longer to his family. WECAN was tasked to rearrange the dynamic with some good old-fashioned law-dog enforcement. They'd been imbedded for years and were probably over confident in their surroundings. We couldn't erase the gang's power, but maybe we could shake up the status quo with their power base.

CHAPTER 24:
SHOTGUN

There was a specific incident that piqued Judge Stall's curiosity and enticed her to contact our lieutenant and ultimately meet Roger and the rest of us at Chicano Park one afternoon. The event that sparked the meet began with one of the local TV news affiliates, Channel 10 News.

A news director asked to go out with one of our team members and film the graphic criminal behavior in Chicano Park. Roger had an abandoned office building in mind to hide the TV camera for some hidden filming. He obtained keys to the place, which bordered the west side of the park, and snuck the film crew inside. They set their gear up looking out eastern windows with commanding views of La Central Market and the kid's playground and sandbox across the street.

The press didn't have to wait long. A heavily tattooed Latino man ran out the front door of La Central and crossed the street into the park. He was carrying a long, narrow cardboard box. He hopped over the sandbox retention wall and knelt to sweep aside some sand. He buried the box and covered it with the same sand. Finally, he retraced his steps and took up a position leaning against the market wall.

Roger waited to see what would follow, the cameras recording the whole time. When the time to move on came, the news crew followed Roger back to their concealed vehicles. Nobody from the park saw the group. Roger and the crew drove up to La Central and tried not to look too intrusive and frighten any bad guys away. The guy who concealed the box didn't move. Roger and another officer stood next to the guy to FI him. The cameraman held his camera on his shoulder and set it up to film. Roger detained the box burier, so if something came of this, he'd be able to hold the guy accountable. Any other hoodlums that stuck around scurried away like roaches when a room light turns on.

Roger felt certain in his bones the box contained either drugs or a weapon. He placed the guy, an OG, or original gangster Red Step member, in his car and walked over to the sandbox. The news crew ran the camera and witnessed the entire event. The newly disturbed sand marked the location of the box. Roger uncovered it with his hands and opened it to the amazement of the film crew. Inside was a loaded twelve-gauge shotgun that was like the shotguns we carried. The news guys ate it up. The story would be aired as sort of an expose on gang crime on the TV news that evening. The press was ecstatic. Roger's newest prisoner turned out to be a parolee. Parolees don't get to carry firearms. He'd go back to prison with a parole violation and a fresh set of charges.

The news network got a plum assignment out of that afternoon's surveillance. Neither they nor Roger bargained for such a juicy piece of live film. La Central wasn't figured in as part of the Red Steps home bases, but now it was. The placement of a shotgun in a kiddie sand box played well for the police department's emphasis on gang problems at the park. WECAN got great airtime since it was our Roger and our team that got the press credit. Any qualms anyone in my chain of command had about enforcement at Chicano park went out the window and we were given free rein to pillage the Red Steps in the park. Judge Stall stood under the bridge with us and spoke casually about her encounters with street gangs. She sat on the bench and stared down the mostly male gang members on many occasions, but to her, Chicano Park was a place that only cropped up in the news when someone died or got caught with drugs and weapons. The park was a big mystery to her. How evil were the people in the park? How did all the good people there cope with thug gang members? Lt. Becker commented on WECAN's effectiveness with a few positive examples beyond just the shotgun story. Mostly, he deferred to us to speak for ourselves. The subject of community activists that didn't welcome any additional police presence was barely addressed and then passed over as a non-issue by the judge.

Rachel Ortiz was a prominent Logan Heights activist and executive director of Barrio Station Youth and Community Center. Her roots were in the Heights included succumbing to crime and spending time in custody. Her life's mission was to serve the youth in her *varrio* and do her part to keep clean the kids she could reach. She spent five decades fighting for justice, which included the gangs to a degree.

Rachel was invited to a WECAN assembly where she agreed to speak about the differences between her view of the community and the impact of the police. Not surprisingly, she was no fan. She regarded WECAN's mission statement with skepticism. WECAN's formation to answer the gang problem seemed more like another attempt at heavy-handed justice in the Latino community. She all but stated that the police would mete out unbalanced justice to the teens in Logan. Many WECAN cops felt that the gangs deserved justice, alright. Justice followed by time off the streets for bad behavior. We suspected Ortiz was the person responsible for pressure on the department to keep WECAN out of Chicano Park.

Like I said earlier, drug sales drove the gangs. The crimes were simple to commit. They didn't get as messy as armed robberies, or as cumbersome as burglaries. LHG Red Steps sought fortune from PCP sales, along with the other drugs. Users were not hard to find. Just look for some spaced-out pedestrian in Chicano Park, probably an incoherent teenager, and you've found someone under the influence.

CHAPTER 25:
A CASE OF PCP IN ACTION

Four of us rolled into Chicano Park in Weber One, one of WECAN's mobile offices. Manny and I were joined by fellow WECAN officers Mike Cash and Rick Schnell. For the time being, they were assigned to Central WECAN with the rest of us. We'd teamed up together in the van to prowl all the Heights hotspots on a relatively quiet evening. Chicano Park was on our agenda.

We parked it in front of La Central Market to be as intimidating and burdensome as possible. We weren't looking to make any colossal arrests. We figured we'd hang out a little while and be the deterrent the gangsters hated. Our goal was to snag any gangster who was up to no good. This night, the park across the street was nearly empty. We lounged around on our feet for a bit, stretching and jawing about one thing or another. A lone teenager walked out of the La Central Market and crossed the street.

A PCP user has an odd, deliberate gait. The steps he takes make his walk appear like he's on autopilot as he looks and moves straight ahead with even, staccato steps. The four of us looked dubiously at each other. Nobody was eager to chase down a fourteen-year old, dusted up kid. At the last moment I said, "I'll get him."

I crossed the street quickly to catch up to the boy. He was a Hispanic kid, probably from the neighborhood. I told him to stop, but he didn't react. He just kept his steady pace across the lawn under the park lamps. I already knew he was dosed. I could smell the telltale odor of ether flowing from him as he exhaled. Right there I suspected this next set of moves would not go well for me. I got behind him to grab his arms and secure him. PCP is no joke and there's no time to think like this is a normal citizen contact. The kid was already tensed up, stiff as a board, a condition of a PCP user's high. I couldn't bend his arms. I tried to talk to him, but his mind was elsewhere. He began to put up a little silent resistance as I tried to urge his arms into a position where I could slip on my handcuffs. His arms were like unbendable iron rods. He left me little choice. I'd have to take him to the ground.

Back then, I weighed about one hundred and ninety pounds, mostly muscle from years of power lifting. The kid didn't even break one-hundred-ten, yet somehow, I couldn't gain control. I broke a sweat with my generous attempt to just overpower just his arms. He didn't say a thing and he didn't acknowledge my presence. I don't think he knew I was even there. This wasn't going well. I looked plaintively over at my comrades. They were mildly amused at my struggles. At least I managed to force the kid to bend at the waist. My "friends" across the street cheered me on. There was no sense of alarm in their minds. I used my bodyweight to force him to the ground and almost succeeded.

The kid was on his knees and I had one of his arms pinned behind his back. If I could put his chest into the grass, I should be able to pry his other arm out from under him and get him cuffed. Instead, he held himself off the ground with me on his back. With my combined gear and body mass I weighed about two hundred and thirty pounds. He lifted his weight and mine with one skinny, little arm.

I yelled across the street, "A little help!" and received laughter in return from my pals. Maybe they knew something I didn't know, but I was gonna lose this contest of strength if I couldn't get the kid to cave in. I continued to struggle with the duster as he had me flopping all over the place when I tried to get a foot anchored to the ground for leverage. His body was sweaty and tough to grip his slippery arms. I was beginning to tire. I sensed that he was fatigued from all his effort, as well. Thank the fates for that relief. PCP gives you a feeling of strength because you don't feel the muscle pain. Users do get exhausted though. The kid finally wore down. This was exactly why I lifted weights, the strength and conditioning gave me an edge to survive a physical struggle. My "partners" only now began to mosey over when they saw me laboring for oxygen. Those guys were all chuckles.

"Gee, thanks fellahs," I drew out slowly through ragged breaths. The comment was meant to be droll.

"We knew you had him, dude," replied Mike Cash. "You know we'd never let anything happen to *El Cabeza*." Mike mocked. He was a fighter without hesitation. He'd seen me get physical in the past. He never imagined a skinny kid would get the best of me. He and Rick made a formidable duo.

Mike was a stocky black man with a kind voice and a wide grin. He grinned even when we went hand-to-hand with some local thug. Rick was a sandy-haired white man with a perennial beach tan and an almost nonsensical way of speaking. I remember the way he described an arrest he and Mike once made:

"We were headed east on Market Street. I was in the passenger seat. I looked to my right and saw a guy on the sidewalk walking the same direction. I turned to Mike and said 'Boy does that guy look fucked up. Let's pull him over.' Mike made a U-turn and parked facing the wrong direction, just ahead of the culprit. I got out and rushed to head the man off. He turned to bolt, but I stopped him with my extended hands. As if by fate, though, the man stumbled backward. I tried vainly to protect him from a painful fall to the ground, but my actions were to no avail. I blame drugs for his plight." Mike and Rick were two well-matched cops if ever I met any.

I got the now-fatigued lad into handcuffs and pulled him to his feet. He didn't struggle or try to fight back. The end of the battle was a blessing. The results of a PCP high could never be predicted. The users frequently ended up trussed up in cord-cuffs in the back of police cars after a huge fight with several officers. Sometimes they were so far out of their heads that cops had to pull the car's upholstery out of their mouths.

The quiet rhythm of the night returned now that the laughter and wrenched breathing was over. I wasn't overly upset about the lack of help. I certainly didn't want to exhibit too much emotional concern. Cops need to retain a mantle of strength to maintain their peers' respect in a job that would eat the weak alive. I did want to know what they were thinking. They calculated I had it all under control and didn't see the need to jump in. "Ahh, you had this easy," Rick emoted with faked concern. That's the nature of cops. We live between the lines where toughness and confidence can't be judged by outsiders.

Like most, this juvenile PCP users' behavior was unpredictable and so powerfully resistant that I could easily not have been equipped to take him down. There's every excuse for overwhelmed officers to use greater, even deadly force, if it means stopping a human turned into a senseless animal. This skinny Mexican American kid could have gone for my gun or clobbered me as I tapped out from weariness. My guys knew there could be a moment of worry and they'd jump in. From their point of view: "Nah, Jamie had this."

The story seems funnier when I look back.

CHAPTER 26:
NYSTAGMUS

Manny Rivera was my partner for many months on WECAN. We worked PCP with greater exclusivity than the Central team had performed before I arrived. The insanity of PCP in the Heights had grown, only partially abated by patrol and narcotics detectives. Neither group could attach enough time to give the problem the needed attention.

We picked a Sunday during a surprisingly wet January to take our families up into San Diego's mountains for some snow-time escape. Mt. Laguna is one of San Diego's highest peaks at over 6,000 feet in elevation. Manny's wife Maria and my wife ran our kids up the slopes, dodging the sledders skidding downhill with complete abandon. My son and Manny's girls were ecstatic. The moms were getting worn out trying to keep up. The ladies looked at Manny and I plaintively for a little relief. He and I had taken seats on a fallen tree to chat about work. The subject of the streets rarely stayed buried for us.

We discussed the current fiasco of PCP within our midst back at work. The chill in the air was hardly noticed as we churned some thoughts around about where we needed to be when we returned on Monday. The Crips hadn't stirred up the trouble we'd expected since WECAN got involved. There'd been no drive-bys and no consistent levels of street violence within their zone. Perhaps now was the time to continue our crusade against PCP. John, Chuck and Roger would likely find the change refreshing and more challenging than babysitting Crips who seemed momentarily subdued.

Our wives caught wind of our "business-talk" and urged us to play with the kids. "Manny, you brought that camcorder for a reason. Take some pictures!" Maria admonished. My wife was too busy trying to remain on-track with her speedy sled and miss an upcoming tree.

Manny and I shook off the stiffness from sitting too long in the cold and got into the adventures with our children.

The camcorder was fated to fail when Manny took it along for a video of one of his downhill runs. When he got tossed by a snow-covered tree stump, he and the sled went one way and the camera flew off in another. We'd later learn that less than fifteen minutes of an hour-long video recording survived the mishap.

As a result of our mountain-top chat we shifted part of our workload from the West Coast Crips to the LHG gangs. One of the hot streets for PCP sales was a short stretch of Evans Street. Evans was mixed residential and industrial, just the place for wayward youth to learn urban survival. We stumbled across more action around the intersection of South Evans St. and Harrison Street than other parts of the Heights. The rec center was always abuzz with cops for a variety of reasons. If WECAN wasn't there for the dopers, patrol was for every other problem. WECAN repeatedly flipped over to Evans and kept landing on dosed Latino teens that crossed our path there. Evans was a focal point for the source. There seemed to be no police control and I imagined the parents of these kids and young adults were flustered by their sons' mysterious behavior.

Manny and I took a trip around those blocks on one of our change-up days and stumbled across another PCP user. He moved with the typical stiffened, measured gait those users do. He looked quickly in our direction but didn't react as though he saw us. The angel dust blocked normal thoughts and responses, which should have been to run or hide on the streets of Logan Heights when the police sniffed around. We could both see the odd eyeball action of the young guy. Even at the short distance between him and us, we could see the distinctive metronome action of a PCP user's eyes. We call that eyeball action vertical nystagmus.

Nystagmus is an involuntary, rapid movement of the eyeballs. A lot of things cause horizontal nystagmus when the eyes bounce up and down. Alcohol causes it and cops use that to measure intoxication during field sobriety tests on drivers. Only one thing causes vertical nystagmus. It was PCP and our guy had vertical nystagmus.

We parked the police car behind him as he stepped up onto the side-walk. We wanted him ahead of us so we could maintain better officer safety. If we got in front of him, he could launch himself at us after finally perceiving we were a threat. There wasn't any point in talking to him. Our best chance to get this guy under our control was to handcuff him first and study him later.

The trick was to move fast. The PCP user was already as taut as a steel pole. If we could catch him unaware, there'd be no fight. I liken the analogy to fishing for sharks, but the fisherman is in the water with a hold on the shark and the fishing pole is useless. We didn't get lucky as the guy turned to face us. At first, he seemed sober. He talked to us calmly and answered a question or two. We were both hit by the PCP smell. His eyes slid up and down and left and right. No doubt we had a winner. Suddenly, the guy became resistant and tried to push through us to continue his course. We grabbed his arms to stop him and apply the cuffs. He didn't want any part of that. Regardless, we had to turn him back around to control him. He pushed us off balance and backward, until we ended up at the rear of our parked patrol car. Manny managed to get a handcuff on the guy's right wrist. I had a good grip on his left arm. We were just about there.

Our man stretched his thin arms and shook both of us off like we were fleas bothering him. Manny gripped the cuffed right arm and I tried to catch his flailing left arm. The guy tried to turn to face us. We managed to keep him faced toward the car. We couldn't get him bent over the trunk and off-balance to control his upper body. Instead, he pushed off from the trunk into our bodies. We countered and combined our body weight to bring him to his knees. At least we got that far. Manny held the man's right hand, so the guy only had his left hand ready to use. Once again, we were almost there. With that left hand he pressed against the asphalt and raised himself up. Our combined weight of about four hundred and fifty pounds of bodies and gear on his back did nothing more than slow him down. As we all rose from the ground, both Manny and I had had enough of this risky combat. We whipped out our batons and whacked at the guy's legs. The blows had absolutely no effect. Even worse, we'd let go of complete control of his arms. He was free to take swipes at us and try to get away. The batons were a fail, so we re-holstered those and attacked his arms again. Time ticked off and we were both growing tired.

We grabbed his arms again. This time he lifted us off the ground. We looked like clothes hanging on a clothesline. We held onto his arms for all we were worth, Manny had the left and I had the right. Unbelievably, he lifted us like we weighed a few pounds each. He weighed less than one hundred and fifty pounds, yet we were in serious trouble.

I pulled my radio off my belt to call for help. I tired with each foot-pound of exertion and could not catch my breath. I had to let go of the man's one arm to get my radio out. Manny was in a predicament. He had to work harder to control the guy. Both of us fought this guy in near silence. He barely made any sounds at all, while we grunted and gasped without saying a word. I couldn't make a decent transmission for help because I was so out of air.

I dropped my radio on our car's trunk lid and used both hands to hold onto the thrashing, resistant asshole, again. Manny tried to shift his reach to gain leverage and force the man to bend down at the waist. The guy popped right back up. I had to tamp down panic. We might lose this battle. If that happened and he turned on us instead of running, our guns would either save us or be the objects he'd go after.

Neither of us could later recall how long the fight lasted. A couple of minutes? Five? More? Who knows? All we could do was to dig in and outlast the bastard. What about him? He must have been feeling the exertion by then. He had to tire.

The man was spun up on the *loco* drug. We forced him forward at the waist one more time and pressed him over the trunk lid with the last remnants of force either of us could manage. Manny got the guy's right hand behind him. I used everything I had left to force the guy's left hand behind his back. At last, we connected the two hands to fit the handcuffs. The sense of finality and relief overwhelmed us. I could breathe again.

Manny got his radio out to announce we were Code Four, or no longer in need of cover, failing to recall that I never got the call out for help in the first place. The dispatcher had no idea what Manny's broadcast referred to. I heard the quizzical inflection in her voice when she responded, "Ten-Four."

The strangest end to this fight was the prisoner's comments after we hooked him up. In the most relaxed, cheerful voice I didn't expect, he said, "Alright. You guys got me." PCP still had control of his mind, but his spirit had changed. It was like the drug's effects stopped simultaneously. The battle was over for us. For him, it was a pleasant afternoon. He even cooperated and directed us to the park to locate his dealer.

Our prisoner chatted with us about drug use and about the drug problem, all in normal, rational tones. There were few remaining indications the guy was under the influence of PCP. The telltale odor weakened, and his nystagmus was slight. This example of unpredictability and random violence is the strange and frightening aspects of angel dust. "Why'd you fight us?" I asked.

"I don't know. I didn't want to go to jail. I was feeling real good when you guys stopped me. What did I do? I wasn't doing nothing."

"You don't remember fighting us like a madman?" Manny joined in. "Did I?"

I looked back at him through the cage, "Really? You put up enough of a fight to wear us down. I thought we were going to have to break bones or kill you." He just stared ahead as though he was trying to remember ten minutes ago. "You don't have any idea, do you?"

"Nah, man. But I'm good now. I feel really mellow." This is the kind of shit about PCP that drove cops crazy. All the struggle and fearful concern for our lives with a guy who felt good because he just got in a workout he can't even remember. Now he's relaxed.

Whereas heroin was considered a depressant and cocaine was designated a stimulant, PCP was considered a dissociative drug that distorted the senses. I'd never heard of PCP until college. Nobody in my neighborhood knew anything about some drug named phencyclidine. Medical experts and Law Enforcement euphemistically refer to PCP as an "inside-outer." PCP's unpredictability and the chaotic human reactions it generated scared experts who believed the drug figuratively turned a user's mind inside out. When we fought the guy, he barely made a sound. I remember an occasional grunt or growl. His face was placid throughout most of the struggle. His Frankenstein Monster like demeanor before the calm displayed the face of PCP. His behavior after we got him subdued put the tranquil in tranquilizer.

We drove through Sherman Hills Park with our prisoner. He gamely sought to help us catch the real bad guy, the dealer. At least he faked his concern well. Obviously, that guy was in the wind. The park was filled with families and friends playing soccer except for a few Sherman *vatos* who wandered in our direction to see who we had in the back seat. Our prisoner was still somewhat chemically detached from any concern about what the gang members would do if they thought we'd taken a snitch on tour for arrests. I wouldn't say he was giddy as he tried to spot the dealer from our backseat, but he strained really hard to see the park at three-hundred and sixty degrees. He lectured us in a fashion about the evils of drug dealers and how bad PCP dealers were.

Our intent was not to parade him around. We really wanted the dealer, the greater of two evils. We made the choice to get our prisoner out of the park before he became some Sherman gangster's little target in the future. We took our prisoner downtown for processing.

CHAPTER 27:

CONTACT HIGH

There was a tantalizing origin point for PCP sales further south on South Evans Street from the block where we tussled with the guy who nearly wore us out. The intersection generated a lot of PCP head cases, but they currently flew under police radar. Once our unit caught wind of it, we set up plans for occasional stakeouts to learn the sales structure and identify the players.

There was an advantage for us we rarely ever received. It was a gift in the form of a surveillance spot right on top of the sellers. The hiding place was a San Diego Gas and Electric utility parking lot. We'd worked with SDG&E Security people in the past. If we needed a hideout to work from, they'd provide access to most any of their properties. In this case, the utility parking lot was used to store work trucks. The property was chain-link fenced all the way around. Slat boards were inserted into the links vertically to inhibit the view into the lot. With SDG&E Security's help we were given access to the lot.

Our team consisted of five of us in uniform. Roger wore a long, civilian coat over his uniform to hide his identity as a cop and protect SDG&E's from any retaliation.

Roger took up position in the fenced-in parking lot at the southeast corner of the SDG&E lot. He wore the undercover coat since he'd be exposed for a brief amount of time to anyone who happened to watch the lot. The dealers operated in front of two homes on the northwest street corner less than forty feet from Roger. Chuck Davis and John Tangredi staged a block away in their chase car. They'd roll after any car Roger saw the occupants buying drugs from. Manny and I were hidden on foot, close enough to race up and catch the sellers.

Roger watched a car drive up to several Hispanic kids who were suspected LHG members. The driver handed money out the passenger window. The guy taking the money signaled one of his pals. That guy pulled a bag out of the top of a tall cinder block wall. He removed something from the bag and handed it to the car occupant.

John and Chuck waited for the car to leave the area. Roger broadcasted the car's description over the Nalemars radio frequency for the chase team. We weren't supposed to use that radio frequency because the wavelength was reserved for multi-agency operatives. We found Nalemars handy for inter-car contact and no one was ever on it but us. We'd beg forgiveness rather than ask permission if the time came.

John and Chuck rolled on the buyer's car a block away to keep the action out of the dealers' view. The two officers stopped the car well away from the dealers, so they wouldn't know we were onto them. Manny and I had a perfect hiding place and a dead-on view of the sale at car window height. We were concealed across the intersecting street, behind the fence of a piece of commercial property. We climbed a fence and over some stored cars in the driveway of that commercial lot to get right up to the street-side fence protecting the property. We had to perform a bit of athleticism and accept the risk to get to that cherry spot. Our uniforms would have to be laundered after this night. Between Roger and us, we had the perfect vantage point for courtroom testimony.

The dealers hadn't closed up shop after the previous dope deal. Their ignorance of our presence gave us time to stick with our plan. John and Chuck confirmed that the car occupant had purchased PCP in the form of a "wet" Sherm when they arrested their guy. The wet Sherm, by the way, was half of a Sherman Cigarettello freshly dipped in liquid PCP.

Manny and I hotfooted from our hiding place across the street from the dealers. We left the property over the back fence and trotted out from out from the alley and around the corner. Our hidey-hole was dark and out of their line of sight. They wouldn't know where we came from when we stepped next to them.

There were several LH Red Steps buddies in the mix, but we only had enough probable cause to nail the two guys. Manny and I surprised the gang members. They confessed later that they never expected two uniformed officers to appear on foot in the early evening's darkness. Manny took down the one who manned the stash, while I grabbed the guy with the money. The plan went well, except my guy was also in possession and dropped a few Sherms into the gutter. There was a light rain and some water traveled down the streets. I had to react quickly and grab the cigarettes before they were ruined by fast-moving gutter water. I grabbed two wet Sherms before the rain destroyed them.

Roger remained in place to provide us with the location of the stash. Roger had the superior "eyeball" on that spot. Still using Nalemars, we all listened with the volume turned down as he directed Manny to the portion of the block wall where all the attention was given. The cinder block was built years before and never finished with block caps. Manny lit up the wall and peered down into each brick until he found the paper bag. He opened the bag and saw a foil-wrapped cylindrical shape. The bag and its contents gave off the potent ether odor of PCP. Manny would open the foil wrapping later when he had a chance to don gloves. The operation was over for the night. The third gangster was high and arrested for the under the influence of PCP charge.

We coordinated a return to HQ with our three prisoners. There was no sense in prolonging the evening to score more sales arrests. One sale of PCP was enough to satisfy the DA's office and these young gangsters had short-term memories. We knew they'd be up selling again until they figured out we'd never stop arresting them. I rode with Manny and our two guys. The PCP and the bad guy's money were in the trunk of our car.

Since PCP is skin soluble, a person can be physically affected by skin contact. The wet Sherm cigarettes I'd collected from the gutter began to affect me as Manny and I headed to HQ. This was a first for me, so I thought the oncoming headache and dizziness were from a lack of energy or hunger. The disorientation grew in prominence. Luckily, the trip to HQ was short. I headed to the bathroom to wash my face with cold water. I hoped the shock to the skin would kick-start normalcy. That did not work. I'd absorbed some of the drug from those rain-soaked butts. My head felt "thick" and unclear. There was almost a hangover feel to the effect. All the post-joy of booze, without the joy of booze.

I was the acting supervisor and my boss was long-gone for the evening. I had to report my condition to the Duty Lieutenant and fill out a Minor Injury Form to document the "poisoning."

The rest of the team had a lot of work to process. Manny opened the foil package and found a one-ounce glass bottle filled with liquid PCP. There was a pack of Sherman cigarettes not yet dipped but cut in half for quick dousing and sales. The sellers were adults at just eighteen years of age. They'd see jail time for PCP sales and possession for sales, both felonies. Chuck and John's prisoner would be pitted for the felony of possession of a controlled substance. We had two good felony arrests for a short night's work. The third guy would get jail for being on PCP.

I had to sit around for a while until my head cleared. The contact high left me feeling detached from what happened around me. I felt like I saw and heard everything through a blanket. The stupid headache came on as a dull pain. I rubbed my temple to find some relief. The high didn't get worse. The aftermath left me dulled and annoyed. I'd washed my hands at the station for all the good it did. I could still smell the ether odor. The scent conjured memories of doctor's offices when I was a kid, scared to death I was going to get an injection for my sore throat. I daydreamed under the mild influence of PCP. I can imagine what a full-blown high must do to users. Just a couple of moments in my hand and I had to fight off a hazardous high. It would be a few hours until I felt decent enough to drive myself home.

Bob Hovey was a patrol officer at Southeastern Division prior to reassignment to WECAN. Southeastern was one of two divisions hammered by epidemics of crack and PCP use. Those who used those drugs were the motivators that would soon lead to the establishment of WECAN in Southeastern and Central Divisions. Crack was a gang drug that notoriously hooked users the first time they puffed on a pipe. PCP's effects on people led to all kinds of dangerous wackos that dropped into neighborhoods and caused random mayhem. The overwhelmed communities within the boundaries of those divisions cried out for help from the police. The divisional response was to select out a group of Southeastern patrol officers and form up a "Flying Squad" of officers trained to target drug dealers. The officers were already talented at the task. Bob Hovey and Ron Featherly, an old F Troop patrol partner of mine, were two of the selected. The two men paired up in the same roving police cruiser.

Bob and Ron were on specific patrol for crack business near a large apartment complex impacted by drugs and gangs. The property owner-ship had finally assigned uniformed security guards to its perimeter to keep the bad people out and keep the good people safe. Two security officers shared responsibility over that complex to work shifts with other guards around the clock. Their job was to turn around the lives of the impacted and fearful residents. They were under siege on all sides by flurries of gang members, junkies and dealers who infested the complex. The 45th and Logan apartment building was a blighted jungle of low-grade apartments in need of constant police attention. The residents who partook of dope and spread it around their neighbors and friends were summarily kicked out of their apartments and banished from the property. Trespassers who conducted drug business within the confines of the complex were the targets for the armed security. The city kept a careful eye on the problems that continued.

Bob and Ron took up the responsibility of adding firepower to the security apparatus in place. They routinely parked their car for a purposeful stroll through the complex. Foot patrol was the last thing the denizens of the complex expected from the cops. This tactic frequently caught the bad guys off guard. Within minutes of entry, Bob and Ron ran across a guy on foot through the complex who was high on PCP. The odor of the drug was strong.

Nobody wants to confront a guy on PCP. If the fight was on, the ordeal could be catastrophic for Bob and Ron. The second worst case scenario is a foot chase. If the guys not too zonked out to recognize his plight with the cops approaching, he might bolt. When they grabbed him, if he resisted, he could choose to fight. The target had the look of a rabbit, or a runner, written in his saucer sized eyes. The much taller Ron didn't hesitate to grab him before he took off.

The user was insanely strong. Ron wrapped his arm around the guy's neck and applied a carotid restraint to temporarily shut down blood to the brain and knock him out. The user managed to stay alert long enough to pull a small vial from his pants pocket. Ron struggled to squeeze down on the guy and force unconsciousness. The skinny black guy kicked, wiggled and thrashed about with ferocity. Ron couldn't get a firm grip as they writhed on the sidewalk. Bob found no angle where he could wedge his way in and help Ron. He danced side-to-side and tried to find an opening to help take the guy down.

The dosed user held onto that glass vial as Bob made a move and caught the man's legs like a tackle dummy. Bob was now behind the man after Ron lost his grip. Bob tried to hold the user's legs, unable to stop the fighter from breaking the vial on the ground. The guy looked back at Bob and tried to hit him in the face with the remains of the broken bottle. He missed him with the glass but hit him in the face and mouth with a capful of liquid PCP.

Ron got back in the scrum and handcuffed the wild man, taking some measure of control. Bob knew he had to get the poison off his face quickly. Ron had control, so Bob got to his feet and looked around for a garden hose or hose bib. Seeing none, Bob stemmed his panic and hurried into one of the apartment complex's laundry rooms to find a sink. He found one in the first laundry room and grabbed the handles on the old fixture and was distressed when the sink didn't pump out water. The well-used laundry tub wasn't even hooked up to the water lines. That surprise was a pisser. Bob could feel the deadening of his normal senses, and dizziness from the chemicals entering his system through his pores and eyes. Bob rushed over to a coin-operated washing machine and cut the cold-water line with the utility knife carried on his gun belt.

PCP won't ever be confused with any other drug, especially in liquid form. It's pungent, noxious odor will flatten a man fast. Even a light touch of PCP with naked skin can cause irritation reaching the brain. Bob took too much to the face to walk it off. With the sliced water line in hand, he flushed his face and mouth for a minute or two. Ron had called for cover to come and help. Ron handed the prisoner over to a pair of newly arrived officers so he could look for Bob.

"How're you feeling buddy?" asked Ron.

"Gah! I gotta get this shit out of me. The water isn't helping. I got some in my mouth and eyes."

"I'm gonna have another unit take you Code Three to the hospital, Bob. That shit is going to mess you up. Hopefully, the hospital can deal with it."

"I already don't feel good. I think it's hitting me pretty hard."

"Don't worry, Bob. The hospital will know what to do," John replied. He didn't know what liquid PCP, even a capful, would do to someone. Nobody really knew what the drug's limits were before an overdose could be identified. Bob might be in serious trouble. Other units were called in and an arrangement was made to get Bob to a hospital immediately.

The hospital received their patient and made no early attempt to stem the PCP effects. For wasted minutes the medical staff monitored his vitals. When the immediate problem was addressed, his blood tested positive for the drug. The first symptom to impact Bob was light-headedness. Soon enough, a headache began to pound away. Bob didn't panic openly, but he felt it under the surface. Knowing Ron had the jerk who did this to him in custody, helped Bob steady his nerves. He figured that if he retained mental acuity through this ordeal and stayed focused, he might be able to ride this out easier. He believed that a firm, mental grip prevented his body from having a severe reaction. The thought that he could be fully engulfed in the shit and lose his mind scared Bob. The hospital didn't seem to have a counteractive agent to tone down or reverse the drug's effect. The staff explained to Bob through his wavering concentration that the only real curative was time. The drug wouldn't do real damage in the long term. The revelation was no reassurance to Bob. He felt physically awful and wanted to be rid of it. Bob would be in the ER for hours of observation.

The prisoner was eventually charged with two felonies, possession of a controlled substance for sale and assault on a peace officer. Bob suffered a poison induced effect from PCP for months with constant, blinding headaches. Few officers have ever dealt with the internal disruption of PCP. I've felt it and so has Bob Hovey.

CHAPTER 28:

THE REC CENTER

Three WECAN incidents stand out as memorable that started with PCP sales to people at Memorial Rec Center.

Roger and the rest of our five-man team watched a street transaction take place near Chicano Park between an LH gang banger and a young white guy in a compact car. We arrested the buyer and discovered he was an elementary school teacher from the suburbs, not far from where I grew up and my folks still lived. He liked to thrill himself on his days off with a few puffs of lovely. I really had to chomp on the bit not to contact the San Diego Unified School District and go after that idiot's job. Due process would have to come first.

His blood test came back positive for PCP's active ingredients. The court system would see his job description and place of employment on the top sheet of my arrest report. If he pled guilty, the city Attorney's Office would decide what to do about his job. If he opted to take his case to trial, he'd expose his background to a sitting judge. Any self-respecting judge would have issues with a schoolteacher using PCP to relieve tension from daily contact with a room filled with eight-year old children.

Memorial Recreation Center continued to be a collection point for all kinds of PCP users looking to score. Two of us watched a deal go down outside the gym. We nailed this buyer, a Hispanic man headed to work after he copped some angel dust. We stopped him in a dirt lot across the street from a bakery on Main Street near the large 32nd Street Naval Station. He remained seated in the driver's seat when I asked him where he was headed. He pointed across the street at the bakery and said he worked there as a baker. He worked nights and kept awake with PCP, instead of coffee.

We arrested the guy and drove him across the street to the bakery. I wanted to meet his boss and see what kind of guy didn't know his employee worked dusted. The shift supervisor greeted me just inside the plant. He was used to cops because of the times his business had to be bailed out by the police for the local trespassing miscreants. He was shocked when I told him I had his night guy in my car for PCP. He was vaguely aware of the drug. He didn't really know anything about its use or effects. I gave him credit for that. Too few people know anything about PCP. I do know my prisoner would have some 'splaining to do just like Lucy.

The third adventure involved a woman also purchasing some lovely before work. She was bagged on exit from the rec with her purchase. Per our arrest, we admonished her of her rights. She freely told us that she liked to get a bit dusted before she showed up for work. I asked her, "Where do you work?"

"Do I have to tell you?" she asked nervously.

"Yes, you do. The prosecutors and the judge will want to know." She could have said nothing. I can't charge her for not speaking. I am there to get answers, though.

"I'm going to be prosecuted?" she stammered.

"Well, yeah. You bought PCP, which is a felony."

"But I don't do it that often and I've never been arrested. Am I going to jail?" She was clearly distraught. She still hadn't answered my last question.

"I still need to know where you work." I kept my tone even because she'd slowed down her cooperation. I wondered why she stalled.

She looked contemplative with her head tilted down and finally said, "I work at a church day care."

"So, you babysit small children?" The muscles in my neck tightened and my jaw clenched. I could feel the heat rise inside me. My partner Manny stifled a curse word. She gave us the church location, which wasn't too far away from the Rec Center, a place of worship near Kearny Street.

Manny and I made a show of driving our handcuffed prisoner to the church to verify she worked there. We parked the car on the street in front and wondered aloud if we should contact a priest. Unlike the schoolteacher's arrest, we chose not to just put this daycare worker through the criminal justice system. We were greatly concerned with the thought that the law might not step in and protect the school children from her. The first incident was the last time I didn't intervene on behalf of children. A little direct action was called for.

One of the priests saw our highly visible prisoner in the back seat of our car. Our in-custody was horribly frightened, just like the schoolteacher from earlier. I couldn't directly tell her bosses, the priests, why she was under arrest. But I could sit there in front of her workplace to verify that she told the truth of its location. Happenstance is the only explanation for a priest from that church who was out and about. He saw his church's employee in our car. He stood a few feet away with the beckoning look of a man of responsibility with concern and a question. I left the car in Manny's hands and walked over to the priest. "Yes, she is in trouble," I revealed, but I politely explained that whatever the private nature of her arrest was, it was up to her to confess it to the church.

The necessary seed was planted to protect the kids of the parishioners she governed over.

CHAPTER 29:
PCP MOM

Rosa Cuevas was the mother of a Logan Heights Gang member, Jose Cuevas. His subset was Logan Heights 30th Street, which overlapped the other LH gangs to dominate the old San Diego barrio of Logan Heights. The working-class populace was hemmed in by freeways, docks, warehouses and low, low-income homes and apartments. The gangs had a captive audience and could ply their trade with the children of those families. In quite a few cases, the parents were gang members or part of the larger gang family. Their children were continuations of gang legacies.

Logan 30th gangsters already had a ruthless reputation thanks to one David Barron. Barron was a leader within the gang, where he recruited his pals to work across the border in Mexico for the Arellano-Felix brothers of that Tijuana Cartel. Barron was trained in paramilitary tactics by the Tijuana Cartel, which included heavy weapons training. This regimen helped to make Barron highly proficient in the crimes of kidnapping and murder.

Brazen Barron was such a callous killer he'd murdered a Roman Catholic Cardinal in a case of mistaken identity. The intended victim was the famous Juan "El Chapo" Guzman, head of a rival cartel. Barron received intelligence that El Chapo would drive into the Tijuana Airport parking lot in a white Mercury Grand Marquis town car. Barron's crew of hitmen wiped out the Cardinal, who was in a nearly identical town car, leaving Tijuana and much of Mexico in shock. The Cuevas family was part of that gangster world.

Barron was a major player within San Diego's Hispanic gang world and attracted massive attention because of the rise of the cartels just across America's southern border. Barron was a huge burden for San

Diego's and Mexican Law Enforcement because he was a recruiter for deadly cartel muscle. We just hadn't put all the pieces together yet.

WECAN had its run-ins with Barron. He was a clever man and had picked up habits on the streets with great alacrity. Manny was gone to Investigations and I shifted over to partner with Roger. Roger and I were split up months later and assigned new partners. I had Darby Darrow assigned to me and Roger got Todd Sluss. Darby and I had just cleared Memorial Rec form a parking lot sweep when Roger and Todd radioed that they were behind Barron in a car around the corner. We sped to their location and got in line behind them as they cranked on the overhead lights to pull the car over. Barron was the passenger. The car made a smooth right turn into an alley and continued moving, strangely at an unhurried pace. There was no warning when Barron's ride stopped, and he slid out. His driver skewed the car so that it completely blocked the alley and allowed Barron to charge off ahead of the car. We couldn't follow, and by the time Todd and Roger slipped out of their car, Barron was in the wind. The driver was a teen, but with a valid license. The car was registered to Barron, but he had a suspended driver's license and was not likely to get caught behind the wheel. He knew how the game was played.

Todd and Roger took Barron's escape roughly. We all knew he had no reason to flee unless he held contraband, probably a gun in his case. He had no warrants and no one in law enforcement to our knowledge was looking for him. They spent the next afternoon searching for him around the neighborhood.

They got lucky and saw him reclined in an easy chair on the porch of a cottage on 30th Street. Once again, Darby and I got called over to back them up. This time Barron did not run. He relaxed comfortably in the chair when Todd stepped up onto the porch and Roger flanked to the right. Todd was frustrated and let a lot of anger spill from his mouth. He had Barron pivot to be searched and ran his hands through his pockets and around his waistband. Socks were checked, too, but the man was clean. Darby and I rolled up and got out to stand by, keeping wary eyes out for perimeter trouble from any other gangsters that showed up.

Todd raised his voice and warned Barron that he wouldn't tolerate any future antics from him. Barron didn't seem fazed and didn't look like he cared a whit about what Todd and his awkward warnings. I sized Todd up and figured he was trying to rile up Barron so maybe he would lose his cool and do something stupid. Todd was solidly built and probably had the advantage in a fight without weapons, but Barron was a thug. He wouldn't take on a cop unless he had some unfair advantage up his sleeve. Barron showed no outward signs of discomfort and didn't get roused.

Todd was former military. Barron did reply coolly to one of Todd's taunts when he told him he should watch his back in the Heights from now on. The heat came off Todd in waves as he held himself back from tearing the man's arms off. Todd told him he'd seen heavy combat and wouldn't hesitate to kill him if given the chance. Barron just sucked on his teeth and told Todd to "Bring it."

Roger measured off where this clash was headed and quietly joined Todd on the porch. He tapped Todd on the shoulder and advised Todd in a low voice that they needed to go. "I'll get an FI on him and note this address as a place he hangs out."

Barron sat back down. The four of us collected at our cars. Todd was seething, so Roger suggested we take off and unwind at dinner.

Barron would not out live any of us. His violent path would one day come to bloody end.

Rosa Cuevas' *vato* son Jose was a typical banger associated with the worst a street gang has to offer. Along with whatever else the gang commanded him to do, Jose dealt PCP. Gang connections could reach back several generations in many Hispanic households in the poorer parts of San Diego. The police were only certain of Jose. If his mother was part of that scene, then the Cuevas offspring was at least second generation bad.

The San Diego Police Department had its own street narcotics team made up of specially trained detectives partially tasked with the capture of street-level dealers wherever they were in the city. Because drug dealers know few boundaries, the Street Team worked with other city and county law enforcement agencies. The municipal levels of narcotics enforcement spread upwards to work with state and federal agencies. In San Diego, heavier dope investigations could be handled within an umbrella organization called the Narcotics Task Force. NTF was laden with agents and officers from across the county. Help also arrived from the DEA at the top of the food chain and the state-level District Attorney's Narcotics Division. This multi-agency task force included detectives from the SDPD, the Sheriff's Office, and police from smaller San Diego cities. Neither David Barron, nor the Cuevas family was on WECAN's radar yet. WECAN hovered between the SDPD's patrol cops and Street Narcotics detectives. Patrol had no specific use for WECAN, and Street Narcotics only considered us relevant for prisoner control, or maybe to take dictation. Central WECAN struggled for a little respect.

WECAN's street experiences developed rapidly. Our arrests and drug and cash seizures, when measured monthly, often rivaled Street Narcotics' captures. At first, there was some rivalry, even animosity directed at us. We were accused of being amateurs, interlopers, or just underfoot. Grudgingly, the detectives eventually accepted us, even worked with us. Some of our officers were promoted out of WECAN and right into Street Narcotics. Manny would be one fortunate WECAN veteran to move up. The advancements helped smooth over the rest of the detectives' ruffled feathers.

Street Narcotics formed an operation, with a search warrant, around Rosa Cuevas' house at the dead end of L Street, off of 33rd Street. The detectives had been working Jose, and a younger man thought to be Jose's brother, for distribution and sales of PCP. The two Cuevas boys were prolific at outfitting street dealers with enough PCP to attract constant business across the county. Their activities landed them in Street Narcotics' web after Cuevas unwittingly sold Sherms to a confidential informant.

The narcotics detectives gathered enough evidence against Jose to go after him at his family dwelling, Rosa's home. Jose was the named target, but everyone at the tiny Cuevas house was subject to arrest if all the pieces fit together and pointed to them as well.

The detectives were hammered with other pressing work and couldn't settle on a date to serve the warrant. Street Narcotics' target-rich environment was like finding coal in a coal mine. There was always more to be dug out.

Besides trying to set a date to hit the Cuevas home, the lead detective, a guy who once thought of WECAN was a nuisance, had to coordinate with SWAT for the attack. Narcotics had picked up rumors and tidbits of information from their CI that 30th Street was a heavily armed gang. Stories floated around that some OG in the gang, which turned out to be David Barron, was a hitter, an assassin, a killer. He brought guns into the gang and taught younger thugs how to shoot. SWAT had to be attached to any operation that involved that gang, especially if the SDPD was to hit one of their homes. The little fortress could be an armed camp with shooters ready to fire on any cops who broke down their doors.

After exhausting efforts to settle on a date and time, Street Narcotics farmed off the project to WECAN. The Street Narcotics detective in charge of the case met with us to share all necessary information. SWAT was in the meeting, too. Their job was to make the forced entry through the iron screen door and make the house safe for us. The Cuevas brothers and other 30th Street gang members, because of Barron, were dangerous with their ties to Mexico's *narcos* and the prison-born *sureno* Mexican Mafia. Nobody knew who we'd find inside when we landed on a satisfactory date and attacked the home.

Normally, WECAN handled its own search warrant entries. On rare occasions, we called on SWAT to make the hazardous entries if we were concerned that we might be met with armed force. If the SN was so concerned about the Cuevas search warrant that they planned SWAT into the mix, who were we to question sound judgment? The nighttime date and hour were set, and the wheels set in motion.

The night of the warrant service, SWAT and WECAN staged a few blocks away for last minute preparation and timing. There were about eleven officers split down the middle by WECAN and SWAT. We got all the conversational planning out of the way first. When it was go-time, all the vehicles lined up behind the SWAT van and headed out in a single file line of five vehicles.

The van and its trailing cars screamed onto L Street and screeched to halts at the dead-end at the Cuevas residence. All our vehicles were left in the middle of the street while the passengers emptied out of van and cars. The six or seven SWAT officers tasked for this assignment passed through a low chain link gate into a large dirt front yard. The property extended around the back of the house with no fences or other impediments. This was the last house on the block that was built below a hillside embankment. The SWAT guys spread out and pointed guns to react to any people coming out of the darkness from the back of the house. WECAN officers crowded into the yard with our weapons at the ready.

SWAT was heavily armed with automatic weapons, some set on the three-round burst selection. WECAN had handguns and shotguns. If this house erupted in gunfire, the attacking SWAT and WECAN officers would destroy the building. As the SWAT guy with the heavy metal door knocker prepared to pull down the security door, a barking, angry pit bull zoomed around the corner of the house aimed at us.

The steel security doors that are so common to houses all over the country were even more prevalent in San Diego's poorer neighborhoods. Burglaries and armed home invasion robberies were common enough to warrant the strong metal obstacles. WECAN didn't have the door-pulling equipment SWAT was trained with.

WECAN joined SWAT for another forced entry weeks later. That SWAT entry didn't go as planned. SWAT went first into the yard and up to the front door. The team members are all outfitted with SWAT gear and protective equipment. SWAT Officer Luis Colon was assigned to use a specific tool to crack the steel security door lock and pull the door open so the others could rush through. He hooked his tool into place and pulled on it like a sonofabitch. The door broke at the hinges and unexpectedly dropped on top of Luis like the drawbridge to a castle. He was clobbered badly and had to be pulled to safety so the remaining team members could get inside before they lost the element of surprise. Luis was knocked unconscious and suffered what was later described as a grievous head wound. He was rushed to the hospital in such fragile condition that his priest was called to the hospital to perform last rites. At one point, his wife had been told that he'd died!

Luis went through weeks of healing and rehab before he could return to full duty.

WECAN guys piled into the yard at the Cuevas' home behind the SWAT officers making a fine pile of cops for the Cuevas's dog to chew on. None of us were prepared to repel an attack dog and scrambled to escape it. One of the SWAT cops, Don, was armed with an H&K MP5 rifle capable of firing single shots, three-round bursts and full auto. His gun's selector switch was levered for single-shot bursts.

Don realized we were all in danger of being mauled. He raised the rifle's butt above his shoulder so he could point straight down and squeezed off rounds at the dog. The deafening Blam! was followed by two more nerve rattling Blam, Blams as we all darted about trying to get away from Don, the dog and the gun shots. The uncooperative dog weaved in and around our legs trying to bite somebody. We all danced as hot lead hit both the dog and the ground at our feet. Most of us didn't make any sounds as we rushed to escape the cauldron of action in the front yard. I heard a "Yargh!" here and a "Look Out!" there, but it was all gunshots and barking until the dog laid down wounded and the rattle of gunfire ceased.

I saw the dying animal at our feet through the dust that kicked up. Don put the animal out of its misery with one fatal shot. The officers who flanked the raging chaos stayed on point the whole time. Nobody escaped the house.

Meanwhile, half of the SWAT team crashed through the wooden front door after breaking open the security door and spread throughout the house. With sudden quickness, the escapade was over. WECAN entered to find Rosa Cuevas, Jose Cuevas, his brother, a girl, and a baby, all guarded by SWAT officers.

WECAN took control, allowing SWAT to clear out and head back to their HQ. The family was seated in the living room now, all of them shaken by the cacophony of gunshots outside and the swarm of cops.

Rosa and her two sons were handcuffed. The mother of the small child remained hands-free to hold her baby. They were all in mild states of shock. None of the Cuevas household had ever experienced a police raid. They were not yet calmed down enough to start asking us questions. Their dog's fate stunned them into silence. We were there and we meant business.

I had the lead on this project, so I held the search warrant in my hands and read the content of the judge's order to the family. They hadn't complained about the police raid or begun their protests about out entry. They were definitely upset about the dead dog. The SWAT guys were gone so it was up to us to talk them through the unfortunate death of their dog. There'd be no family accusation. The dog was there to protect the home and family. If they hadn't involved themselves in drugs and the gang life the shooting never would have occurred. The relentless search for PCP and other contraband could begin.

It's hard to disguise the smell of PCP. We were in the house, filtering throughout the small property, but had yet to smell PCP's malodorous scent. The lack of odor was worrisome because the strong odor means we have something. No odor means we have *nada*. We want odor. Without that telltale clue that PCP was within reach, we had to conduct a long search in this tiny, but overstuffed house. Luckily, there were enough of us to watch the family and hit each room. I chose the master bedroom.

This was Rosa's small bedroom and was packed tightly with baby stuff. The woman with the baby was Rosa's daughter and shared the bed with her mom. A crib was forced into a nook between the bed and a wall. Cursory searches in the room gave up nothing. The other cops came up blank, too. Our exploration wasn't looking too good until I opened clothes hamper for the baby in Rosa's bedroom.

The hamper was filled with white bedding and baby clothes. The contents didn't smell like used baby poop. This was more to store clean baby things than the departure point for the laundry. I had no little poopy surprises to fear as I dug down into the clothes and felt around for harder objects. Dopers and gangsters will hide weapons and contraband anywhere. They don't always care about the sanctity of their loved ones.

I once stopped on Webster St. to talk to a Crip who was fresh out of prison. He stood in front of his mother's home with a baby carriage filled with said baby. His wife or girlfriend was seated on the porch surrounded by a couple of other thugs and their women. Rumors had it he was already slinging rock cocaine. I was backed up with other WECAN cops when I told him to assume the position. The Crip wasn't holding, so I decided to play the long-shot and search the carriage. The baby's momma leaped off the porch and collected her kid. Nobody said a thing to me or the other officers. Usually there's some complaint, some rampant mouthing off from the peanut gallery all around us, but not this time. Something was up. All of us could sense the tension in the air. The Crip was silent, too.

I removed the first layer of bedding and there it was a loaded revolver. The fool had concealed it below his baby. What an asshole. He got hooked up fast while I spun a web of shame about him in front of his woman and cronies. Nobody took aim at us for harassment. The silence from a normally hostile crowd was deafening. The mother asked if she could give her man a phone number to call from jail. Go figure.

Back at the hamper at the Cuevas place, I felt the lid and structure of a glass jar buried beneath piles of clean cloth. I gripped it and eased it out of the hamper. The jar turned out to be a sports juice bottle. The thirty-two-ounce jar was mostly filled with a yellow liquid. The label on the jar was for a juice that would have had a different color. Why was the juice colored yellow? Not particularly worried, I unscrewed the cap and took a whiff. The strong aroma just about knocked me on my ass. This was PCP, roughly thirty ounces of the drug. What the hell? I capped the bottle quickly. I didn't want a repeat of the PCP dosing I'd received some time back. I surprised the others when I announced I had a jar filled with "juice" that was not juice.

We hooked up almost everybody immediately. The unprecedented amount of liquid PCP alone worried me that we had more here to worry about than some dope dealers. These guys had some direct connection to a lab. The cautious search for weapons proved fruitless, which did surprise me. There should have been guns here. Or, maybe they were so feared across the Heights the Cuevas' were immune from transgressors.

I assumed their *Eme* connections immunized them from attack. Not even the reckless Crips were foolish enough to ignore that level of protection. We stripped the couch before the prisoners were confined to it. One of the crew set up a stepstool and lit up the crawl space above the ceiling with his flashlight. Still no weapons. There was money, but not a whole lot, maybe three hundred and change. The quart of dip would have to suffice.

Baby-momma was left to deal with the aftermath of raising a baby in a house of convicts. Jose was the prime target for this adventure. Rosa sat stoically on the couch, but she would burn because the stuff was in her home and in her room. All the Cuevas' were booked into jail for possession for sale. The younger brother had just turned eighteen and would enter the legal system early in his adulthood. We estimated the jar contained enough liquid to dose hundreds of users, more liquid PCP than any of us had ever seen. We were proud of that evening's accomplishment. The Cuevas' unidentified supplier would be mighty angry about that night's events.

The fate of the dog was in the hands of County Animal Control who collected the corpse.

David Barron didn't fare so well in life, either. He escaped the law enforcement net for years and thrived as one of the Arellano-Felix Tijuana Cartel gunsels. He ran fellow gang members back and forth into Mexico to turn them into additional paramilitary soldiers for the Cartel. The LHG members reaped the whirlwind, kidnapping and murdering people at the Cartel's orders. Barron worked his way into the position of a lieutenant within the ranks when his luck ran out. The world was still furious over the Cardinal's murder by Barron and his team. He was wanted in two countries for the murder of Cardinal Ocampo. Three LHG shooters were eventually charged with the murder. Barron escaped capture and continued to fight the Cartel's drug war. Barron was part of a hit team that tried to take out a Tijuana journalist with heavy weapons on full auto. The Mexican police intercepted the gang and opened fire. Bullets flew all over the place when one of them found Barron and killed him on the spot.

LHG took a hit in its supply chain and its command structure. Too bad for the world, new shooters would come up the ranks.

CHAPTER 30:
SPANISH MANNY

Central's WECAN team consisted of six of us for a while, plus the two we rarely ever saw, Boyd Long and Richard Grano, who had a mandate to work autonomously from the rest of us. Mike Cash and Rick Schnell were temporary Central WECAN members when I joined the team and then they moved on before we met Agent Chuck. We were talented at gaining the cooperation of the Mexican men imbedded in dope houses by their narcotics bosses. Agent Chuck from the FBI had provided us with occasional feeds while we developed our own leads to the dopers' locations. Team members Chuck, John, Roger, Manny and I were grew closer as a unit and were supposed to work street gangs and corner dealers. Instead, we were tantalized by the prospects of those little drug fortresses. The number of locations seemed legion. There was always another one to be discovered. No matter who we hammered, or what doper we took down, the paths that connected always seemed to lead to a home or apartment. Clearly, the dope didn't walk itself to a street corner from Mexico or L.A. The drug dens were the ends of tentacles from larger repositories that were tied to more mysterious origins. Those "factories" were out of our WECAN pay grade. Street Narcotics and the law enforcement legions up the chain worked those big-league drug emporiums.

We continued to do the occasional neighborhood walks to reinforce our presence and frazzle the gangs. In conjunction with the other WECAN teams, we sometimes changed up our activities to stay fresh, relevant and unpredictable. We snarked street sellers for larger drug sweeps, hit the gangs hard and anything else we could cobble together in between. Snark is a cop term for spying on someone. There's no dictionary reference other than the noun snark which refers to a "mysterious, or imaginary animal." Sometimes the unit's lieutenant organized us at

HQ for a group plan. One of those mass meets packaged us all into our cars for a caravan to the border with Mexico.

San Ysidro is a community of San Diego separated from the city proper by two other towns, National City and Chula Vista. Since San Ysidro never incorporated as its own entity so San Diego got the border with Mexico. San Ysidro was small and had a sense of independence from the rest of the city. The largely Hispanic population had its own economy, strongly dependent upon the business ties to Tijuana across the border. San Ysidro had its SDPD station within Southern Division and its own way of dealing with gangs and drugs. Our LT thought we could spend a day down there and give those officers a hand.

I had Manny with me, whose Spanish lingo became a necessity when all the WECAN teams flooded the commercial heart of San Ysidro. I'd spent little time down there in my career, but I knew a lot of the Spanish speakers spoke little English.

Suddenly, the neighborhood was filled with cops on foot who had little clue as to where they were needed. The plan to shoot us all down there to saturate an unsuspecting community was more of power show frill. We got to have some fun parading down the freeway in an army of patrol cars. But once we were on foot we figured out we were on holiday because the bad guys weren't going to be so easy to find. The goal was to make a scene with all of us officers. We made the scene, all right. We left a lot of people either scurrying into better places to be or scratching their heads and wondering where all the cops came from.

None of the dead time bothered any of us. We scratched out some FIs, patted down a few questionable people and ate great roadside tacos. There were thirty-six of us lounging about or peering into alleys and alcoves in the hunt for anybody that required agitation.

Manny happened to talk to a clerk at one of the gas stations, partly out of boredom. The Spanish speaker warmed up to Manny, as most Spanish speakers did with a cop who spoke their language and looked like them. The attendant hinted to Manny that we were in the wrong spot. If we headed up San Ysidro Boulevard a couple of blocks toward a certain set of motels, we'd worry a lot of people.

The experience was fun for a few hours. Thirty-six cops spread out over a large swath and FI'd the hell out of a lot of people. Quite a few people were in the country illegally. If they had dope on them, they were screwed. Nine of them, some who haunted the area daily, had never expected a sweep for bad people in San Ysidro. Their concerns primarily entered on Border Patrol and deportation. They seemed scantly aware of Southern Division's small contingent of cops. One or two spoke to Manny in their native language and asked what was up. One told him that he, "crossed the border all the time, legal, or, you know, not legal." He was involved in crime by his own admission, "I been busted before, man. I got nothing, on me now. You cops came out of nowhere today. Is this a new thing down here?" This was all spoken in Spanish. Basically, this trip was more like a day-picnic for WECAN. The LT wanted to show us off to Southern Division and to the people of San Ysidro.

Manny knew this was a lark. He'd spin some yarn about the New Centurions bringing the rule of law to the lawless border and such. We got paid to parade to the border in marked police cars and cause a big sensation just north of the border. Those of us who'd never worked Southern got to see a town that appeared almost exactly as it did in the 1960s, minus the Taco Bell. "We'll be here to check up on the bad guys from time to time, my friend," Manny said in Spanish.

Most of us lost interest when we came up empty-handed. Even the dirt bag motels Manny was warned about seemed mysteriously quiet. Word travelled fast up and down San Ysidro Boulevard. We weren't given specific targets. A pair of Southern Division cops caught wind of our swarm and rolled up to chat. I spoke to them for a bit, candid with the confession that we didn't know heck about the players down there and that we had no specific targets. The passenger officer chuckled. The driver commented he'd heard about WECAN and wondered if we released clouds of cops every day. I admitted this was more of a sanctioned lark then a bona fide plan. Our lieutenant literally tasked us with making a massive stage presence, and then we were gone never to return.

We travelled over the freeway to the western portions of the South Bay area and bothered some gang bangers in the community of Nestor.

Those guys had to worry about the PD and the Sheriffs. WECAN cops as thick as flies stifled any objectives that those bad gang boys had brewing that evening.

Day turned into night and then late night. Central WECAN remained behind while the other teams split for their territories. We wandered down to the actual border to watch the nightly show. The klieg lights, Border Patrol vehicles and its helicopter all go silent after dusk. Crowds gathered on the other side of the concreted creek, the Mexican side of the border, astride the border fence. We watched in awe as all the lights came back on and listened to the sounds of truck engines, ATV motors and the whine of a helicopter turbo revving up and fly over. The mania of hundreds of people making mad dashes for the northern bank and the terra firma of the U.S. was astounding. Manny and I parked on a dirt path in the darkness without any lights on to indicate our presence. The night was moonless so we couldn't see anything once the border lights were extinguished.

Suddenly, we heard the motions of bodies passing by as their clothing rustled and their feet scuffed the dirt. What began as a few people exploded into a flood of humans all headed north and past us. The oddest part about their rapid journey overland was the absolute lack of voices. Our car windows were open and my eyes had adapted to the darkness so I could make out distinct figures. Large figures and small scurried by without uttering any words. I found their exodus a little spooky and unnerving. I had the car keys and turned the engine over to crank on some lights. The bodies, identifiable now, scattered to avoid us. No one turned back for the border. We moved ahead slowly until we were certain no stray person was in the way of our car. I thought there was a forlorn quality to all those fleeing people. The best they had to look forward to now were lives perhaps marginally better than home. Or maybe marginal would be barely subsistent here, too. Lives lived on the fringes in the U.S. could get rough.

According to a BP agent we spoke with that evening, this observable madness went on nightly. This was no place for unprepared gang cops. Back to the Heights!

John and Chuck continued to gather their intel from the ladies of the evening that tramped up and down 32nd Street. Whatever knowledge they collected was aimed at more dope den houses, mostly homes with indiscernible landlords. The prostitutes seemed to hate those places as much as they probably hated the police. One of those sources sent us to a house on Market Street. Typically, the only people in the house were Mexican nationals in this country illegally, who sold cocaine and heroin to junkies. The neighborhood had been beaten down and ignored by the city-proper for so many decades that crime could flourish under everybody's noses that would never get off the ground in most other neighborhoods in town. Cops like us could walk the streets and not get much attention because the sight was not so uncommon before WECAN. Now, when we walked, it was just another Tuesday. When we walked up to another potential dope house, few eyes were on us. Our only decision was, is this house or that shack worth the efforts for search warrants or should we just knock on the door?

The "knock and talk" worked when Manny spoke, because of his Spanish-speaking fluency and cool Brooklyn bred nature. Manny's shtick was to stand at the door in full uniform and warn the occupants we'd been told drugs were being sold from this place. The Hispanic men, it was always men, almost never spoke English. Of course, they would innocently deny that drug sales happened in their midst. Manny would then sell them on the idea of allowing us to come in and search, just to satisfy our curiosity. The normal pattern was absolute cooperation with permission granted. Sometimes they even thanked Manny for being polite! The concept of a knock on the door followed by acquiescent permission to enter was perfectly legal. Two men spoke, one a cop, the other probably not from this country, and an invitation to walk inside was provided. Never mind the dweller's uncertainty about his role as the occupant in the face of a swarthy uniformed Latin man. We asked and he consented. The rest would be up to the courts.

The two guys in that Market Street hovel allowed us to search, thanks to Manny's polite schmoozing techniques. I wondered if the Mexican nationals weren't used to a police officer's politeness when he'd straight-up ask for permission to step inside and look around. There were no heavy-handed threats, no abuse, and no gestures with guns to intimidate them. Manny was direct and soft-spoken. The dealers were used to direct threats from the law back home. They were perplexed on our side of the border when the WECAN cops did not bring fear and abuse. The dealers either feigned skin-deep indifference, or they kept their mouths shut and gave us the open-door policy.

These two guys weren't as clever as others we'd encountered. They didn't get Cartel Tech training on how to properly hide their dope inside a dwelling. The stuff was on a coffee table inside the doorway and almost within sight of the door. We seized small amounts of heroin and cocaine and arrested the two dealers. Normally, we knew all the hidden spots the dealers used in these sparsely furnished rentals. The months of drug house take-downs taught us well. The dealers had to put up with small cadres of meticulous WECANers intent on finding the hiding places no matter how long it took.

We took an opportunity to play house with this Market Street escapade. Our marked police cruisers were a block away to avoid announcing our presence in the house. Predictably, while we were there, junkies came up to the house to buy dope. This dope house arrangement was street-fed to junkies by other junkies. "Go to a broken rear window in the back of the house to buy the dope," they'd say. Ask to buy *blanca* and *negra*. Spanish words for white and black; cocaine and heroin. Presumably, undercover cops wouldn't know the street code at this location and would blow their cover when they asked for anything other than *blanca* and *negra*. Our sources helped us with the smallest of details.

Manny looked the part of an expected Hispanic dope peddler. Even if he didn't, it didn't matter. The junkies weren't picky about who sold them drugs. One of us suggested I turn my black police jacket inside out and wear it at the window. The buyers expected a Mexican to greet them. With this half-in-jest experiment, they would get blue-eyed, sandy brown haired me.

I spoke some pidgin Spanish. I took Spanish in school and retained a little. I could remember the words, but I was shit at conjugation. Manny gave me some phrases that worked with any *gringo* trying to *sabe* proper Spanish. I only had to fake it to the point that the buyer was convinced and popped money through the broken window serving as the drug portal.

I could mimic a cross-border drug dealer well enough to succeed. Besides, the junkie buyers were there to cop dope, not argue with the dealer about blue eyes and a terrible accent. I would tell them to wait for the dope *uno momento*, while a pair of my teammates ran outside to grab the junkies and haul them inside. One officer guarded the occupants, and another would run the additional bodies for warrants and document their identities. We always had two officers free to grab more junkies who attempted to buy dope at the window. This mode worked so well we tossed around the idea of manufacturing prop heroin to sell. If one of us could hand something immediately to the junkies, they wouldn't get nervous and suspicious. We'd freeze them in place a little longer instead of obviously stalling for time.

I went to a bodega market the next day and purchased a bag of toy balloons. I knotted them so the toy balloons looked just like the favorite form of packaged Mexican Brown heroin. Brown heroin was in powder form and could be easily extracted from an unknotted balloon. The sticky tar heroin worked better when it was twisted up in cellophane. Balloons were simple and could be swallowed to avoid seizure by the police. Later, the balloons would be released through defecation, unaffected by stomach acids, ready for instant use.

I'm really into doctor avoidance and shun "light duty" or time away from the field due to injury. Four of us hit an apartment one afternoon in Logan Heights that was "up" selling heroin. The fenced-in, two-story building housed four apartments with a courtyard separating another single apartment. Our target was a ground-level apartment with a broken window that faced the common-area patio. I pounded on the steel screen door hoping to induce permission to enter. Loud-knocking cops do tend to get people's attention and induce them to open doors. The broken window next to the door was missing a substantial amount of glass except for the shards that remained in the frame. That window was also covered from the inside with tattered, dusty drapes. Manny was with me and he tried to gain a little cooperation with some conversation through the window in Spanish, correctly assuming that Mexican nationals were inside. We could see shadows through the drapes, but nobody spoke. We needed to get that door open.

The broken glass made for a protective portal for the dealers. To reach inside without due diligence was to risk severe cuts. I figured the guys inside broke it to provide an open gateway to move dope and money back and forth. If I just reached inside carefully, I could grasp the door lock and turn the tumbler. The other guys were less confident than I was. That glass was jagged and, what was to stop the drug dealers inside from grabbing my arm and pulling it into a glass shard? I told myself I was going to do it. I told them to shoot the guys through the window if they tried to harm me.

Of course, nothing went as planned. I reached in and managed to grab and twist the door lock uncontested. My guys were all behind and next to me. As soon as the lock clicked, two of my team members pulled the door open. At the same time, sudden voices and motion inside warned me to move. I pulled my hand out of the window fast, but somehow missed the clearance and scraped my right index finger against a sharp point of glass. The three team members went inside and secured everything quickly. I looked at my finger and saw a massive gash from knuckle to joint. The wound filled with blood that dripped in rivulets onto the floor. Jeez, I knew I should have taken precautions, but in the moment, I shot from the hip and got a war wound.

Quickly, I reached back inside and tore down some drapery. I wrapped the filthy cloth around my finger, and then my whole hand to staunch the flow. I was still integral to the reason we were there, so I didn't dare find an excuse to leave.

Manny and the others found a bag of heroin balloons and took two Mexican nationals into custody. Manny came back out to check on me. My hand was a bloody mess, but the wound was somewhat compressed from the pressure I used with my left hand to suppress the flow. The torn drapery was aged and dirty to begin with. Now it was a bloody, nasty mess and I needed to clean the finger before infection set in.

One of our two police cars had a clean cloth in the trunk. I discarded the ad hoc drapery bandage and took a good look at my finger. Before I rewrapped it, I used the complexes' garden hose to wash out blood and debris. That was the first chance, albeit a quick one, to see the damage. I was momentarily shocked when I could saw my finger bone through the pooling blood. I'd literally cut a gulley down the center of my finger from the knuckle to the first joint. I was lucky the pain felt more like a sting than a devastating injury.

We collected the arrested bodies and drugs, packed up our police cars and headed to HQ. Once there, I rushed to the bathroom with the first aid kit from our car. I un-wrapped the wound and let my hand soak in the sink's hot water. The water turned pink as it water disappeared down the drain. I'd gambled with the cleanliness of my first aid back at the drug place. I was still gambling with it when I managed to get the bleeding to stop long enough to study the wound. That was indeed my finger bone I'd peered at earlier. It was no longer as visible as some of the swollen flesh that closed the wound a bit.

From my past experiences in construction as a carpenter, wounds like this have a good chance of healing without stitches if the right aid is applied. My favorite medicine for such an occasion was Neosporin. John warned me that I should go to the hospital, that a cut that bad would probably get infected.

"I'm good, John. I'll clean it out at HQ."

"It's your business, but that really looks bad. I could see the bone, too, when you washed it off with the hose."

"If it still looks bad to me after I fix it, I'll take myself to Sharp Hospital," I told him. John wasn't used to my sort of first aid. Maybe his caution was warranted, but I ignored it.

I went upstairs to a quiet bathroom to work my medical magic undisturbed. Despite John's nagging, I medicated myself with a thick bead of the Neosporin salve and filled the trough in my finger. My remedy was good enough for government work. Despite John's commonsense medical approach, I healed correctly and quickly with no infection. The subsequent scar is still a trophy I wear for show-and-tell when I relate the story to people with sensitive stomachs.

CHAPTER 31:

REVOLVER

Manny and I worked a tip we dug up from a dissatisfied heroin addict. We detained him when we caught him on a bus bench nodding off. With no operation to pursue at the time, we shook him down and got him off the street. Frankly, The Heights were filled with bad people and behavior that children shouldn't have to witness. A junkie on a bus bench that school kids passed by was too much reality. They should go be high somewhere private.

This guy snapped out of his funk the moment I tapped him on the shoulder. He'd shot up less than ten minutes prior but wasn't as high as I expected. He explained that he wasn't so much high as just feeling normal. He wanted to get high and paid for two spots of tar heroin, but the dealer cheated him and only gave him one. He couldn't sustain an angry thought despite his unhappiness. His blood system had still devoured enough dope to close his eyes. Manny suggested he give us the address and we'd be his avenging angels. He stopped mumbling and looked into Manny's eyes. "Really?" he sounded dopey and dumbfounded at the same time.

"If the place you say is actually selling right now, we'll let you go and check the place out." I was busy on the radio with my request for wants and warrants on this chap. He was clean, so I suggested to Manny we drop him off near the methadone center close to C Street. Maybe fate would steer him into the clinic.

The chore was quick. The guy gave us an address deep down on South 33rd Street. We didn't bother with a drive-by in case they had lookouts. Even the sight of a police car driving leisurely down the road could "hink" up the dealers and send them scramming. We had to drop the car around the block and walk in as nonchalantly as possible.

The time was about three in the afternoon. The dropping sun cast a few shadows but didn't hamper the easy identification of the given address. We stood and stared at the small house from the front yard of the house next to it. There were no sounds and no signs of movement. The kitchen door was conveniently open. The property was old. I thought the tiny double-door garage at the rear of a long driveway dated the place back to around 1910. The garage was detached from the house and the driveway abutted the side of the home with the kitchen door. We walked quietly through the door and then spread out to cover two rooms. There was food on the stove, little furniture and no people. Maybe they had made us. Somebody who saw us could have ratted us out. Manny said he'd wait for their return and began a cursory search for dope. I told him I'd go back to the garage and check that out.

The garage was weather worn and had a slight lean to the frame as though the front dipped into the foundation. The doors were those old-fashioned dual, wooden jobs that opened in the middle. The wall on the right sight was battered and holes were broken through that I could peer into.

I could hear low tones from voices inside. I took a chance and peered through one of the holes to see three men in dimmed light at work on an old fold-down workbench and saw a sight I'd not seen before. Two of the guys had wrapped tiny booger-sized dollops of tar heroin in cellophane cut down from a larger sheet. I had the men dead-to-rights. I took a step to the right and gripped the double doors.

Defense attorneys will pounce on an officer over the simple rules of search and seizure. I had probable cause to be on the property. Up until this moment, we'd met no one to either stop us or provide permission. Manny and I were at the beginning of an investigation. If I manipulated nothing to find or see objects in question, I was home free. The holes in the wall gave me optimum, legal visual access. If the holes were covered, I'd have a conflict over the warrantless search if I moved the cover aside. The same principal would ruin an arrest if the hole I peered through was over my head. I'd lose the arrest through legal doctrine of the fruit of the poisonous tree if I borrowed a stool to raise my line-of-sight and see what I saw.

I needed both hands free to pull on the door handles. I intended to be quick enough to step inside and then unholster my gun with my right hand. I tugged on the doors but should have regarded the sag of the sunken building face. The doors didn't budge, and I'd lost the shock and awe moment. The next tug was mightier and with urgency. The doors opened with a reluctant scrape along the concrete, to a shadowy interior lit with one weak light bulb. My eyes would need split seconds to move from sunlight to darkness. I didn't have that much time. The tallest of the three men stood less than two feet away with a gun in his hand pointed at me.

I had quick reflexes and the tight police training to fill my hand with a gun in a split second. The armed man gave me no time. He raised the pistol to waist-height and pointed it straight ahead. The barrel was less than eighteen inches from my belly button. I had a fraction of a moment to accept that I was dead. I didn't even have time to feel fear, only surprise. Then, the strangest thing happened. The gunman tossed the gun into a corner of the garage. The sucker was heavy and made a loud clatter on the concrete pad. I wasted no time and lunged at the man and hit him so hard with my body-check that he stumbled back into the workbench and sunk to the floor.

Three things happened at once. I pulled my gun on the other two dealers, shouted for Manny who was still in the house, and kicked the dazed gunman in the stomach. The two companions saw their guy in pain on the ground and my gun as I waved it at them to get on the ground. I had no idea how much more danger lurked around me. I nearly screamed for Manny the second time and kicked the gunman again for good measure. He was my real threat. He had the gun to defend their drug den. I had no idea if he was a shooter or the guy entrusted to repel the various pirates in the neighborhood, including aggressive addicts. I only knew I took the measures to remove the fight from this one real threat.

Manny was at my back in an instant and in time to see me destroy a man senseless, on the floor and vulnerable. "What are doing?"

"Look behind you in the corner!" Manny had one hand on my shoulder to stop me from my rampage. He looked back quizzically and saw the gun in the shadows. "He had that pointed at me." I stopped hurting the guy who writhed in pain. The beating was better than a gunshot, to either him or me. I was lost in anger and fear. I was frighteningly upset with myself for being in this position and out of control with rage.

Manny shouted at the two men prone on the floor. He was alive with the tension in that small space. His shouts snapped me out of my frenzy. I was livid, my fury aimed at the gunman and even more furious at being at the wrong end of that gun because I was cocky.

I handcuffed my guy and left him face down in the dust. Manny searched the other two and found wads of cash, but no additional weapons. I picked up the gun and stared at the thing for thirty seconds as I tried to come to terms with my brush with mortality. This was a big gun. All six cylinders loaded with forty-five caliber bullets and a barrel the length of a Bic pen. My Kevlar vest was supposed to shield me against rounds this big, from a distance. This gun had the power to smash into my armor at close range, shatter my ribs and mash my internal organs into jelly. If that joker had pulled the trigger, even once, the vest wouldn't have prevented my death.

A Street Narcotics officer once took a gunshot to the abdomen in Ocean Beach during the service of a search warrant. He wore a vest identical to mine. The would-be killer shot him from about eight feet away. The nine-millimeter round struck him in his torso-covered vest. The shock of the shot knocked the detective back through the door he'd just burst through. His team pulled him to safety and shot the suspect, a drug dealer popular with rock groups who performed at the Sports Arena. The detective showed me the aftermath of the hit to his body days after the incident. The vest took the bullet just above its bottom edge of protection and spread the impact over his waist. He suffered massive bruising and a soreness that took weeks to dissipate. The purple and black contusion was almost the same girth as a basketball. He was extremely lucky to be alive by just an inch of material. One inch lower and the bullet would have missed the vest. The bigger rounds my potential assailant had in that gun would have killed me at that short distance.

I took the few moments to decompress from terror and anxiety and looked at the table. The engineers of this event had bagged about thirty doses of heroin. There was a larger amount stuck to a plastic wrapper they'd scraped off with a butter knife. These lively entrepreneurs were more than just dealers. They were low-level suppliers, or maybe the gunman was the supplier and he watched over the other two as they prepped the dope for sale. We had three hardcore dope peddlers in custody and the one would get the enhancement from the prosecutors for the gun.

Manny and I attended the prelim for the three border-crosser dealers of poison. Each man had a translator, and each faced serious prison time. Obviously, they were sellers stuck with possession for sales charges. Through the interpreter, the judge announced that all three were bound over for trial. The gunman asked his attorney what he was charged with. He could read Spanish. The English words on the page in front of him were in legalese and made only slightly more sense to me than it did to him. I watched the neutral expression on his face screw into a look of deep concern. He leaned over to his attorney and spoke quietly in Spanish. The translator listened in and then the three-way conversation focused on the translator. The lawyer asked to address the court. "Your Honor, may I address the court on behalf of my client?"

"This is an unusual request, counselor. Is this of import to the court?"

"You Honor, my client wishes to speak to Officer Newbold. He feels he doesn't deserve the penalty if found guilty in trial."

"Officer Newbold?"

"Yes, your Honor. He can speak to me." What the hell was this about? The translator spoke on the man's behalf. He addressed her quietly in his native tongue. She stood in the jurors' box and related the following:

"Officer, why are you doing this to me? I didn't kill you. I threw the gun away. I did not want to shoot you. Why are you sending me to prison?" He didn't know American justice. He also had no idea who ran this court. His admission answered the Golden Question. He didn't kill me because he didn't want to shoot a police officer. For this, I was supposed to forgive him.

The judge gave me the opportunity to retort. I sat stunned by the weird display of hubris and naivete. Manny was outside in the hallway, so I didn't have a trusty set of eyes and ears to reflect on. "Uh, you sell heroin and carry a gun." My point was succinct. The translator had little to say that probably didn't need to be interpreted. The judge stepped in and asked the three different defense lawyers if they had anything to add. The forgone conclusion among the three ended the proceedings.

The gunman pled guilty between the prelim and a trial date. He got three years and useless deportation.

I had to let the event simmer the day it happened. I still had to tell my wife. She would need to know why I didn't sleep well for a few nights and the brush with death occupied my thoughts constantly or weeks. She was horrified and her mind instantly ran ahead in time to the next time something like this could happen. I promised her I would be more careful. My son was young enough where he wasn't so much distraught as excited to hear more about cops and robbers. I soft-pedaled the gravity of the nightmare to him so he could continue to be a kid that thought his old man was in complete control on the mean streets.

I became a more cautious cop after that. I still put myself in precarious situations, but with a gun in my hand.

CHAPTER 32:
INTESTINAL FORTITUDE

Roger was my partner the afternoon we spotted an addict walking on Broadway past 10th Avenue in downtown. The face was familiar. She was a heroin addict we'd seen coming from the area of a dope house in the Heights weeks before. Roger drove and made the quick U-turn to come up behind her. We hoped to get to her before she swallowed any drugs she might possess. She'd watched us approaching and her cupped hand went to her mouth when we stepped behind her.

I knew what went down her throat and it wasn't a cough drop. She swallowed what was more than likely a couple of balloons of dope before we could seize it and arrest her. This movement was standard junkie etiquette; swallow the balloons of heroin and crap them out the next day. Heroin use causes constipation in many users but a laxative will help speed the balloons on their way to the exit port.

I grabbed her neck and applied some pressure to prevent her from swallowing and shouted at her to spit it out. She grimaced from the C-clamp I put around her throat. We were trained to prevent the evidence from going down the pipe, but we could only take that force so far. Choking the addict wouldn't look good on television and was too excessive just to nail a lowly addict with a monkey on her back. I saw three colored balloons on her tongue. She couldn't develop enough saliva to swallow them with my hand around her neck. I let go when the sheer act of defiance could have caused her throat damage at my hand. The balloons went down her gullet.

The woman was clearly under the influence of heroin. The pinned pupils were dead giveaways. Roger cuffed her for the Eleven-Five-fifty charge, the Health and Safety code for being under the influence of certain illicit drugs. We tagged on Destruction of Evidence and heroin possession to her charges. I smelled the distinct odor of vinegar when the balloons were on her tongue, which is common with brown heroin. We figured the City Attorney's Office would drop the last two charges. The allegations would only stand if the courts wanted this woman in custody. I stuck with them because I believed my narcotics experience would be challenged by a defense attorney. I wanted that challenge so I could articulate the facts in court and push the envelope. I had amassed a lot of drug experience and loved to use it to argue on my behalf in court.

The communications operator let us know over the radio that she had an arrest warrant for a previous Eleven-Five-fifty caper. We took her to women's jail and told the deputies about the stomach full of heroin she carried. Instead of just saying thanks and goodbye, the intake guards told us they'd stuff her in a cell with nothing, not even a drain. They would contact us the next morning if they recovered the balloons.

The morning arrived with the unlikely call from jail since my name was listed on the booking slip. The sheriff's deputies had collected the female prisoner's feces at dawn. "Do you want to come out and search the collected biologics?" the deputy asked.

I dithered over the concept of searching nasty shit for contraband. Fuck it. I'm a rabid dog when it comes to finishing something and that lady junkie had stolen my evidence! I called the other Central Division team members.

Chuck, Roger and I decided this unique experience would be a first. We met together at HQ and drove out to the suburb of Santee in a supervisor's car to Las Colinas Women's Facility to meet the challenge. Las Colinas is the main criminal holding facility in San Diego county for women. The Men's facility is downtown, conveniently close to HQ. Las Colinas is a pain-in-the-ass, twenty-five-minute drive from HQ.

When we arrived, we were met out back by a guard. She directed us over to the jail's docks where a hose and shovel had been conveniently arranged for us. The jail has a protocol for feces extraction and scrutiny. The deputies had bagged up the feces and placed the sack near the dock. The guard was instructed to tell us to collect the shit bag with the shovel and carry it over to a drain in the parking lot. The hose was attached to a hose bib so we could pressure-wash the prisoner's feces. The chain of evidence technically dictated that one of the arresting officers be at the scene to collect the evidence. But truthfully, the deputies didn't want the assignment.

In the parlance of the moment, "You caught it. You clean it."

I had the hose while Roger took the shovel. This was some funny shit we got ourselves into. The few guards around passed by and smiled. I could see some jail employees gazing at us through the windows and laughing. We were the morning show at county jail. We decided to play it up for a couple of photo ops. We photographed Chuck pointing his gun at the mound of human by-product as the water hose assaulted the poop.

My job was to break up the clumps of poo until we could identify the colored balloons. Roger kept the shovel at the ready until something surfaced. We broke down the former contents of the woman's intestines quickly. There was nothing there, no balloons. We knew she'd swallowed them. The cell had no plumbing, no running water and no place to conceal anything.

I asked the guard to call the shift deputy who'd monitored our prisoner's behavior through the night. She was still on shift and met us in the parking lot. She said everything was monitored until the moment the prisoner defecated. The deputies rushed in and moved her to another cell while they bagged the stuff. We looked at each other baffled. Then it dawned on everyone. She had plucked the heroin out of her droppings and put the balloons back into her mouth before the deputies entered the cell. They'd already done a cavity search after re-confining her that included vagina and anus. Nothing. Our prisoner took a dump, plucked out the balloons of heroin and re-swallowed them without the deputy's knowledge.

There should be a commendation or citation for "working below and beyond the call of duty." We thanked the Las Colinas staff that found humor in our parking lot antics and called it a day.

CHAPTER 33:

BUNK DOPE
AND RHYTHM

We'd had early success when we posed as dealers and sold bunk dope. We repeated the scam periodically at dope houses. We figured the act was a great deterrent against drug dealing. If a junkie's trusted dope houses collected cash for dope but failed to produce said dope, who the hell could that junkie trust? Many of the buyers went to jail for any charges we could levy against them. If we had nothing, they got FI'd and went into the computer system. The locations got burned because we were involved. The addresses went into the system so every cop working Central Division could learn about them. This was the imaginative police work WECAN was encouraged to delve into.

We impounded addict's money at the police station on a regular basis. All the cash we seized went into Police Impounds. We didn't keep a dime. We might push the envelope on our capers but didn't risk our integrity. We made sure one of us had toy balloons in possession every workday. Our arrests were up in quantity. Our dope seizures increased, and more bad guys went to jail. We'd even encountered gang members within a few of these houses, but their presence was a rarity. Usually, the only gangsters in these Mexican-run joints were overdosed users passed out on the floors and ignored by the dealers.

In one knock-and-talk entry, we found two West Coast Crips seated together in a standard Mexican dope house. There seemed to be no connection between the Crips and the dealers. The Crips didn't budge an inch when we showed up. I'd seen these two young Crips on the streets crisscrossing this portion of the Heights before. They had to live in this neighborhood to be this bold. Their staid, calm demeanor bugged the hell out of us. This was an odd foursome if I ever I saw one. Crips do not hang out at Mexican drug dens. Were these guys afraid to move or were they concerned we'd attack, thinking they were armed? We tried every which-way to discover their intent. We couldn't find anything. Still they sat there. The search for weapons yielded nothing. We stripped the sofa they were on and still found nothing. They wouldn't talk to us and the Mexicans didn't either. It was one of life's little mysteries.

The dealers wanted us to go away. I'm pretty sure they wanted the Crips to leave, too. One of our guys intently searched the place for the magnets that brought everybody here, dope and money. Eventually, John found balloons of heroin in a plastic bag hidden in the drapes. We hooked up the two Mexicans because they'd acknowledged they were the tenants. We knew this was a skinny pinch. The City Attorney had to make the call on prosecution. We sent the Crips packing for want of an arrestable crime.

We repeated the knock, talk, find dope, and arrest the occupants at another tiny house. Manny set himself by the broken window that was sure to be the hole the dope buyers would go to. He dropped a few toy balloons into his jacket pocket, now turned inside out to hide the distinct police officer clothes profile. As expected, we caught users who bought our fake stuff and added a few more bodies to the two Mexican dealers we took down inside. We had enough prisoners to fill two cars, so we ended the day back at HQ to process bad guys.

Manny was targeted for promotion to Investigations. Roger was earmarked to become my new partner. The team-up was put into practice to cover for Manny when he took a series of extra days off before the transfer to Investigations. Roger was as savvy as they came and a WECAN veteran from the first wave.

I liked the tough guy a lot and found his courage to be remarkable. Neither partner was adept or even interested in cracking jokes, but both enjoyed good laughs. I was always the smart aleck with the snide and funny comments designed to elicit at least grunts of approval from both guys. Manny was the serious, *rico suave*-type and often attracted the eyes of the ladies. His uniform fit tighter than mine with tailoring meant to give him that Latin-trim physique. Roger was stockier, a little wider in the belly and hips than I was. Both of us wore shirts that were a little tight around the girth. Underneath the shirt our bulletproof vests just made us look beer-belly plump. We became better friends off the job when I teamed up with him to go off-roading on our Honda 250 Fourtrax in San Diego's desert.

Roger loved a good practical joke and never hesitated to make light of a cop situation if he could squeeze a laugh out of it.

I remember working with him when we transported a mental case to County Mental Health for the seventy-two-hour hold evaluation. We captured the guy at 25th and Broadway when he stepped in between two of us drinking coffee at the 7-11. He was a crazy street creature, buggy as a loon and tried to stomp on our booted feet. "Let go of me, Satan. I will be rid of you!"

"What the hell, man," I exclaimed.

"You'll not get the best of me, crocodile, because I have places to be and you can't stop me!" he yelled.

Roger jumped back to protect his feet while I dropped my coffee and reached out to grab the guy. He turned around and shouted more zealot gobbledygook into my face. Roger took him from behind and tried to cuff him. The guy flipped around and tried to kiss Roger's face. Now, it was my turn to end this. I wrapped my right arm around his neck and pulled him backward and down to the asphalt. He struggled and spat at us. I pinned one knee to his back and turned him onto his chest. The man continued to rave as lunatics do. Nothing he said made sense. I couldn't tell if he was high or insane. The only drug that I knew in the Heights that would create this madness was PCP, but we determined he wasn't dusted. Our man was batty, pure and simple. He'd need the help of pros at County Mental Health.

The old Hillcrest facility was where the police stood around and did their intake paperwork alongside mentally disturbed people. Some were already medicated by the staff to make them docile. There were medicated drop-offs from other police officers and agencies.

My face was buried in my Intake detention report. The reports needed to be articulate with a modicum of correct grammar, not my strong point. I wanted our man to get the commitment he needed. My report had to sell that wish, down to the finest details. I paid no attention to Roger.

Roger got bored. He looked around at the doped-up inmates awaiting a trip through The Door every detainee must pass to get to the detention rooms. Five men and one woman in a robe sat in low chairs, their eyes opaque and their jaws slackened. The other officers were gone by the time I looked up and saw an animated Roger standing at a wooden lectern. Roger rotated the podium to face the Haldol and lithium crowd. A few of the patrons let their eyes drift in Roger's direction. Roger gave a slight cough.

"I'm glad you could all make it here this evening," he announced. There was no reaction. The psych meds really zonked these folks out. Most were there because their previous behavior mimicked that of our detainee. The staff had already injected our guy with something antipsychotic and he'd already turned into a vegetable.

Roger surveyed his audience for any signs of life. "You're probably wondering why I gathered you here tonight." Roger began a recital of the *Declaration of Independence*. I stared at him in disbelief. What the hell was he thinking? What would the staff do if they didn't like it? I looked over at the reception window and saw that the lone staffer wasn't paying any attention.

Roger ran out of material with the second sentence of his speech. He pulled out the PD 145 notebook we all carried and read the Miranda warning that was printed on it in a sing-song voice: "You have THE right TO remain SILENT! IF YOU give UP the RIGHT," and so on.

I got hit right in the funny bone. All the detainees who were conscious focused on Roger. He played to his rapt audience with a rendition of the facility's mission statement he'd found printed on a sheet of paper in the lectern. I lost all perspective and caught myself laughing a little too loud. The staffer behind the window looked up puzzled. She looked blankly at the comedian at the podium. She was only intent on focusing on business at hand. Anything else was somebody else's problem. She might have been drugged, too.

Roger encouraged audience participation. Maybe one of them would be cognizant enough to get the joke and react with a chuckle or two. I laughed at every facial tick and twist of the dry words Roger performed. He kept up the shenanigans for as long as he had source material. He read the notes he'd written for an old urinating in public citation he wrote ages ago, that were still trapped in his notebook. He switched to a high-pitched voice and quickened the pace like a hummingbird in flight.

"I saw the man behind the liquor store using his head as a brace against the wall. The stream of urine was steamy on a cold winter's night."

The door suddenly opened and out came the doctor. He looked up over his glasses at Roger, now red-faced and a little embarrassed. I had a wide grin on my face as tears watered my eyes from laughter. Roger just looked at the professional psychiatrist and said, "Hiya, Doc!"

I bailed Roger out fast and stood to shake the man's hand. "I'm the detention officer, Doctor. You want to talk to me," I said as I looked over the man's shoulder at Roger, who was suddenly in a chair reading a magazine as though nothing happened.

The crazy man who attacked us and tried to kiss Roger was a regular there. The doctor recognized him and asked us few questions. We left through the back door of the facility giggling like children when out of range of the doc's hearing. Roger and I took the slow road back to our turf as we composed new speeches for Roger when he hits the lecture circuit. I prodded him about that out of character buffoonery. "That was some funny shit. What got into you?"

"I thought a little humor along those lines might be entertaining tonight."

You bet.

The next workday, we got word of a dope house on 33rd Street around the corner from Oceanview Boulevard. The five of us got permission from the Mexican dealers to enter. We found heroin concealed in a ratty couch cushion, arrested the dealers, and set up shop. Manny got into costume when he reversed his black SDPD windbreaker, while Chuck and John hid outside as our arrest team. Manny was still a few weeks away from the transfer to Investigations. I would be prisoner control with Roger.

We parked our cars around the corner on Oceanview Boulevard. We didn't bother to conceal them. We were confident we'd catch prisoners.

Our logic was that when the junkies were dope sick, or afraid of the withdrawal pains, they'd risk police duress to get "well" again. If we shut down one house, the dopers weren't impacted. The dope places were plentiful in the Heights, so the buyers would find one through the grapevine soon enough. If we closed out a dope house, chances were it would be up again within a day or two. We figured turning it into a bunk dope house might impact that spot's reputation and drive the junkies elsewhere. We'd ruined that joint's reliability permanently.

In quick time the buyers appeared at the broken window used in this tiny house as a portal. The window was partially boarded over with a used portion of thin plywood. The remnants of the glass were covered with the wood as well. Only a tiny opening through the wooden cover offered a way for seller and buyer to exchange money for dope. Manny's colloquial Spanish always relaxed the dopers and lulled them into buying what they thought was real heroin. Money exchanged hands and they walked, not knowing they bought an empty, knotted toy balloon. My Mexican-speaking novelty act would be a back-up ruse. Roger would assist, but his accent and red-headed appearance was a more preposterous Mexican routine than mine.

The purchasers arrived almost on top of each other. Chuck and John were busy. I had to tie up more toy balloons because none of us wanted to handle the ones the junkies briefly held. They could keep them. The buyers kept coming like it was a fast-food joint. I filled up one room with people and Roger was going to fill another. We had nothing but a few pairs of handcuffs.

The prisoners were seated and silently watched us in action. Nobody was combative. Some squirmed as they tried to find comfortable positions on the floor. Only the first few were handcuffed. The rest were admonished not to become nuisances. We agreed we'd end this after just a little time passed. Who knew catching illicit narcotics buyers would be the spree it became? The task was a simple as casting fishing lines in a sea filled with biting tuna.

The buyers approached the window with all kinds of things to pay Manny, tools, brand new Levis in stacks with the tags still attached, even liquor bottles just boosted from some market with the anti-theft

device still locked on. At one point one of the sketchy buyers walked up
to Manny's window and warned him police cars were parked around
the corner. They were our police cars. Manny said, "Fuck them po-lice!"
and continued with business.

Roger and I did our best to identify the people we detained. Most
of them had driven into the Heights from other parts of town. Those
people had licenses and were interviewed first. Those without identification were told their fate could be determined only after longer waits
than the others. The tactic almost guaranteed these people would tell us
the truth. A couple of the people had warrants and they were formally
arrested.

Time grew short as our shift would end soon. We'd need to return to
the station soon to process the prisoners and avoid overtime. We Field
Interviewed everybody and added the two resident dealers to the group
going to jail. Several were borderline for eleven-five-fifty on opioids. We
made the mutual decision to not process them for the charge. It wasn't
worth working overtime.

We got everybody outside under the moonlight and saw that, as
usual, nobody'd tried to see what the po-po were up to. No one in the
neighborhood was out and about. There seemed to be few people in
view of our location. The only signs of life on the block were a few
lights in living rooms across the street. What were we going to do with
these people? We didn't want them just walking off into these poor
people's neighborhood. Ever the showman, Roger had an idea. We
would encourage them to sing or face the repercussions of being stuck
with us longer.

Sing what? Four of us snorted a little over the thought. John was
dubious about anything with untoward behavior on our part. Roger had
that mischievous look on his face, meaning this act was going forward.

These drug addicts might not see the humor, but we'd have some fun
at their expense. Maybe, just maybe, we might impact future addict
thoughts about a return trip to the Heights to cop dope. The neighborhood didn't need the strain of constant streams of junkies who invaded
their streets to destroy the fabric of their community. I watched Roger
play this out. He suggested we have them sing a pleasant rendition of

the children's song, "Mary Had A Little Lamb." The idea was absurd, of course. This prank could also get us in trouble. John, the worry wart, wasn't interested in participation and thought we'd all get caught doing something along the lines of Conduct Unbecoming an Officer. What the hell, we gave it a shot.

At first the detainees didn't understand. Were we going to embarrass them if they sang and humiliate them more? Why yes. Maybe they'd learn to stay off this street and away from the good people on the block. Certainly, having us in their faces was not an affair they'd want to repeat. So, the chorus began to warm up with some coaxing from Roger. John and Chuck stood back, while Manny and I were on each side of the group. Some of the people had problems remembering the words.

"Sing so the neighbors can hear you. They know what's happening here. You can give them some satisfaction that no bad deed goes unpunished," I warned them. Roger led the chorus with the first stanza.

The first chorus was horrendous. A few singers chuckled at what was going on. They got the message and were relieved, I suppose, that this comical bullshit would get them out of jail. The rest mumbled and shuffled their feet anxious to be out of there. Roger told them to bring up the volume and line up in a chorus. The second attempt elicited more participation. Several of the voices rose above the others in resigned acknowledgment.

On the third chorus, the singers were in some version of harmony and everybody sang. Black, Hispanic and white, male and female, young and old, all performed in crooked harmony. A couple even got into rhythm and blew out their pipes. Roger finally led them through the last chorus with something just about as close to gusto as a nervous junkie can get. With the last lines the five of us bowed and thanked the singers.

Distant applause and shouts rang out and shocked all of us. We did three-hundred-and-sixty-degree turns with our eyes trying to locate the source of the distant ovation. Chuck and I pinpointed the origin of the sounds, an apartment complex behind some houses across the street. Residents erupted in cheers and clapped for our benefit. We even got whistles.

The balconies of the two-story complex faced us from less than one-hundred yards away. All the balconies were filled with people standing under porch lights illuminating their faces. All black and Hispanic faces, they cheered for us. They were in on the joke. I knew the people around this, and other dope houses wanted justice. They hated the daily invasions of dealers and drug buyers. The police could never stop them all. For so many of the locals it felt like justice was selective and favored other neighborhoods. Many of the folks in the Heights thought they got singled out for a different kind of justice, or "just us" as our targets. WECAN never subscribed to racial typecasting and let the people around know we had other ways of doing things.

We speculated they knew about the house and wished the police would do something. We had no idea when they caught on and watched our actions nabbing those dirt bags. All we knew was they seemed to love us in that moment. None of the five of us wanted to milk this event and chance ruining a good thing. The always-stoic Chuck smiled and even John got a feeling we'd done something momentarily extraordinary. The feeling was almost a personal thing. The audience got a show in a manner they'd never witnessed before. For the moment, the people on 33rd Street saw that the police who fight against the forces of evil didn't always involve weapons and shouts in anger.

A couple of us waved and Roger did a bow before we went back to our duties. We kicked the junkies loose with warnings not to return. We waved goodbye to the folks on those porches and decided discretion was the better part of valor. We returned to our cars with our four prisoners, some heroin and a great story.

Because those people welcomed our intrusion into that dope house, Manny and I decided to check on the place regularly. If the owner was in control over the drug sales, we'd hamper it. If the dopers thought they could let things blow over and return, we'd reinforce the negative. I'm proud to say we gave those neighbors enough of our attention to return their support. The dope house was boarded up right after our escapade. Months later, the dwelling was reopened and rented to a good family. We stopped to chat with the current residents, a Hispanic family of four. They knew about the lousy reputation of their new home. The father boasted that the seedy history helped keep the rent low. We never had to return to that address for another rendition from the chorus line.

Three weeks later, I opened the local newspaper to a scathing rebuke of the LAPD. The story blasted one of the LAPD's narcotics team. Seems, they'd herded a bunch of junkies together and had them line up for a chorus line. The detectives rehearsed the drug addicts with a show tune and then had them perform sans orchestra. The *a cappella* ensemble performed without a contract and somebody complained. The LAPD being what it was, the department drew lots of attention around all matters of behavior. This act was a song for the books. The cops got the joke. The press did not.

Whoops.

CHAPTER 34:

EGGS AND NO BACON

John and Chuck were gifted with the kind of gab that could pry information out of the most tight-lipped street prostitute. Their next dope house tip required a team-up. They got a hold of Manny and me because four meat-eaters can tear up a dope house quicker and safer than two.

A B-girl gave the partners an address on 28th Street not far from Market Street in the Heights. Stop me if you've heard this one before. Two Mexican nationals were holed up in a sparsely furnished, single-family home and dealt drugs through a window on the side of the house. The place was a poorly kept rental in need of an owner other than a cartel, prison gang or blind landlord.

The four of us took a trip to the location, scoped it out from a distance and then parked our cars out of the line-of-sight of the target. The daylight was dying, and the cars would disappear into the inky evening. I took the lead and knocked on the front door, while the others flanked the house for runners, tossed contraband or worse, an attack from inside. The two men inside were workers formerly of the agrarian region of Jalisco, Mexico. Neither man looked like a farmer.

We ran our routine, with the stone-faced residents looking on, but the place turned out to be a disappointment. We got zilch, zero, bupkus for our efforts. The four of us found nothing. We came up empty-handed. About the only items there in abundance were chicken eggs. Specifically, a couple of trays of eggs for someone's meal. I thought it odd that they had pallets of eggs. Unfortunately, the eggs were the only objects of any value. The two nationals had the rolled-up twenties so often indicative of dope dealing. They were obviously there illegally and up to no good, but we preferred to solidify detentions with at the least a modicum of evidence or guilt. We'd wasted too much time and had some solid gang prospects down in Chicano Park that needed attention. We decided to leave things be and head out.

Manny and I walked out the front door ahead of John and Chuck. The night was young, and the surrounding neighborhood was relatively still. Only a few people were about. As we stepped off the curb an egg sailed through the air and hit our patrol car, followed by another egg. Manny looked up in the air as I swung around to see the two human chickens launching eggs from inside the house. John and Chuck each had an egg in both hands and wound up to chuck the yoke bombs at us again.

I yelled, "What the fuck are you guys doing?" as Manny turned to shout back at them to stop. Those guys laughed at their merry pranks and hurled another round of bio-bombs at our car.

John was laughing when he chucked another egg, in our direction and shouted, "Look Out!" I had to sidestep to avoid a sure hit.

"Fuck you, John!" I hammered back.

An incensed Manny demanded, "What's up Bro?"

John shouted, "We're throwing a going away party for Manny!" I got the joke with the play on words. One egg sailed dangerously close to the dapper Manny. He danced a couple of steps to avoid the splatter. The next egg was clearly thrown at me. I moved like a serpent and avoided the missile by a couple of feet. Those guys had a full pallet of eggs and meant business.

"Almost gotcha!" John was content to toss some near misses to mess with us. Chuck's wry laughter followed another shot at our car. Splat! Right on the rear window. Now the car looked like it had been under a nest of seagulls.

Manny had a bitter grin and shook his head. His eyes said, "I'm going to murder those guys."

We waited for them to knock it off. I said something about getting even, but neither Chuck nor John believed I had a way to one-up them. Silly men.

Sometimes, you just need to up the ante in a way that explodes with the most shock value. I decided not to wait for another day to get my revenge. I chose now. I walked over to their car, took a quick look around and then unzipped my fly. I let loose a powerful stream of urine and soaked their driver's side door handle. My back was to the attackers, so I didn't see their reactions. When I moved to the passenger side, I saw the shock and dismay, "Hey, that's gross!" John whined.

Simultaneously, we all heard some guy up the street shouting "Hey, that cop's pissing on the cop car!"

I finished my revenge, leaving the door handles soaked. I was already busted by a witness so there was no sense in panicking. I needed a show of force to teach those boys a lesson. The urine upped the ante and put the onus to respond on their shoulders. I highly recommended they didn't consider increasing the stakes. I was already in trouble. There was nothing worse they could do to me that a citizen's complaint wouldn't accomplish. John and Chuck ate their pride and backed down.

My behavior was thoroughly unprofessional, and I knew I'd burn when the inevitable grievance hit my boss's desk. John and Chuck ceased the egg-chucking. They had to wonder what I'd do next, or if I had an off button. But they had a problem. They had no way to get cleanly into the front seats of their car. Chuck solved the problem when he hired a passing homeless man to clean their ride for five dollars. The man didn't balk, five dollars was a lot for a man not used to a bonus for being in the right place at the right time. Neither officer had any rags. The street person didn't hesitate to use the sleeves of his own shirt to clean off the door handles for the two desperate officers.

Manny and I next met up with them at the downtown police department car wash. To this day, Chuck still can't believe I did it. I know. It takes balls to be a cop sometimes! Strangely, I received no civilian complaint. I think the one witness figured out what we were up to and why. He must have reasoned I justly got even for some sleight. At least that's how I viewed it.

Dope-finding can be a tedious ordeal. Nothing is more disappointing than the search for dope, hours of laborious hard work and then no score. We always found the dope. I mean: WE ALWAYS FOUND THE DOPE, or the guns or the money. Rare was the incident that got our hackles up when the dope just wasn't there. Even then, we had tools for the occasion. The ever-ready canine officer with the nose for narcotics.

The day after the egg toss, Roger and I checked out an upstairs apartment in the Stockton portion of the Heights. Manny had taken a couple of days off for a deep-sea fishing excursion. There was only one guy present in the tiny walk-up. We had trouble finding the dope, at first but found lots of cash. Frustrated, we elected to cut our time short and have a canine officer assist us.

The canine officer was called out to meet us with his dog, a highly trained specialty animal. The dog's handler held the lone baggie of dope in front of the dog's nose and let him sniff it. Once he caught the scent, we were sure he'd find the stash we knew was there. The dog took a couple of heavy inhales. He must have really liked what he smelled because he opened his jaws and took the baggie out of his handler's hand. Then he ate it. His perplexed handler had no recourse, but to humbly apologize and figure out how to extricate himself and his partner from this big fuck-up.

I was pissed. The stupid dog ate our evidence. Now, the dog was of no better use to us than a bag-less vacuum cleaner. We all stood in the tiny kitchen and tried to figure out our next move. Roger was as disgusted as I was. We'd already tossed the apartment. What next? The lone occupant was seated on a short sofa with a blank look on his face.

Roger kicked at the gas stove behind me because it blocked his path in the cramped kitchen. That was odd. Why was it out of place? The stove door fell forward, and the top popped up. I reflexively looked at the seemingly decrepit stove, only to see that the hidden spaces under the stovetop were filled with bagged kilograms of marijuana. There was enough dope there to pit the tenant for possession of marijuana with the intent to sell. The newly minted prisoner wore a dejected look. His day was good until a cop trumped a police dog.

The canine duo left the scene with their tails between their legs.

The contact with the public began earlier in the day. That's when officers Roger Barrett and Jamie Newbold, another WE CAN team, walked through the neighborhood south of Lincoln High.

"In the first week, we had a pretty good response," Barrett said of the month-old patrols. "When we first came down here, the park (John F. Kennedy Park) was empty. Now people have barbecues on the weekend and they can walk their dog or whatever."

Roger Barrett and I walking near Lincoln High School In Southeast San Diego. Virtually every cable wire to a residence had been cut by the cable company for pirated connections or non-payment. Accompanying Union-Tribune article.

Guns, drugs and money seized from an address on Martin Street.

The Ford assigned to Woody and I. The car was comfortably large. Plenty of space for prisoners in the back and a trunk to hold more (kidding).

Guns, crack and cash from a crook's apartment on Franklin Avenue.

Bill Woods and I when we were still on the Beach Team together. Our unit was assigned to work car prowls and shoplifters at shopping malls during the Christmas holidays. We were a happy couple and would be again within a year when I transferred into WECAN.

Back in the days where quantities of marijuana bagged for street sales put people in jail. Bill Woods, Ray Beatty and I. WECAN seizures tended to eat up a lot of table space in the work areas outside prisoner control.

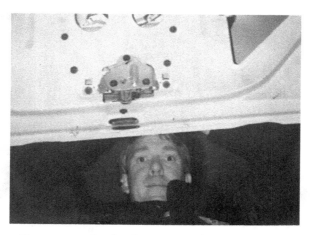

Roger Barrett mugging for the camera. The trunk of our car was comfortable enough to lay in and be a shutter bug. Of course, a mountain of police gear had to be removed so I could climb in.

Manny Rivera and I hamming it up for the camera. The caps were stored in boxes outside the Duty Lieutenant's office for a donation to the Tijuana Police Department. Only the most grizzled patrol veterans still wore this style of hat in the field.

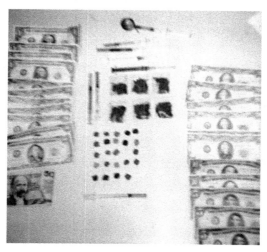

The contents of the pockets of an "International Traveler" from Mexico selling dope at 25th and Imperial Avenue. He'd serve some local time in jail and then get a free ride back to his country courtesy of Border Patrol.

Heroin and cocaine seized from the back half of a duplex in Logan Heights. The parolee would get prison time for the two guns, working or not, for the violations of his parole.

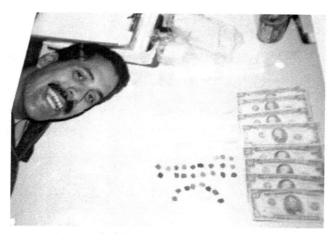

Manny was quite proud of the seized dope. The dealers were two women in an apartment on Broadway. They not only sold "speedballs," but one of the two ladies shot up the combo in her neck several times a day.

The day I nearly scored dope from a guy in a house on Imperial Avenue in full uniform. If only my radio hadn't gone-off. Union-Tribune columnist Neil Morgan was fed the story by our department's Public Information Officer. I woke up to read it in the paper two days later.

HOT DUO: The old movie teaser on Channel 69 was of a close embrace, and the announcer said the co-stars were Henry Fonda and Gene Autry. Bob Tschirgi didn't think that likely, and looked up the movie. Not Gene Autry. Jean Arthur.

DRUG WARS: James Newbold tapped on the high, west window of a known drug house in the 2800 block of Imperial Avenue. "Cheeva," he said, the word for heroin, and held up $20. The man inside was about to take the money; bindles of cocaine were within inches of Newbold's fingertips. Then Newbold's police radio crackled. The dealer slammed the window shut, and Newbold's police partner, Manuel Rivera, waiting at the front door, made the arrest. So what made this deal different? Newbold was in full uniform.

Rosa Cuevas got SED in the newspaper. I'm holding the jar of liquid PCP I found in her bedroom clothes hamper. The newspaper was fed a steady diet of WECAN/SED exploits.

Logan Heights woman arrested after drug raid

Police arrested a 43-year-old Logan Heights woman over the weekend after discovering 30 ounces of liquid PCP during a drug raid.

The illegal substance, used to lace cigarettes, was found during a search Saturday evening of a house in the 3300 block of L Street, said Sgt. Jim Long, of the San Diego Police Department.

Members of the Special Enforcement Detail led the 9:15 p.m. bust. A pit bull terrier that attacked the officers was shot and killed during the raid, Long said.

Nearly $1,000 in cash and several weapons were also confiscated with the PCP, Long said.

Rosa Cuevas, who was in the house during the raid, was arrested and booked at Las Colinas Womens' Detention Center for possession of PCP for sale.

The home of a Crip where we served a search warrant. No dope, but two guns were taken out of the hands of a potential killer.

ANOTHER S.E.D. OFFICER HARD
AT WORK FIGHTING THE
NEVER-ENDING BATTLE AGAINST
NARCOTICS !!

I spent long hours at work and too many days in court virtually every week for three years. I was tired the day the Desk Sergeant caught me with my eyes shut outside the Duty Lieutenant's office. My work was done as my partner handled our reports. The silly sergeant took the photo to play a prank on me. His intent was to lay his "funny" photo on my chest with his clever inscription. When he returned I wore the same dour expression. He handed me the witty photo and then scrammed.

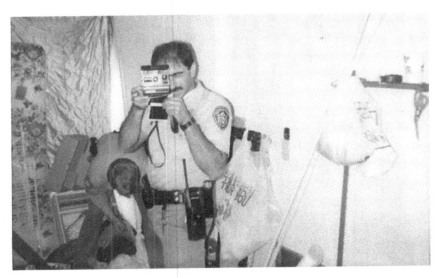

The late John Tangredi and I play dueling cameras as
Roger climbs through the garbage of a dope house search.
Notice the window décor. That's not our doing.

More bags of pot smuggled from across the border.
Logan Heights was a smuggler/dealer's paradise.

Four of us were inside the mobile WECAN office we named Weber One, parked
at 22nd and K Street. I looked out the rear window at the juxtaposition
of Sherman Heights gang tagging and weird local guy staring at us. I got
out and tried to shoo him away. He moved off several feet and then looked
in on the van. This went on for forty-five minutes. I stepped back out of
the van and asked him what was up. "I ain't never seen the po-lice in a
van. If'n you guys aim to stay here I aim to stay put. I figure I'm safer
around you guys and that big white van." I couldn't have agreed more.

Roger and I took a day-trip to California's Salton Sea on our
Honda FourTraxes. We made frequent trips out to the Imperial
Valley desert to escape the daily turmoil at work. The Honda
quad was a lot of fun, but would eventually take a toll on me.

Manny and I at a Christmas fundraiser at the Home Avenue Police pistol range. The local families brought their kids for a night of love and celebration. This photo was pinned up all over the place until I finally rescued it from puncture oblivion.

Roger Barrett, me, and Manny in 2019 at a bar in eastern San Diego County.

Cinda Jauregui and I in 2019 celebrating the memory of "Our Giant," Tim Fay, who passed away a few months earlier.

Manny, me, and Chuck Davis in 2018. All the memories flood back over beer and companionship with my fellow street warriors.

CITY of SAN DIEGO
MEMORANDUM

FILE NO: 445

DATE: August 25, 1989

TO: Cal Krosch, Commander, Field Operations, Zone II

FROM: Jim Sing, Captain, Special Enforcement Division

SUBJECT: SED Unit's First Six Months of Statistics and Combined
              Seizure Effort of SED, and Narcotics Section

On March 3, 1989, the Special Enforcement Division (SED) was formed. This Division is comprised of the Gang Unit, WECAN, SRT and the Tactical Squad, totaling 86 personnel. The formation of this Division is in direct response to the street violence committed by gang members.

The high profile tactics employed by SED has been extremely successful. In the first six months 2,535 arrests have been made. In direct correlation to this high number of arrests, driveby shootings have dropped 39% from 62 in 1988 to 38 for the same time period this year.

The officers of SED have contacted 7,094 people on the streets of San Diego, 3,892 of whom were gang affiliated.

The following is a list of seizures made by the SED Unit in the six month period.

ARRESTS	2,535
VEHICLES	21
CURRENCY	$163,297.47
WEAPONS	
Shotguns	17
Rifles	39
Handguns	92
DRUGS	
Marijuana	111 lbs.
Heroin	29.98 oz.
Cocaine	4429.48 oz.

SED *Memorandum. The captain of* SED, *Jim Sing, sent this memorandum to his commander, Cal Krosch, to apprise him of* SED's *statistics in its first six months of operation. The stats for arrests, seized vehicles (or recovered stolen vehicles), money and drugs reflect the* WECAN *core of officer activity.* SED *looked good on paper, but the memo could just have easily read,* "WECAN *Statistics since* SWAT, *Gangs Unit and Tac bikes joined the unit."*

Eastern WECAN *suits up for another work day in the Wild East. Mo
Parga, Tim Fay, Frank Hoerman, Doug Collier and Cinda Jauregui.
Six-foot, seven-inch Tim was forced to sit to fit into the photo.*

WECAN *is suited up and ready to march in the annual Martin
Luther King Jr. Parade. It figures, the only obscured face in
the photo is mine (rear, far left next to Manny Rivera).*

CHAPTER 35:
STAY IN SHAPE

Manny and I had a few more weeks together in the same car. We knew our time as a duo was short when Manny made the Investigations list. Some cops would be picked off that list quickly while others might languish until the list expired. Manny's standing amongst cops in general and, specifically among narcotics officers guaranteed he'd get an assignment rapidly. The department needed qualified Spanish speakers in every rank and division. Manny's life and skills clicked all the boxes.

He and I drove up 31st Street from Imperial to come up the back way and surprise our old "friends" on 32nd, at least the ones not in custody from our big sweep many months ago. We never made it that far. Manny looked over to his right through the passenger window and saw a tall and lean black man pounding on the ground floor windows of a Victorian two-story house. The guy screamed at the top of his lungs, but I couldn't make out what he said. Manny could. The man, dressed in dark clothing, with a blue "do-rag" over his scalp, was yelling something about his dope. Here we go, I thought. We get a two a two for one, a druggie and a Crip for the price of one stop.

I pulled to the curb half expecting the guy to bolt, but he didn't. He kicked the wall of the house in a frightful rage until he refocused on our marked unit and the two of us in uniforms with business written all over our faces.

No one in the house had reacted to the pounding. Nobody was at the windows peering out with concern. No one stepped out onto the porch to thank the police for magically appearing in their moment of need. The place was a tomb, with barred windows and doors. The suspected Crip shut his vehemence down when Manny spoke in his cop voice "Stop! What's happening here, Bro?" The guy looked over his shoulder at him as I approached from the flank.

"Fuck these guys and fuck you!" The man wasn't fazed by two cops cramping his attack on a perfectly peaceful home. With no more preamble, the man bolted.

I was a decent long-distance runner in high school. I was a three-year member of the cross-country team and in tip top condition. In my senior year, I broke the five-minute mile with a time of four fifty-eight. Seven years later, and a few dozen pounds heavier, I managed a five-thirty-one mile in the police academy. All that endurance was gone now. I'd chosen weight-training over running for my daily workouts. If I'd had more time in the week, I might have attempted both, but WECAN and family made that more a chore than a habit. When the guy ran, I jack-rabbited after him with only a glimmer of hope of a successful capture.

I had no chance and didn't even know what the pursuit was all about. All I had for probable cause was a perturbed guy and a beaten house. I sped after him anyway with all the gear on my belt and the not so light-weight Kevlar vest. The rabbit had a lead that widened as he raced to an alley entrance in a bid to lose me. I was thirty feet behind him and slowing. I felt like I was encased in concrete and my boots turned to irons weights, but I kept him in sight. I had no idea what Manny was doing.

Chase Party One kicked up dust in the soil of the never-paved alley. Chase Party Two, me, had the energy, but too much inertia. He looked back and saw the distance between us increase. The sudden roar of an LTD engine fast approaching motivated Chase Party One to run even faster.

Manny was behind the wheel and right on us. Chase Party Two made a tactical decision to hop a wooden six-foot fence into someone's back-yard. Before Manny could speed past me to drive around the block, I heard the ferocity of an attacking, large and angry dog from the yard on the other side of that fence. There was nothing festive when dog met fence-climber. Chase Party One hauled his butt and flailing legs back over the fence to save his life and ended up in my loving arms as Manny jammed the car in reverse and braked to a dusty stop.

Chase Party One was amped up on pure adrenaline. I manhandled him to the ground as Manny came up from behind and added his body weight. I muscled his right arm from underneath him and wrapped the link of the cuff around his dirty right wrist. "All right, all right. I give up," he said.

He was face down in the dirt when I lifted him to his knees, then to his feet. I breathed in and out deeply as I tried to find purchase on some air. Manny asked the guy, "What the fuck was all that about?" Manny wasn't drained and could hold a conversation.

"That dog nearly killed me. That's what's up!"

"No, I'm talking about you and that house. Why'd you make us chase you?"

He looked down at his feet and checked out his soiled shoes. "Man, I just got these kicks. Now they're all fucked up."

"I asked you a question. What was that all about?"

Streetwise and none too intimidated by the cops, Willy, as he called himself, said, "What are you charging me with?" His bravado was on the rise. He knew we had nothing on him.

I stepped in and apprised him of his predicament, "We're going back to that house and talk to whoever lives there. Maybe they have something to tell us."

"They ain't sayin' shit, officer," Willy answered. "They be dope dealers who ripped me off and that's all I'm going to say." So, the truth came out. Willy, now known to be Willy Perndergast, had a small-time warrant for his arrest. Manny put him in the car and then we had a brief pow-wow over this revelation.

We drove back the way we came and parked Willy on the 31st Street side of the corner lot. I stayed near the car and angled my position so I could cover two sides of the house including the front door. Manny traipsed on over the dirt front yard and examined the porch to the front door. I walked a little off point and tried to peer inside the windows on the west side. There were blankets tacked up on the inside covering the windows. I stepped a few feet to the right to look down the narrow stretch of land between the old building and a chain link fence. I could hear the pissed off Willy in the back of our car. I marched back to my first position and mad-dogged Willy into silence.

Manny stepped up onto the porch and tapped on the door to see if he'd get a response. No surprise, nobody acknowledged. This was a dope house, for sure. Willy didn't lose his mind over the place because he was nuts. He was heated because he felt he had a valid reason to be so. Manny returned to our car. "Let's pit him for the warrant and bring the boys with us to check this place out tomorrow," he recommended. I agreed.

Willy would go to jail for a jaywalking warrant. I loved those piddly laws. We got a big favor from the cop who wrote Willy up for that pedestrian violation. I bet the officer that cited him had experienced Willy's hostile attitude, I'm sure that officer just wanted to get past this clown with a little bit of justice in the rearview mirror. He'd get incarcerated, but probably for one lousy night.

I met the crew for line-up the next afternoon. We were privy to Central Patrol's briefs and read the same notices they did. Otherwise, we'd never have learned of the homicide on 31st Street earlier in the morning. Homicide detectives were still on the scene of a bled out dead man. The name was the shocker, but murder in the Heights was a necessity to keep the drug biz operational. Willy Pendergast had taken a round to the chest, allegedly from the occupant of a Victorian house. Yeah, that house. A lone witness had heard a commotion across the street from her home. She knew better than to step outside, and watched Willy try to force his way into the house through the front door. The witness heard his shouts and threats. She did not hear any matched response before she heard the bang of a gunshot. I had no doubt she knew what a gun sounded like. The Heights can sound like a pistol range on any given violent day. She watched Willy stumble backward. He stumbled to the street and collapsed. Two Latino men ran out the same door and fled in two directions.

Homicide stood outside while they waited for a search warrant. Whatever the Mexicans didn't take when they split, would soon be in the in the hands and evidence envelopes of Homicide. Central WECAN would prowl and growl another day.

CHAPTER 36:

ATTEMPT CRIMES

One tip after another led to new places to explore. Manny, Roger and I made our own inroads into CI development. John and Chuck had dedicated more time to the development of those two-legged resources than the three of us. The connections were easier to make than a lay person would imagine. The Heights were filled with dealers. Therefore, the Heights were filled with addicts and snitches. The addicts had little in the way of scruples, especially when they were dope sick and needed a fix to stave off withdrawals. This time, Manny and I scored some news from a street urchin about a hopping place near the border of Central Division and Southeastern Division.

The snitch was a twenty-year old African American woman who'd bound herself to crack's grip. We saw her troll down 32nd Street for johns and decided she might be worth talking to for some information. Jennifer, as she called herself, bore no identification, and was sober and lucid when we rolled up behind her. She knew the routine and stopped to face us. There was no outward hostility and we didn't intend to intimidate her. "What's your name, ma'am?" I asked in the least threatening tone I possessed.

"Jennifer, officer."

"I'm gonna cut to the chase, Jennifer. We're looking for any dope houses you might be willing to give up to us. Are you interested?"

"What do you mean, officer? I don't know anything like that." Her feigned innocence was a stall tactic that we all knew wouldn't play. She wore large sunglasses and I asked her to lift them. I would best describe her humanity under heavy and cheap make-up as worn and tired. She might have been twenty, but she had fifty-year-old eyes. The creased skin surrounded deeply sunken eyeballs that rarely ever closed in precious sleep for more than a couple of hours at a stretch.

"You can drop the glasses down, Jennifer. Is it heroin or crack?" I asked.

She paused long enough to register that we were only there for one thing. I kept the conversation business-like and waited for her to drop her pretense of innocence. She probably figured she'd be looking at jail, depending on her answer. "I hit the pipe," she answered in a much more subdued voice. "Are you going to arrest me?"

"Not today. I'd appreciate you answering my earlier question instead of trying to dodge it." She knew what I meant. There'd be no more games.

"There's a place down off this street but after Oceanview. I think some cops hit it before, but it's up again."

"What are they slinging? Is it crack, or *chiva*?"

"It's *chiva* and a little coke. You're not gonna say anything about me telling you, are you?"

"No. We don't burn our sources and nothing about you goes on paper. Ask the other girls on the track and they'll verify it. Is there anything else about the place we need to know?"

"It's always two Mexicans selling the stuff through a hole in a boarded-up window. I sometimes get high from there. I used to be a junkie, but I'm not like that anymore. The H helps me come down from crack when I get strung-out. I mean, you know how it is right? I hate those motherfuckers anyway. They're always ripping me off. I went to buy a twenty-five-dollar bag, gave them a fifty, and all I got back was a twenty. Them fuckers never give me back my change. If you get them, I wish you'd fuck them up good."

"Sister, you're a mess. You look like you need to move along to another part of town," Manny stated flatly. "If the drugs don't get you, one of those Mexicans probably will." She nodded in comprehension and asked if we were done. Manny told her she could go.

Jennifer's directions brought us to a small house at the corner of Durant and South Payne Streets. She'd said the place was active, but we had no proof. If it was true, then a quick drive-by of the building would allow us to see the sales portal plain as day. The little dope places were always locked up tight, windows too. Sometimes, a hole was cut into the steel door's screen. Sometimes the windows were barred, and business was done through there. Mostly it was broken windows, their thought being they'd only expose one hand through the window. Dopers who dared to reach in without the dealer's consent could be stabbed or shot for. The dope houses were places of evil and the occupants were expected to drive off infiltrators, killing them if necessary. Each place WECAN inspected seemed to carry the same genes as the last one. The template always consisted of the usual arrangement: dual Mexican aliens, minimal furniture, barred windows, and little food except for a few take-out containers, and drugs hidden somewhere. This time, we'd put a theoretical experiment into action.

The California law codes assigned various law descriptions to criminal acts, 187 was the penal code for homicide, 5150 of the Welfare and Institutions Code covered mental cases, and so on. For our purposes, we dealt a lot with 11350 of the Health and Safety Code for possession of controlled substances, 11550 H&S for being under the influence of a controlled substance and 11352 H&S for sales of controlled substances. There was a range of drug charges all built into the health and safety enforcement platform. The three H&S codes above governed heroin and cocaine. Our jobs were to target gang members and drug dealers moving these drugs and get them identified, then stopped, then arrested if possible. To achieve these goals, we really needed to be free of other police duties and to use our imaginations.

During the planning for the operation on Durant Street we debated an idea I'd mulled over after we'd hit the last house. In theory, each time a doper puts his or her hand through the opening into a dope house, he or she does it to buy dope. The dope we encountered was all felony drugs. So, the buyer was entering a building to commit a felony crime.

459 PC, Burglary, is defined as entering a dwelling with the intent to commit a theft or a felony crime. Therefore, the junkie who stuck his hand through the hole in the window is a burglar. On top of that, when our seller handed back fake dope, we could additionally charge the suspect with 664 PC/11350 H&S, attempting to possess a controlled substance! We all thought it was clever using 664 PC because it was designed to charge a person with attempting to commit a crime.

There were no guarantees San Diego's prosecutors would relish this literal interpretation of a couple of laws mashed together. We knew it was a stretch. We stuck with the old saw, "Beg for forgiveness, rather than ask permission." Maybe we'd get an Issuing D.A. who would bite on the novelty. Hey, WECAN cops were encouraged to use our imaginations. Sally forth, I say!

We hid the police cars out of view of the Durant Street home, although there was no such thing as hiding anything police related around this set of blocks. The locals had the most sensitive mental cop radar in town. Infestations of gangs, their anti-police families and friends, and the drug dealers completely saturated this neighborhood. When police cars slowed down on any street in this part of town, the street-watchers hopped into holes and their heads and ears popped up like prairie dogs. Everyone was alerted to our presence. Whistles, phone calls, pagers and runners were quickly mobilized to protect their own. However, they were not that tricky to sneak up on. All their security ended at the walls of the building. They were like forts with no posted sentry.

The local, concerned residents rarely burned us to the dopers. They had no connections to these pop-up dope storefronts and even welcomed the infringement by police to bust "those scumbag drug dealers." Getting to the Durant house unnoticed was a piece of cake.

The five of us in full uniform surrounded the house to reduce the kinds of surprises that could get us killed. The information we had matched every other drug house, a couple of Mexicans sold heroin through a bedroom window. Before Manny performed the knock-and-talk, we identified one back door exit and the barred bedroom window partially open to pass money and dope back and forth. These affairs may have seemed boiler-plated, but WECAN teams never compromised our safety and nothing tragic had befallen us, yet.

The illegal occupants behaved sedately as hoped. Three officers went inside to set up and sell bunk dope while two of us remained outside to catch the culprits "burglarizing" the home.

Manny prepared his disguise to work the dope threshold. He turned his black SDPD windbreaker inside out to reveal a quilted, non-police looking liner. The people who approached the house to buy dope would not make him as a cop. John and Chuck were inside as prisoner control and cover. Roger and I were outside on either side of the house.

Before I could even settle into my hiding place, some guy approached the window. We weren't ready so I walked back to the side of the house to detain the probable dope buyer. The guy, a young Hispanic man, saw me and veered quickly to his right. There was a trail up an embankment that led to the homes and street above. The trail was a little steep and wound around the hillside a bit. My target sped up to get ahead of me for the uphill trot. I rushed up behind him just as his right hand dipped into a jacket pocket. The sudden movement was enough for me to drop him where he stood with a body tackle on the narrow trail. He hit the ground belly first, me on top of him as I grabbed at his right hand. The guy wasn't particularly strong. I had him pinned so he couldn't maneuver his arms. I had a tight grip on his forearm and held him flat to the ground while I extracted his right hand that held a gun.

Things can go to hell just that fast. My cover officers weren't even aware of my absence because this grab happened so fast. One minute I was there, the next, I was not.

My suspect was pressed facedown into the dirt where the treads of countless dirty shoes had trodden. He spat out dirt and gamely tried thrashing about to dislodge me. I pushed back with greater force and yelled at him in English and pidgin Spanish in the hope he'd just give up. When I threatened to shoot him, he looked back over his shoulder and saw my hand on my holstered gun and knew he wasn't going to win this battle. He stretched his empty right hand out along the path without his gun. I pulled out my handcuffs and hurriedly bound him behind his back. The gun, a small .25 caliber semi-automatic, was pinned under him, part-way exposed out of his coat. He really tried to put it into play. I picked it up and tucked it into my back pocket. I wrenched the guy to his feet and marched him back down the trail.

Roger met me at the bottom of the hill, "What happened. Who's this guy?"

I displayed the little gun. His eyes grew a little wider when I told him the story. I nudged the prisoner ahead to get all of us out of sight. I had a chance to examine the gun and found the safety off and the weapon fully loaded with a bullet in the chamber. There wasn't one gun-operation step left for the suspect to kill me if he'd had the chance.

This would be the first of several detentions of this Durant operation. The others would be snatched one at a time as they put their hands through the barred window and into the house to hand in the money. Manny made sure they reached across the windowsill to fulfill the 459-component based on entry. After that, they got knotted toy balloons filled with absolutely nothing, followed by handcuffs and a seat on the floor with John and Chuck keeping watch.

We knew this kind of operation could go on all day. We had obligations to work other bad guys, the street gangs foremost. We made a small number of arrests to test our 459 plan and took everyone with us, including the undocumented Mexican men and my armed guy and ran the whole circus to HQ.

I thought we were clever about our sage comprehension of the law. The indoctrination of this new legal instrument seemed like a game changer. We even had a surprise meeting with one of the Assistant Chiefs, Mike Rice, who dropped in on our line-up a day later thanks to an invite from our sergeant, Chuck Sleeper. Sergeant Sleeper was one of several sergeants who walked in the door one day as our sergeant and then out the same door months later to be replaced by, of all people, me. I had a couple of stints as the acting head of our unit.

Sgt. Sleeper had boasted about the burglary arrest test to the Chief when he braced him in the hallways of HQ. The Chief was probably being polite when this curious three-striper urged him with a "tug on his sleeve" to sit in on line-up. None of us knew Chief Rice personally and were a little uncomfortable in his presence. After all, the big bosses rarely came down to our floor to go one-on-one with the troops.

The Chief was in our leadership chain and really wanted to know where the increases in drug and gang arrest stats came from. Sleeper loved to pump up his elite squad's reputation. He'd bumped into the Chief minutes before and talked his ear off about us all the way to line-up.

The Central guys were the only men in the room. Since it was a Sunday, the *two who were never there* were on days off. Those glory hogs would miss out on some Chief time. The afternoon was rare when they did show up at our line-up. The convenience of being in the same building as the Chief was the initiator. The other two WECAN teams had even fewer chances of seeing any chiefs at their substation locations. We spoke about the achievements of all WECAN teams but took credit for our own innovations. We knew we pushed the limits of the law and were not sure how that knowledge would be received by the next to the top person in our command chain.

In our business, cops were used to management telling us not to do things that could cause trouble. We're apprised of the risks of civil litigation and the press who misconstrue our actions to make cops look bad. We were all jaded by lectures on behavior and told not to rock the boat. So, it came as a pleasant surprise when Chief Rice dropped his game face and commended us for our motivation to take chances and push the envelope. He confided that, if we got into trouble doing the right thing, he would not only respect us, but do his best to protect us. The Chief was from a different time in history. He commiserated about his days in the field when he and his coworkers were willing to take risks to get the job done. He'd already lamented the passage of those times with the SDPD.

Our fledgling 459 PC, 664PC/11350 H&S case first had to pass through the investigators at Central Division. WECAN did not have its own detectives. All our paperwork went to the area command we worked within at any given moment. The investigator's jobs were to prepare a formal report to validate the law and facts within our cases. The follow-up reports went up the chain to for review by either the City Attorney's Office for misdemeanors, or the District Attorney's Office for felonies.

When WECAN first began, some area detectives were none too keen about the increased paperwork. I'm sure some were angry when WECAN maxed out at thirty-six members. We heard occasional complaints, mostly indirectly, from some detectives. One Central Division detective, Det. Chub, was more vocal than the others. We heard his complaints through the grapevine. He thought our arrests were bullshit. We generated too many arrests. Why couldn't we process our own paperwork? Blah, blah, blah. Whatever the previous daily arrest statistics were at

Central, Southeastern and Eastern Division, we probably doubled them. Regardless, our command decreed something like, WECAN Shall Go Forth Unhindered by Area Commands and Do God's Work.

A lot of our reports were funneled through the area commands with little review or oversight. So, our Burglary charge experiment ended up directly in the hands of the deputy district attorney assigned to review our reports. His response was the dreaded CRE, or Complaint Request Evaluation.

Normally, a rejected case from up high required some simple additions and a retool job to make the case doable. On rare occasions, the cold-hearted DDA told us we'd brought in a fouled-up case and it was doomed to disappear. Not with our case. We reached the pinnacle of audacity and got back a blood boiling CRE from a pissed off attorney. In no uncertain words, he admonished with, "We have enough laws on the books to keep us busy. We do not need any new laws from you officers."

Somewhere in the body of the CRE were exclamation marks to really drill home the disdain this attorney had for us. The CRE was passed around our unit and ended up as story time with the other WECAN units. The 459 was a no-go for the future. The DDA relaxed a bit after that intrusion. We never saw another CRE and WECAN continued to haunt gangsters and drug dealers alike.

CHAPTER 37:

REACH FOR THE SKY

The five of us caught wind of another illegal alien dope house in the Heights. This one was a granny flat that shared the back half of a property on Clay Street. A primary house was built on the front half of the property. Our informant painted the stereotypical picture, a couple of Hispanic men selling balloons of heroin through a window on the side of the building. Pretty standard stuff.

The best way to approach the house was from the alley through a gate on the east side of the building. We made our approach in the usual way with no demonstrative effort to get where we needed to be. Slow, steady and quiet was the best way to reach a target undetected. Perhaps no one would signal our approach if they didn't know which place was the target. Once we entered the alley, we all saw the seemingly ubiquitous, startled rat race across the alley. Simultaneously, a rough looking alley cat sprinted across in pursuit. I commented on the frequency of rat sightings in the Heights and the volumes of feral cats. Rats and cats, were a metaphor for cops, gangsters and drug dealers, representing the unending struggle for domination between hunters and vermin in the Heights.

We crept forward in broad daylight to the gated destination. John followed Chuck around to the front of the house. Roger remained in the alley so he could peek through the wooden fence and watch the windows on the west side. Manny and I stood on the shaded east side of the house. We could hear John and Chuck knocking on the door while speaking at the same time. Suddenly, Roger saw an arm reach outside a window on his side of the house and made an underhanded toss of a plastic bag onto the roof that was peaked at the center. The object sailed over his side of the crested roof and landed on the opposite side. Unfortunately for the guy we'd later arrest, the roundish bag fell short of the guy's attempt to dispose of it. The bag rolled down my side of the roof and landed on the ground at my feet. Treasure from Heaven. There was a bag full of tiny, knotted balloons of heroin.

Three things happened at once. The WECAN team at the door was speaking to one guy in the doorway. Roger was directed to stay put because we had exigent circumstances to hit the house without a warrant. Manny and I ran to the front and pushed past the first guy to get to the room Roger saw the pitcher throw from. John and Chuck secured the guy we almost knocked over. I reached a bedroom and saw the second occupant still at the window. We handcuffed the guy for the easiest possession of heroin for sales pinch I'd ever made. The entry into the house was completely warrantless and completely legal. All the probable cause for the arrest literally landed at our feet. Perfect search and seizure circumstances were wrapped neatly.

Both residents, and I use residents loosely, were undocumented Mexicans. There was a third guy in the house, a black man with a long-time heroin habit. His timing was just bad. He was there to cop dope and got caught up in our maelstrom. Roger went around to the front when we gave the all clear signal from the other side of the house. He was tasked with identifying the black guy.

Of course, no self-respecting junkie who thinks he could get out of this dilemma was going to be straight with the police. With no identi-fication on hand, the guy didn't satisfy Roger. Roger handcuffed him for being in the dope house and decided to grill him downtown for his real name. The other officers began the look-see around the rooms for anything of interest. Roger wanted to see the room the dope was pitched from, so I stepped up to watch the prisoners seated in the living room. The two Mexicans sat on a couch, while the black guy sat on the arm of a chair next to the front door.

I made one little mistake next and never heard the end of it. My part-ners scoured the house until John let out an exclamation of success when they found some drug money. I turned away from the man seated on the arm of the chair and stepped over a few feet to see what they'd found. The handcuffed man near the door took advantage of my inattention and launched out the doorway. I looked back and saw emptiness where a man once sat. I yelled for help and ran out the door after him.

I caught a wisp of the guy as he bolted for the alley behind the house. By the time I cleared the gate he'd already reached the alley's east end. Roger was now behind me in this frantic chase, desperate to get his handcuffs back. I caught another flash of my quarry as I reached the cross street and he headed to the right, down another street. The guy boogied faster than I could move and with his hands still cuffed behind his back. All my gear made me race like I was jetting through a pool of Jell-O. By the time Roger and I made the same turn the escapee did, he was already gone. Roger and I stopped to catch our breath. The guy disappeared between the houses. There was nobody on the street, no witness to surreptitiously point the way for us. Our quarry was gone and so were Roger's handcuffs.

Roger was pissed at me. I'd have to make up for the loss of those handcuffs down the road. I only took my eyes off the guy for a second. Things happened fast in the Heights. If there's any upside, it came about three weeks later when we were subpoenaed for court. A prelim hearing was held for the arrest we made of the guy who chucked the dope over the roof. The evidence would be tested for one charge of possession of a controlled substance for sale. Roger and I were the ones who nailed the seller for the prosecution when we testified at the hearing.

We'd both done that courtroom dance hundreds of times. I calculated my three years in WECAN resulted in over four hundred subpoenas. Of those, roughly one-third copped pleas before the hearings. The rest went to preliminary hearings. Everyone arrested was bound over for trial. Of the cases headed to trial, all but four took plea bargains. Of the four that remained, two went to appeals. Of those two, I lost one. The other three were subsequently scheduled for trial. I never had to face them in a courtroom: The defendants pled out right before the trials selected juries.

I mentioned earlier about the success rate of prosecutions for the arrests I was involved with on WECAN. Out of all the city attorney and district attorney cases there was only one that got away from me.

The event began with a familiar formula. Snitch plus WECAN equaled finding a dope house. This address was in Sherman Heights off Broadway, not far from an apartment where I caught a woman for being on heroin. She was the first person I'd met that actually shot up in her neck. The tiny puncture wounds and ugly track marks over her jugular vein made her look like one of Dracula's mistresses. Scarier still, she lived with her sister and her own three-year-old daughter. She bought a respite from prosecution when she "dimed" off the roadway address as her supplier. We left the child with her sister in their home. The sister was clean, and it was her place. I preferred the risk of family over the trauma of separation and a sad trip to a county placement way station for the three-year-old.

Roger and I were on this assignment. We didn't ask for help and Manny wasn't available. We walked into an old 1940s apartment courtyard and studied the perimeter of the target apartment. The ground floor pad was tiny and shared a wall with another place. Entry could only be made through a front door into a living room studio or the back door that entered a bathroom, which I thought was an odd arrangement. This antique bachelor pad had a kitchen built into the studio which doubled as the bedroom. The bathroom connected to the kitchen, on the other side of a privacy door. The abbreviated living space had all the comforts of an ensign's quarters on a battleship.

Roger took position at the front door. I stood beside the back door-bathroom exit to seal the trap. On my go, Roger knocked on the door. I tried to peer into the bathroom window which had a clear, curtain-free view of the toilet. As predicted, I saw a head quickly enter the bathroom to flee from the cop at the front door. I figured he must have spied Roger through the peephole. I couldn't see the man below the neck. Conveniently, there was a large cement block near the flowerbed below the window. I lifted the block up and dropped it in the turf below the window. I stepped up onto the big brick and gained a full view of the suspect. That's when I saw the toilet for the first time as he dumped a handful of heroin balloons into the bowl. I stepped down, turned the corner of the apartment, a mere three footsteps away, and kicked in the flimsy bathroom door. The force of strike hit the suspect with such a blow that he got knocked backward and lost his grip on the toilet handle.

I rushed inside as Roger heard all the commotion and hurried to me. The suspect's stash floated in the bowl and he was forced back through the privacy door into his kitchen. "Roger, I got this guy. Get the dope outta the toilet." We would not lose the evidence to a lucky flush.

My guy was scared and stunned into submission by the shock of the two troops that were on the march. Roger rescued the dope, about thirty multi-colored balloons. My prisoner let me handcuff him without any complaint. We had him and his dope under the legal doctrine of exigent circumstances and that was that.

The preliminary hearing was two weeks later. The judge listened to both sides and bound the case over for trial. Normally, the trial would be in a month, maybe two. The history of WECAN arrests of this nature usually resulted in some plea arrangement between both sides. The suspect would cop to a charge and take his licks. Very business as usual stuff for me. So, when the unexpected subpoena issued by the defense attorney ordered me into court prematurely for an appeal, I was taken aback.

I'd never been a party to a court appeal in all my years on the job before this court order. Apparently, the defense exposed a weakness in my case.

Roger and I appeared in the Appellate Division of the District Attorney's Office and met the woman who would fight for our case. The Assistant D.A. sat in her office with us and went over the arrest report very business-like. She examined the defense attorney's appeal which highlighted the argument. The block I'd stood on was the crux of the matter.

The various rules of search and seizure in California have been stated, argued and re-stated that police officers can enter dwellings without warrants if they see a criminal act where destruction of pertinent evidence is imminent. The balloons seconds away from being flushed produced the warrantless emergency. The D.A. pointed out that if I'd been able to stand in that stretch of soil and peer down through the window, without standing on the block, I'd have been okay. The problem was, I wasn't six inches taller and the block was an enhancement not allowed by law.

The appeal took place in court an hour later. The defense planted the seed in the rebuttal and the judge mulled over the complaint. I was honestly surprised that the block was an issue. I know I'd been in similar situations with other arrests going back to my patrol days. This dilemma had never cropped up. Either the rule was missed by attorneys or the rules were arbitrary. If previous defense attorneys hadn't noticed or cared, the prosecutions didn't bother to highlight any case weaknesses.

The judge was impartial. He called the case as he saw it after the weight of the defense attorney's presentation was weighed. That stupid block was firmly planted on my chest and I couldn't escape its load. The case was dropped.

The prosecutor felt for me. Roger was just plain pissed off at the defense, the judge and the whole rotten, patchwork system. "The rules are made to be broken by both sides," he spat out. His vehemence struck a chord because the law is sometimes grey, not always black and white.

We went back to the prosecutor's office where she shared some after thoughts. Roger and I flew some scenarios past her about other searches. "What about the cops in the air that spot a marijuana grow and get a warrant?"

"The air is common space, and anyone can have the right to be there. The grower is not protected and should have covered the plants," replied the experienced attorney. "If a guy is committing a crime in his house and an officer uses a ladder in the neighbor's yard to see through the windows, the police have a case. That's assuming the officers had a right to be on that neighbor's property. Even an empty lot that's open to anyone is valid grounds to spy on the criminals. Your problem, Officer, was the dirt flower bed you stood in was private property to that resident. You created a vantage point that didn't exist before. If you stood on the block in the common walkway where you found it and saw what you saw, you should have been okay."

"So, my height and the lack of a stool were the elements that worked against me," I said rhetorically. Roger didn't bother to sit out of disgust with the law at that moment. He'd get out of the office and head back home to cowboy country where things made more sense to him.

"It's all about where you have a right to be without enhancements on private property if you don't have the warrant. I know it's a grey area and these are the kinds of cases my division handled. We argue for and the other side argues against. Believe it or not, I've won similar cases in Appellate court and seen them go all the way to trial. You lost this one, but you could win the next one," the prosecutor said.

Arbitrary, like I said.

CHAPTER 38:

COURT

I took court seriously. Right versus wrong and good versus evil played out there like a stage play. Easy prosecutions make for easy testimony and less stress. The drug cases WECAN constructed rarely failed a victory. We were all good at what we did. On the other hand, court took us all away from our families and our free time on a too frequent basis. Our unit was forever seated in the hallways of justice awaiting our turns to testify. We made a lot of money in overtime but struggled to find quality family time. I saw my wife and son only in the evenings a few days of the week, and rarely on weekends. So, court became its own social life.

Officers like me and my friends wasted hours seated on low wooden benches in the hallways of San Diego's Municipal Court biding our time and people-watching for amusement. We'd crack each other up with snappy comments and observations on the various flotsam and jetsam of humanity that flowed through the hallways. Perhaps an attractive attorney would shimmy by and we'd all adopt shit-eating grins. Another attorney might slide by with a Cheshire grin or a scowl like they'd entered a gauntlet. One defense lawyer walked by dressed in the most garish of outfits. We thought he'd repurposed the seat fabric of a 1957 Chevy for his courtroom attire. Every time we saw him in a suit it appeared to be from another vintage automobile. Secretaries, defendants, witnesses, gawkers, families, crooks yet to be arrested and the rest of humanity paraded past bored cops.

I brought books to read, as did other officers. We had to keep our voices in check when the nearby courts were in session. But the ebb and flow of people was a constant circus. The halls were filled with people until all the cases were assigned to courtrooms by the presiding judge. The hallway crush thinned out a bit then. We might have seen a sudden burst of activity when jurors were called upstairs for an assigned court room. Then, quiet again. I spent years and hundreds of hours in those hallways and felt the pulse of the criminal justice system's mundane reality.

WECAN cops spent so much time in court that we made acquaintances, even friends with attorneys on both sides of the aisle. We peaked behind the proverbial curtain with lawyers on all sides of the law. Lawyers were rough on witnesses, victims and the cops who supported them. But the attorneys were also rough on each other and loved to gossip. I could be alone in one of the halls for a few moments and then just as easily be around the attorneys after a court case just to shoot the breeze. I knew which lawyer slept with which lawyer, who was cheating on whom, and which one was on a short leash with which judge over some courtroom behavior.

Some of the prosecutors ingratiated themselves with WECAN cops and gossiped about our SDPD peers. They'd warn us about who was in trouble with judges, who was a shit to work with or who faced censure from the court over bad behavior in the line of duty. We were rarely privy to that kind of juicy talk through our normal channels. We even gleaned sensitive information about a cop or two, caught flat-footed on the witness stand lying before the court. This kind of mistake went straight to our department brass.

Court was no picnic when cops were raked over the coals for hours by the defense. The pressure was worse if there were no independent witnesses or corroborating evidence. The defense only had the cop's word, so the cop became the real target. Attorneys would spend hours to tear open a cop's testimony and make him or her squirm until darkness began to seep through cracks in the officer's rosy statements.

Court preparation couldn't be emphasized strongly enough. Officers could forget facts in the interim between arrest and court. A light refresher of the police report could save a police officer on the stand at a preliminary hearing or a trial. You had to be as good or better than your opponent as he or she faced you down for hours trying to rend your case to shreds.

Roger and I were partners on a case that ended up in court. The caper involved two Hispanic men from Mexico we arrested for drug sales. We were subpoenaed for morning court for the first hearing on the case. I started my morning at the police station getting a copy of the police report and a photo of the two suspects. Court was going to ask if I could identify the two men, so I was to say, "I can."

Roger didn't make it downtown in time. He didn't get a chance to refresh his memory about which guy was which. He caught up to me inside the courtroom with no time to go over the police report and the photos I carried with me. Ordinarily, court would be held in one of twenty-plus Municipal Court rooms, modest-sized rooms with small audiences, especially for preliminary hearings. On this day, all the rooms were busy with cases. Our case was going to be heard in Presiding, the much larger room normally busy sending out cases to the other Muni courtrooms.

We did it all there in front of a large audience. My partner and I sat to one side before the case was called to order. I stepped through the stubby barroom style doors and slipped into seats on the prosecution side since I wrote the report which made me the case officer. Roger sat in the gallery with the general audience. The defense attorneys entered as the defendants were escorted in by Sheriffs from a prisoner area behind the court. Both defendants sat interspersed between the two defense attorneys. Proceedings began when the judge called everyone to order. After attorney introductions, Roger was sworn in. Roger was randomly chosen first, his bad luck of the draw. He left his seat in the gallery and walked through the double doors to take his seat next to the judge. Nice and close to his Honor. The room was open to the public and no call had been made by the defense to exclude other witnesses to this case, including me.

The prosecutor's job was to introduce the officer and then ask some preliminary questions. At a certain point, the prosecutor would ask about the defendants. The very next question came from the prosecutor, "Do you recognize the man, or men in court today?"

The answer would always be, "Yes." When there are two defendants, the officer must be able to identify who is who. My partner had not looked at the suspects' photos for that needed refresher. Weeks had passed since the suspects' incarceration. Roger looked at the two defendants when asked if he recognized a defendant named by the prosecutor. He mulled it over knowing he had a fifty percent chance of getting the answer right. With trepidation, he pointed at the defendant on the left as the defendant just named. The defense attorney instantly drew a smirk across his face. The two defendants smiled wryly while I sank into my chair. My partner switched names. He'd forgotten which bad guy was which.

The prosecutor wasn't even certain a problem was brewing until the defense attorney gleefully announced that my partner got it wrong. Roger instantly realized his error and that it was too late to walk it back. The audience of about twenty people waiting for other cases woke up when the defense attorney snapped the unexpected trap shut on my ill-prepared buddy. Some of the people in the gallery laughed out loud. I was embarrassed for my partner. I kept my eyes firmly on the action as it played out in front of me. I saw people glance at me. I knew they expected me to provide them with a potentially humiliating second act.

Fortunately, the prosecution was able to stop the case from hemorrhaging. I was quickly sworn in and straightened out the confusion. That kept the case from being torpedoed. My partner's ruddy complexion was now an even darker shade of red. The judge was not amused as evidenced by the glare he gave my brother officer. We got out of there with a modicum of self-respect. The lesson was learned. You had to be prepared all the time.

CHAPTER 39:

HIDING PLACES

There was a house on Kearny Street in Logan Heights facing Freeway 5 that was known for drug sales. The inhabitants all seemed to belong to some *narco* gang we saw at other residences. Nobody ever seemed to live in these places, and nobody spoke English. There were no bills, no paperwork, no mail, and nothing to link anyone inside with any real tenancy. Some of the guys had distinctive facial features more Indian, *nativos mexicanos*, than Hispanic. Many claimed to originate in Southern Mexico.

We'd hit the place on Kearny Street thanks to countless tips, yet we never found a thing. Repetitive searches in the attic, throughout the house, even under the house brought us *nada*. We even bumped into the pair of WECAN officers at that house who worked independently from the rest of the Central Team. They were also unable to find the elusive dope. This was one of the rare moments when we all crossed paths. Those two had a vast record of dope seizures, but mostly from locations the rest of the team didn't approach. I was frustrated. They never shared with us, offered their assistance, or asked to team-up in brotherly fashion. I saw the pair as glory hogs who worked skillfully at forging their destinies first and dogging crime second. I accused them of poaching while standing on the porch of the mystery dope house. I got a cooler head later when I told myself there was certainly enough dope for all the cops to seize in the Heights. We all reached the same frustrating end, though. Where was their secret hiding place?

Like I said, those narcotics dealers were at more than one location. Another was a problem apartment complex at the dead end of 32nd Street just above Freeway 5. We'd see the same *narco* guys loitering around the entrances into specific apartments at that large complex. We tried to nail them there, with the same empty-handed results. If we had cause to go in, we'd still come out with zilch. Even other apartments in that complex ran dope and got caught, just not THESE guys.

The TV news gained permission on a separate occasion to ride with us. Roger had a source provide this specific address. The press lucked out because the first half of our team made the entry and got into a brief brawl with the dealer on the apartment porch. The overconfident drug peddler seated himself on his lawn chair throne with his door open for quick access to his stash. The news cameras got action footage of the takedown as real as the "Cops" TV Show. The dealer had two options, smile for the camera and then give up. Or go ballistic and chuck the pebbles of crack off the second-floor walkway. He chose the first option, a poor decision. The flurry of action was a fog of unbridled activity. One of us collected the crack, pebble by pebble. The others kept residents in check or aided in the arrest. There was something about the brazenness of the dealer that signaled to us this complex was more than met the eye. Within several days, word got to us that a Central cop got into a fight with another dealer in this complex. That man was armed. He and the cop wrestled violently as the bad guy tried to get a proper grip on the officer's weapon and shoot the officer. That officer managed to shoot him first. WECAN was engaged with a target-rich building.

One day, several of us headed to that complex to try our luck one more time. Roger was in the first car, while Manny and I followed in our cruiser. Roger drove up close enough to recognize one guy standing at the foot of a set of stairs that led to an upstairs apartment. He didn't see us until it was too late. Roger braked to a stop and rocketed out of his car. The guy reacted too slowly when he split and charged up the stairs. Roger was right on his heels when he broke the plane of the doorway leading inside and out of Roger's sight.

When Roger reached the landing, he saw the guy through the doorway with a straight view into the bathroom. The runner stood on the bathtub rim as he grabbed at the top of the bathroom door. Roger raced in and pulled him down for a good handcuffing. Charges would be figured out later.

Roger stepped up onto the rim of the tub to see what the guy'd been up to. He looked down at the top frame of the bathroom door. Strangely, the frame corner was loose, like somebody had sawn a cap out of the wood. Roger could see an open space below the cap that was filled with balloons of heroin.

Roger suddenly grasped the pieces of the confusing puzzle as they fell into place. He quickly passed the prisoner to me. Roger didn't say a word and ran downstairs to an identical apartment. He opened the door unannounced and ran right past the Mexican drug suspect seated inside. He hit the bathroom and stood on that bathtub's rim to examine the door and found more heroin. Geez! How pervasive was this hiding technique? The whole complex could be individual drug dens with bathroom doors that had been tampered with.

We only had the two apartments to work with legally, or semi-legally. We slowed everything down and looked at other doors in each of the two targets. Nope. They only monkeyed with the bathroom doors. We recognized two of our prisoners and realized we'd seen them at the Kearny Street residence. One stood out facially with an aquiline nose and Aztec features. Those two wouldn't say a word to us. In the past, they said nothing and kept relaxed demeanors that told us they could withstand our attempts to find their drug stashes. This time, there was a tension in their faces not there in the past.

We took the two prisoners and drove straight back to Kearny Street. Not surprisingly, nobody was home, and the doors were left standing open. The occupants knew we were coming. That didn't matter. We only wanted to solve the Kearny Street house mystery. We left our car doors locked and ran inside like crazy men. The three of us spread out and reached up to touch the top of every interior door in the house. Out of seven doors, two had the telltale tampering, including the bathroom door. There was no dope now, of course. But the bad guys now knew that we knew. Their *narco* enterprise would have to work up a (w)hole new hidey-hole for the future.

CHAPTER 40:
BASS-O-MATIC

We hit an address on L Street more than once. The two-bedroom, one-bath, wood frame house was built circa 1930 and bore layers of white paint going back to World War II. The house was a drug den through-and-through. There was never a time in the three years I worked that neighborhood that the place was rehabbed into a comfortable home for non-criminals. The house couldn't present itself any more clearly as a drug sales den, all day and every day. The people in control should have skipped any pretense of suburbia and mounted a Dopers 'R' Us neon billboard.

Each visit WECAN made there, and there were at least three on my watch, was always the same. Two Mexican nationals slung dope from the same barred windows in the kitchen. Every time we went there, the furniture was sparse with take-out containers from Mexican fast food places strewn about and the same worn-out couch that looked like it had been rescued from curbside trash pick-up. Each time we knocked on the door, the inhabitants held it wide open for our entry. They either didn't know any better or didn't care. We knew from our months of encounters with dope houses that many of the dealers inside really thought we'd never find their stashes once they gave us permission to search. Often as not, their permission amounted to a shrug of the shoulders and the Mexican words for, "Go ahead."

On this evening, the Central team sent an officer around back to cover escapes or tossed dope and guns. The rest of the team gained permissive entry through the front door. Yet again, different Mexican nationals, but the same worn couch. Virtually all our detainees sat on that couch each time we rolled in. As always, our police cars were out of sight more than a block away. No one in the surrounding homes gave off any clues to the addicts that cops were onboard. Our trap was set.

By now, the neighbors were either hunkered down lest they get caught up in some drug sting, or they watched us bust these drug dealers and junkies. Hopefully, they got great satisfaction when we did our jobs. By the same token, I hoped they believed we were the cops they could trust. Obviously, people in the Heights could be suspicious of the police. Maybe they considered us renegades and thieves. Our actions indicated otherwise. We were apt to pile up too many witnesses to be crafty, crooked cops that siphoned off a taste of the booty for our own greedy purposes. No, we were in it for the law and the action.

Once satisfied we had the place under control again, we went back over the repetitive chores of nabbing junkies while we searched the house for the dope, guns, and money stashes. While the search continued, Roger acted as the dealer at the window. Junkies arrived and seemed not to be suspicious their dealer was white with red hair and wearing a police jacket turned inside-out. We went with the toy balloon gambit a couple of times. The money collected would be impounded and the buyers would be detained pending warrant checks or charges we could scrape up against them.

Roger ran out of balloons and the rest of us forgot to pack extras. We had nothing to lure the cash through the window. Roger, always easily inspired, looked around the kitchen for some prop. He opened the refrigerator and saw a paper-wrapped fish that awaited preparation for the dealer's evening meal. The fish was a large, fresh bass. He laid it on the kitchen counter and opened the paper that sealed in its freshness. Now he had something to sell.

The very next junkie at the window, a black man, asked for "two *blanca* and two *negra*." He'd do a speedball with one of each and either sell the other or double-down and probably overdose. With the utmost sweetness in his attitude Roger collected the cash and handed the man the fish. At first the buyer laughed. Here was a dope house with a sense of humor, he must have mused.

He asked, in all seriousness, for his dope. Roger just stood there and motioned with his hands at the fish as though he'd made a wise purchase. No longer humored the guy shouted, "Fish? I don't want no stinkin' fish! Where's my dope?"

Roger couldn't fake the simplest Spanish words. All he could offer in retort was his patented wide-mouthed bass grin and hands open in apology. John and Chuck decided to take the guy into custody before he blew a gasket.

I watched the whole comedy from the living room. John and Chuck had avoided the backyard until now. The lawn was just a swamp of grey water. The bathroom plumbing somehow was disconnected from the sewer and the outflow from the sink and toilet ran right onto the grass. The sight and smell were disgusting, yet the junkies walked through it with every drug buy. The WECAN duo skirted the pond and grabbed the "fish man" before he could send the bass flying back through the window at Roger. Roger smiled with a toothy grin partially obscured by his Tom Selleck-thick, red mustache.

Chuck walked the handcuffed man around to the front and through the front door. Once inside, we identified the still-fuming dope buyer. We all got a chuckle out of that. After an ID check we found nothing we'd hold the man for and let him go. This was his first dope house with funny cops inside. We even got the guy to admit he thought it was cool that he got to keep the fish.

SDPD worked in cooperation with Border Patrol back then. We weren't tasked with searches for undocumented aliens, but if we encountered them, especially those suspected of crimes, we took custody and turned them over to BP. The accepted practice was to radio Communications and ask them to set up a meet at a destination labeled Point Seven. This was a parking lot in Chula Vista about halfway between SDPD HQ and Border Patrol's border facility. Communications relayed our request for a meet with BP to send a cage unit to Point Seven to meet us.

Once we all arrived, quiet greetings usually opened the procedure. WECAN had little contact with BP beyond the turnovers of the undocumented. We operated in two different worlds of law enforcement. We released the handcuffs on the detainees. BP attached new ones and sat them in one of their vans. BP headed south and we headed north. BP would process them at their station and likely release them at the border gates into Mexico. We would encounter some of these same illegals again in the future. They had criminal jobs to do on our side of the borderline. The border fence and law enforcement were not much of a deterrent to them.

The place that resembled a dump at 3120 L St. was a real burden. Our team didn't have the time and resources to single out this place for permanent closure. The name on the deed was Hispanic with a residence in Mexico. We felt certain the name was a bogus front for gangster overlords. In frustration, Roger dumped a second bass in the blender the alleged tenants used to process drinks. Roger cranked it on high and mulched the fish into a soupy liquid. He poured it over the couch and the two dealer assholes seated on it before the rest of us could react.

I smirked at them because I didn't care what they thought or said about it. Chuck's lips were a thin line. I worried John would get nervous about the bass bath. The *narcos* didn't budge or show any emotion. We imagined they'd seen and done worse to others. John usually was the first to point out we could get in trouble over some tarnishing act we might pull off, but even he was glad we stuck it to those two dope peddlers. We all stared at them for a moment. There wasn't much of an odor from the bass purée. I took pleasure in the sight of these guys covered in fishy yuck. I felt no guilt, but a sense of sweet justice fucking with the worst element to cross our porous borders and slave our citizens to drugs. The ironic aspect about the dousing was if they hated America before we got to them, we probably made them twice as mad at the United States than before. If we'd had stronger borders, we wouldn't have to worry these two clowns would return to manifest their hate and sell their poison.

We turned those guys over to BP as they were. The agents didn't bother asking what happened. They smiled at us in common knowledge. They hated these *narcos* as much as we did.

We expected the couch to be gone on our next visit. *Narcos* don't get maid service. The couch was still there and a marvelous mess. Chances were this place would be up and running in no time.

Two days later, we got a guy out of a dope location that provided us with a connection to another place. The dealers at the new place were in an apartment on 27th Street and upstairs. Our sourced told us two Mexicans pedaled small quantities of coke and a little heroin. They seemed low on the criminal food chain like they weren't being run by some larger dope faction. They were kind of do-it-yourselfers. Whatever they were up to was insignificant. We made our way inside and confronted the occupants.

The place was bereft of contraband. Their only sin so far was the extension cord they'd wired into the downstairs tenant's electrical subpanel. Manny went downstairs and asked those tenants if they knew they were being ripped off, after he divined that they weren't culpable.

The downstairs folks were working class people who spoke good English. They knew the people upstairs were trash dope dealers and were afraid of them. Manny became incensed. He returned upstairs where I baby sat the two miscreants from Sinaloa, Mexico. The cocky sons of bitches acted like they had not one care in the world. If they had masters, American police were much less threatening.

Manny took me aside and expressed his outrage that these asshats stole power from a young couple with a baby. The husband was a waiter in Old Town. They were innocent, documented migrants, viewed as weak in the eyes of the dealers and taken advantage of. The power to the dealer's apartment was furnished and paid for by the family below. They couldn't afford to move out until the husband's job gave them enough bank for another rental deposit elsewhere.

Fuck this. I took out my knife in frustration and cut the cord to the dirt bag's power. That might have been a little impulsive. The knife jumped out of my hands when the 110-current bit into the blade. I got a nasty jolt through my arm. The blade suffered more than I did, with a blackened, jagged chip in the metal. I was in pain and frustrated. How could we protect all these people when life and the *varrio* were stacked against them? Every time we had a win, I found ten more losses which was the reason we fought every day. The honest residents needed to know all was not lost.

Manny concocted the plan that we could "produce" a crime. I wasn't above the thought. We almost always had drugs in the car waiting to be impounded from earlier arrests in the day. Hell, I'd found pot in our car we'd lost track of more than once. If we were going to do this thing, it would be the first time. Could we live with ourselves?

No. That wasn't us. The best we could do was turn them over to Border Patrol if we had nothing criminal our courts would handle. We shrugged our shoulders and took the Sinaloans downstairs to our car. I had one ace-in-the-hole that could defeat them if they returned. Nothing complicated. I took a key I found in the apartment, locked the door, and broke the key off in the doorknob on the exterior side. The act was more symbolic than anything. But if it turned out these bad guys were trespassers; they'd not be able to get back in. That was something at least. Manny gave his business card to the downstairs couple and asked them to call us if the nuisances returned. We never got the call.

Recent gang violence in the Heights was low. With few active targets to look for in the gang world, we slipped back into type and hammered away at dope houses. A time or two later, we reacted to another tip on L Street. The same place was hot again. The place never seemed to be in the hands of legitimate tenants. Our teams were not investigators. The identification and pursuit of the homeowners was a pay grade above ours. We were given the flexibility to do many things but targeting the people who set up dozens of these dope locations was more than our team was built to accomplish.

Once again, Central WECAN grouped together to take down the same dope house. This time, Roger was tethered to a trainee named Randy. Randy was still in the academy and would go on to great things with our department, even reach a rank none of the rest of us would. For now, he was just a rootie-poot rookie, an empty chalkboard waiting for experiences to fill the board with writing.

John, Chuck, Manny, and I set out in two cars with Roger and Randy behind us. We left the cars around the block and followed the usual path to the dope house. We made contact in the usual way, covered the perimeter in the usual way and gained entry in the usual way. As usual, we met a fresh pair of Mexican nationals who shrugged and spoke poor English. In we went.

This time, somebody had warned them to use a new hiding place. The curtains, curtain rods and stove were already known to us. Four of us spread out while Roger and Randy stood guard. All this was new to Randy. He had questions about our methods. Roger explained the intricacies of laws of arrest, fourth waiver searches and other aspects of procedure. Randy grasped at the concepts. In a nutshell, the rookie was told to watch and learn.

As the search progressed, it was clear all the old hiding places were untouched. We knew dope was there or should be there. Otherwise, there'd be no dealers. While the others worked at floor level, I decided to stand on a chair and push open the cover to the crawl space in the ceiling. That might have been a mistake. As soon as I pushed the wooden cover aside, bugs began falling on top of me. I was so grossed out I nearly hurt myself when I dropped from the chair. Undeterred, I used my PR24 police baton with a side control handle to push the cover off and away from the opening. The bugs, mostly small roaches, disappeared. I put a pair of gloves on for further exploration. The bugs didn't seem eager to stick around.

I wasn't tall enough to see over the ledge into the crawl space above the ceiling. I reached up and over the ledge and felt my way around for contraband. Very quickly, I felt a roll of bills and plucked them from the piles of old asbestos insulation filling the ceiling. I called over for help from Roger and Randy stood beside him. They stood below to make sure my perch didn't shift.

I dropped a wad of bills to Roger and continued my search. The next find was a revolver I identified with my fingers. I gingerly picked it up, noted it was loaded and handed it over to the guys below. These were good hauls for deposit at Impounds, but I wanted the dope to seal up the two dealers for a drug pinch. I needed more height and light to see further into the crawl space.

We determined the only way up was to lift one of our guys into the crawl space. Of the six of us, I don't think any of us weighed less than two hundred pounds with all our gear on. Only one appeared thin and wiry enough to make it over the ledge, the choice was Randy. When he figured we had something up our sleeves, Randy developed a sinking-feeling that showed in his facial expression and questioned if this was going to be legal and safe. Uniformly, we all nodded and agreed it was fine. The only hazard was the asbestos. We solved that problem by furnishing Randy with a disposable paper suit we used to suit up naked prisoners, and a filter mask. Randy's dubious concern was overlooked by all of us. Randy was stuck with us and our devious ways.

Randy was lifted into the crawl space by his legs and handed a flashlight. He'd removed his gun belt for easier crawlspace agility. His instructions were to search every square inch of the space above the ceiling. We also warned him to stretch out along the ceiling beams to spread his weight evenly. If he stepped on the ceiling boards, he'd fall right through since the house was built before sheetrock was common. Instead of plaster, three-quarter inch planks were nailed side by side to make the ceiling. To be honest, we didn't think the bad guys would be energetic enough to hide dope any further away from the opening than they could reach. However, to avoid discovery, it was possible they tossed the dope far across the crawl space and would return to retrieve it once we were gone.

Randy crawled and searched, searched and crawled. He finally shouted down to us through the ceiling boards that he'd come up empty handed. He was clearly miserable and begged to end this futile affair. Roger finally gave him permission to come back to us, when a sudden crash sent ceiling boards dropping all over the living room. Randy lost his balance in mid-turn and braced a foot a little too strongly against the boards. His leg broke through the ceiling boards. His leg protruded down like an Abbott and Costello sight-gag. I think we were all alarmed at first, but Randy's plaintive cries for help broke laughter out from all of us.

I stood on the chair and pulled myself up over the ledge to light his way and figure out how to bring him back. The others pulled down loose boards, making the hole large enough for Randy to extract himself. We got him out safely and brought him back to earth. Now he was angry. His paper suit was torn, and the uniform underneath soiled with dust and asbestos. The ceiling was destroyed, and he was fearful of blame and Department trouble.

We explained to Randy the unwritten rule of dope houses and cops. Nothing ever came back to haunt us if no one was hurt and nothing was stolen. He'd be fine and we'd take any heat. Since we didn't think it was appropriate to leave broken ceiling boards in the living room, we took turns carrying the boards into the backyard. The plumbing still drained into the yard leaving a nasty swamp. We dropped the boards into the mire and reasoned we'd be doing the next group of travelers living there a bit of a favor when we created a bridge to cross the swamp. The Army Corps of Engineers we were not.

We did wonder what the owners thought of cops in their houses breaking their buildings. Would we hear from them? Would a complaint be registered?

Nothing ever came of it. Randy wasn't so certain and probably still worries our escapade will come back to haunt him. A month later, several of us returned to the place with our sergeant to check on its criminal status. We found the same equation we'd repeatedly solved, two Mexican nationals and all the rest. Curiously, the ceiling was repaired. For the property owners it would seem building repair without making a complaint was just part of hosting a lucrative drug trade. The members of the Bass-o-Matic Club certainly never brought their drenched heads to light. This L Street house was a place of pure cross-border Mexican troublemakers. Nobody would ever complain to the police or even their attorneys in Mexico. By the way, the tattered living room couch had finally disappeared, only to be replaced by a likewise crappy sofa pulled from somewhere of questionable origin.

Bugs are a facet of the daily encounters of cops in some neighborhoods. Spiders, flies, mosquitoes, worms, moths, and everything else that plagued those neighborhoods plagued us. But the worst for me was roaches. I hate 'em with a passion. Having them drop from a ceiling into my hair and onto my clothing was as disgusting as it got for me. Working Logan Heights was no treat for a man that detested creepy-crawlies. Roaches were everywhere. Some of those old buildings seemed to breed generations of roaches that were so bold they marched around outside with no fear of people. I'm serious. I've seen roaches move in colonies outdoors, on sidewalks in broad daylight. I've never seen anything like that anywhere else.

There was an old decrepit house near lower 30th Street in the Heights, a place so worn out it was ready to fall apart at any time. This was also a dwelling inhabited by junkies who'd long since taken over. Whoever owned it failed to do anything for the place or to the trespassers inside. The house crumbled away decade after decade. The windows were constantly covered to prevent sunlight from peeking through. People I talked to said that the windows had been covered against light and prying eyes for as long as anyone remembered. You can imagine the bug problem in that place. Unfortunately, tipsters said the place was up for drug sales, so we felt obligated to check it out.

Four of us teamed together and drove to the address. The house had to be ninety years old and mistreated from day one. We walked in through the open front door. The frame of the door was torn to shreds from legions of cops and crooks kicking their way in for who knows how long. The door was in such bad shape it didn't close properly and couldn't be locked.

The interior rooms were covered with makeshift beds for junkies and not much else. The place was a crash pad. The gas was shut off ages ago, so nobody cooked on what passed for a stove. And, of course, there were lots of bugs. There were the usual assortments of spiders, termites and something I couldn't identify, some kind of albino creepy crawler. Whatever these things were, they were under everything. If one of us disturbed any of the furniture these white bugs scrambled for a replacement dark place. After a little watchful observation, I finally figured out what they were, albino roaches! Some mutant metamorphosis had allowed nature to breed at least one white roach in this disgusting den of inequity. Years and decades of roaches later, whole generations of them called this one house their own. These things had probably never even seen the sun.

The guy purporting to live there was an old, black junkie with diminished mental faculties. He was surprised when I pointed out the albino bugs. He mumbled he'd never noticed them before. I had to get out of the place. There'd be no arrests out of that house today, or ever. Albino roaches. *ARRGHHH!*

Some Central patrol officers felt the same as me. They began the process to allow the city to render the property unsafe. The city seized the property and demolished the house. I can only imagine the shock to the albino roaches thrust into the demolition survivors' new world.

We all grasped the irony and madness that was the dope world. We understood that the origin of the term dope was an accurate jab at the people who used drugs consistently. Dopers could become complacent, reckless, dangerous and stupid. The dope dealers on the streets and in the buildings provided WECAN with plenty of examples of bad people behavior. The complacency aspect kept working in our favor. The bad people just didn't anticipate or know what to do with a bunch of rambunctious comedians in uniform with street savvy and bottomless energy and smarts. Manny and I chose a day where we'd really put complacency to the test.

This day's project was a single-family sized house on J Street near 29th. We'd figured this place out on our own because of its visibility from the street. Manny and I had borrowed a pick-up truck from the police garage used for undercover work. The truck came into play down on 32nd for some on-the-scene fact gathering for a later sting. We watched some Crips work a corner without them making us. We'd turn the notes we made into an escapade with the rest of the team at a later date. Our way back to the station took us past the place on J. Manny spotted a guy coming out the side yard of a house on the north side of the street. He knew the man from prior contacts and voiced out loud that any place he was in any way connected to was a dope house. We didn't bother to stop him and left well-enough alone. Since we were undercover, I swung around the block and made a second, slower pass to get a better look at the suspect building.

The front yard was barren and bordered a late-style Victorian designed home. The entry was on the side of the house instead of the front. The opposite side of the house had tall, double-hung sash windows that were part of the original construction mounted into the walls at about shoulder height at the sill. An idea pooped into my head.

Manny and I talked about the audacity of buying dope in full uniform. We laughed about how dull the dealers were. Supposedly, they were trained to behave a certain way by their masters. We'd learned they rarely deviated from that behavior, see the buyer and sell the dope. Their work didn't require much in the smarts department and little in the way of imagination or independent thought. They just had to sell dope and hand the money up the chain.

"Roger managed to sell dope and a fish on K Street and while in uniform. I bet I could pull it off on J Street," I told Manny.

"How are you going to pull that off, dude? You are one *guero* cop," was Manny's retort.

"I saw how high those windows are off the ground. That guy you saw came from that side yard. I bet they're dealing through those windows. How about I put on a cover over my tans and make the deal? I bet I could pull it off. If I hunker down a bit, they'll only see my shoulders and my head."

"What're you going to wear," Manny asked.

"Everybody from the junkies to the *cholos* to the Crips wear Pendleton's. I've got a red and white one at home. I'll toss that on when we get out of the car and shake a leg into the backyard before anyone catches on. What to do think?"

"I think you have one mucho set of balls, brother."

The new day brought our little scheme to fruition. We stashed the marked unit a half-block away and walked into the alley behind the house. I carried the shirt in my left hand until we'd swept the yard for people who might concern us. The coast was clear. The detached garage provided cover from the prying eyes of the people in the house we were after. Manny watched the front porch while I donned the slightly frayed Pendleton that I kept around the house for a work shirt when I built furniture in my garage at home. Outfitted for the kill, we concocted our plan.

Manny would do the knock and talk at the door when I gave him a signal over Nalemars. That radio frequency was almost always unused so it was unlikely some broadcast would interfere. I slunk around the building and set myself up below one of two windows. My camouflaging shirt was buttoned up but tucked in behind the butt of my gun so it wouldn't interfere. The radio was also unencumbered for quick reach. So far, the occupants, who were hopefully there, hadn't been spotted so we were in the clear. I took my position just below the window, my chin at sill height.

The plan was for me to click the transmitter just once to let Manny know I'd begun. If there was trouble, I told him rather than waste time with the handy-talkie I'd just shout like a madman.

I tapped on the window for attention, figuring that was what the buyers would do. A Hispanic face looked out at me and then lifted up the window. Hopefully, the fingers I'd run backward through my hair provided some dishevelment. The guy inside looked squarely at me as I asked for "*uno negra* and *uno blanca*," with the worst version of a Spanish accent any guy from Clairemont has ever uttered. I held up a couple of my own twenties and fives since that was the going rate for a speedball. He stared at me rendering judgment. Moments ticked by and he made the call to hand a balloon and a bindle out the window.

Fate and coincidence can be so unkind. The ever silent Nalemars hosted some innocuous transmission from somewhere out in police radio land. The sudden transmission burst startled the seller. He leaned out through the window to see where the noise came from and withered away inside when he recognized the bottom half of a police uniform. I was burned.

"Manny. It's on!"

I heard the front door getting pounded on with a size twelve Hi-Tech boot. I pulled my gun out and pointed it through the window at the dealer. I shouted things that probably sounded incoherent to the dealer, but he got my meaning and froze in place. I think I shouted "*Alto*" at him. He got the meaning of my temperament and the nine-millimeter barrel he faced.

Manny was through the door in seconds. He grabbed a second guy in the hallway standing dumbfounded and tore into the room. He had both guys secured and a handful of dope. I trotted around to the entrance and joined the crowd.

A small amount of both heroin and cocaine were seized, maybe five hundred dollars' worth. Luckily, there was no gun. The scenario could have been caustically different if those clowns were armed. Manny was panicked in the short term. "What the fuck happened, Bro? I heard you scream and thought all hell broke loose."

"Somebody broadcast on Nalemars, for fuck's sake. The first time I hear anybody on that freq other than us, and it's some other agency. I almost made the deal. We were inches away from getting it done when the radio blasted."

"I heard it too, but I thought it was you. I was confused because that wasn't the signal."

"Yeah, I went into panic mode and drew down on the guy. I was surprised he did what I shouted at him to do. Anyway, we got the dope and the bad guys. I'm even going to charge him for sales because it was *that* fucking close."

We charged both men and booked them into county jail. Two days later I got a call from the sergeant at the Duty Lieutenant's office. Sergeant Nehrich had called up to Central WECAN and asked if anybody in our office had seen that day's newspaper. Nobody had, but I heard Rich's call and went downstairs to meet him. He showed me a blurb in one of the local columns about a strange drug deal in the Heights. I looked at the clipping and saw my name. That was a surprise. Cop's names in the newspapers could just as likely be a bad thing. Mine was a good thing.

Our department's Public Information Officer, or PIO, had discovered the arrest we made at that house with the tall windows and thought it made good copy. He'd gotten ahold of my arrest report and thought it was the funniest thing he'd read in a week. He turned the story over to his column writer buddy Neil Morgan at the Union–Tribune and it hit the paper two days after. The title of the brief story was something like, SDPD Officer Buys Dope in Full Uniform. The part about my wearing the Pendleton was glossed over and the Nalemars guffaw was ignored. I loved it. I got some attention and had a host of questions from my peers.

Manny could only shake his head in abject recognition that Newbold got in the press... again.

What antics would WECAN pull next?

CHAPTER 41:

THE NAM

A couple of us stopped a crack head on 30th as he scurried out of the side yard of a house by hopping the backyard fence. His actions gave us the impression we might have a burglar in flight from a crime. The guy didn't get far and put his hands up almost immediately when our car made the U-turn. His name was Robbie.

Robbie was patted down for weapons or obvious contraband. We didn't have enough to legally enter his pockets. I pinched the cylindrical object in one of his shirt front pockets. I knew instantly what it was, but there was no rush to retrieve it.

"Why'd you hop that fence? What were you doing there?" Manny asked, as he straightened out his gun belt. Robbie might have misinterpreted Manny's actions as a threat. Who can say? Robbie was instantly motivated into honest conversation.

"Honest, officer, I live there. You can check with my mom."

"Why did you go over the fence?" I wanted to know.

"I didn't want my mom to know I split."

"Why's that, Robbie?" Manny sensed this guy was only going to speak in short clips. "You going to give us the whole story, or do we have to go ask your moms?" That did it.

Robbie looked from Manny to me. I drilled my gaze into his and then stared at the pocket with the crack pipe. Robbie got the message. "I was gonna go score some rock. Are you gonna bust me? I didn't do anything yet."

If only we could serve justice with pre-crime arrests. "Nah, Robbie, we're not gonna bust ya, but I'm seizing the pipe," I directed him to take it out of his pocket and hand it over. Of course, he was saddened by the loss of the pipe. That was his lifeline. Now, he'd have to cop crack and a replacement pipe. More money out of his pocket.

"You can do one thing for us that I'll consider a debt paid, Robbie." Manny said.

"Yeah, what's that?"

"Give us a dope house." Manny made the request plain and simple. Robbie's mouth turned down at the corners, disappointed only free him at a cost. His hesitation warranted a sterner request from Manny. "Don't think too hard on this, man. We haven't released you yet."

"Aww, officer, I don't know any dope houses. I score off the street."

"Yeah, I don't care." I reprimanded. "Look, Robbie, we're serious. Right now, we're being cool with you. Do not make us go from good cop, good cop, to two bad ones. You know what I'm saying?"

Robbie quickly came to terms with his dilemma and volunteered, sort of, "There's this old man on Clay Street. I know he deals in junk, man." Robbie described the house with plenty of detail. That was good enough for us. We kicked Robbie loose without another word. The glass crack pipe got crushed under my boot.

The target was a granny flat behind a larger stucco home on the north side of Clay. Our approach would have to be through the front of the property. The back gate was mounted to a six-foot grape-stake fence. Apparently, business was done over the fence. The dealer kept his front door open and could hear buyers call out to him.

The two of us accessed the back house through the front yard. Manny and I surprised him when we walked up onto his wooden front porch in broad daylight. His name was Joe. Joe's pupils were pinned compared to his shocked, wide eyes. I kept the conversation brief. "Hey. We got word you're slinging here," I admonished. "I can see you're a user and are high right now." I waited for his reaction. Manny stood to one side and tried to peer into the tiny living room. Joe was caught between my pronouncement and Manny's curiosity. Joe stood in the doorway. I had him dead to rights for the eleven-five-fifty.

Joe was about fifteen years older than both of us. He was a disheveled, boney black man with droopy eyes and a slight bend at the waist. He looked old and tired. I didn't want to be hard on the guy, but our role as dope cops came first. "Joe," I said, "let's skip to the end. You're under arrest for under the influence. Turn around."

The handcuffs went on and the search of his clothing began. Joe wasn't cautious enough. He had several balloons of heroin in a pants pocket and our arrest got kicked up from misdemeanor to felony. He stayed quiet when I told him we had the right to search his home within his reach, which would have been right inside the doorway and a few feet in every direction. I told him we'd probably have to get a search warrant for the rest of his home.

"You don't have to do all that. You can search my place. You won't find anything, though."

There was an air of honesty about him, like he didn't want to fight battles anymore. I told him I appreciated his cooperation and asked for some identification. He didn't drive and provided me with a worn military identification card. The card read "U.S. Army." "When were you in the service, Joe?" Manny asked.

"Yes, sir."

"I asked you, when did you serve?"

"I joined the Army around, Fifty-Eight."

"Did you go to Vietnam?" I was genuinely curious. Joe looked up at me and seemed to brighten up a little.

"I was, sir." This was an awkward moment for Manny and me. We were both close to draft age when Vietnam raged. I turned eighteen in 1973 and signed up for my draft card at the Selective Service Office. The U.S. military was no longer sending troops to Nam, but I was still worried. Eight years of the news on family television in my house gave me a good sense of the brutality and volatility of Vietnam.

"I was an advisor with the Army, part of the first group of specialists with MAAG." The acronym stood for Military Assistance Advisory Group-Vietnam or MAAG-Vietnam. That was 1959. "The Viet Cong made things hotter for us in the South. I stuck around when Kennedy sent in more advisors."

"What happened to you?" Manny wanted to know. The stretch from a form of Special Forces to heroin addict was a curiosity.

"I was over there too long, man. I did a couple of tours and watched things get worse."

I wanted to know his drug history, but I felt it was respectful to be delicate with the questioning. "Did you find heroin when you were there? You don't have to tell me if you don't want to."

"Yeah, man. I played around with it, everybody did back then. We smoked pot, hash, and the like. Dope got me out of my head and mellowed me out. Then, it was too late. I got discharged because of dope. The Army just cut me loose. I came back to the world a damned junkie."

"Didn't the Military help you get clean?" Manny was disturbed that a warrior got used up and seemingly spit out.

"There's programs. Better ones now through the VA. No one wanted to deal with users back in the day. I tried methadone and didn't like it. I've tried getting off the dope, but it never lasts. I know I'm going to jail. I've been there before. Maybe this time I'll get clean. I'm tired of it."

Manny and I both sympathized with old Joe. He'd been through the hell created by others and lived in the continuation with a hell of his own making.

With all the dope houses raided by my WECAN team, it seemed abnormal that we didn't encounter dope sick junkies. The dead and the dying sometimes never made it a block from the place they copped *chiva*. WECAN dealt with few overdoses. Many of the dope houses frowned upon even letting the dopers inside to cut the deal or get a fix. I'd seen junkies fix right outside of the source of the dope in desperation. Manny and I once watched a guy standing in low apartment shrubbery prepping the needle, virtually out in the open. He was yards away from his connection. He'd just scored and didn't bother to hide the fact.

His hunger for heroin overwhelmed him. He cooked the heroin for needle infusion without running the solution through cotton to filter out unwanted debris. He was so consumed by the act of getting high he didn't even notice us walking out of the darkness behind him. By the time he was aware, I'd snatched the needle from his hand. His goose was cooked. He was near dope-sick and off to jail.

The debris from dope use littered the Heights. We constantly saw discarded dope baggies, syringes, balloons, crack pipes and every other piece of flotsam that dopers left in their wake. I felt sorry for the decent people in that part of town that had to teach their kids to avoid all the poisonous refuse. This travesty was more publicly visible than in many other parts of San Diego. The only consideration given by any junkie was the possibility of a needle for re-use because he or she didn't know when they'd get a clean one next. HIV and AIDS were in full effect. However, junkies lived by codes of desperation and did wanton things to get high, their health and their lives constantly at risk.

What was odd was the places I most expected to find these dope discards. The dope houses were the cleanest places around. I rarely found more than burnt matches. Maybe I'd see an empty balloon or two on the ground. The telltale needles and other evidence of felony dope were rarely seen. The dope bosses may have instructed the dealers to push the junkies along to minimize exposure to the police.

Crack was handled differently in the parts of San Diego I worked. Crack was sold hand-to-hand in pebble form, rarely ensconced in a wrapper or a container. The East Coast news stations always pictured tiny vials with colorful caps strewn across sidewalks, alleys and streets. They used the visuals of this detritus to illustrate the pervasive crack epidemic. The vials were rarely a tool in the crack trade in San Diego. The sellers here were less interested in the vial's use. Maybe it was unnecessary overhead. Bits of wax paper or Saran Wrap seemed to suffice if they choose to bag the crack at all.

Dope sick junkies, or those who tried to stave off the hunger, were common in the areas that serviced them. They were all over the Heights, on foot, in cars, and desperate and struggling to make their connections. The users not indigenous to the Heights and took taxis or got other rides to cop dope in the heights as unnoticed as possible. If WECAN wanted to raise its 11550-arrest quota, all we had to do was watch the cabs dropping people off, especially if the passenger was white. Much of the Heights' population was non-white and white junkies stood out like the full moon at night.

WECAN rarely had to deal with overdosed junkies. Those matters usually ended up as radio calls to patrol or to paramedics. Physicians and Surgeons Hospital, P&S in our parlance, was planted right in the middle of the Heights and drew collapsed addicts from ambulance rides before WECAN ever caught wind.

Junkies preferred to go to ground rather than be out in the daylight and advertise their habits. The 25th and Imperial spot attracted more heroin users than any other intersection in the Heights. WECAN's afternoon to evening team rarely found reason to hound the nether people or street urchins there unless we were hungry for a snitch. The source material was easy to spot. Look for the white person who seemed to be asleep standing up. Addicts didn't practice patience unless they copped dope long before they needed the needle in their arms. The people in dire need shot up as soon as available and headed toward 25th either to catch a ride back to their zone, or because they felt safe there if they were high and vulnerable. Ambulances caught regular calls to that intersection by anonymous phone tips to pick-up a person passed out on the sidewalk. Too often, the relief came from an injection or inhalator filled with the heroin-neutralizer, Narcan. CPR may have been applied if the paramedics couldn't determine if the prone victim's malady was only heroin. Down there, a speedball was as likely the culprit. The hospital was the next step. I was never called upon by fate to apply CPR to save a drug addict's life.

The sum of my academy-trained CPR field experience amounted to one field episode.

Two officers were called to an old apartment building to deal with one of the tenants, a loner with bad behavioral traits who frequently upset his neighbors. The two officers, Stone and Martino, broadcasted they were on-scene. Minutes later, one of the two officers called for help over the radio. Female officer Martino announced there'd been an officer-involved shooting and that her partner was hurt.

I was close and got there first. Paramedics and the fire department were close behind. I rushed inside and saw the body of a man on his back, the man that was poised just moments earlier with a knife over Stone's chest. The man that Martino shot in defense of Stone. The would be attacker's chest still rose and fell with shallow breaths despite two or three bullet holes in his chest. Officer Martino was the shooter.

The officers had responded to a radio call involving the man on the floor and a disturbance with a neighbor. The man had made loud noises in his apartment, giving his neighbors the impression he could be in real trouble. They worried he was dangerous and about to explode into violence. The officers found the guy inside his apartment and asked him to tell them what ailed him. He stepped back from the door, giving the two officers space to step inside.

The subject of this commotion, now known as Roy, was hostile and irrational. He was clearly on something and acted like a weirded-out nut-ball. The two officers tried to reason with him. The care they exercised came to a shocking end when he produced a long-bladed kitchen knife. He didn't give any warning of his intentions when he raised the knife and charged Officer Stone. Stone was too close to the raving lunatic and couldn't impede the charge. Roy had the knife in the stab position over his head when he plowed into Stone and they both toppled to the ground.

Officer Stone was on his back as Roy straddled him and stabbed at the nearly helpless officer. Stone attempted to repel the attack and pushed at Roy to dislodge him. Stone wanted to pull his gun and shoot the man in a quick one-two move but needed both hands to push back at Roy and stop the downward movement of the knife into his chest. Roy gnashed his teeth and snarled at Stone.

Officer Martino didn't hesitate to jump in and try to insert herself. Roy was strong and stabbed into Stone's chest area, trying to penetrate the light body armor. The Kevlar chest shield would stop the full penetration of the knife, but his throat and face were exposed. If Roy shifted to those vulnerable spots Stone would be grievously hurt or killed. Officer Martino pulled her handgun and sited on Roy's chest. Three shots rang out, leaving a tight group of holes in Roy's chest. Stone pushed the wounded man away and rolled away to get clear. Stone was more stunned than injured.

I was the first cover unit there and made it to the door of the apartment just seconds after the gunshots. Paramedics were right behind me. The suspect might have still been alive. My duty as a police officer induced me to begin CPR on the shot-up man. I made a choice to begin chest compressions just as a paramedic knelt next to me. The paramedic placed a resuscitation mask over the suspect's face and squeezed air into his lungs. I continued compressions to his chest to try and retain heart action. Roy's body was dying, yet some part of him clung to life.

This was the first time I experienced death in front of me of any kind. My heart pounded. I literally felt I had this man's life in my hands. He wasn't wearing a shirt and I clearly saw the bullet holes. Officer Martino must have been close when she shot him. I saw powder burns around the bullet holes. Remarkably, I stayed on task and didn't flinch from my duty. My police training simply kicked in. I was proud of myself later. For now, though, I saw how terrified Officer Stone was. He was exhausted and had the distant look in his eyes of a person in shock. He needed space to recuperate from his near-death experience. His body and mind needed a time-out. I was afraid his mainframe was going to shut down. He looked like he struggled to stay in control of a desire to panic. Martino was with him, but he simply stared at the floor as he regained his composure.

The paramedic and I did our best to stabilize Roy. I knew it was wasted effort when blood oozed out of the bullet holes with each chest compression. Roy's breaths were shallow and the span between them grew longer with each inhalation. His eyes were closed. I listened to his ragged breath and guessed it was only a matter of minutes before his life escaped. Quietly, his breaths slowed to quick gulps. Just as he slid into darkness, his eyes opened and seemed to stare straight into mine. I would be the last person he saw on earth. Then it was over. The paramedic knew it was pointless and called it finished.

Most of the people I know watch their elder relatives die in their care at home or in a hospital, but my first witnessed death was violent and justified. I'll never forget that night.

Four of us teamed up to do a knock-and-talk on a new dope house. Formulaic as always, the illegal Hispanic occupants, a pair of males, allowed us entry. The house was almost bereft of furniture, even more sparse than the other dope houses we'd seen in the past. So, the prone junkie on the floor in one bedroom did not go unnoticed.

The young, late twenties-something guy was unconscious. The shallow rise and drop of his chest meant he was deep into a heroin sleep. Not surprisingly, he was one of the local Logan Heights 30th Street members. His tattoos marked him as a gang member.

In the world of thugs, some gangs, like the Hells Angels, live by codes. One Angel code bans the use of heroin and needles. The Logan street gangs produce occasional junkies that remain part of the gang family as soldiers, despite their unreliability. This real-life gangster was crashed out on the floor. His breath was slow and ragged. We'd finally tripped upon a doper in physical distress in a dope house. He was probably close to death. That fact that he'd been allowed to fix in the dealer's dope chamber told us the gang exerted some influence over this place.

The dealers in the house would have let him die and later taken the body out of the house pending orders from their handlers. To move him out would be more trouble than it was worth. They might get orders to leave him there and bail on the spot. Somebody within their dope organization would set up shop again, days or weeks later and in another location.

I was snide about the man's condition. Did I care if he was dead? Did I even care if he was dying? Did any of us there, care? The man was fading, ever so slowly. Chuck Davis kept an eye on the two culprits detained on the couch in the living room adjacent to the bedroom. John played angel's advocate to the moral debate Manny and I waged. Did we intend to sustain the life of this gangbanging piece of shit on the floor?

We didn't carry Narcan, the treatment for heroin overdoses. So, there'd be no easy solution to keep him from succumbing to the drug. Our moral compasses pointed towards our duty to save this man. A violation of our own self-imposed protocol was a test of our honor. Did anyone of us have the colder heart to stall getting help? Time slipped by. I wanted the man to die. I felt I could live with his exit. I was that callous. But I had no experience with the aftermath of a death that I'd allowed to happen. Was I impervious to the demise of a person I was trained to "detest and arrest"?

John argued we'd gotten away with all kinds of borderline conduct in the past. "We have to call paramedics. Leaving him here to die, especially with those two *pollitos* in the other room will come back to haunts us." John's reasoning was sound and moral.

If we did nothing and waited a few minutes he'd die, I supposed.

Manny stood by sucking air in through his teeth and didn't say a word at first. Then, "Hey Bro. I wish he was already dead. This *cabron* shouldn't even be here. Why'd they let him fix in here? Who is he?"

I recognized his tat. So did the others. It was the big, gothic styled "30th Street" on his stomach. "This fucker's *Treinta*. Better to let this gangbanging piece of shit die and save us from dealing with him later." My intonation said that I was serious when I was really testing the others to see what they would do. This guy was barely alive. Manny waited to see what the rest of us would do.

John looked through the doorway at Chuck who'd heard what went on between us and shrugged his shoulders. John made the decision and got out his radio. He put out, "Unit Twenty-Fourteen. We need an 11-41 for an OD at our location."

"Ten-Four Unit Twenty Fourteen. Paramedics en route." The decision was made. None of us fretted too much over the two sides of the debate after we moved on. Our morality wasn't in question. This incident demonstrated just how jaded we'd become after years of police work. Those internal arguments we had within ourselves would be considered and addressed throughout the rest of our lives.

I had my three pals around me, but that didn't validate kissing off this piece of shit from his "mortal coil." One vocal slip of a theoretical cover up if we'd let the guy die and we'd all punish ourselves over the wrong decision, not to mention we'd face criminal and department discipline. But still, doing nothing and watching the man die quietly seemed an easy thing to do. The two detainees were out of sight and couldn't see the drama unfold. If they talked, they'd be implicated for poisoning the guy and leaving him to die in their company.

One of us knelt to do a sternum rub. The painful pressure to the chest plate ordinarily forces collapsed people to react, an indication they're not completely zoned out. This guy didn't react which was another sign of his degrading plight. At least paramedics were headed our way. If the man failed now, we'd at least have done the bare minimum. We'd finally made a decision that forced the choice. From this point on, we'd be responsible for the gangster's life. If he stopped breathing and CPR was required, one of us was going to do mouth-to-mouth resuscitation.

For a few moments, I wanted to return to the debate of discovering the dead man when we arrived. This all sounds cold and inhuman, I know. But cops live in that world. We tread across the worst elements of society. The seduction of letting go of our humanity can be tempting, if even just one time. Our consciences were supposed to win the moral conflict on the side of justice with principled judgment. Individually, the four of us could have argued internally with our own decency, but it could only come out one way for the group. We had to try and save this lousy fuck. Fate and God would make the final decision.

Paramedics were close and got to us as the man sucked in and blew out puffs of oxygen and carbon dioxide. They had the Narcan we weren't issued. One medic checked the vitals and quickly came up with our conclusion that he was on heroin, so Narcan was the treatment. I hadn't seen Narcan applied. I was fascinated to see the addict regain consciousness so quickly. As soon as he was awake, he pushed at the medics and fumbled with a canula they'd inserted into his nostrils. They had ruined his high.

As weak as he was during recovery, he still complained. "You assholes fucked me over." He spoke in a weak voice. He had different priorities from the rest of us.

The spiteful street punk would still get a ride to the hospital and out of our hair. In retrospect, none of the Central WECAN guys at that scene have ever chosen to talk about that day. I don't even know if the other three remember the incident.

CHAPTER 42:
WALKING DEAD

One of the brazenly public Logan Heights streets for crack sales was the short stretch of 3200 Martin Avenue. Our team hammered away at the drug dealers on this block for over a year. We hit the homes. We hit the apartments and we hit the streets. No amount of police pressure made permanent dents. This was simply the place for crooks to be, cops or not. We could always tell when the street dealers had a new load of crack to sell, the crowds of "walkers" would be out in force surrounding the guy with the drugs, just waiting for something to dribble their way. I call them walkers because some of their crack-head behavior resembles the zombies on television.

Manny and I were out on patrol on an extremely rainy afternoon. The cloud bursts were consistent, and the rain made stepping out of the car a non-starter. Still, we could at least scare up something if we kept moving around. Somewhere, somebody was outdoors and catchable.

3200 Martin was a prolific target zone. This was the same block that produced all those jumpers from the warrant and searches we'd done months prior. We headed down 32nd St. to make a slow left turn onto Martin. I figured the wet skies would leave Martin empty of bad people on the street. I was wrong. No sooner had we turned then we faced a literal herd of people standing on the sidewalks and blocking the street. What the hell? It was pouring out! Manny was our driver but stopped immediately to take stock of the scene in front of us. The crowd, by comparison, was packed together and seemed to undulate in movement like one big, live thing.

Our presence there created the effect of a television zombie distracted by a sound. First, one of the crack dealers recognized us as a threat and shuffled away from us. Slowly, the herd followed in ones and twos and then more until the pack moved as one. The dealer only drifted another fifty feet ahead of us before he stopped in the soaking rain. None of them seemed to mind. Like one brain, they all housed the same single thought. Get crack in me.

The blank stares on the faces of the thirty or more crack heads nearest us reminded me of thoughtless cattle. If one led the herd for a different patch of land, the others tended to follow. But they were crack monsters instead of beefsteaks. Their cravings united them all. They stood close to the dealer and somehow hoped to entice him into some kibbles and bits tossed in their direction. If he moved, they moved. When he stayed, they milled about like the living dead. If there was a loud noise, the herd reacted as one and shuffled away until they lost focus on what they were walking away from in the first place. If they were startled by something besides the police, they scooted into the shadows until the coast seemed clear.

I was creeped out when I moved among them. The downpour was no impediment to their needs. We left the car in the street and felt the cold rain through our rain gear. I wore a yellow poncho designed for uniformed officers with slits on the hips for holstered gun access. Manny wore a raincoat with matching pants. We meandered rather unthreateningly down Martin St. and into the herd. Most of the people wore the clothing they put on daily, tattered shirts and ill-fitting pants. Nobody wore any outer clothing designed to protect against the rain. I looked at the faces of those people, amazed at how few of them seemed to notice their soaked clothing and chilled skins. They looked back at me with vacant stares, gazes that looked past me and not at me. There was nothing going on upstairs. Maybe we were less recognizable in bright yellow raincoats. The addicts just ignored us for the most part like we weren't real. Certainly, no cops would ever stroll into a large group of street people on their terrain in the pouring rain and then do nothing.

This surreal atmosphere was like taking part in a social experiment. We threaded our way into and through a mass of dangerous people with not an ounce of trouble. As long as we didn't manifest intentions to jack-up anybody, we were fine.

There was more than just one dealer. He had his friends, bodyguards, and mules around him. Some of the guys flashed just enough blue to advertise they were West Coast Crips. This was their turf. Wary of us as always, they still weren't perturbed by our presence. This was more of a curiosity for us. Neither Manny nor I were gonna get worked up enough to make some skinny junkie pinch. We just wanted to scare them off, but like the walking dead, their desire was to get crack and they moved toward that scent. They noticed little else. Unlike the walking dead on TV, loud noises had the opposite effect and sent them scurrying away. We discovered this when we returned to our car and put it in Drive.

Just for the hell of it, I switched the siren on as we slowly crawled through the herd. Even a marked police unit in their midst didn't faze them. The loud wail of the siren seemed to wake up a bunch of the dazed junkies. Now we saw angry and frightened faces. They got the point and made serious attempts to adjust and move along. They ambled even farther away as our car's headlights laid a glow across their bodies. Some disappeared into dark shadows.

Manny drove the car off-site. We wanted to see what damage we'd done to the crack trade there. After five minutes we spun back around and re-entered 3200 Martin. The rain was even heavier now. To our surprise the crowd not only hovered around the Crips, the size of the herd seemed to have increased. I looked at Manny and suggested we find the other Central WECAN guys and go get dinner. We'd get them another day.

CHAPTER 43:
TRAINEES

WECAN's superiors deemed it innovative to have team members with FTO pins, Field Training Officers, paired with trainees. The intent was to expose raw recruits to the toughest neighborhoods, teamed with veteran street cops gilded with vast gang and narcotics experience. The trainees would ride with us for two weeks and then report their experiences back to their Police Academy Advisors.

In theory, it was a dicey idea. We were a highly mobile force that moved at lightning speed, or with cautious planning. We targeted the worst elements of criminality and hit them hard. The trainees wouldn't comprehend everything that happened in front of them and we didn't plan to stop to teach them. In practice, the trainees were as inconvenient as theorized.

WECAN officers worked in pairs. Our partner was our protection on the mean streets. Trainees were not partners, and not salty. They had no sixth senses honed by the streets. They certainly weren't ready for hordes of Crips, Bloods, and the factions of Logan Heights' *vatos* that careened around the lower-income neighborhoods next to downtown.

The San Diego Police Academy conferred with the department's administration to puzzle out new techniques to educate their crops of student cops. An idea that reached fruition was to give the classmates time in the field during the academy. The notion was that those officers could relate better to the training if they could see classroom instructions put into practice. The administration decided that the eight-week mark in the academy would have provided sufficient time for the new officers to function in the field. The recruits were tested in defensive tactics and firearms to assure their readiness for the streets. This would be their first time in uniform patrolling San Diego's streets, albeit with an FTO in charge.

The decision to split the recruits up among various units, Patrol, Traffic and WECAN was believed to give them the necessary exposure to the jobs facing them when they were on their own. WECAN was more of a flying drug and gang squad than a teaching unit, yet we would get our fill of trainees.

Whoever tasked WECAN to babysit recruits was off their meds. We were an elite unit. We were highly experienced and motivated quick movers. The teams moved so quickly and with such experience that the new people were baffled. Each FTO on WECAN got stuck with trainees and I was one of them. Within the earliest months of assigned trainees, we FTOs made it clear through our actions in the field that the trainees were not learning enough. Our gang and drug focuses were too narrow. Our proactive plans were quick and not decipherable to the newbies. We were not responsible to the radio. We didn't take crime reports and traffic accidents. We didn't always move in the same circles as patrol officers. Patrol, by the way, is where the trainees needed to be if they were to learn the nuts and bolts of police work. When comments from the trainees began to filter back to the Police Academy, the WECAN FTO program dissolved quickly.

Here's a bit of feed-back provided to the Academy Administration by the trainees: "Our FTOs would be driving down various streets when they suddenly stopped and yelled at us to jump out and arrest that guy, pointing at someone we hadn't even noticed."

Another comment was, "We were behind another WECAN car when the driver veered across Imperial straight into a liquor store parking lot. My FTO jumped out of the car and ran into the store with the other officers. I didn't know what to do. The car doors were open, and the engines were on. Jeff-the other trainee-returned and told me we were to sit tight. Another WECAN car drove fast into the parking lot and told us to secure the cars. Those two officers also ran into the store. Then, a lady ran at us screaming about her son. I had no idea what was going on. The officers inside came out with three guys in handcuffs. One of the officers had a gun in his hand. My FTO had a bag of crack and a wooden club. The WECAN officers opened the cars and put prisoners inside. My FTO yelled at the angry lady. Her son was one of our prisoners. She was freaked out until my FTO got her to calm down. He let her talk to her son. Then she apologized for something her son did and left. I found out after that the same prisoner flipped the bird at the WECAN car in front. That was all it took. We ended up with three Crips, a bag of crack, a billy club and a gun."

One scintillating written account that one of the trainees delivered went like this: "We were piled into a WECAN van. Three FTOs and three of us trainees. There were two other WECAN cars behind us. Suddenly, the van's driver, FTO Newbold, slammed on the brakes. Our FTOs shouted at us like it was back in boot camp. They yelled 'get out and arrest everybody wearing blue.' We got out but I had no idea what I was doing. The other two cars were all WECAN officers. We just did what they did and stopped everybody in blue. Officer Newbold and my FTO, Officer Rivera, gathered everyone together and lined them in front of Mullen's. Then, one-by-one, the WECAN officers told the Crips, I guess, that they were all being detained for disturbing the peace and wearing attire designed to provoke a fight. Officer Barrett explained that these guys were hardcore Crips. The FTOs figured as long as they had extra manpower, they'd take advantage of it and hot stop 30th and Imperial."

The FTO Admin interviewer asked, "Attire designed to provoke a fight. Is that even a law?"

Trainee: "I know, right?" A second trainee echoed the first. "WECAN had this big van. Sometimes we would all jump into the thing. It looked like a bread truck. They called it Weber One. There might be as many as six of us in the van, driving around Central territory looking for gangsters and dealers. The guys I rode with just called out the names of Crips they knew to each other and debated stopping them. When we stopped at a red light at Thirtieth and Imperial, everybody jumped out of the van running in every direction. The FTOs shouted at the trainees to grab anybody dressed in blue and detain them. We had no idea why we were stopping them."

Other recruits tried to explain their experiences, but so much of what we did was like a counterpoint to their academy training. No one could prepare them for our speedy and effective crime-fighting antics. WECAN's practices and tactics were a bit too advanced for the trainees.

Trainees that asked questions in the feedback sessions sometimes had difficulty explaining our actions. Others asked the FTOs at the academy for explanations that stumped them. WECAN was an entity in a league all its own.

I'd completed the program to become an FTO two years before I joined WECAN. My year and a half long stint on the Ocean Beach Beach Team curtailed the number of trainees I got assigned. We were Beach cops in name only. The men and women on the OB team were specialists first, and beach enforcement ticket-writers second. How else do you explain that four of the eight1986–1987 OB Teamers went to WECAN, Bill Woods, Cinda Jauregui, Tim Fay and me? WECAN would be the destination for my very first academy recruit.

My first trainee on WECAN was Derek Diaz, former military and former Special Forces. Derek's presence split me from my partner. By this time, all of us WECAN officers were well-versed at policing the drug and gang issues. We were proficient in any designated area. We were good at what we did. Partnerships were so well-honed that each could finish each the other's thoughts. That provided inherent abilities to react and move quickly. We had no radio responsibilities so there was no hourly distraction from everyday toils. We'd zip in, get the job done and take stock of what we'd just accomplished. The trainees saw things differently.

They reported that WECAN officers "acted and reacted so fast that trainees had no idea what was happening. One minute my FTO was driving down a main street. The next, we've skidded to a stop and I'm running after him chasing some guy into a yard."

All the trainees from the various WECAN teams reported their experiences in much the same way. Some admitted that they were overwhelmed and didn't really learn anything. WECAN officers piled up arrests and wrote miles of reports. The trainees couldn't grasp all that went into the process. The WECAN officers developed such rapid probable cause with each detention the trainees never got properly schooled. One trainee tried to describe an episode with his FTO: "I'm looking out my passenger window while my FTO is driving. Suddenly, she shouts, 'Did you see that?'"

"I'm looking around trying to see what I missed." She points to a black guy in blue walking down the sidewalk.

"'He dropped a cigarette pack. Go get him,'" she said as she slammed on the brakes and dropped me at the curb. I hurried to catch up to the guy and asked him to stop.

"'What'd I do?' the man asked.

"I had no idea and just told him to wait there. My FTO was behind me now, telling me to cuff the guy. I did, but I just went along with what she said. I was in the dark. My FTO held out her hand holding a small plastic baggie. I'm pretty sure it was rock, it had to be illegal, or why would I have arrested the guy. Everything happened so fast."

Derek recalls loving every minute of it. Every day out of the barn meant another set of doors kicked in, another foot chase, another gangster traffic stop, with yells and suspects tackled to the ground, followed by more confiscated drugs. According to Derek, he was never quite sure what led to any of our actions. He knew he was along for the teaching moments, but it was a blast for him to work WECAN and represent the kind of action he joined the San Diego Police Department for. "Thank God I didn't have to go to Traffic," Derek recalls. He looks back now with humor at his earliest WECAN team-up.

When FTO Admin assigned trainees to WECAN officers, I was still paired up with my former OB Beach Teamer, Bill Woods. I got stuck with a trainee at a time when Woody and I were a happy pair. We were assigned a large Ford LTD with a long bench seat in front. We were required to split up into two cars since there were three of us. Woody and I considered that option undesirable, so we put Derek between us upfront. His timid complaints were ignored. There was no articulate department policy to prevent such an arrangement. Hell, I'd seen motor cops in Tijuana ride two on a seat. Eventually, our command got wise and sent Woody one direction, and my trainee and me to Central WECAN where Manny and I partnered up. Derek was now in the bowels of Gang Town, USA.

I drove as was the norm with trainees and WECAN. Derek happened to look one direction when I looked the other as we scoured 32nd St. southbound. I saw a crack head I'd dealt with toss a small baggie into the front yard of a corner house. I studied the guy's motions as soon as I set eyes upon him. He'd obviously ejected the bag when he saw our car. He didn't react as though he knew I caught the movement. He certainly didn't want to get caught with contraband but wasn't slick enough to escape my notice.

I braked quickly and told Derek to stop the guy. Derek got out and intercepted him. Derek was an experienced combat soldier from the conflict in Panama and took orders well. The crack head, Melvin, feigned innocence and didn't balk at Derek's blockade. For the moment, Melvin stayed put and didn't seem bouncy like he was ready to rabbit. I stepped out of the police car and saw a garden just over a short, wrought iron fence. The baggie lay on top of the soil of a sparse rose garden that bordered the cinderblock wall.

The tines welded to the wrought-iron fence atop the wall were wide apart. I reached in between the metal staves and collected the baggie. The soil was damp from a passing rain cloud, and the baggie was the only dry object in the yard. To no surprise of mine, the baggie had a couple of pieces of rock cocaine.

I told Derek to arrest Melvin and handcuff him. Derek didn't react immediately. The event unfolded a little too quickly for his comprehension. He didn't know how I knew the guy was dirty. Recruits who rode with WECAN officers tended to be stumped by our deeds, but Derek's hands were already in Melvin's pockets before the cuffs went on. He pulled out a glass crack pipe as his contribution to the arrest.

Melvin wasn't ready for jail. He decided right there, this was the moment to resist. I was only a few feet away when the guy slapped the pipe out of Derek's hand. The glass tube shattered on the sidewalk, but that wasn't good enough for him. Melvin stepped on the glass and pulverized it to dust. Derek was stunned into action and tried to push the guy back. Melvin's hands were still free. I cleared the eight feet of distance and closed in on the pair just as Melvin made a shocking move. The man went for my holstered gun.

The spun-up fool had to be desperate to do such a stupid thing. As he gripped the butt of my holstered sidearm, my reaction was to turn and twist away from him. He strengthened his grip and attempted to

tug the gun out of its carrier. A typical police holster is built to retain a
weapon under these circumstances. Pulling the gun straight up from the
holster wouldn't work because of the holster's retention design. Melvin
had time to give the gun a couple of good tugs before I knocked the
fucker backwards and separated him from my weapon.

Derek couldn't wedge in between us and was uncertain how to attack.
He tackled the guy when I forced us apart. Derek and I flipped Melvin
over onto his chest on the damp concrete. The fight was over fast.

Any patrol officer will tell you this kind of confrontation can go
dangerous quickly just as it did for us. WECAN's two-officer sets were
paired for this reason.

The drugs, the pipe, and its destruction, all carried some light jail
time. I carefully described the man's effort to take my gun in my arrest
report. I hoped we'd see the guy get real jail time. This was a near-tragic
moment of realization for Derek. Talk about things happening fast on
WECAN, this was the type of going to shit fast incident that befell many
cops in their careers. I had four struggles for my service weapon in my
career.

Derek was a decorated soldier before he became a police officer.
But the unpredictability and surprising speed of Melvin's assault was a
complete surprise to Derek's sensibilities. He reacted to this skirmish
with reflection, asking himself what he could have done differently. I
told him the gun was always a tool for protection and a weapon in a
battle but could become a burden. He had to worry about the damn
thing anytime he was face-to-face with an opponent. I suppose he
already knew, but I emphasized the danger of drug users.

The events of the day easily mimicked the daily circumstances of
every patrol officer in the Heights. There were hosts of bad people with
the will to off cops. The number of attacks on police, in one of the most
violent neighborhoods in the county, was blessedly small. This one crack
head had some gang affiliation as a minor player. The dominant black
gang in Central was manned with many dangerous men, most ready
to make reputations by doing a cop.

Incidentally, the feedback the FTO Administration and police officials at the Academy received from Derek's fellow recruits fed a lot of

imaginations. As the last of the WECAN trainees were debriefed, it was clear to everyone that WECAN provided hot spots for police action. Now all the recruits wanted to be cycled through WECAN. Derek added his WECAN experience to his plans for his future. He chose SWAT as a lasting destination figuring it had to be at least as much entertainment as WECAN.

CHAPTER 44:
CRIPPIN' IT

The West Coast Crips were THE street gang west of Interstate 15. Their territory loosely bordered Downtown San Diego. Across highway 15, the Neighborhood Crips were their allies in crime and violence. Like all the Southwest regional African American street gangs, the WCC had their roots in South Central Los Angeles' historic gangster powder keg.

The WCC had the local distinction as the most tenured Crip set in San Diego, formed in 1972. By the time I'd graduated from training and hit the streets of Central Division, the West Coast Crips were already eight years old with plenty of members who wore blue like a uniform color. Central WECAN was designed to hamper the West Coast Crips on their turf. The crack epidemic encouraged black gang violence city wide, but Ground Zero for the Crips was the hunting grounds for my team. The Hispanic gangs shared the same turf and had little conflict with the black gangs. Their stake in crack sales was still minimal compared to flourishing black gangs.

WECAN used existent knowledge to pledge an end to gang violence. The black street gangs were the foremost targets for the time being. The drive-by shootings were getting a lot of press coverage. Since the shootings were within the black gang sets, they were our prime targets. Every cop who worked in gang-infested neighborhoods knew the hotspots and many were capable of quelling some of the violence if they only had the time and manpower. WECAN cops were assigned to take the time and make the plans to do what other cops could not. Once we moved in on the problem locations inhabited by the Crips in Central Division, we gave them hell and headaches.

A particularly annoying magnet for WCC activity was an apartment complex at the intersection of South 33rd and Durant Streets. This place was across the street from the house where we initiated the inaugural arrests for heroin balloon burglary that irritated the District Attorney's Office just weeks prior. Some of the residents living in this new target area were WCC, others were family and affiliates. Part of the reason for the draw was the connection to two notorious WCC Crips from that neighborhood, the Rogers brothers.

Curtis and Leslie Rogers were OGs, commanding respect and fear from the neighborhood they lived in and intimidated. Both men, in their twenties, were cruel, physical giants somewhere over six foot four and beefy, in the high two hundred range. I never met Leslie. He was in prison by the time I reached Central WECAN. He would die wielding two machine guns in a shootout with Central patrol officers not long after his parole from the penitentiary. Leslie's younger brother, Curtis, was a handful to deal with, too. He lived a block over from the S.33rd and Durant hangout. His homies took up a portion of the intersection almost every day and were constant irritants to the ordinary people who passed by.

The thugs and gangsters hung out for recreation and to move pot and crack. They typically spilled out into the street to do business with the vehicles that stopped to throw some brotherly love or pop for a dime bag. The antagonists within the gathered homeboys sometimes felt mean and formed a gauntlet to harass anyone foolish enough to drive through them. Every driver was scrutinized as either allies, customers, or the enemy. Drivers sped past, found other avenues, or wished they'd stayed home. The problem was pronounced and pulled Manny and me away from 32nd and J.

Along with other WECAN partners, we worked that intersection to contact, annoy, detain, arrest and generally be nuisances to the Crips as often as we could. One significant memory is when Manny and I stood in an abandoned house near the intersection where Curtis and his gang hung out. We'd parked out of site on Imperial Avenue and hiked in about two short blocks to get to the rear of the house. We'd jimmied the backdoor lock and got inside. The day was warm, but the sun had passed its zenith two hours before. The Crips outside had late afternoon shadows to potentially conceal their actions. Our vantage point was a drape-covered front window. Today was to be a good day. Curtis Rogers was on scene with an entourage of blue wrapped men around him.

I understood what gang members did to a neighborhood. Their actions ran good people off their turf. The house we stood in was one of the many homes abandoned since the Rogers brothers took up roost. The rental sign in the front yard must have irritated someone. The smashed wooden advertisement for new tenants was splintered all over the ground.

Manny and I watched Curtis and his cronies from behind drapes that covered a bay window at the front of the small home. With a simple nudge of the drapes, we could see the enormous Curtis seated on the front, left fender of his Cadillac Seville that was parked across the street. Curtis had put on some more weight. Manny and I tossed our guesses back and forth. We'd know soon enough if we detained him. Better yet, if we got enough on him from this operation to jail him, we'd know what his hugeness amounted to for sure. We watched Curtis enjoy a mid-afternoon snack, chomping down on the meaty contents of a giant bucket of Church's Chicken. The man's frame carried so much poundage that the poor car's bumper was buried into the asphalt.

We hoped to see some dope sales action, or an act of crime worth a contact, but it was not to be. The worst thing that happened was the disgusting pile of gnawed chicken bones Curtis left in the street. On a warm day like that, we could see the grease from the bones staining the street an inky black beneath Curtis' feet. When the excitement from this operation couldn't top Curtis' greasy appetite, Manny and I decided to collect out car and roll up on these guys for some good old fashioned FIs.

Our arrival came to the surprise of no one that ever hung around Curtis. Curtis was a magnet for the cops. Those people likely to carry dope or weapons sauntered off rather than deal with us. The others moped around to wait for this session of cops and gangsters to get over with. Naturally, big Curtis yapped at us for the sake of his diminutive brothas. The show was mandatory so he could maintain the image of top dog. "Why you five-o always be messin' wit me? Y'all got nothin' better to do than harass a brother 'cause he black." Curtis played his race card and his cohorts closed in to see what would happen next.

"You being black, brotha, has less to do with it than you wearing blue," Manny posited. And he phrased it quite astutely. Manny was a swarthy man with deep brown skin. Curtis just looked like an ass when he complained to another man of color. Manny's retort left Curtis flattened. He looked away from us at some distant point that didn't inspire him to a witty response. He kept his mouth shut and shrugged. His friends saw a dark-skinned officer challenge their leader, and the leader backed down. The others that didn't drift off and stood their ground, imitated some form of defiance with their arms across their chests and glares that mimicked prison yard stares. Manny and I weren't put-off. The puffed-up chest shenanigans no longer made much impression. We'd been there and done that, as the saying goes, way too often.

One new element did enter the situation. A large black woman appeared in the front yard of a house caddy-corner to, and behind us. I hadn't seen her enter the picture, but I sure as hell heard her shout. "Get home, Curtis!"

I looked back at him. He hadn't moved an inch since Manny spoke to him. He now looked sheepish and mumbled something to his friends. The woman was Mrs. Rogers, mother to Curtis and Leslie. Mother Rogers was wary enough to keep an eye on Curtis and try to protect him from the police and his own damn self.

Her sons were the junior versions of mom. I suspect the absent father was an older, male version of his sons. Mrs. Rogers was six-foot four and two hundred plus pounds herself. She wasn't fat, but she was big and intimidating. She protected her son when she yelled at him to come home and stay out of trouble. She wasn't doing it for our sakes. She held no love for the law. She didn't want him to get into trouble and end up in prison like his brother. Poor Curtis didn't challenge her. He released the pressure on his car and stood. He made a show of pulling up his waist, size fifty pants. Curtis strolled across the street in no real hurry and took a path parallel to his mother, in step next to her. He was done for the day.

The associates faded into the growing shadows and recesses of the big apartment complex across Durant as the sun took its journey west. The chicken bucket Curtis left on the sidewalk was the only evidence he had been there. Well that, and the sigh of relief I swear I heard emanate from his Caddy.

I looked at my watch and realized it was dinnertime for us. Mrs. Rogers surely had Curtis on the same schedule. I surmised that he'd worked up such an appetite arm wrestling with all those drumsticks that he was ready for supper, too.

Complaints from the honest folks in the neighborhood laid out the problems with Curtis and the gang. The ever-present crack sales attracted more crack heads than even the most liberal residents wanted to handle. No property was safe in that area. Thefts increased and addicts refused to stray beyond the distance necessary to get high quickly. The gang bangers from around the neighborhood were prone to hang out there, under the protection of Curtis. They yelled and played music at unheard of decibels and picked fights with anyone they wanted to. These Crips were embedded similarly to the others at 32nd and J. WECAN dealt a slight blow there. What else could we do here?

The fed-up neighbors who complained took a real big risk. Nobody complained about the gang members and remained safe and they knew it. These folks kept their identities secret to skate past the expected retaliation should their names be uncovered. We got the message because WECAN could filter through this portion of Crip turf at will and interrupt their daily business to the point that they'd have limited ability to sell drugs or hurt people.

The day came when I had a new trainee that separated me from my partner for a couple of weeks. Still, we all had responsibilities and 33rd and Durant was high on my list. My trainee, a guy named Rob, needed some exposure to the street gang world, so I drove him down to Curtis Rogers' 'hood to see what could be seen. When we got there, nothing much was shaking, the only thugs gathered were in front of the apartment complex. I saw three guys in blue Pendleton's and other blue attire, the usual assortment of hangers-on. I didn't see any a threat.

When an officer gets out of a police car in a war zone, he or she draws gawkers. In this case, Crips wandered outside from their apartments in the complex, followed by everybody else interested in what we were going to do. Rob was in strange territory. He'd had little exposure in life to gangs in their world. I told him to watch my back and stay close. I'd do all the talking. Most of all, I needed him to stay calm and look frosty. The worst gangsters would see any fear he generated and capitalize on it, which was a very unsafe prospect.

Straightaway, I was face-to-face with a large guy in blue, later identified as Leon. The guy was three or four inches taller than me and heavily muscled. He was also high. Leon's eyes were dilated in broad daylight. He could have gotten that way from booze. However, the man wasn't drinking. My expectation was that crack was the culprit when I considered where we were. There was a slight incoherence about the man. He was clearly on the upside of a smoke from a crack pipe and felt the full effects. I reasoned this would be a good sample arrest to teach Rob how to identify and solidify an arrest for 11550 H&S. Rob had yet to go through the procedure.

Rob stepped up next to me to observe. Leon didn't pay any notice to Rob. He concentrated on my voice. Leon was docile, at first. Rob began to get nervous as more people gathered around to watch the show. The action was at a time on a hot day where tempers could flare, and the lookers now could be the doers with just one wrong move or comment as a trigger. Volatility was always just a match-strike away in tough neighborhoods.

Rob worried for us and asked me if he should radio for cover. I told him not yet. These people in this place had seen me many times. I made it my mission to stay cool and display no weakness. We were not in a pressure-cooker and I told him not to worry.

A cop has to stay cool under pressure to maintain control of situations. The challenge to do so can be daunting for officers who had little experience with groups not pleased with the police on their turf. I work from the confidence that when I give respect, I expect the same in return. I hoped the gathered handful of people recognized that. If we called for cover prematurely, we could break that wisp of peace I was building here. Leon was the crowd's focus. His actions could dictate a peaceful outcome or a scrum that could get people hurt.

The sun made it difficult for me to demonstrate Eleven-Five symptomology to Rob. I'd seen what I needed to see from Leon, the dilated pupils in broad daylight. His eyes were sensitive to the sun and he tried to squint to reduce the irritation. He must have smoked in the past ten minutes to have eyes declare his under the influence so distinctly. I told Rob to handcuff him for arrest. Rob stepped around the soon-to-be prisoner, but that motion roused Leon. I needed a new approach and I could see Rob's flirtation with panic begin to surface.

Leon may have been aware of the circus that unfolded around us. He was in his zone of artificial contentment. Agitators began to speak up from the crowd. A few people horsed around and told Leon not to listen to us. The crowd noise tried to incite Leon to rebel. He seemed to slowly focus on resistance. He said he didn't want to go with the police and that he wasn't high. When he showed twitches of reluctance to follow my lead, the noisy crowd picked up on the signs.

The Crips in the complex appeared in larger numbers, crowding out some of the residents on the two floors of the apartment building. The disruptive crowd became larger, emboldened by the other guys in blue who challenged our authority. I told Rob I still had this. I made a show of transmitting a request for my WECAN partners to join us on the radio. I said it loud enough to make the group around us back off. Rob struggled to tamp down his nervousness. I could feel it in his demeanor. His eyes darted about, and his stance was stiff as a phone pole.

Leon was the apex man in this enlarging confrontation. He repeated that he wasn't high. I told him he was, and we were way past letting him walk with all the hostility that swarmed around us. I told him that the only way to prove or disprove his sobriety was a trip to Police HQ. If he didn't show the symptoms there, I swore I'd bring him back right there to that spot. He thought it over and surprisingly liked the deal. That must have been one happy crack high.

He wasn't angry. He didn't try to incite more trouble even as the others tried to stir him up. "Don't listen to the po-po, brotha."

"Fuck the po-lice. You ain't going with them."

"The po-lice be fucking with you, man. They got nothin' on you. Don't listen to them."

The crowd tried to egg Leon on and get someone in their midst to mix it up with us. That would be the call to action that would turn everybody loose on us. If they wanted a riot, they wouldn't get it. I spoke quietly and deliberately. I instructed Leon on my protocols. I told him, "The way this works, Leon, is we're taking you downtown where we can see your eyes proper-like. I know you think you're not high, but I need to know for myself. Are you good with that? If you're not, then those people around us are gonna make this one messy afternoon." I told him I was doing my duty with respect toward him. I expected the same in return. He had denied and debated my right to arrest him while the crowd got hotter. After the mutual respect speech he lightened up.

Leon looked around as though he was completely unaware of the mob that wanted trouble and depended on him to light the lighter. "I'll go. You're going to bring me back here if I'm not high? I'd rather not come back here."

"You got it, man." Nothing was going to deter me from the trip downtown. The crowd sensed things were not going to erupt in their favor. Some voices, more women than men, took direct verbal shots at me. One irate lady shouted, "Don't let that cracker take you in. You didn't do nothing. Don't let him arrest you!"

Rob swiveled and put his back to me. He faced the crowd with his sunglasses in place. The little things can matter in a conflict. The tinted glasses will mask fear in the eyes of a nervous man. Leon looked away plaintively at someone in the crowd for only a moment. Whatever tempest swirled through his mind, he knew he was enjoying his high, and he knew that I knew. This was not going to be the day he fought the police. Rob was focused on the crowd, probably praying for a miracle. I felt the tenseness inside begin to fade. I wasn't entirely sure I could pull this one off. I was deeply relieved when I put the handcuffs on. I hoped no one in the crowd could see the measure of relief on my face.

Slowly and deliberately, I walked at a nonchalant pace to our car. I wanted the witnesses to see confidence and no fear. I've seen people pour out of their apartments in neighborhoods like this when cops are at disadvantages while they try to do their jobs. I found it a struggle sometimes to keep my cool, but it was imperative. Any move that's likely to incite the gathered throng could be answerable to the Command, the press, the hospital or the morgue. I would return there soon, and I wanted today's impression to sink in. The drive to HQ was quiet. Leon wasn't ready to burst his high by talking to either of us.

Leon was processed for being high and went to jail. Rob asked me a lot of questions. I got the distinct feeling he was not ready for the confrontation that almost happened. I'm sure when his tour with me was over he'd spill his feelings of the day to the FTO Administration. If you can stand your ground against an antagonist, an opponent that hates you, and maintain muscled determination to quell a potential physical confrontation, that's a win. I have no idea if Rob took the message to heart. Once his tour with me was up, I never saw him again.

The blocks surrounding 33rd and Durant were dotted with dope houses, gang residences and a palpable hyper-awareness among the residents. They lived on tense streets yet had few alternatives while living on subsistent incomes. Many of the people who resided there were Spanish-only speakers, but all felt that the neighborhood had fallen through society's cracks long ago. Central Patrol, Central Investigations and WECAN knew that no one from the city Administration would publicly refute the knowledge.

My WECAN partners and I kept an eye on that intersection and apartment complex. Curtis Rogers and the other bangers were magnets for trouble. Since some poor soul felt it necessary to leave their comfort zone and complain to the police, not about the police, we would strive to provide some level of satisfaction. The complainant probably represented dozens of silent voices.

Manny and I were back together again. We returned to S.33rd one afternoon and headed north toward to Durant. The spies and lookouts were everywhere and fluttered into action. Pagers, animal sounds and shouts of "Five-Oh" rang through the streets. I imagine the cacophony was much the same in prison when guards are on the floor. We drove slowly to one block before Durant. We didn't want to miss a thing.

Curtis leaned up against his car with his bulk protruding into the southbound lane. I drove and Manny had shotgun. I saw the common bucket of KFC chicken, but it was all alone on the sidewalk behind the Cadillac. Typical. The bucket must have been empty trash and Curtis just dumped it in plain sight. Curtis leaned forward off the car and clearly said, "Fucking cops, always hassling us."

We hadn't done anything, but the "mad-dog" exchanges we gave and got back from Curtis were a red flag to a bull. I stopped the car.

I saw a large potato chip bag on the other side of a low chain link fence. The chicken bucket was on this side of the fence. Man, if that didn't look staged I don't know what did. Manny had a conversation with the ever-loquacious Curtis while I looked at the bucket. Hell, there was still fresh chicken in there. Why'd it get dumped? I leaned over the fence and saw the potato chip bag was full, too. Only, the innards weren't chips. I lifted the bag and discovered it was filled with dime bags of weed. I looked over my shoulder at Manny to see how he was doing.

Curtis jawed at him. That is, until I had the chip bag in my hands. I looked around at the other gangsters. They all moved on like something bad was about to happen. I looked at the bucket and saw more zip-loc baggies of pot mixed in with fried chicken thighs. I couldn't help myself. I laughed out loud and got Manny's attention.

"Check this shit out," I exclaimed as I held up my two trophies for Manny to see. Both of us looked back at Curtis to see his reaction.

Curtis was a mask of indifference on the surface. He had to be pissed off inside. I took out one of the chicken-greased baggies and wiggled it all around. The last of the hangers-on had his hands in his pants pocket and shrugged like it was no big deal. He also shuffled off since his plans for the day were crushed.

Curtis stood straight up and shambled off in the direction the others walked. I'm pretty sure I heard him say, "Fucking cops."

We had no one to pin the dope on. The weed would get impounded, anyway. I didn't know what was sweeter, taking Curtis's dope or his chicken.

CHAPTER 45:

SPEEDY DUNCAN

Manny and I briefly overlapped with assigned trainees. He had Linda and I had Cathy and we picked a day to slip back onto South 33rd and walk the neighborhood as WECAN was wont to do when a grander presence was necessary. We parked two cars on Durant next to the apartment complex that had become a headache. It was the same complex that was a haven for Curtis Rogers and his cohorts when they slung dope from chip bags and chicken buckets. Many of the occupants were relaxed on folding chairs in a small parking lot in front of the living quarters of the two-story building. Other residents and hangers-on stood on the second deck. Their attention was centered on a couple of men in suits. There was no sense of urgency, so Manny and his trainee strolled around the complex while my trainee followed me into the parking lot.

The two suits were distinguished-looking, older black men. They stood in conversation with a couple of the complex residents, the ones not wearing too much blue. The two men saw our uniforms and directed their attention to us. Some of the apartment denizens faded away or kept a distance from police scrutiny. Nobody at that complex ever wore suits. Most people there were either working-class renters or no-class thugs. I rightly guessed those two gentlemen were the responsible types.

I took the initiative and introduced myself to the "suits." The older man of the pair reached to shake my hand and introduced himself as Leslie Duncan. Then, on a side note he asked me if I ever watched the Chargers. When I said I did, he smiled at me and told me he was Speedy Duncan. THE Speedy Duncan.

My parents had been Chargers fans since the team relocated to San Diego from its one-year tenancy in Los Angeles after the inaugural American Football League season of 1961. My folks bought and retained season tickets since the inception of San Diego Stadium. Of course, I knew who Speedy Duncan was, and up to this point he was the only NFL player I'd ever met. The encounter was cool! I was a bit star struck standing next to the Chargers legend. He was one of the Chargers all-time most popular running backs from the 1960s. Unfortunately, Speedy wasn't there for a celebration. He and the other suit were owners of this problem property and doing an inspection. The police weren't the only recipients of complaints about the bangers in occupancy at this complex. Speedy was there to inspect and rectify a situation that would continue to gnaw away at him and the co-owner until something was done.

Manny and his trainee made a loop around the block to give his partner a "ground-level" view of one of the toughest blocks in San Diego. They finished their tour where I stood with Speedy Duncan. Speedy explained the dilemma of ownership of a rental domicile in such a tough neighborhood. This complex was designated sometime in the past for Section Eight housing per the U.S. Department of Housing and Urban Development, or HUD. Section Eight housing was geared towards low-income people. Hopefully, for families that needed to find residences they could afford. These Section Eight opportunities were geared to families otherwise trapped in the confines of places even worse than South 33rd and Durant. This apartment complex was a place HUD designated Section Eight and properly maintained by property management.

I'd seen the worst living places the poor had to settle for and this South 33rd complex was an improvement. For those residents that came from the Heights, this place allowed them to live close to their roots and their families. The problems on South 33rd weren't the buildings, it was the people. In this case, the children of some of Speedy's tenants were gangsters content to ruin the lives of others in the building and on the block. The complaints that filtered through to Speedy indicated he currently had problems with one or two of the apartments. Those troubles were magnets for all kinds of problem people with the Crips at the center of the maelstrom.

We all agreed that the neighborhood was smack-dab in the middle of gang territory. Speedy and the guy with him were not naïve. They didn't feel safe being there and were grateful the police happened to show up. Speedy recited that no matter how well he screened tenants, he could never know the whole truth about them unless he dug deeper. Up until now, Speedy thought he'd done his homework well. Clearly, we agreed his intuition could have been better honed.

The solution for him was the best solution for us. He lowered his voice and singled out the two apartments he was sure were the bad elements infecting the rest of the building. He'd spoken to at least one of those tenants, but they put the blame on others in the area and tried to throw Speedy off the scent. Nobody denied there were Curtis Rogers-types all over that neighborhood. Speedy let it be known that the problem tenants would lose their housing vouchers.

Poor people allowed to live under Section Eight protection paid no more than thirty percent of their income for rent. The loss of their vouchers could put them in worse places to live. And there were places worse to live in the Heights than South 33rd and Durant. Speedy promised the tenants who did not respect the place they lived in they'd find life on the streets much worse when they got evicted.

I watched some of the people take stock of our presence and begin to disappear when they sensed Speedy was referring to them. Some of the tenants wanted to see the outcome. Maybe they hoped our coincidental meet would lead to some good for them and their loved ones. They knew the day-to-day strain on their lives could get better. Some had come from those places worse than South 33rd and Durant.

I thought this happenstance interchange with Speedy Duncan was a fateful moment. He didn't enter the ownership of an apartment complex to have to police it himself. Our presence took some weight off his shoulders because it looked like we were there to share the responsibility of turning the status of the apartments around. We gave him our WECAN unit phone number and told him to call anytime. The tenants saw the mutual sharing of phone numbers and probably understood the problem-people's days were numbered.

I know that coincidental hook-up that afternoon prodded Speedy and other owners to take aggressive action against their problem tenants.

After about a month we saw fewer guys in gang blue loitering around the complex. Even sightings of Curtis Rogers seemed to be fewer in number.

I've mentioned that Curtis' brother Leslie was shot and killed in a gunfight with police. A direct assault on police by Crips with weapons in the Heights was rare. Leslie Rogers' attack on the officers was more a reaction than a plan of action.

Several officers drove up on Leslie as he stood around his car that day. As the officers got out to speak with Leslie, who was on parole, he reached through the open window of his car exposing two machine guns of the MAC Eleven type. He blasted away at police and one officer was wounded while shooting back at Leslie. Officers from all over headed into the fray. Bullets flew in all directions, but at least one fateful round plowed into the large ex-con and killed him.

A subsequent increased police presence tipped the scales in favor of the good people who lived in that neighborhood. This was a prime example of letting a problem fester and of the power of a street gang with dominant leaders. When the head was lopped off, the remnants scattered, if only to shuffle off for two blocks north to South 33rd and Imperial Avenue and the ubiquitous corner liquor store.

I was always impressed by the professional level of policing instituted in such a violent warzone. The department had so few officers who managed to hold the Central Division neighborhoods in-check from day to day. Central Patrol was a litmus test for new cops. This was the place to learn how to deal and work with people who lived within a rugged city sector. Gangs and drugs took away their peace and security. Toss in the constant throngs of drug dealers and users and it's a wonder both Logan and Sherman Heights didn't tear apart at the seams.

The police were charged with the protection of a public that couldn't do much to ensure its own safety. If the people drew negative attention from the local villains, their lives were at stake. If they fought alongside the police, they risked vengeance from gangsters ready and willing to kill. A win-win scenario didn't seem to exist in that climate.

The gangs were an entrenched army that ran crimes, their family members, and allies. All we could do as police was battle with them constantly. Some community activists and leaders believed that less policing was be the answer. They argued that the presence of police officers instigated trouble. This paradox occasionally found airtime on television news during election campaigns. Meanwhile, the police stood in defiance of the gang problem and did what we could. Our chance meet with the great Speedy Duncan might have been the motivation he sought to push out the bad elements. Foot patrol and happenstance paid off. The complex was quieted to a degree and tenant complaints to Speedy lightened.

Walking police officers were the epitome of drawing a line in the sand. WECAN knew we'd added a measure of pressure that had a small impact. Changes in the Heights were no easy accomplishments. And for once, the trainees had something to relate back to the FTO Admin that wasn't incomprehensible.

CHAPTER 46:
OVERWHELMED

With all the contacts and snitches that slithered about, we never took long to uncover our next lead to some dope house. One lead came from some random resident who lived on the busy commercially zoned 2800 block of Imperial Avenue. The concerned man saw us in our parked police car and made the bold step to approach us in front of a lot of passersby and a few men playing pick-up basketball in the courts next to our car.

I was a little surprised anyone would want to volunteer any crime information in the Heights. In retrospect, I suppose there was such a large police presence down there that, to the average person on the street, a man talking to the police was not out of the ordinary.

The gentleman complained to Manny and me about a house behind a taco shop on Imperial. The shop was just around the corner from our current parking spot. This bolder-than-most local said the place was always busy with lots of people coming and going. He volunteered that he was a hard-working man with a mortgage. He knew he lived in a dangerous neighborhood, but he didn't fear the gangs. He didn't bother them, and they left him alone. Those "lousy drug dealers" were what bothered him enough to talk to a policeman. He warned that the police needed to know, so they could stop them. We now had an address and gathered our forces to check the place out.

The sun was at five o'clock and dusk was two hours away. We remained in our car to make the contact look a little more coincidental and perhaps give the impression the talk was impromptu and meaningless. The savvy street creeps watching us might get suspicious if the verbal exchange led to direct action on our part. Luckily for us, that part of the 2800 block of Imperial was cluttered with people used to seeing cops around. They hardly paid attention to us.

John, Chuck, and Roger met us one block up and around the corner on L Street for a confab. Our marked units were around the block, away from prying eyes that could connect us to our mission.

The house was an early 20th Century Craftsman with a granny flat behind one of the seemingly ubiquitous Roberto's Taco Shops. It was sided with wood lathe and built with a generous front porch. The porch-end of the house was covered with ivy and other plant growth, giving the impression the place tried to hide itself. Vines, overgrown trees, and bushes hid the small dwelling in an elfin forest. The yard was surrounded by a fence tall enough to hide it from the street. We made access through a gate off the alley.

The five of us took up caution points around the house until we could figure out the lay of the property. The plan was interrupted when a Latino man stepped outside through the side kitchen door for a smoke. When he saw us, he froze long enough for Chuck to step up face-to-face. Manny stood next to the guy and asked him the usual questions in Spanish. He was clearly not from this country. He had no idea how to respond to American police and politely allowed us inside. Two of our guys stayed outside to cover us. The house was larger than it seemed from the outside.

The sight inside astonished us. There were over twenty-five people crowded against each other throughout the front half of the house. Everybody was Hispanic with more men than women. Some of the men and women were huddled in pairs. Everyone looked nervous with us in the room. Most of the people sat on the floor. The lone couch and chair were for the lucky few. If I had to guess, I'd say the bundles and backpacks these people held onto held the total of their belongings. We'd stumbled on an alien drop house.

For the uninitiated, a drop house is a stop for smuggled undocumented nationals, mostly Mexican in this case. However they arrived, they were there to get rides to their next destination which was usually Los Angeles. Our tipster probably knew this when he fished around for our help. If drugs were coming out of here, it was unlikely this crowd selling them. That was not what they were there for. We found more people in the kitchen where food containers from Roberto's

Taco Shop filled the countertops. The smugglers couldn't have picked a more convenient place to temporarily house Mexican border-crossers. I suspected Roberto's knew about the house behind it and what it was being used for. They were making a fortune as the caterers.

Quietly, we moved about the house and sent all the people into the living room. Chuck and John initially stood guard in the doorway. John kept the post as events unfolded indoors. I asked Chuck to come inside and cover us. John had a clear view of the back door to Roberto's. One of the cooks stepped out that door with a cigarette in his mouth. He took one look at John and spat the butt out. John made eye-contact with the man and John later related that he looked back in anger. Then, his face went neutral and he slipped back inside the taco shop, probably to tell the others their largest customer base, the fearful dependents of his menu, might dry up and go away soon.

Back then, the San Diego Police Department's policy on the detention of undocumented foreigners gave its officers broad range to get involved. If we discovered undocumented people during the performance of our duties, we would either transport them to Border Patrol, or call for Border Patrol to come collect them. This enforcement was approved by our department and was up to the discretion of the officers. There were rarely any projects when we were sent into the field with the express purpose of rounding up illegal border crossers.

The only time I can recall when we were induced by the department to snap them up was when the new development around downtown San Diego's Horton Plaza Shopping center was red hot. The city wanted to sweep clean the streets of people that distracted from their goal to clean up downtown. The thought was that the throngs of street people and the illegal aliens would detract from the Horton project and drive away tourists and prospective business. The department was directed to pay officers overtime to clean the streets. We were sent out on foot in two-officer units to roam the streets within a four-block radius of Horton Plaza. The months-long program was euphemistically called, "Walking for Dollars." I added those hours to my normal WECAN week. I walked for dollars and I walked against crime. The overtime pay I earned would eventually go into my buy-a-house fund for my wife and son.

Right now, we needed to figure out who oversaw all these pensive souls in this decrepit house. Was it some *coyote*, or smuggler, trying to blend in with this crowd to throw us off? How many people in this house were potential dangers to us?

They all seemed docile. We had them stay seated on the floor and made cursory searches for weapons. The guys on the couch and chair were moved to the floor. Those seats would have made enticing hiding places for guns and we reasoned only the bad guys would get those seats. Nothing was found. The men were patted down one at a time while we looked on for any change in the group's demeanor. We searched personal bags, backpacks, and everything else these people had with them. We were not going to let any weapons remain unnoticed. So far, everything was status quo. I'd been among large groups of people all massed for one reason or another. My radar had developed into a well-refined device that could single out and home in any troublemakers. The sounds I picked up on, the utterances under the breath and the vibes of bad intent all clued me in to a problem brewing within any circle of people around me. The rest of my team all had deeply intuitive senses that warned of peril. This uncanny ability had kept the five of us going this long. There wasn't a blip of concern between us for a threat from these worried people.

I decided to check out the rest of the house. There were still two bedrooms and a bathroom we hadn't scoped out. I made it my duty to secure those rooms before we decided our next moves. The five of us had the house contained outside. My team could spare me as I cleared the other rooms.

The first bedroom down the hallway from the living room was empty of people but filled with temporary beds. The bathroom checked out okay, too. The second, furthest bedroom was furnished with just two beds. I peeked in and saw two guys relaxed on the separate beds. I stepped into the room and determined they only faked sleep. Both guys laid on their backs, one with his right arm behind his head and under his pillow. They were both Mexicans from the other side of the border. I tried a little Spanish with them. The guy on the left with his hand behind him acted like he didn't understand. The guy on the right understood English. He played dumb when I asked him questions. He didn't know why he was there. He didn't know whose house it was and yadda, yadda, yadda. His cool demeanor bugged me. Why wasn't this guy as nervous as those in the big room up front? His companion seemed calm, too.

The guy on the right sat up. I didn't want to be outnumbered so I shouted for one of the other officers to come to my location.

These little mysteries always make me nervous. The back of my neck began to itch. Something was wrong here and it all had to do with that guy's hand under his pillow. My instincts screamed at me to pull my gun out. I pointed it at him and braced myself in a shooter's stance. Using pidgin Spanish, I demanded that he remove his hand from concealment and show it to me empty.

"*Levantase sus manos*," was the closest I could come to making my directions clear.

His facial expression didn't change. His eyes narrowed like those of a man on the cusp of sudden, hostile action. Beads of sweat formed above his brow. I knew this guy was bad at that moment.

The other guy was still a problem for me. His hands were in plain sight across his chest. I had him in my peripheral vision. My gun could cover either of them with just a nudge of my right wrist. I felt my tension rise. My outstretched arms were taut with my semi-auto at shoulder height. The right-hand side dude was frozen on the bed. He didn't risk a move. The left-hand side guy gave off ambient energy that crackled. I'd felt that sensation before with other people I thought were a clear and present danger to me in the moment.

Manny and Chuck looked in through the doorway and saw my gun out of its holster and pointed in a death grip at a guy on a bed. Manny told the guy on the left in Spanish to get up. The other guy froze with his hands in the air. Both men were on their feet and faced Manny's gun, as well. Once the guy from the left bed was clear of it, I holstered my gun and lifted that pillow that bugged me so much. There was a loaded pistol underneath. The gun was a semi-auto with the safety off and one round in the chamber. That effing guy was going to shoot me if the opportunity arose. Thank the stars my threat warning system kicked in when it did. His lips were twisted into a cruel smile. That look neutralized as I unloaded the pistol while staring into his eyes. He let his mouth flatten but his eyes never lost their cool menace. If I could read anything from his gaze, I'd interpret the man's thoughts as a reflection on the use of a gun before. A stint in county lock-up for the gun didn't bother him at all.

We figured out these two guys occupied the presidential suite, which made them the *coyotes* in charge of this operation. These men were part of an organization paid to move all these people onto their next delivery point. The gun was to keep their charges under control in case they still owed money. The other Mexican nationals were literally prisoners of some human smuggling cartel. The man with the gun could have been an experienced killer. I am not. I am highly trained and ready to shoot at a threat. These human smugglers are about as evil as they come. Who knows what bodies this gunman had left in his wake?

We are not outfitted to arrest two guys for holding twenty-five other people hostage. That was the bad news. The good news was the gun's serial number indicated, through Police Communications, that it was stolen. My guy was going to jail for that. His companion and the rest of the party were turned over to two Border Patrol vans called up from their border headquarters. Manny and I pointed out the smuggler we didn't take to the BP agents. BP got too much shit from critics. They were consummate pros and did their job with care and efficiency. They knew many of their detainees lived in hard times across the border and beyond.

To this day, I mull over what might have happened if we hadn't caught the guy with the gun by surprise.

CHAPTER 47:
REMOTE VIEWING

WECAN cops got to play spy all the time. We were constantly on surveillance and awaiting the golden opportunities to catch bad guys in the act. On top of all the other equipment handed to us through our fat budget, high-powered binoculars were on the list. With those, we could watch a dope deal go down from a hundred yards and still tell the court what the drug was and how much money exchanged hands. WECAN cops met many challenges to get gangsters and drug dealers off the street with the full backing of the law. The binoculars were the powerful tool we needed to stay within the confines of search-and-seizure laws and still make cases that would stand up. We were no longer restricted to close contact to pull down dealers and bangers. Stealth was introduced to such a degree that the crooks probably still don't know where we were when we watched them engage in crime.

One of the newer challenges to police work in the downtown area was the protection of trolley riders. The trolley made many stops downtown, but none were more nefarious than the stop at the intersection of Twelfth and C Streets. That trolley stop was next to a convenience store, three schools, a busy McDonalds, and was notorious for gangs and drugs. Like so many other places in town, this stop was ripe for WECAN pickings.

Across the street was a YWCA building, with a door to the roof that overlooked the trolley stop and the busy Circle K convenience store parking lot. With a few words to the YWCA staff, we were granted access to the roof. The staff was almost all women. They showed us consideration and appreciated some uniformed cops within arm's reach. Some of the women housed there were domestic violence victims. The staff warmed them up to the idea we were not there because of internal issues at the Y.

We were only at the Y periodically, and exclusively to occupy the rooftop. They knew we weren't there specifically for their needs, yet they showed cooperation without contesting our presence in a facility with patrons in transitory periods in their lives. The only men in the place were the maintenance people. We always made a point to greet any women we encountered with a "Hello" and a smile. I got a warm feeling when the occasional staffer or resident gave a smile in return. One or two hugs were given, and we made it a point of giving the hugs back.

Our plan was simple and repeated often. The rooftop lookouts would spot dope deals and send in the chase teams to arrest both parties. The miracle Bushnell 7x50 binoculars we carried allowed us close-up, focused views of the money and drugs that changed hands. And we were five floors up! No one on the streets below ever gave an outward indication that we'd been spotted. The eye in the sky operation required a couple of chase cars so the arrest teams could rush in and take down the actors. Remarkably, the cars would disappear with their charges, listen to the instructions from the rooftop to turn over another exchange, and return lickety-split to nab another pair. The bad guys in the cars could hear the conversations between their captors and the voices over the radio. But the bad people were so numerous that they replicated each time we returned, as though nobody feared or understood the scope of our operation.

We racked up the felony pinches as criminal illegal aliens and gang members alike went to jail. The bad guys could never figure us out. Our position on the roof was never burned. What a great surveillance spot. For my money, it should go down in the books for originality.

The action there was constant in the daylight. We could pick them off all day if we didn't have other responsibilities. The bad guys arrived constantly by trolley. We watched Mexican nationals exit the trolley after the ride north from the border. They frequently hopped the ride without paying and rode the trolley to drug-deal central. The trolley would soon extend all over the county with new tracks being put down. The bad guys of Mexico could travel for crime to places they normally wouldn't reach without a car or the bus.

The fun was in popping countless dope dealers, but the time constraints from the paper flow and prisoner transports took its toll on other spots we needed to be. We held onto that daytime-only location to bust guys until something even more entertaining and more important surfaced at my gym of all places.

I was at my membership gymnasium one morning when greeted by a fellow exerciser I got to know there. He was older than me and lived on the water-surrounded resort city of Coronado, across the bay from downtown San Diego. He knew what I did for a living and felt himself a strong supporter of the police. On this day, he showed me a copy of the Coronado newspaper. Some intrepid reporter had discovered that the transit authority cameras on the Coronado Bay Bridge hovered over Chicano Park.

The bridge and pole-mounted cameras were controlled by Caltrans, the state freeway and highway authority for California. Caltrans cameras monitored the bridge for emergencies from one end of the bridge to the other. The reporter got to watch and note how the informative bridge booth operator toggled a camera and pointed it down towards the park. The reporter knew about Chicano Park's reputation for gangs, drugs, and violence. The reporter offered in his article that it was, "a cool tool for the police to use to catch bad people."

I brought the article to work and held it out to my team. WECAN's bosses saw the wisdom of WECAN intrusions into the gangster-ridden park. And since the park was notoriously difficult to spy on, the Red Steps and their cohorts had seemingly free reign over that patch of earth. All our previous successes at the park were either happenstance arrests or occasions when we hid in bushes and got lucky. We couldn't resist the opportunity to chip away at the Logan Heights Red Steps responsible for all kinds of evil, with the gift of a single Caltrans camera mounted on a light pole directly over the park.

We used the same basic scheme we'd used on the roof of the YWCA. The Caltrans office was in the old Coronado Bridge Authority office when the bridge still had operational toll booths. The many cameras were steered remotely from a series of consoles and pointed in various directions. The few nighttime employees gave us carte blanche to work the system whenever we wanted. One or two of our team manned the camera control console. The camera used toggle controls to rotate and maneuver it horizontally three hundred and sixty degrees, vertically, and with zoom. The picture was in black and white which didn't really affect us. We just needed to be able to identify people and vehicles. The other team members would create vehicular choke points to cut-off and stop the cars we wanted.

Logan Red Steps claimed Chicano Park as their turf. This violent gang was allied with the *sureno* Mexican Mafia prison gang and was an entrenched mainstay in a community that bred the members. Aside from all their other dubious activities, the Red Steps were prolific at drug sales. The community activists had an accord with the gang, but not with the individual gangsters. Nobody had control over them, but the *La Familia* bosses.

High on the list of products they moved was PCP. Chicano Park was very much a community and family park. People kept their distance from the gangsters, which was unfortunate for the kids who should have been able to play there untouched by the gang's violent reality.

We'd picked off a few dealers and users in the past, like that fourteen-year old maniac I'd sparred with. But we missed the cruelest players, those that would sell to the fourteen-year old. WECAN had removed a handful of OG bangers prior to the camera's introduction. The best arrests came about through luck more than skill. We caught a guy with a sack of "lovely" foil bindles in front of *La Central* because he was a heroin junkie, not because we were good at subterfuge. His people allowed him to sell PCP without any lookouts. He was too stoned to pick out our spy, so we got him in a deal with a car. Just like the shotgun episode from weeks prior, patience and luck trumped skill. The bridge camera was the blessing we'd waited for. Now we could stage in more than one place and work the daytime, just like the YWCA, and sanction real players.

Our first act utilized five team members. Manny and I worked the cameras and radio to relay observations. John and Chuck sat in their car a block away, while Roger took another position in his cruiser. Manny and I made ourselves comfortable in the chairs provided by the Bridge office and became accustomed to camera operation. We tested the camera's limitations and judged its optimal attitude in relation to what we could testify to in court. Once everything was dialed in, we toggled our way to work. None of us felt confident we'd pull this off. Maybe the cameras weren't good enough. Maybe someone in the Bridge command structure would object, like we experienced with the FBI. Would color images matter? The cameras transmitted to black and white monitors. I worried remote viewing from over a mile away would prove a logistical weakness. If the guys needed help at the park, we would be too far away.

Chicano Park is a beehive of activity in the daytime. Everything changes at night. The Red Steps hang around La Central Market across the street and increase in number. Nighttime was gangster hour. The Red Steps used the darkness to sell drugs to motorists who floated up and sped off. The customers seemed more likely to buy "wack," another street term for PCP, under the cover of darkness. We would depend on the strong park lights and those fortunate La Central exterior lights to enhance our view. Many cops had monitored the actions of the criminals at the park in the past, but not like this. The camera opened a whole new world. Within moments of operational inception, we watched drug deals in motion.

The first pick was a southbound sedan that stopped in front of the market. The gang member who made the deal approached the passenger side and handed a silvery bindle through the window to the driver in exchange for cash. The camera saw everything. The detail and zoom capability worked like I was only yards away. The market's lights were bright enough to reflect off the foil and the camera picked it up. I was presented with veritable stage-lighting and the stage. Manny called the shots to the chase cars while I used the camera's zoom to note the car's license plate. When the car left, the stage was set for a take-down.

John and Chuck stopped the car out of sight of the seller. They made the legal search and recovered a foil bindle of PCP-laced marijuana. After another prisoner takedown, they handed off their prisoner to Roger as he became the designated prisoner control vehicle. The first scenario worked so well we decided to keep it going. Roger drove his car farther off to escape any chance a prisoner would be recognized and send back alerts to the Red Steps. The seller hadn't moved, and we figured we'd let him hang himself with a couple of more sales.

Pretty soon, another car rolled up and we repeated the exact process with the same result. Still, our seller was clueless and remained in front of the market with a couple of his pals. So far, he was the only player among that crew.

Our final buyer that inaugural night was a guy on foot. This time, the same seller signaled the buyer to stay put. The seller walked a few feet down the sidewalk past La Central to a fence that fronted a house next to the market. He reached down behind one fence post and retrieved a crumpled paper bag. From my camera mount I could see him extract another foil bindle and then replace the bag in its hiding place. The closest streetlight illuminated the aluminum foil so that it sparkled in front of the camera. I steered the camera back to the buyer.

The pusher stepped back over to the buyer and another cash deal took place. Satisfied, the buyer walked across the street into the park. I pointed the camera to the left and followed his path. Manny gave out the description. John and Chuck rolled up a block and waited for the unsuspecting buyer to cross their path out of view of the park. My observations generated enough probable cause for a legal detention.

The buyer's purchased bindle of lovely was confiscated and he was arrested. This time we all coordinated via radio for the seller's arrest. He hadn't moved on and was calm when both police cars left their posts and surrounded him. I stayed with the camera as a safety issue just in case I spotted some ambush or other villainy out of the arresting officers' sight lines. The WECAN trio radioed, "All is well." Manny and I thanked the bridge techs and cleared the control booth. The trip across the bridge and down to street level took fewer than five minutes.

The seller was a documented OG, Red Steps gangster. He was hand-cuffed while the team members rearranged their prisoners to separate him from his buyers. The officers froze the scene until Manny and I got there. I was the spotter witness to the dope's location. I reasoned the "chain of custody" of the evidence would retain a level of indisputability in court when the guy who spotted it also collected it.

We returned to the camera over a period of weeks and made more arrests. Chicano Park turned into a Cherry Patch Park as we racked up the felonies and snared a few baddies, including two Red Steps on parole for, wait for it... sales of PCP! One operation sent two WECAN guys into the backyard of the abandoned house next door to the market. The dealers were antsy by this time. We didn't want them to be too alert and toss contraband on the roof of the market should we drive up all sudden-like. Two of us entered off the alley, while others staffed the camera. The guy they targeted was holding bindles in his hand to count them, under full view of the camera. So far, no bites among the wack public. A woman sauntered up to him and led him by the hand into the yard my partner and I were in. We ducked into the shrubbery figuring they'd see us soon enough. Instead, she led him into the house. What occurred next I'd never witnessed before.

We looked through the curtain-less windows and saw the two seated on the carpeted living room floor. The place was barren of furniture. She handed him a balloon of heroin. He set up his rig to prep the drug. To remove his drug paraphernalia from his pants pocket, he had to pull out a paper sack, the one he stored the PCP in. He set that on the floor and went to work to get high. The woman leaned in to plant a wet kiss on his cheek and in closer for the lips next. He was intent on the chore at hand and seemed ambivalent about the bout of affection. She became more assertive and ran her right hand over his Levis, sliding the hand up his thigh and over his crotch. He wore a dopey expression and momentarily took his eyes from the needle still in his hand. She had his attention when she unzipped his fly and reached inside his pants for his manhood.

I was stunned. This guy had to be dope hungry. I understood sex was the furthest thing from a user's mind when about to fix. He didn't abide by that rule and allowed her to tug his penis out of his pants.

At this point, the two of us had remained silent, just waiting to go in and nab them. The guy and his actions were fascinating. We watched a junkie go through the routine to shoot heroin as though we watched a documentary. The addition of the woman made the whole shebang seem voyeuristic. When she withdrew his "special purpose member"

I looked at my partner with eyes wide open and mouthed the words. "What The Fuck?" Meanwhile, she had his penis in her mouth and began to work him like a pump. He was still trying to figure out how to get his rig prepared as she went down on him and skewed the dynamics.

We broke off our stares and decided to walk in before things got, umm, messy. We surprised of them, of course. She recoiled in fear and separated herself from Loverboy. He had his hands full and just gave up when I told him to stay still. We let him collect himself and then hand-cuffed him for the PCP and the heroin. She went down for heroin too.

We made other worthwhile arrests and gave the Red Steps a pretty good drubbing over the few weeks we stung them. Court was looming as the subpoenas for the first arrest began to float into our office.

We chose a subsequent night to set up and snare more drug deal-ers. Roger took camera position, so, Manny, Chuck, John and I could be the arrest teams. This time, Roger had a guy in front of La Central slinging PCP from a bag he kept hidden just over the front yard fence of that abandoned house.

Manny and I drove up on this caper. Manny babysat the dealer and I became the designated "finder." Roger pinpointed the bag and directed me via Nalemars. I approached the dope's concealment as though I was poking about with a random search for contraband. I gave an Oscar worthy performance when I acted as though I'd searched around for the crumpled bag before I fortuitously stumbled onto it. We wanted the mystery of the camera to remain for as long as the subterfuge would last. The bag was right where I'd seen him conceal it from my camera haunt. I had latex gloves on to prevent skin contact with the chemi-cally volatile PCP. I opened the bag and counted out twenty-three more bindles of the same type and substance as the three seized from the buyers. That was that.

The seller was charged with sales of a controlled substance and possession of a controlled substance for sale. The District Attorney's Office would later decide if they'd apply a gang enhancement clause to the seller to guarantee an increase in the time he'd serve after conviction.

We wanted to protect the camera from the bad guys and their attorneys. The defense attorney's knowledge of the camera's mounted location could end the ease of these surprise arrests and probably get the camera damaged. The attorneys would combat our case throughout court and potential appeals because of the distance, the use of electronics, and any other way they could figure to fence with the prosecution and disrupt our case. The gangsters could only guess at how we discovered their movements.

My team members and I knew the bridge camera was a great tool if its secret wasn't revealed to the people we targeted. Once that happened, we'd lose the advantage. To keep it secret required just enough explanation in our reports to keep the camera's existence unknown. We hoped we could stall defense attorneys with vague verbiage about our surveillance nest. The five of us debated what to write and hit upon the following: "I took up a position of surveillance with a view of the park from less than one hundred yards away."

Technically, the camera's distance fit the measurement. We camera monitors did not. We would protect the camera for as long as we legally could. Our first preliminary hearing for a Chicano Park bridge camera arrest came in the form of a DDA subpoena two weeks later.

The case was the State of California versus Salvador Ascencio Sanchez. He was the guy I nailed for the bag of PCP bindles stuffed in the yard. Each bindle contained marijuana laced with PCP. The two felony charges stuck, but there was no gang enhancement add-on. The DA would use that boost for leverage if this case went to trial. The attorney for Sanchez had the police report and cautiously studied the observation point I'd barely described on the pages. This was only a prelim. All the court wanted was the facts to judge if they lined up for a prosecutable case. The prosecution side interviewed me on the stand, and I regurgitated what I'd already written. The prosecution doesn't want any surprises like comments that weren't on paper. The defense craved facts that weren't written. Attorneys pounce on anything after the fact. The report lost credibility if the officer providing testimony added some color or filled in holes that seemed to be suspiciously added to fix a screw-up. The old saying goes: "If it ain't written down, it didn't happen."

I sat solid on my report. The defense side tried to blow it apart. I was too experienced not to see the attorney's angle of attack. When he tested the authenticity of my observation post, he strained to ask the right questions to pin me down. His problem was my strength. His imagination did not send him looking up a pole. He could only articulate ground-based questions. So, I gave him answers that didn't elevate my line-of-sight. I read his narrowed eyes to mean he was dubious over my answers. He smelled something that reeked of mystery. The defense challenged our position through an *in camera* hearing.

In camera allows the judge to exclude jurors and spectators from the courtroom. Things intended to be kept secret would be disclosed in front of both sets of attorneys. Our secret was the bridge camera. If a savvy attorney suspected we cloaked a secret, he or she would have the advantage. If the judge forced us to reveal the bridge camera, two problems would be created. One would be the gangsters' realization of the camera and a change in their tactics. Two, would be the defense attorney's desire to see the camera in operation to build a defense to argue against it.

The many arrests we made resulted in preliminary hearings that bound the defendants over for trial. Only this attorney contested our surveillance location. He sensed a way to wedge into the prosecution's case for drug sales if he could figure out where we'd hidden ourselves the night of the operation. The attorney cross-examined me until I was coerced into defining the spot. I played with generic versions of the truth and admitted to "seeing everything from the Coronado Bay Bridge overlooking Chicano Park."

The attorney seemed satisfied when I was forced to surrender my hunting blind. He stopped short after that revelation. If he'd dug a little deeper the secret would have been uncovered. I would have been compelled to tell the whole truth because the judge would see the stall tactics and compel me to give it all up. Out of the numerous arrests the camera yielded in the park, none ever resulted in the disclosure of the magic camera.

We arrested every violator we'd seen on camera. Only one guy bothered to put up a struggle. He was a Red Step holding the bindles in his hoodie the evening we watched his dope move for cash. He was easy. In fact, they were all easy. No other police officers knew of the camera.

That tactic was brand new and the cast of Red Steps and their flunkies fell as prey to us every night we trained the lens on them. The gangster that thought otherwise when the arrest team confronted him, a Red Step called Flacco, was already in hot water. He was on gang probation and wasn't supposed to be in the company of other gang members. He was cautious about getting pinned by police in front of La Central with other Red Steps, so he stood right inside the market's entrance. The other thugs would signal if a police car was on deck and he'd pop into the gang-friendly store. The Chaldean store employees had little choice but to comply with Red Step gangsters' directions. Nobody in that gang looking up at that bridge ever saw anything other than a giant, concrete obstruction.

I watched Flacco make his sale and sent the cover team after the buyer. The night was kind of quiet. We expected more action, but nothing was shaking. Flacco surely felt tonight would make him a lot of money. PCP was an attractive drug for psychological reasons only. There's no opioid like addictive qualities to the chemistry. Users love the zoned-out escapism the drug provides. They really want to get out of their heads for a spell. Other than a possible headache, there's little in the way of bad-aftereffects and they don't need a needle.

Flacco saw the first police car roll up from around the corner of the market. That was Roger and he'd stopped the car in front of the door. Flacco turned tail and walked lively toward the front yard of the house next to the store. If he made it through the gate of the picket fence, he'd be gone out the back, into the alley where he could hop a fence to escape.

John and Chuck had planned for that with Roger by radio. John hit the gas and jumped the curb to drive right at Flacco. He hit the brakes with the cruiser's driver door inches from the picket fence. Chuck could exit, but John was trapped. Roger was already out of his car. Between the car at one end and chuck approaching on foot, Flacco had nowhere to go. Flacco hesitated. I could see his head pivot to each obstacle. John remained behind the wheel in case Flacco jumped from the starting block and ran across the street. Chuck reached for Flacco just has he climbed onto the hood of the car and flung himself over the fence. John was ready for that move as well. He jammed the car in reverse and moved backward. Flacco lost his balance and fell off the car, right into Chuck's arms. Before Flacco could twist and fight, Roger had one arm around his neck as Chuck cradled Flacco like a big baby. Manny stood behind me and watched the show. We both died laughing.

While our partners concentrated on the capture, I pivoted the cameras to cover the area around the market. Manny and I watched for potential threats allied to Flacco. I saw three guys on the side of the market facing the towering bridge. One peeked around the corner, but his ever-threatening hands were in sight and empty. One of the market employees stuck his head out the door. He receded when John rearranged the car and walked away from the scene to cover their backs. Manny radioed, "We gotcha, bro. Everybody beat feet outta there."

"We'll stay with the camera until you guys are Code Four," I added. Code Four was the code that officers needed no help.

"C'mon over," John replied. "We got the dude and the drugs. He's already given up." Chuck snagged the bag, taking the air out of the guy.

"Manny's gone to get the car turned around," I replied. "We'll be there Code Two and a Half. No red balls to stop us." Code Two and a Half meant to drive like a bat out of hell without announcing ourselves to the world with lights and siren. Red Ball meant red traffic light, but red ball sounds cooler. The term was one of those typical cop-isms that would never appear on any police department radio code card. The captures after this bust would slow down activity in the park. The dealers finally got the message and hunkered down. They either moved to another point we hadn't discovered, or they bided their time as did we. The camera wasn't going anywhere, and neither was WECAN.

CHAPTER 48:
CENTRAL PATROL

WECAN officers were having a ball. All three teams shared their stories and conferred on Friday's, unified line-ups. We ran around the city with no radio responsibility and arrested the worst criminals. We all worked with minimal field supervision. Although most of the sergeants were tight with their teams, they did ship-in and ship-out as they transferred to other assignments. Each replacement was a new story. WECAN continued to receive a lot of citizen kudos no matter who ran the teams. The unit shined but not everyone in uniform was gleeful about our success.

Rumblings from patrol cops throughout the department reached back to WECAN and told us we were not loved by all. Some groused that we didn't really do a whole lot. Some patrol officers who looked in from the outside had no concept of what we did every day. The fact that we dismissed radio calls as part of our mandate left many patrol officers believing we milked a useless assignment. Those officers who spent a lot of time at the sally port where prisoners were processed would have had a different opinion. WECAN cars were always taking up space in the narrow confines of the prisoner parking lot. And our constant parade of gang and narcotics in-custodies clogged up the Duty Lieutenant's Office with booking approvals.

Cops loved to bitch. Anything perceived as new and untested was strange and bad to some. Cops certainly didn't care if it showed in their comments and attitudes, either.

At some point, a couple of us complained to our sergeant. John Tangredi and Chuck Davis were at a scene they were not comfortable with. When they called for a patrol unit to cover them it took too long for Central cops to show up. The sergeant agreed that kind of behavior was not only stupid, but dangerous. We couldn't imagine a cop calling for cover and not getting immediate help from his brothers and sisters. Several other WECAN officers shared the same problem. Our sergeant asked us to tell him what we thought was happening. Eight voices blurted out at once: "They're jealous!"

"Some of 'em are just drones with something new to bitch about!"

"They're all assholes!" followed by laughter from the mingling group.

"Nah, they're not all assholes," chimed in another. "Well, some of them are assholes."

"I think it's just a few, at least at Central."

"Yeah, a few others are just mimicking the complainers, but don't really mean it."

"Then they're assholes, too!" More laughter.

John added, "I talked to a couple of guys yesterday. They didn't have a problem with WECAN. They said others thought our work was over-rated and that patrol could do the same job."

"Then why didn't they put in for WECAN? We all came from patrol, too."

"What whining assholes."

"They said we should get around to patrol line-ups and talk about WECAN. Maybe explain to them that WECAN is in position to supple-ment patrol while facing down the problems we encounter all the time," John added.

"Supplement them? We got away from Patrol to get away from that shit!" some said.

These conversations took place in the line-up room that Central Patrol used. That didn't help the attitudes of some of those cops. On this day they were outside the room impatiently waiting for us to leave since they held their line-up after ours. We were warmly greeted by some of the patrol officers while others stared coldly at us or avoided eye contact. I heard some mumbles and grousing pass through the ranks as I walked through the gauntlet of men and women. Some of us caught one or two degrading comments: "When do guys go on break from doing nothing all day, 'cause I'd like to get that job."

"Assholes," was one WECAN officer's reply.

Central was a tough division. Some of the department's finest meat-eaters came from Central. I've worked and partied with many of them. And then there's some who succumbed to the dark side of ego. Those black-gloved, mirrored sunglasses-types carried huge egos that never shrank. To some of the cops, WECAN must have looked like easy pickings for a mouthy bully, or a Grade-A whiner. As time went on, their attitudes were seen by many as two-dimensional and foolish. The chaff gets separated from the wheat.

We worked around patrol and shared the same pathos. We slipped in some "me time" with Central Patrol whenever it was convenient. Most of the WECAN teams did eventually attend patrol line-ups which encouraged aggressive cops to apply to join us. Despite our selective status as a team disconnected from radio duties, they knew we'd respond to calls for help in a heartbeat. WECAN cops came from that breed in Patrol. Disenfranchising us from our status as hard chargers was wrong and insulting. Dialogs were opened in the field with patrol officers. Most of us knew each other to some degree. Ruffled feathers were smoothed, and good partnerships resulted. A Central Patrol sergeant thought it would be a good idea to blend WECAN and patrol together for some training.

WECAN was a year old, now. The concept seemed alien to many at first. The brass had little trouble recruiting members at the inception. The lieutenant had sergeants he wanted who picked the men and women they wanted. WECAN registered interest from patrol in the form of increased applications after the program matured past its infancy. The fantasy that the teams took advantage of a cushy assignment appealed to patrol officers who looked for a way out of their current assignments. We were gifted with a formidable challenge, to be free to target the worst criminals, use our imaginations to send the baddies to confinement, and to hold them accountable because we were coming for them if they committed crimes.

The budget for WECAN was over a million dollars. We were spoiled with a lavish bank for superior equipment. The true test of the team members was in how we utilized the equipment and the money to attack the gang and drug problems. True efficiency, smarts, and gusto reeled in quite a bit of the violence. That was our mission statement.

Central WECAN sat in on a couple of line-ups with patrol. We also teamed up on some surveillance busts. Our intent was to teach central patrol officers our techniques and courtroom strategy if they weren't already prepared, to teach them how to frame their actions and reports for success in court. There would be simple refreshers if they were already tight with their testimony techniques. The goal was to show them scripts that matched their arrests to produce consistent wins in court. They could concoct their own operations as their supervisors saw fit.

I was enticed to transfer from patrol into WECAN for the Special Forces aspect of the assignment. Patrol rarely got to run ops like we did. They were slaves to the radio. WECAN wanted them to write efficient cases that would butcher defense attorneys at prelims. Central Patrol had a lot less prejudice toward us after we worked together.

One of the innovative recruiting concerns with WECAN was its selection process. The first group was the people who bothered to read the Department Announcement and volunteered. The next wave, my group, got voted in. The third wave got voted in and that was the one time I got to take my seat in front of the chalkboard and say "yea" or "nay" after each written name was presented. All twenty-four WECAN officers were collected in the room and voted for the next and last wave.

The sergeant pointed to a name and the audience made their decisions. People not known were not strongly considered. If one WECAN officer voiced a strong opinion one way or the other and no one else spoke up, that was all it took to accept or deny. A few names were easy non-selections. One applicant did everything in his power in patrol to not be singled out as a stand-out officer. He didn't make it. One officer was known for constantly volunteering for calls. She was voted in. This wayward course meandered through the list and the sometimes-awkward confessions from our people when there was a split decision. One potential recruit might have one of us in his or her camp, while another WECAN vote was a strongly worded negative. When asked why, we all learned a little more about someone many of us didn't know. If that officer didn't make the grade, then he might always wonder why

WECAN guys in his presence tended to avoid him. Twenty-four cops and the sergeants tried to be democratic, but we were all gossips at heart.

To my knowledge, there's never been a unit like WECAN where team members were voted in. There are generally no democracies in police work.

CHAPTER 49:
CRACK HEADACHES

One of Central WECAN's tips fleshed out a little differently than most. This time we were headed to a crack house. The culprits were described as black women. Hey, that was a new one! Manny, Chuck, John and I would handle this case thinking this would be a milk run.

The house was another Craftsmen-style home that showed all the wear of a sixty-year-old building. The Craftsmen homes were ordered from Sears catalogues ages ago and described as easy to assemble. They were common in the first half of the 20th Century in the sunny climes of Southern California. The Heights was lined with blocks of homes in that architectural, single-level design until post-World war II San Diego allowed developers to knock them down. The replacements were cheap, dual story, twelve unit apartment buildings that would release torrents of problems for law enforcement for decades to come in the form of single-parent families with uncontrollable kids, battling domestic couples, easy access for burglars and cheap rent for bad guys.

The target house was situated on a corner of a stretch of Commercial Street. Commercial ran through a light-industrial part of the Heights. The San Diego Trolley ran a line down Commercial St. that made the length of asphalt a little tight for traffic at times. The old residences that still existed had lower property values because of the noisy zone. Light-manufacturing plants and low-income homes lined the street for blocks. Out target was at the tip of a wedge-shaped street block that intersected Commercial and had virtually no neighbors. This spot was a perfect location for a dope house attempting to avoid attention.

The tipster was a regular snitch for one of our department's Narcotics Street Team detectives. The assigned detective, Detective Max, had the CI make a couple of controlled buys from the crack house. The seized crack from the dual buys granted the detective just cause to obtain a search warrant. The detective didn't have the time to work the place right after the warrant was granted. Max gained his superior's permission to hand it off to us. He'd done the hard work that gave us all the background we needed. Max already did the court time to get the search warrant. All we had to do was serve the warrant. There wasn't any evidence of a dangerous entry so, we figured we'd approach as calmly as could be and ask the people inside to open the door. We just didn't anticipate a violent response from female crack dealers. Max was the same detective who had a hard-on for WECAN and wanted a civil war between Street Narcotics and us. We shouldn't have trusted Max.

We set the usual placement in motion, surround the house, make entry, then take control of the occupants. The action went according to plan. There were three African American women in the small two-bedroom. Neither of the three acted thuggish. Two were in dresses and one wore slacks and a blouse. This was decidedly not your standard crack house. We showed them the search warrant and discussed our next moves. Yep, it all went just fine. I told the women we would have a female officer meet us to search all three ladies. That's when they all giggled and told us, "We haven't had the operations yet."

"What operations?" I asked. The tallest of the three pointed toward the area of "her" genitalia and made a slicing gesture with the right hand. I hadn't made her for him. In fact, none of us had any inkling they were all men. We should have noted the masculinity in their faces, but crack can change a person's looks and make some women look like hardened men.

John said he figured they were guys. He just wanted to see what would happen if we didn't learn the truth, but I'm not sure I believed him. I wondered what was up with the large, manicured hands. Deep down I guess I really didn't want them to be men. That would mean cavity searches. These three were happy, giggly men in women's clothes who acted like they didn't have a care in the world. This was already going bad for me.

We handcuffed everyone and sat them in the furniture-cluttered living room. The space was cumbersome to move around in because the occupants' belongings took up every inch of floor. There was so much clutter and so many objects to search we were doomed to a lengthy, messy nightmare of time-consumption. Our prisoners never acted alarmed by our intrusion. They seemed to enjoy our company as they socialized and awkwardly flirted with the four of us. Their lack of concern for potential incarceration worried me. Were there even drugs in this house?

I began thinking we'd been pranked by Max the Magnificent and his Street Narcotics unit. There was still a certain rivalry between WECAN and his unit. Both had accused the other of poaching in the past and there were occasional overlaps that either interfered with Street narcotics or WECAN operations. Short feuds erupted over accusations about poaching each other's seizures and arrests.

Either way, we were stuck in this one and had to handle it appropriately. We did manage to find a small number of crack cocaine rocks. That was enough to nail the occupants for possession. Whether the arrests would stand up in court was up for debate. A big downside to these arrests was that these were crack dealers who might be willing to conceal the dope in their rectums. We couldn't risk that discovery made at jail, so one of us had to cavity search all three of the prisoners.

None of us had been in this situation. We'd performed cavity searches before, but never with prisoners who looked forward to it. These three individuals tossed quips back and forth about which officer they'd like to search them. Ugh, how humiliating. Manny was high on the list. He stuck a toothpick in his mouth and hissed through his teeth. John was mildly amused, with Chuck leaning toward the "it won't be me" as shown through his blank expression. The four of us were resigned to a random choice for the lucky cop stuck with the chore. One of us would have to take a "crack" at the cavity searches. We decided to draw straws. I drew the short one.

One at a time, I brought the subjects into another room for privacy and removed their handcuffs. Quietly, with as little conversation as possible, I had them drop their pants, or dresses, and bend forward. I held a flashlight for the sensitive search process when they spread their cheeks. When the snarky comments came, I just wanted to fold up shop and climb into a hole. "Officer, do you want me to do it? I can hold the flashlight and you can look," one said with a grin on his face as wide as a canyon. "I'm glad it's you. You're much better looking than the others. Although, that Puerto Rican officer looks like he could be a real tiger," was followed by a wildcat purr.

"We don't sell rock cocaine, Officer" one said while peering at my nameplate, "Newbold. Maybe we get some extra and make a little money. We do that so one of us can get the operation. We think it should be Sheila. Right honey?"

Sheila was the second of the three. "Look, officer. We make money on the crack. Crack ain't no big thing and we ain't no crack whores. It's just that we can't make enough money from the johns around here. They ain't got no money neither. I'm saving up for the operation. After that, my girls will get theirs. Honest, none of us have crack inside us. At least, not where it don't feel good!" This was followed by laughs and snickers.

"Can we not talk and get this over with?" I pleaded.

The third lady squinted to read my nameplate. "Officer Newbold? I want you to know I'm as embarrassed as you. I know this is awkward for you. Me too. When this is all over, I would really like it if we could meet sometime when you're not at work."

"Nothat'salraightI'mmarriedandperfectlyhappy." I crashed all my words together, trying to speed up the search and get one hundred miles away from this place. Boy, a cold beer in a dark lounge somewhere in the mountains sounded real good right then.

The individuals came up clean. I experienced an aspect of the job that proved I was a professional. My teammates loved the escapade for the flotilla of wisecracks, pardon the pun, that they would sail at me for the next two days. Worst of all, there was no contraband. I performed three anal cavity searches for nothing. My partners' ribald humor was ruthless for the next few days. We'd been had by Street Narcotics and within a couple of weeks Manny Rivera would be promoted to the very same unit.

The next day showcased the contrast between one crack house situation and another. John and Chuck had a source spill the beans on a tiny home on 28th Street that busied itself with crack sales. The occupants were a weird combination of two Hispanics, one male and one female, and an older black man in his sixties. The way John explained the arrangement to me, his source explained that a couple of junkies "borrowed" space from Cleveland, an old alcoholic, and set up shop pushing crack from one of the bedrooms. The window on the side of the house was the portal. We teamed up, made contact at the door with Cleveland and entered the house with his sodden acknowledgement. The three of us found our targets and ruined their livelihood.

I went outside for some air knowing that 28th was a busy street with plenty of people about to buy dope. I took up a guard position just as a Cadillac Seville rolled to a stop at the curb line in front of me. The stoop was a few feet higher than the street. The driver may not have been able to see me on the porch.

I cautiously took the three steps down one at a time with my eyes pointed at the Caddy. I was only about eight feet away when the driver's pant legs and right hand were in view. The passenger window was rolled down. I made it to the sidewalk before the occupant, a black man in a Panama hat and sunglasses, bothered to look to his right. His right hand slithered down between the center console and his seat. I had my gun part way out of my holster judging that this was more than a pit stop for the guy. "What's in your hand, man?" I asked him.

There was an "Oh Shit," moment when he realized I truly was a cop.

"You have something in your hand you better just leave it where it is," I said as my handgun was out and at the ready, pointed at the man in the car. To protect the gun from a rabid grab from that guy, I held it to my ribs so that it was steady and out of reach.

The only body part still moving was that damned right hand. He kept pushing or pulling, I couldn't tell which. "I'm guessing you are either grabbing something bad or trying to hide something bad. If it's a gun you better just leave it alone. In fact, get the fuck out of the car, slowly. I can see you through all your windows as I come around your car. My buddies are in the house, so you best be warned you are outnumbered."

He did as ordered and climbed out of the front seat. Traffic was light, but I made him shut the door and hug his car. I wasted no time with the handcuffs and then radioed into the house for one of the guys. Manny came out. "What's up?"

"My man here got jiggly in his car when I walked up. Hold onto him while I search it." I opened the passenger door so my butt wasn't hanging into traffic. There were several rocks in a plastic baggie inside the center console. Maybe the seizure would be legal, I didn't know. Yet.

What had he been fiddling with when his hand was slid down into the cushion? I had the drop on him so whatever it was in his hand when I surprised him was still there. I gingerly reached down into the tight space. I had to be careful in case it was a blade or a needle. Quickly enough, I gripped the butt of a .38 Walther handgun. I painstakingly wrapped fingers around the gun wary of hooking the trigger and removed it.

Manny had my prisoner and they watched my actions together. When Manny saw the gun, so did our prisoner. Manny stared daggers at the guy who swore under his breath and then sagged at the shoulders. The gun was loaded with the safety off and a round ready to go. Even though I hadn't read him his rights I was suitably pissed off. "Were you going to shoot me?" I asked as a demand for an answer. He kept his mouth tight, but I could see the surrender in his posture. He would not talk to me. I could only surmise that he held the gun and fought with himself to make that decision. Luckily, my cop radar warned me probably seconds before he made that call.

CHAPTER 50:
THE WORKMAN

The Workman Hotel was one of those low-brow hotels built when Wyatt Earp called San Diego his home. The architecture of the historical San Diego dwelling looked like a 1890s structure right out of Dodge City with its functional structural design, roof-edge dentil flourish and basic amenities. The Workman resembled a three-story shoebox and might even have hosted Earp as a guest. That legendary figure was a temporary fixture in the Stingaree district of downtown. Time was not a generous fan of the old wooden structure and neither was ownership. The old darling was only fit for junkies and the downtrodden long before I worked WECAN.

Older patrol cops remembered the Workman as a pit, with constant problems inherent with any fleabag Bowery hotel. Unsavory types flitted through the hotel's doors and made the place ripe for anti-crime action. Local SDPD legend Al Massey had made that place his project for years. He constantly dragged out the spores of humanity that grew like mold inside the Workman's two floors.

Manny and I found ourselves in circumstances when we could work a day shift. That rare day allowed us to work from early morning to late afternoon, when we normally worked from afternoons into evening. Since this shift took us away from the peak production hours, otherwise known as best arrest times, we decided to help a couple of Central cops with one of their problems. That problem was the Workman and the officers hoped WECAN could help use its talent to run through the hotel and make a few arrests. They hoped we'd add fuel to a project they sponsored to urge the city to condemn the place as a health and crime hazard. We agreed to give the place a look-see.

Both of us had been in the Workman in the past, back when we worked downtown independently of each other. The place was a flophouse for indigent souls, good and bad. If you lived there you were either two ranks below down-on-your-luck, or you were a scumbag. The best residents were the ones that got back on their feet and moved on. The few decent people left were poor ones and victims of harsh situations. They had my sympathy.

Among all the other toys WECAN was gifted, we had our own prisoner van. This paddy wagon was an extended Ford van with no rear passenger windows. The interior was bisected by one wall to separate two prisoner compartments. Both were lined with benches for the prisoners. Manny and I shaped a plan to start with a sweep of the Workman and then fill the van up with Eleven-Fives at various stops throughout the morning.

The Workman was a hotel, but with an SRO certificate for Single Room Occupancy. SROs attracted low-income tenants with cheap rooms outfitted with few luxuries such as kitchens and bathrooms. The communal bathroom on each floor was at the end of the hall. Naturally, drug users, criminals and other "low lives" sunk to this level of survival to get off the streets, if only momentarily. Dealing dope from a hotel room was preferable and safer for some illicit retailers than the streets. The fixed-income tenants that had few choices for shelter elsewhere were constantly under siege from the flow of criminals and the dangerous homeless and, or mentally ill street people.

Manny and I checked out the prisoner van for the day and parked it around the corner from the Workman. We entered the hotel through the front door. The backdoor would have suited us too, but we wanted the front desk manager to know the police were on deck. One guy sat behind the check-in window. He barely looked up at us before he tilted his head back down. We walked the first-floor hallway and looked for strays, but they were barren. The rooms on the first floor were quiet as well. There were stairs at the far end, so we climbed those to the next floor. We surprised a woman on her way down. We stood face-to-face with her for only a moment, long enough to see the pinned pupils of her eyes.

Tiny, fixed pupils are a classic symptom of heroin use. Without much interruption, we hooked her up for being under the influence.

We brought her back up the stairs while we swept the second floor. The evening hours might have been more productive. Thursday morning at the Workman was legitimately quiet. Perhaps our van was spotted, and the fleas hopped off the pooch before we got inside.

Our prisoner lived on this floor. We pushed her resolve a bit and tested her to see if she'd snitch for us. She had to know at least one dealer in this place. She opted to hold fast against coughing up any scoop and played dumb. For now, all we'd accomplished for the patrol officer's sake was a lone, scrawny trophy.

San Diego's Police Department policy does not allow male officers to search female prisoners unless exigent circumstances justified hands on. Even then, any touch in the proximity of a woman's genitalia, buttocks, or breasts is performed with the knife-edge of the hand. The best we could do was ask if she carried something that required a female officer's presence. Our prisoner coyly stated she was clean. There were no female cops at work downtown that morning, so we'd have to drive the short trip to HQ and search for a woman officer there.

The prisoner van was designed to prevent the handcuffed prisoners from the surreptitious removal of contraband kept hidden on their persons. There were simply no places to hide anything they discarded. The prisoner areas were just empty metal boxes with cages and narrow benches. If some bad stuff mysteriously appeared, the item would end up on the naked metal floor and the prisoner was screwed.

We got our prisoner through the gates into the secure prisoner parking area at HQ and settled on a place wide enough to park the van. Manny headed into the Duty Lieutenant's Office to collect the necessary forms to fill out while I rolled open the van door to take our prisoner out. I opened the interior cage door and saw her calmly seated in a corner. Habitually, before I climbed in to assist any prisoner, I gave the inside a little inspection. One never knew. When I looked to my left, I saw a plastic bag that wasn't there before. I looked suspiciously at her. She stared nervously. "Aw shit, is that yours?" I asked exasperated.

"What?" was her reply. That was the best alibi she could concoct on the spur of the moment.

I bent at the waist to avoid bumping into the low roof and reached down for the bag. In a moment of conscience, the woman warned me not to.

"Those are mine. Please don't pick them up." That's the moment when I saw that the bag held two diabetic hypo syringes.

"Where'd you have these? You don't have any pockets."

"They were inside of me." She seemed sheepish and embarrassed.

"Where?"

"In my vagina." We had few secrets between us now.

"How'd you get them out?" Her hands were cuffed behind her back and she wore long, tight jeans. She had to be a magician or a contortionist to pull off a trick like that.

She was suddenly bashful and a little ashamed to disclose her womanly talent and hinted that it took a little effort. "I did have to wiggle a lot to push them down my pant leg. I was hoping you wouldn't see them. There's something else you need to know. I have crabs."

My feet braked to a full stop. I left her and the bag in the van until I put on gloves. Manny saw me glove up and asked, "What's up?"

"Look in the van. There's a bag of syringes."

"Ah, I see them."

"The gloves are on because she had them up her pussy."

"Ohhh…"

"That's not the worst of it. She told me she has crabs."

"*Hijole* Holmes. It's all yours! I'll sit her over by the DL's Office."

"Gee, thanks bro," was all I could say. I got a sanitary evidence bag from Police Impounds and picked up the syringes with a paper towel squeezed between my fingers. The tiny vermin infestation could be seen with the naked eye. At least she saved me my own indignity by warning me.

I had to take the nasty contents of the bag to the Impound room downstairs. The civilians at the counter in Impounds were none too pleased to see my evidence, but like all police departments, this seizure was nothing new. The Impound folks kept special, biohazard containers for just such occasions. They used a magnifying glass to confirm what I'd learned. I saw the live buggers crawling all over and inside the bag.

Disgusted, I knew we weren't done with them yet. We still had the nest in our custody, and she had to be searched. Let's just say we found a female officer to screen her before a long trip to the women's jail about thirty minutes away. Manny and I made no friend with that lady officer that morning.

CHAPTER 51:

THE GUNSLINGER

Central WECAN's turf included a handful of small neighborhood parks for families and small children. Those little patches of green lawn were designed with sandboxes, playgrounds, and trees for shade. They belonged to the families in the day and to gang members at night. The street gangs, many spawned from these same families, sometimes shared the same patches of green on any given day. The gangs existed in sort of a parallel world where they didn't often bother the families in the parks directly, but those neighborly citizens knew who controlled the parks, and it wasn't the police.

WECAN worked in tandem with the department's Street Gang detectives. We were the enforcers and the dicks, short for detectives, were the investigators. We were the arresters and they were the processors. Our uniforms were the more visual targets. The detectives wore street clothes. Because of our higher profiles, officer safety was drilled into us with more training than I'd experienced in patrol. Our entire workdays, aside from court, put us in the sightline of any street enemies we'd generated. We all worked with a stronger sense, a sixth sense, of potential danger and wired ourselves to be better prepared. The SDPD hammered away at Patrol with occasional refresher training but WECAN generally got training every other week.

My team continued scrutinizing the Sherman gang. The Shermans were seen by Gangs as less of a threat than the Logan Heights thugs. They controlled turf north and west of Logan but were more likely to follow Logan's lead than battle their soldiers in the streets. Shermans were the Logan gangs' closest rivals. The *Varrio* Encanto *Locos* were the main enemy for both gang sets, just across Freeway 15.

We rarely had call to roll through Grant Hill which was considered Sherman gang turf. Sherman Heights is the sister neighborhood on the slopes above Logan Heights. We were always consumed with Logan Heights and found little time to hammer the villains in Sherman unless we were asked to or just got curious about what the street punks were up to. My team caught a rare opportunity to collect a whole group of Sherman gang members when we surprised them one evening in Grant Hill Park. A Street Gang detective was in the area with a tip about a wanted Sherman gang banger who was in the group at the park. He asked us to cover off and assist him.

Five of us drove up in the early evening in three marked units and cut-off any escape for the fifteen teens and men who lounged around or stood nonchalantly in tiny huddles. We knew the park well enough to box in any runners. A patrol unit was in the area and volunteered to cover us and add to our numbers. None of the gangsters were in positions to bolt or toss anything we wouldn't catch. We caught them unawares in and around a playground sandbox and froze them in place.

Strangely, the detective was missing. We called for him and he came up on our frequency to advise he was close by. He was in seclusion awaiting our arrival before he made his presence known. He had his own agenda. He seemed to like playing gang detective more than being a gang detective. In fact, none of my team ever really worked with him in his gang detective capacity and wondered why that was.

The detective drove up just below the large sandbox we'd corralled our detainees in. The rim of the sand-filled enclosure was a raised concrete wall suitable for seating, perfect for fifteen hard cases. My teammates and the patrol officer patted down each subject and returned them to seated positions. Nobody copped attitudes and no one carried weapons. Chuck and I sifted the sandbox with our boots searching for any objects, guns, drugs, or other contraband to impound.

The dick sat in his car longer than he needed to, maybe for dramatic pause. When it was show time, he slowly got out of his G-ride and gave the panorama around him a seasoned, "Here I am, world," steely glare. He straightened his hair and his pants, then turned and focused his sights on the tableau ahead of him. He had all of us watching like we were his private audience.

We all knew his big ego was set design for his stage entrance. That didn't mean he couldn't get the job done. We just had to put up with his insufferable self-importance. When he was certain his gig line was straight, he turned to his right, walked to his car trunk, and opened the lid.

I figured he was going to pull out some paperwork, perhaps a camera or some other detective stuff. Instead, and with all the rapt attention of the mixed audience of bangers and cops, the dick removed his huge pearl-handled, nickel-plated semi-auto handgun from the trunk. Shit, the man just advertised to fifteen hostiles and his fellow officers that he didn't wear a gun in the field!

Roger watched with rapt attention and then leaned over and asked, "Do you remember the nickname he used to tell people to call him?"

I furrowed my brow and shook my head no. "The Panther," he reminded me. Geez, I thought, what a clown.

The dick holstered the damn thing after chambering a round. I didn't just see that. I just saw Magnum P.I. in action. How "television" of him. All of us officers were shocked. What the fuck was he thinking? We're all looking at each other with dropped jaws. The bangers stayed stoic, probably taking mental notes. Somebody in that group, maybe several somebodies, were dangerous individuals. These were hardened street gang members mixed in with younger, impressionable teens, for God's sake. They didn't need to see this supreme act of stupidity, for the Panther's sake, as well as our own.

The goal of this op was to nail one particular dude. We'd already frisked every one of them and found a minimal amount of pot. There were no hard drugs to be seized. We'd scoured the ground for any discards and sifted through the sandbox and prowled the shrubs around us. Still nothing. We'd genuinely surprised them before they could conceal anything. There was just no contraband to be found. You'd think fifteen gangsters could feed us a little better than dime bags of pot for personal use.

The target the Panther wanted was identified and handcuffed for a crime of violence against another gang member. He'd be pitted for Assault with A Deadly Weapon. The others were FI'd and cut loose.

Sadly for us, the pickings were slim. Despite all the potential for crime in this large group and we didn't get squat.

The Panther was conciliatory and thanked us. Two of us agreed to take the prisoner downtown so Panther could question him about the violent crime. We cleared to return to the field. I have no idea what became of the arrest. I do recall sharing this story with another gang detective. I hadn't even gotten to the meat of the story when I mentioned the Panther by name. The detective rolled his eyes and shook his head as though I had no need go on.

Please, please, please don't let my career cause eyes to roll around in the heads of my peers, I pleaded to the Fates.

County Parole Agent Steve Duncan was a new face to Central WECAN. He was assigned gangsters all over the county that were on the streets under some forms of parole or probation. We met him at one of WECAN's Friday line-ups when all the team members were together. Steve came in to introduce himself and solicit some help. He worked with a small contingent of fellow agents, but none of them had the information sources for a small army in the Heights. Steve got a hold of Manny and me and began to feed us the names of wanted gang bangers on his "to-do" list. Two of them were Shermans. We told Steve not to worry. Give us two days and we will have your men.

Of course, Manny and I had no idea where they were. We'd only recently begun to get familiar with that gang. We let the others on the team in on what we were up to. Chuck and John were on another mission, but said they'd cover if needed. Roger was on a day off for his family.

The two of us began our search in Job Number One's neighborhood. Number One, Pedro, was known to "hang out", the classic catch phrase for wanted poster descriptions, around 22nd and K Streets. The same 22nd and K where we used to park Weber One. We didn't stick our car under the neighbor's noses this time. We hid it two blocks away and hiked in with our radio volumes turned down and any clanging keys stuffed into back pockets to silence them.

The Shermans tended to hang out on the steps of a 19th Century apartment building. Probably a mansion once, it was now re-walled into low-rent, low quality crash pads for low-income workers. The two-story apartment building barely met the needs of the mostly Hispanic folks in residence. Whoever the owner was, he or she had created "slum-lord chic." The two of us found a neat spot to conceal ourselves in the overgrown brush of a house gone into disrepair on the same side of the street.

We roosted for less than twenty minutes before Pedro obliged us with an appearance. He surfaced from inside the apartment building and stepped onto the front porch with two buddies. His weasel eyes shifted back and forth for cop trouble. He and his friends had beers and relaxed while they sipped from cans of Budweiser. We worked our way through two bordering front yards until we were one fence-line away from Pedro. Apparently, he had more than one beer on board. He stepped off the porch and wheeled around the side of the building to go pee. We slid around the fence and flanked him as he finished a long period of passing water. Steve's target was ours.

We met Steve the next day at HQ. He thanked us for the pinch and asked if we could pull off number two. We had no illusions about our chances. Pedro timed our arrest for us, we just got lucky. "Number two," Victor, had no known address. Manny and I looked at each other with a crossfire of doubt. Steve saw the non-verbal exchange and offered, "You guys drink beer? It's worth a case of any beer you want if you can get Victor. He's a project of mine and a pain in my ass."

I blurted out, "You bet," before I realized what I'd agreed to. Steve had me at "Free beer."

We set out at dusk with Roger back at work and in a second car. Victor was FI'd months ago at Grant Hill Park. We hoped no other cops had bothered with Grant Hill Park and scared him off. We slid that direction in the hopes we could split up and vector in from three different points. Maybe, we'd get lucky again. We set off on foot.

The park was quiet at dusk. The grassy acreage was surrounded by brush. There were trails between some of the plants. We all switched over to Nalemars and kept the volume low. There were voices near the top of the hillside knoll. Three of us entered from separate points and ducked down to lower our profiles. I counted four young guys either standing or seated near a water fountain, sharing a joint. They were relaxed and caught off-guard. Roger gave the signal and popped up. One of the younger guys spotted Roger and told the others it was time to go. Roger drove them like a shepherd right at Manny and me. We had all three within seconds. The faces were those of young *Latino* men in Pendleton shirts and chinos. One face stayed hidden under a ball cap. That guy stared at the ground almost as though he hid his face. I bent at the knees to look up at his face with my flashlight held pointed at an angle not to blind him. I softly lifted his chin with one finger and held the wanted picture Steve had handed me. "Fellas. We've just scored a case of Karl Strauss Amber Lager," I said.

I made the call to Steve's pager. He returned the call with such enthusiasm he seemed to be incredulous. "You men are good!"

"Ha. Tell our supervisors." He did, in the form of a written commendation from his agency and a meet back at HQ the next day with the beer.

CHAPTER 52:

NAILING FIDEL

WECAN teams were frequently fed information about wanted subjects. SDPD Divisions fortunate to have WECAN teams operating in their areas had the option to request WECAN aid. The same was true for outside agencies like County Probation and Parole which was Steve Duncan's unit, and State Parole. Even some obscure local law enforcement agencies would ask for a little help from us. Our success rates at putting gang baddies in jail attracted other law enforcement investigators. They could cast a wider net with WECAN help. Thirty-two gang or narcotics cops were bound to know virtually every player on the streets in the areas where they were most active.

One nasty piece of work was a character named Fidel Mendoza. Mendoza was a multi-national traveler jumping back and forth from the U.S. and Mexico to pair buyers with drugs. He had a reputation for bloodshed and for hurting anyone in his way. State Parole owned his soul but couldn't find his body. U.S. Immigration would deport him to remove one more dangerous character from San Diego, only to have him return in no time at all. Mendoza played the system after he served time for murder in this country. No law dogs could suppress him from his crime life in our city. He was aligned with the Logan gangs who made names for themselves with cross-border cartel alliances and violent behavior.

One Central Division investigator, Joanne Welter, was alerted to Mendoza by a Central patrol officer. Officer Milano had a run-in with the drug-dealing Mendoza. Mendoza was nailed selling pot for some pocket change when Milano tried to take him into custody. They tussled and Mendoza pulled free, fled and avoided arrest. Milano knew him from the streets and set the wheels in motion to obtain a warrant for his arrest.

The wanted picture and caption found their way to Manny and me, care of State Parole. Mendoza, it turned out, had completed some prison time years earlier for a double homicide. His victims were other bad guys he ground into so much meat with blasts from a shotgun. Somehow, our criminal justice system saw fit to let this guy roam the streets after only a few years in the Big House. The lesson he learned, was to continue to be bad news in San Diego. He faced less danger here than in Mexico.

Detective Welter got word to us during our shift one day. A snitch placed Mendoza at an address in our area. If the info was to be believed, Mendoza hung with some Logan Gang members at an apartment complex in the 2800 block of Oceanview, not far from our usual stomping grounds. Manny drove us that direction.

Neither of us was familiar with the complex and didn't know the wisest approach to keep a lowered profile. We decided to do a drive-by down Oceanview and scope the place out before we staged to find the guy. With atypical bad luck, we drove right past the relaxed Mendoza on the concrete steps in front of the complex. He stared at us and then ran before we could launch after him. After a momentary stop around the corner and out of sight, we decided the only way to lure him out for a second try was for us to disappear.

Our plan was to drive far enough so that Mendoza's cronies would think our pass was a nonchalant tour through the Heights. They would hopefully give the all-clear signal and bring him back to the surface. When we figured they'd forgotten about us, Manny dropped me off a block away. He maneuvered the car to an opposite street block where he'd remain invisible to the miscreants surrounding Mendoza. I doubled-back on foot hoping Mendoza would think in the short term and resurface quickly. Meanwhile, I worked my way through the alley behind the complex and stayed concealed.

My luck changed when a resident of the complex walked into the rear parking lot behind the apartments. He saw me behind a low wall that separated the car lot from the alley. Surprisingly for that neighborhood, the guy moved closer to me and spoke in low tones to tell me everything was cool, the bad guys didn't know I was there. He said the guy I looked for stood in the breezeway of that complex above the staircase where we'd first seen him.

I radioed Manny and told him the timing would be critical, "I'm gonna run at him from behind just as you bring the car to the front," I said. He acknowledged as I crossed the parking lot to the backend of the complex and saw Mendoza and two other Logan gangsters on the lookout in a hallway between two halves of the building. Their backs were to me. The hall was an open breezeway front to back with no obstacles to impede me. Remember, this guy was a proven killer and I had no idea if he was armed. To take him down would mean a surprise attack before he could react.

Nobody looked my way when I hit charged full bore at an unsuspecting Mendoza, too focused on passing traffic and potential cops on the main boulevard. He never saw me until I performed a perfect D-line hit and knocked him forward about six feet. He hit the concrete steps with such force the shock and impact stunned him and stalled his ability to react. At the same time, Manny turned back onto the street, hit the brakes and dumped our car in the street. He raced up the steps just as I grabbed Mendoza's arms and jerked them behind his back. The fight was out of him as he shook his head to gather his wits. Mendoza was in some pain and the party was over for him. He had no weapon, which didn't mean a gun wasn't resting in a nearby hiding place. His boys took their cues and loped off into the shadows. I was grateful to the resident that guided me in. Wisely, he was gone to avoid any chance the bad guys would put two and two together.

Manny and I received accolades for the arrest from our department and State Parole. Personally, I felt a triumph of will. The guy was unarmed when I knocked him into kingdom come, but I didn't know that at the time. I simply blew off any crippling concern and got lucky with my timing. Mendoza offered no words of praise for my offensive capabilities and obviously didn't follow football. Surely if he had, he'd have given me credit for that amazing hit. In my entire career I can only recall one other such hit, back in my Ocean Beach days. That prisoner gave me kudos for my tackle. He said nobody ever hit him as hard as I did.

Manny and I decided to celebrate Mendoza's arrest with dinner at the Chicken Pie Shop. There was no better spot in town for down-home cooking and chicken pot pies made from scratch. Then, a typical Jamie Newbold coincidence manifested itself. Seated across the booth from us were three, familiar women, who looked at us with furtive glimpses. I caught the stares because I'd been glancing back at them. Finally, she got up from her booth and walked to our table. My boys and I looked up at a thirtyish Filipina with a warm smile. The woman was my ex-girlfriend from ten years ago.

Anna was more shocked than surprised. The last time she laid eyes on me I had a ponytail, skateboarded everywhere, and worked construction. Her sister and mother made up the balance of the trio. I dated her out of high school and kept our relationship together despite some struggles and more than one lie in each direction. She left me for another guy and broke my heart.

Our relationship was cursed from the beginning. The troubles stemmed from my skin color. Anna wanted a boyfriend and an exit from her dominating mother and emotionally detached stepfather. Mother was born in the Philippines and married an African-American man which gained her passage to the United States. She divorced him in America and married a second black man. His name was Franklin. He expressed to his wife early on in their marriage that he did not welcome white males into his life. Suddenly, and without an invite, I popped up and pleased neither parent. Franklin didn't even want to be in the same room with me. When I made the trek to visit my girl at their Tulip Street address Franklin disappeared deep into the house, or just got into his car and took off.

Anna's mom came around since I was always in her life. She trusted me and saw my love for her daughter. Franklin could be excused for his poor regard for me. He was a pillar in the community. He had a successful real estate business down on South 43rd Street. Anna's mom told me more than once that Franklin knew everybody and people were always calling him for advice. When he finally deemed me worthy of conversation, the prejudice dripped from his tongue. "What's a white boy doing dating my step-daughter? Don't you have your kind where you live?"

Franklin was educated, articulate and cold to me. My dedication to Anna and the fact that I was underfoot on the rare occasions when he was home, was bound to get him to find some use for me. I wanted to be a part of this family and presented my best, most mature behavior when Franklin was around. I really wanted to him to accept me, if not like me. Two years passed before he settled down and hired me to paint one of the small cottages on South 43rd Street that he represented for sale. I told him I was handy. The cash was off the books and I thought he was good with me as a worker, therefore suitable for Anna. Although, Anna and I agreed he didn't give a rat's ass for her or her sister. He showed due attention to the two sons he had with Anna's mother.

Anna's sister was the product of a short marriage to her mom's first husband. Marie was half-Filipina and half-black. When these two girls fought one another, the shouts were vile and portended violence. Anna knew how to get under her sister's skin. Through our repeated dates, Marie was mom's idea of an escort to make sure Anna and I kept our hands off each other. Her mom did not want another generation after hers to birth a kid out of wedlock. Anna once confided in me that her mom's first marriage resulted from and unplanned pregnancy. Anna hated the restriction her sister's presence put on us. She referred to Marie as a "fligger" when they battled. The derogatory term was designed to hurt and anger Marie. I didn't need much imagination to compute the resulting mash-up of Filipina and the N-word. These early pressures combined over several years to torture our relationship. Anna knew I was unfaithful at the end and found a man she could love and have a child with.

Ten years later, her sister and her mom were flabbergasted at my uniform. Never in their wildest thoughts would I become a cop. We made a little conversation in front of my pals and agreed to meet some-time later.

Anna worked at a hair salon. I made a date to go to her business and have her cut my hair. We talked while she trimmed. I thought we might be friends again and left her my number in case she wanted to continue.

The call that came was not the one I hoped for. Anna's formerly two cute as buttons younger brothers were now full-fledged gang members in a gang-infested neighborhood watched over by Southeast WECAN. Anna wanted them out of the gang and wanted to know what I could do. I suggested I find time to talk to them separately when I wasn't at work, but she had more insidious ideas. She asked if there was some way that I could wipe off the criminal record for one of them. Right there, my love-life, my history and my job all crashed together. Any fantasies about togetherness blew away. I gave her a perfunctory answer and told her it would be better if I backed out of this conversation. "I'm sorry, Anna, but where I am now in life is way beyond what we thought we had ages ago. I can't do anything about Tyrone. He's eighteen and an adult and has to own up to his mistakes. Isaiah's a kid and your folks need to dial into that."

"Their father is dead and my mom can't control them."

"That's too bad about your step-dad. What happened?"

"He had a heart attack and left my mom with a lot of bills. She had to sell our house and move into an apartment. Where she lives now, the gangs are bad. My stupid brothers got jumped in and that's where it's at now."

"I tell you what, if they want to talk to me. I will. If I don't hear from them or you after this, that's it. Okay?"

"Sure. I'll talk to them."

"Bye, Anna."

"Bye."

That was the last time I spoke to my ex-girl. My buddies at work pestered me about my time with Anna. They never pictured me as a white guy that dated girls who weren't white. I told them that my dating history was rich with all types of girls. I had one relationship with a black girl named Anne that lasted about eight months, right into my first year as a cop. I sewed my oats aplenty before, during and after my time with Anne. She did too. The future was not in the cards for us. Manny was interested in the fate of Anna and me. I told him about the gang complications with her brothers. He measured off where that would be the drawback to haunt her and I if we got back together. I decided I'd better stick to the future, not the past.

CHAPTER 53:

MEXICO BUS TRIP

Right around the month when WECAN solidified its three full teams, our lieutenant presented us with a team building adventure. Up to this point, there were some bar nights, outdoor gatherings and full team meets. This new venture was an outstanding opportunity to feel appreciated by the department. The LT set up a day when the whole team and their significant others would cross the United States line into Mexico for a feast south of the border.

The treat was more than just a party bus to Tijuana. Our lieutenant arranged to send all of us to the beach city of Puerto Nuevo to dine on fresh lobster and the trimmings with that city's chief of police. We would be feted like kings and queens, all on the company dime. For all those that would make the trip, a city bus was commandeered for our use. Any overflow of bodies would follow in their personal vehicles.

The day of the event was sunny and warm. The launching point for this party was the police substation in South Bay, right across from the US-Mexico border. The bus and driver were waiting for us as the LT took stock of the attendance. We were all in comfortable civilian clothing. Nobody was armed and everybody had the proper identification. Even though this treat was sort of a friendship exchange, nobody was under the illusion that all Mexican law enforcement would be amenable to this force of Americans. American police officers have little or no pull in Mexico. We are as likely to be somebody's prisoner in Mexico as any other U.S. citizen would be under the wrong circumstances.

There were SDPD stories I'd heard about, going way back in time, about local police in car chases that headed across the border at the U.S. end of Freeway 5. The officers supposedly took their exuberance for the catch too far and drove onto Mexico. Mexican police were notorious for seizing any police car from our side of the border that crossed without permission. The car, the officer's gear and the officer were likely to be held captive. The officer would be detained until some ruffled Mexican law enforcement feathers were smoothed out. The officer's gear, gun, badge, and car might be left behind, as bargaining chips to secure his or her release. That was part and parcel for being a law enforcement officer at our border with Mexico. The cops in Tijuana would take advantage. Legendary tales from my department illustrate a certain chaos at the border.

Stories abound about police chases where the drivers of pursued cars crossed over into Tijuana to escapes from San Diego cops. The pursuit police cars were commanded to stop mid-flight before they crossed over too. The poor bad guys thought they were going to escape because Mexico didn't care about what drove into Mexico. Instead, Mexican border cops blazed away at the wanted cars with a classic .45 Thompson machine gun. Whatever remained, either disappeared into the bowels of Mexican justice, or got thrown back into the United States. Do not mess around with Mexican cops.

Those of us who got to the substation early climbed on board the Greyhound-style bus and got the choice seats. A few stragglers arrived in the parking lot late, so they had to be accounted for too. By the time all souls headed south were counted, bus limitations clearly would not seat everybody. I managed to get seats for my wife and me. Others from my team wouldn't fit. Fortunately, we left no man behind. Manny, Chuck, John and their wives all squeezed into John's mid-size sedan. With the bus fully loaded and a trail of extra folks in their cars, we crossed the border into another country.

Two Puerto Nueva municipal police cars met us at the crossing on the Mexican side. The cars pre-arranged an escort for the bus for the hour ride to Puerto Nuevo. The trailing cars were expected to keep up. The police escort ran all the way with their overhead lights on and drew all kinds of attention with their red and blues glimmering along the highway. We all got a kick out of the presidential treatment our southern counterparts provided.

Highway One was a Mexican federal road that stretched from Tijuana to Cabo San Lucas at the tip of the Baja Peninsula. The winding road is narrow most of the way, sometimes two lanes each way with periodic reduction to just one lane for north and one lane for south. The constant traffic down this highway often got jammed with traffic and created plenty of stop-and-go snarls. We found out the hard way as our bus trip's estimated time began to lengthen. The private cars following us experienced the same delays. The last car in line contained Manny, Chuck, John and the wives. They were at ease chatting away when the unexpected lights and siren of a Mexican police car lit them up. Since they were the last in line, the rest of us had no idea they'd been stopped.

The officer was with a Mexican municipal agency. He was informed about the Americans on his highway, but in a bus only. Nobody running this leisure trip had told him there were cars attendant to the bus. John dutifully pulled over. The officer approached from the driver's side. John was the driver and watched the man approach in his side mirror. John was a little concerned to be plucked from traffic this way. He thought it was another escort for our group. Traffic was heavy and slow. John rolled his window down and greeted him in Spanish, a language John had little familiarity with. Luck was on their side because Puerto Rican-American Manny spoke fluent Spanish.

Manny leaned over to make eye contact with the officer and said in Spanish, "Hey, we're just trying to keep up with the other cops." The local cop missed the reference. Some of the local cops in the regions of Baja can't be trusted. The law down there could put the proverbial arm on innocent Americans if a dishonest buck can be made. Corruption of this nature was an odd concept for a San Diego police officer. Cops on my side of the border didn't take bribes from traffic violators.

One of the lessons I've learned, from the actions of two former brothers-in-law is to not rile the local cops or disregard them. Mexico ain't the United States. Montezuma's Law is a reversal of our rule of law down there. You were guilty until proven innocent.

The *policia* reply in Spanish was a cordial, "You were speeding." The others in the car listened as Manny grew a little heated with this officer's untrue response. Manny tersely objected and said that it was impossible to speed in this traffic. He added they were part of the police escort up ahead. Something about paying money in lieu of a ticket rapidly changed to, "No problem, Senor." The policeman swiftly disappeared.

Manny courted the idea that the stop was for la *mordita,* a phrase that means "little bite" meaning it was a cheap attempt at garnering a bribe. If it hadn't been for Manny's Latin social skills, somebody in that car would be poorer a few dollars. The speeding accusation was absurd. The traffic barely moved throughout much of the journey south. Of course, the story was told later at the restaurant. I assume the police chief and host would be on the radio rushing their money back to them if they'd been forced to pay. Word did seem to get around to the host Chief, our lieutenant confided in us later. I wouldn't want to be that municipal cop who urged the bribe.

The Puerto Nuevo Police Chief was a powerful man in his town. He cleared the entire restaurant for the seventy or so people in our troupe and arranged for the party to be comped or paid for by someone other than us. Our LT wasn't talking. We sat to eat and enjoyed ourselves. Once we were satiated on lobster, refried beans, grilled corn and booze we moseyed around the town for a while. The trip was extended to a night at the nicest club in town.

Puerto Nuevo was a beautiful touristy beach village on the shores of the Pacific. The town isn't large and supported only one nighttime party place, a *discotecha.* The cops either got drunk or reflexively watched the doors for trouble. The wives and girlfriends absolutely loved the place. They danced and drank and socialized until the Mexican police lieutenant, under his *capitan,* politely informed us the witching hour was upon us. Those of us on the bus re-boarded while the others returned to the cars. We were back in traffic headed home. This time, we had police escorts at both ends of vehicular parade.

CHAPTER 54:
THE PARKING CONTROLLERS

WECAN was provided locker rooms, office space and a meeting room at San Diego PD's Headquarters building. We'd been elevated physically and professionally from the trailers at Traffic Division. Although the space gave the Central team a little more room to breathe, the office was only temporary and not enough to call it our own. Apparently, room was tight, so we were crammed in as roomies with one unit after another. We bounced around all over the main police station. One of our first placements forced us to share workspace with non-sworn parking enforcement personnel.

Like sworn officers, they wore uniforms and badges. Their jobs range from ticket writers through traffic direction to Community Service officers who performed duties that relieved cops for the more hazardous responsibilities of the day. We patrol officers loved our CSOs who could do anything from traffic accident investigations to translations in numerous languages. The parking controllers were the bunch saddled with the label of meter maids which was a misnomer. Men were equally represented in San Diego PD's Parking Enforcement Division. So, to be correct in the inappropriate designation, the public should have referred to them as either meter maids or meter footmen or valets. Both sexes carried guns. Their weapons didn't shoot bullets. They fired out tickets.

Our two offices collapsed into one at a time when Parking Enforcement was not well liked at HQ. Somebody of rank previously had directed Parking Enforcement to enforce employee parking at HQ, cops and all. The relatively new building was already hampered by inadequate parking. Stalls were narrow and cops and civilians had to park their personal vehicles wherever spaces weren't marked for police vehicle exclusively. Some employees found the stalls so confining they'd park and then get out through their sunroofs. To make parking worse, there were no other places to park around HQ. Street parking was all metered up to and under Freeway 5 just a couple of blocks east. Just past that often crowded street parking, cars were likely to get broken into for radios, cassette/disc players and spare change. That untenable situation was made worse by some of the most overzealous parking controllers I'd ever met. Going downtown to work sucked.

I found the closeted space with the ticket writers tough to tolerate. One of us could be the working stiff that got a ticket for no front license plate in the upper lot at HQ. An hour later we'd be in the office we shared with the ticket writers, seated next to the person that tagged one of our cars. Central WECAN's arrival at our new job station just added more cars to the difficult equation. Some officers, WECAN and Central Patrol and Investigations, discussed solutions over cocktails. The idea of policing the police came up. "Let's write the parking controllers' personal vehicles tickets. We just have to watch their cars until they screw up." was one suggestion.

Officers grew even more riled when the Command suggested parking controllers go after officers and investigators' personal vehicles at every police substation. The state of affairs grew increasingly silly and petty.

A pair of LAPD Homicide detectives in an unmarked car came down from the north to meet with our investigators. They parked at SDPD HQ assuming it was permitted. They were there to coordinate efforts to charge one individual for a series of armed robberies in the Southland. The LAPD detectives' city-issued car got a ticket for parking over the white line of a parking stall. Our department looked ridiculous. The same thing happened to a DEA agent parked at HQ. His vehicle was undercover and wore disused plates. The registration was purposely expired to keep it out of the DMV system. That agent had to meet with the HQ Watch Commander to get the ticket quashed. Apparently, the governor of this parking policy upgrade hadn't thought things through.

Signs popped up in the shared office soon after we roosted with the parking controllers. Somebody made handsome, professional signs cast with universal images depicting a traffic controller in silhouette along with the term "Meter Maid" written underneath. Ruffled parking controllers complained and pointed fingers at the WECAN officers at Central as the offensive parties.

A witch hunt was sparked by somebody of high rank, and the responsibility landed on my lieutenant's shoulders. Central WECAN cops were questioned in private in our supervisor's office. My sergeant, Bill Edwards, got around to me and asked the only question he was directed to: "Did you make the sign."

"Yeah, I did."

Parking Enforcement Officers had no sense of humor. My jocularity resulted in a Written Warning, a page of negative paper that could have marred my career opportunities. What seemingly came out of the investigation was the tighter scrutiny of my antics and the pranks of other Central WECAN people. My poor sergeant had to investigate this, which was the only bummer because he had to explain the facts to the LT. The LT rode his ass a bit about getting control over his people, which meant if we got into more hot water, the sergeant would have to punish us further. Bill liked us and we liked him. He had every reason to be at WECAN with cops he considered "a cut above." The last thing he wanted to do was break up the chemistry of the unit. I'd forced his hand and took my written warning in silence.

The LT was liberal about our behavior. But pressed from his superior because of the parking controller's complaint, he had to discipline me with a formal CUBO charge or Conduct Unbecoming an Officer. The warning was as far as he had to implement my punishment. Pranks within the unit were tolerated across the board within the ranks. We had thick-skins and histories with each other. The parking controllers had greater sensitivities and took themselves way too seriously. Not long after, we were moved to more spacious digs far away from the meter —, I mean parking controllers.

I want to emphasize how pervasive the parking controllers had become. Not only did sworn police personnel assigned to work HQ receive parking tickets on their personal vehicles, the detective's assigned undercover vehicles got tickets too. One undercover detective got so tired of the tickets adorning his undercover city car's windshield, he adopted a CUBO response, as well. One morning, one of his peers saw his Mustang parked in the parking garage below the HQ building. The car was nosed into one of the ridiculously narrow stalls. The detective's car brandished a new, rear license plate frame. His sense of irony matched mine. The frame read METER MAIDS EAT THEIR YOUNG. That was a popular myth around the PD by that time. I'd seen no proof of cannibalism, but they sure chewed up a lot of people's patience.

CHAPTER 55:
ONE TIME

San Diego Police Officers were getting butchered in the 1980s. Several police officers were attacked, some were shot. Seven died before the close of the decade and jostled the department into rethinking its officer safety protocols. The rise in police officer deaths coincided with the increase in gang superiority across the country and the realization that too many street cops were outgunned in the field. Gang fear of the police diminished, and the public perception was that gangbangers roamed neighborhoods at will, often heavily armed. Cops armed with revolvers and vintage shotguns were no match for the street soldiers and they knew it. To offer an even greater example of the unbalanced scales of armament, SDPD officers in at least two cases discovered used rocket launchers in Central Division. These were the shoulder-fired tubes that were good for one rocket launch and then became disposable. Their origins weren't proven, but the discoveries were thought to be used weapons smuggled home from military action elsewhere. Gang threats were more vocal, more out in the open as police officers reeled from greater job restraint thanks to litigation-fearful police departments.

Agencies reined in police officer's use of force. The SDPD had a sergeant, Fred Parenti, teach more crucial forms of self-defense. Fred was a Vietnam veteran with a fierce reputation for toughness, but a kind-hearted communicator to the public and his squads. I worked for Fred at Western Division for a while. This diminutive, sad-eyed man was the guy I'd vote least-threatening looking if I had to choose among a group of cops. That observation couldn't be further from the truth.

Fred had thrived as a hand-to-hand combat instructor as far back as the military. The department used him as an instructor in self-defense for rookies and veterans alike. Classes were held in the academy gymnasium, a suitable classroom with wrestling mats on the floors that extended up the walls. His classes began with little instruction. He was gung-ho about hands-on training and insisted we attack each other in simulated warfare. Fred had a desire to protect his people as best he could. Nobody could be like Fred who could make the strongest man look bad if he didn't compete to protect himself.

One of Fred's showstoppers was edged-weapons training. He was good with swords and kept a few on site for his performances. I loved the exercise where he handed a sharp sword to a volunteer in class and then showed the disciple how to hold it blade-out and buttressed against the student's body. Then, Fred gave the most remarkable live display of a human and a sword. Fred placed his throat against the point of the blade and slowly applied pressure. The person holding the blade was forced to brace against Fred's assault. Fred had no shield to protect his neck. He pressed the assault and pushed harder against the blade with his neck as a ram. Finally, the blade-holder lost his footing as Fred pressed the attack and knocked him off his stance. The climax involved Fred moving an immovable object, the person holding the sword, with irresistible force, his throat. Fred never got so much as a dinged neck.

He intended the scenario to surprise us with his concentration, discipline and mastery over edged weapons. The show got our attention. Then, he embed in us that edged weapons were real threats to cops. Absolutely none of us thought for a second we could hold off an attacker with Bruce Lee powers we did not possess. In fact, an attacker with a knife was more likely to kill an officer than a guy with a gun. He taught that a person running at you with a knife in his hand would not necessarily be stopped by a gunshot. His momentum on the attack could carry him as many as twenty-one feet before the bullet dropped him. If the knife stabbed the officer, it could even penetrate body armor. Even worse, the blade would rip through tissue and keep cutting, while the bullet may only have made the neat hole into flesh.

Gangsters tested police officers in the field with less restraint and more weapons than they might have a decade prior. Crack cocaine sales emboldened gangsters because the money obtained gave them power, and power made them feel invincible. The black gangs that hung at street corners and crack dens watched and learned from police departments who tied the hands of their officers to minimize complaints and lawsuits. Where gangsters once sprang for escape when a black and white headed their way, they now sang out, "One Time!" when they spotted us.

I remember the first time I rounded a corner in my police car and heard "One Time!" shouted over the din of traffic at 30th and Imperial. The comment didn't register, and I didn't know what triggered an exodus beyond a cop on the scene. Hell, cops were on the scene there constantly. Black gangs began to shout "One Time" all over the Heights when a police car drove into view. Cops listened to the manic shouts from virtually every assemblage of black gangsters we encountered.

I asked the origin of the phrase from a talkative Crip as I walked a block to break up the monotony. He explained it to me "You cops used to chase us around. Now, when you hassle us, you tell us, 'If I see you hanging around here one more time, I be arresting yo ass.' We're not scared about you arresting us for being black on a corner no more."

Gangsters adapted to a police officer's new reality. They felt emboldened while police officers tried not to be perceived as impotent. WECAN joined other street officers who forged the will to work energetically within the rules and turn back the tide of gang threats. We "walked among the tombstones." so we could put the squeeze on the bad guys and make them feel discomfort. The dozens of yards of space in all four directions around the intersection at 30th and Imperial resonated with warning shouts every time there was some cop interaction with the Crips.

Thirtieth Street and Imperial Avenue was a busy place to buy and sell dope. This was Crip hangout number one, and one of WECAN's incessant targets. Police officers didn't have to work too hard to nail a pusher. At this intersection, dealers were like buses. If you missed one, another would be along shortly.

One particularly slow night, only a couple of Crips hugged a street corner in front of Bruno's Market to hustle some crack heads. A Narcotics Street Team detective rolled through the intersection of 30th and Imperial and recognized a wanted player among the two. The detective was in an undercover car and no lookout shouted, "One Time," at his presence. The wanted gangster, Willis, was known to be a crack dealer. He leaned against a building on the corner. He looked relaxed while his eyes cross-checked every car for threats or buyers. The look on Willis' surprised face told the detective he was onto him, but too late to gracefully fade out of the picture. Willis had to run like hell if he wanted to stay out of the detective's clutches. The detective wanted him badly enough to slam his car into Park and put foot to pavement.

WECAN was familiar with the man, too. He was a muscled brute with a record of crime that included violence. Willis also had a habit of challenging cops when cornered with contraband. There were a few other gang pals of his across the street at Mullen's Liquor. He could choose to stand his ground and battle the detective or flee. He fled.

Willis zipped across 30th and blew past Bruno's Market and hung a hard right trying to disappear. Unfortunately for the bad guy, the sprinter detective cornered him in no time in the side yard between a house and a barber shop. A six-foot wooden fence blocked the crack dealer's egress. The wary detective wasn't sure if the guy was going to fight. He pulled out his service pistol and pointed it at his soon-to-be prisoner. The detective hadn't yet called for assistance, the events happened so fast. He wanted to maintain one hundred percent focus at this most crucial point. If he took the radio in one hand, he'd weaken his grip on his gun. The radio could become a distraction in one split second. He figured he'd take Willis under his control first, and then get help.

The detective, whose name I don' recall, had the Crip kneel and face the fence to get him properly handcuffed. He made all the commands from behind the guy. His next direction ordered Willis to place his hands on his head. The situation was tense, and the space was ill-lit. The darkness enveloped the movements of both men. Nobody else was around. The detective moved in closer to grip one hand and cuff it. His gun was still in his strong hand, pointed at the back of the Crip's head. The distance between the two opponents closed until there was no gap.

The detective made no mistakes in that moment. He had no idea if his suspect was armed. His rudimentary completion of the arrest should have gone as planned. Willis was compliant once stopped. The detective was in the danger zone, in proximity to a hostile opponent without total physical control. The things could go sideways alarm rang in his mind.

We will never know if the gangster, crack dealer knew how close the detective's gun was to the back of his head. The gun was still aimed because the detective didn't feel safe enough to holster it. The only way the gun could be effective was to bend the elbow and hold it back behind the man in case Willis reared-up to fight in the last second, before the other handcuff was applied.

Suddenly, Willis tightened his shoulders and drove his head backwards. He was too close to the gun he couldn't see and struck it with the back of his head. The detective's finger was in the trigger guard. The force of the blowback reflexively triggered the gun in the detective's tightened fist. A shot was fired, drilling into Willis' head. He was dead soon enough.

I felt bad for the detective then and feel for him now. The unfortunate action of a gang member got himself killed. Ramifications stemmed from the cop killing an unarmed black man and spread throughout San Diego. The immediate fallout landed on the officers stationed in the Heights. The shooting happened there, and the Heights cops were considered the bad guys. Consequences seemed worse for the ever-present WECAN cops. The department had begun to switch over to black and white police cruisers. Only WECAN, with their own personal squad cars, still drove all-white vehicles.

The gangsters hated us. The shooting amplified that hate. They didn't know we weren't involved in the shooting, but they didn't care. They squawked and preened in front of WECAN cops in the Heights trying to incite us for their benefit. Civic leaders fought the press to keep the peace, but they wanted answers. Meanwhile, WECAN officers were firmly aware of the need to work in groups if that was what it took to send a message back to the gangsters.

Department policy forbids officers from carrying unapproved weapons into the field. Cops had to stay armed with what they were issued. The department would not condone unauthorized firearms in the hands of its police officers when at work. Under our current circumstances, we felt stressed and outgunned.

This was a time when street gangs flexed their collective muscles in many cities. Crips kicked up their danger quotient with drive-bys up and down the West Coast. They used powerful and murderous machine guns. Some were so exotic I'd never even heard of the brands. We had little extra protection provided by the department to match firepower. Some of us quietly took matters into our own hands. An extra piece of equipment showed up in the car I shared with Manny. This new "piece" appeared after direct threats to kill us the day before.

Manny and I were at 30th and Imperial on foot in front of Mullen's when a group of Crips marched by and pointed fingers like guns at us. The less subtle, "We all gonna kill you motherfuckers!" shouts told us they were trying to incite the recklessness to do what they said they would do. We watched some of the control we'd exerted over the street thugs at that intersection dissipate as a result of the shooting. Once, when WECAN was established, the criminals would move on if we parked and rooted in place. Now, they saw us, formed up into small groups and paraded past us in full Crip regalia. Mumbled comments meant to convey death messages and intertwined fingers molded into gang signs were held up in our faces. I could feel the heat coming off those men as they had re-emerged from passivity back into an army seething with rage.

The more significant threats came to us through the department grapevine. Gangs detectives and the Criminal Intelligence Unit caught wind of threats against cops in general and WECAN cops specifically.

The detectives often collected threat intelligence. Not everything was credible, but the detectives valued these threats as valid enough to warn our command. The threats also sounded real to us. They felt more real because the Crips incentivized their anger with a common cause. We were targets. The life of any cop on gang turf became a daily grind whenever we crossed paths with Crips and Bloods. The bad guys worked each other up with attempts to start the fires of retaliation. I sensed it would only be a matter of time until one of them tried to take one of us out.

The extra equipment Manny brought to work was a Ruger Mini-14 rifle with .223 caliber rounds, capable of penetrating several Crips lined up together, with single shots. This was formidable firepower and completely against department policy. WECAN team members felt unprotected by the department.

Being dastardly didn't faze us. "Fine, we'll look out for ourselves," was the feeling we ran with.

We entered the field each day with the certainty we'd balanced the scales of risk. The only way that gun couldn't be effective was if we were ambushed in our car or on the street before Manny could drag it out of the trunk. Our daily routine tilted slightly in our favor. Our odds provided us with the confidence to do what we always did, jerk the bad guys around within the parameters of our training and goals.

All good things must come to an end. Word of our additional armament slipped upstairs to our higher bosses. Whoever found out did not want to punish us. Fair warning was steered downstairs to our sergeants then down to us. Unapproved weapons needed to go back to where they came from. End of story.

We were back to square one. All the WECAN officers felt the hate on the streets. WECAN fought back and stopped passing by men "Crippin' it." We jacked them up every time we saw a pile of them. We heard threats which were beginning to look like smoke and no fire. WECAN represented the gangsters' worse antagonists while the air was heavy with danger from both directions. The Crips needed someone within their midst to step up front, go crazy-mean and attack one of us. So far, the WCC showed the teeth of a dog, showed the bark of a dog, but lacked a leader without restraint to force the issue. There was no Li'l Capone, Mad-Dog, or Killer Smurf with the *cajones* to rear up and make a suicide run at us.

Meanwhile, activists pressed for the name of the detective that shot the gang member in the head, so they could strip him bare in the press. The detective, an acquaintance of mine, tried his best to keep his composure under mounting pressure. The department kept his identity quiet for as long as they could. Somebody weighed the peace against the knee-jerk, hacksawing press and saw the wisdom of identifying the detective to the news. The detective was a black man, but the department had no interest in playing the race card. The dire situation with the press stirred up hard feelings in WECAN's communities. After the detective was identified as an African American SDPD veteran, the racial injustice anger fizzled out. The reveal withered the hate and pressure against the San Diego PD. WECAN also felt a draw-down in threats and risky confrontations. Everyone took a breath as thundering anger lowered to a dull roar. The activists folded up their tents and faded away. Within a few days, the pressure in the Heights reduced from boil to simmer.

The lesson all of us agreed on was cops should have been better armed against the increase in gang firepower and aggression.

Southeast Division suffered from a couple of hot zones with streets that were gauntlets of trouble. One short residential island was nick-named, "The Hole." The cops were wary of the tight squeeze when they drove into it. The crowded, low-income apartments that lined the intersecting Uvas Street and Aurora Street had all the warmth and charm of an "ambush waiting to happen" with only one vehicular way in and out. WECAN made a point of going in with more than one car and more than two cops. The gangs considered themselves to be in control.

The other dangerous block the Southeastern cops had to endure was Bates Street. Bates was another dead-end block, but longer and lined with old military housing apartment units. The block and the two-story block structures were in decay and a Mecca for gang prob-lems. The stretch of low-income stacked hovels was so bad that pizza deliveries were no longer made there. To get an idea of the residential block's appearance, rent the movie Training Day. There's a scene where Ethan Hawke and Denzel Washington drive down a gritty street lined with gangsters. There's a veritable army watching the two cops amble slowly through their midst, many of whom are openly displaying guns. Except for the visible guns part, Bates Street was as close to the same level of hostility as any street in San Diego. WECAN adopted Bates St. and frequently teamed all three WECAN groups together to run amok on the block.

CHAPTER 56:

SPECIAL ENFORCEMENT DIVISION

The Los Angeles Police Department has always appeared to me as a massive department with money to spend beyond my department's wildest dreams. L.A. had a large police force in a city with a population five times the size of the county of San Diego. L.A.'s leaders identified the prevalent and increased crime levels that needed specialized units to control the worst of its population. No matter what bad thing happened in San Diego, it was ten times worse in Los Angeles.

The LAPD built the Metropolitan Division, also known as Metro, as an elite. The Metro Division, which also contained LAPD's Special Weapons and Tactics or SWAT team, contained seven platoons of specially trained officers. The division was tasked with numerous crime-fighting duties that included solutions for major crimes, surveillance, provisions for counter-terrorism details and control over high-risk, barricaded events, such as hostage situations. Some ranking figures within our department admired and even envied LAPD's almost supernatural ability to police their city. Some asked, "Why couldn't San Diego field the most exotic personnel and equipment?"

Suggestions abounded for SDPD's creation of its own Metro strike team. One ranked officer studied the situation with analysis of our department's needs. The conclusion saw a cohesive configuration of the department's top-down command construction. Several units already under other commands transitioned into one new Metro-style division. Suddenly, WECAN saw itself renamed the Special Enforcement Unit, SEU, within the larger Special Enforcement Division or, SED. For two years WECAN remained separate and autonomous from the rest of the department. Now, we were joined in matrimony with SWAT, Tactical Bikes and Air Support.

Within the first few weeks, friction arose. The Special Response Team, SRT, subsection of SWAT became absentee players at our line-ups. SRT comprised the full-time SWAT members. The Primary Response Team, or PRT, were SWAT team members assigned field duties as patrol officers at each division.

SEU members realized what it was like to feel like second fiddles when the lieutenant assigned to this new army would gush all over SWAT. WECAN was convinced that Lieutenant John Welter didn't really appreciate what our mission was. Outgoing Lt. Bill Becker was a go-getter and spent time with us in the field because he loved street work and enjoyed participation when we snarked the bad guys before we popped them. Lieutenant Welter's plan to tweak SEU into pure gang enforcement meant we were no longer going to work narcotics. That was fine with us meat-eaters. We were meant to check-down gangsters and they had plenty of drugs for everyone anyway. Problems simmered when word slipped through the mouths of SRT guys that the old WECAN folks were to be replaced by SWAT officers. Suddenly, men with SWAT mentalities, generally more rigid in application, took the places of cops that would operate with more flexibility.

WECAN had begun to believe it was irreplaceable. We succeeded because we had one mission to fight the felons. We were never detoured with other matters. WECAN cops still with the teams had collected as much as two years of dogged experiences and were a force to be reckoned with as it stood. We were not susceptible to SWAT diversions or any other interruptions to our mission. We tried to sell that experience to the LT. We interjected some opinions about our experience, dedication, and toughness to the LT, but he seemed the type not to listen. Instead, we found ourselves teamed up with SWAT patrol officers who were told if they wanted to keep their SWAT pins, they needed to transfer into SEU.

SDPD fielded a minimal number of officers on trail bikes to supplement Patrol. The motorcycles were handy for canyon enforcement and searches, capable of going places Motors Division would be incapable of maneuvering. Trail bikes in trained hands rode through tight corridors on narrow roads, through tight alleys and even between buildings in pursuit of "rabbits" on foot. Each SEU Team had a two-officer Tactical Bike team to shadow and assist in the field. Air Support brought our department's planes and copters under the SED umbrella. Together, the units were combined into a fierce foursome of machine-gun toting, gang chasers playing with dirt bikes and helicopters. Ahh, baby, that was the coolest!

Lieutenant Welter envisioned more than SEU would eventually handle. None of us understood how we would all work together. The power of SED put the lieutenant in charge of immense resources, not necessarily meant to work together. Tactical Bikes could work with SEU on gang sweeps, but SEU would have no ability to follow the bikes into an operation based on their plans. SWAT was there to lead the way if we needed to force an entry for a warrant, but we weren't trained or prepared to cover SWAT on their incidents. None of the units knew what to do with our attachment to planes or helicopters. SWAT cops were SWAT cops because they wanted the toughest of the jobs, but not necessarily the dirtiest ones. Drugs were a dirty business and generated lots of report paper. I didn't know many SWAT bruisers who wanted to get their gloved hands on junky arrests guaranteed to cause more paper flow than a toilet roll.

The partnership of Rivera and Newbold broke up months earlier when Manny got promoted to detective. Roger Barrett and I became partners until SED formed up. Sluss went with Barrett and I partnered with Darrow. We warned the new guys that we were partnered with SRT in name only. We were still hard-charging WECAN cops and preferred to stick with the mission as we saw fit.

WECAN-turned-SED Officer, Doug Collier, was assigned to the Eastern Team. That squad was even further removed from contact with SRT by distance form HQ. SWAT was always at HQ or next to the Pistol range just east of downtown. When they did interrelate, Doug and his partners were amused by SRT's rather lax days at work. Of course, they required constant training to be the perfect SRT officers. All went into controlled hell when they were sent on missions to save people and take down the worst animals in the city. But when they weren't called to action, they had lots of cushy sit-down time. Doug's team renamed them the Snack Response Team, noting their proclivity to eat whenever the mood struck.

Doug's team kidded them often enough, even mocked them. All SWAT officers wore a tiny pin in the shape of a shield on a front pocket flap. The pin was a sign of honor. SWAT was printed vertically down the center of the pin. Doug found out what company made their pins and went there to look around. The owner was there, so Doug decided to play out a prank he'd dreamed up. He asked the owner if he kept blank SWAT pins in inventory. The guy furnished a handful for the grateful Doug and asked how many he'd need for a SWAT pin order. Doug had other ideas.

The next day's line-up saw Eastern SEU officers adorned with pins identical to the SWAT jewelry. From a distance, the line-up sergeant wondered why his squad all wore SWAT pins. Was it something he'd not noticed before? Was this a new directive he'd missed? He was embarrassed not knowing what was going on around him. As he got a closer look at Doug's pin, the sergeant asked Doug to explain what he saw. "What's O.T.S. stand for, Doug?"

"Other Than SWAT, Sarge."

The sergeant was a little perplexed. Doug read the questions on his face, so he explained, "SWAT gets all the attention and people ask why we don't have pins, since we're working on SED with SWAT. Now we all have similar pins." That was a righteously funny and poignant joke, leaving Doug to consider fitting the word, "SNACK" on a pin when the moment was right.

WECAN officers that remained with the teams when it morphed into SED were required to go through a modified, one-week SWAT course ostensibly to get familiar with their tactics. The shooting tactics' training was handy. The ability to fire automatic weapons on full auto was outstanding. Going through the Obstacle Course was not.

The course was roughly four minutes of severe physical anguish. Recruits ran and dove into the dirt and squeezed through, over-and under obstacles. They climbed, dragged dead weight, and generally tested the physicality of perfect human specimens. SEU's old WECAN troops were not staffed with many perfect physical specimens. We were savvy street cops who ran into gang warfare when others scurried away. The SEU officers questioned why this test of our limited physical prowess was necessary. No one ranked above us gave out a credible answer. Leave it up to our friends in SWAT to confide to us that our LT was simply trying to replace former WECAN members with SWAT officers. The LT really had a thing for SWAT. He didn't see the value of a bunch of drug cops hanging around his elite unit.

The obstacle course was tough and cruel for people not trained and fit. The rigorous strain through endeavor, fortitude, and pain left us all to question whether we'd pass the test. A few of the officers struggled to complete it at all, let alone under the time limit. We had to drag dummies, scale walls, climb into buildings and slide in the dirt under obstacles. Hell, we had two officers, Kevin Ammon and Tyrone Crosby with combined weights of close to 550 pounds, directed to do sit-ups and pull-ups! One officer, Linda, suffered a grievous knee injury and had to be carted off to the doctor. Several of us WECAN cops saw the whole charade for what it was, a weeding-out of the Old Guard. The SWAT guys in charge of this mess were sympathetic. They respected us and felt we were being railroaded out of the unit.

I was a conditioning-nut and had workout routines I'd stuck with for ten years-plus. The "O"

Course was a snap for me once I'd gone through one time. I understood the effort and the pace I'd go with to complete the monster and beat the clock. When I watched my fellow officers tackle the course, in pain, I might add, I ground my teeth together in quiet frustration. "This is fucked up," I whispered to the others too tired and too sore to disagree. My friends and team brothers and sisters were put through an unnecessary grinder so a lieutenant could remove them from the Unit.

When the tests were completed, many of my teammates were concerned they'd failed. We all left for lunch afterwards and commiserated over the utter folly of those bullshit SWAT tests. We speculated that our lieutenant was in his office dry washing his hands with snidely glee. HIS SWAT cops would be one gigantic army after the SEU infestation was cleaned away.

I imagine the LT must have been unpleasantly surprised when the test results revealed all passing grades for our O Course run-throughs. Our SWAT brothers respected us and understood those physical tests were improper. We were good, tough cops and this project of the lieutenant's was a pile of shit. No way did they want to replace us and work as hard as we did. The LT preferred to sweep this fail under his rug and move on. I still have no idea if the SWAT guys administering the tests ever let the truth out that all WECAN cops passed even if the truth came up short.

The changeover to SED and team-up with SWAT meant fewer pranks. All the fun we'd had under WECAN disappeared. Few of the SWAT guys had any desire or will to have a little fun during shift. Everyone was just too serious. One of the last pranks Roger and I committed began before we were split up as partners.

Roger and I drove down Logan Avenue one night when we spotted a canvas banner discarded on the street in front of the Green Fly Restaurant. We got out of the car and straightened out the banner, stretching it to a full length of fourteen feet. The banner read, BUY LOTTO TICKETS HERE. We looked at each other and a spark fired off simultaneously. We knew where this banner needed to go! We stuffed it in our trunk and sped back to HQ.

I grabbed a handful of twelve-inch flex cuffs while Roger bundled up the banner. We took the elevator up to the seventh floor, careful not to be spotted. From that floor, where all the chiefs and Internal Affairs were located, we accessed the stairs to the roof. The top of HQ boasted the unused helicopter pad I mentioned earlier. I think it was the only rooftop helicopter pad in downtown, even though no helicopter had ever landed on our roof due to a design flaw nobody noticed until all the money was spent.

Roger and I each took an end of the banner and tied it off to the roof's top rails with zip ties. At fourteen feet long and three feet high, the words were clearly legible from the ground seven floors below. Once it was secure, we scrammed.

We made it downstairs undetected and returned to the parking lot outside the first floor. We admired our work from a viewpoint below the west side of the building. Now, much of the length of the Chief's west windows advertised BUY LOTTO TICKETS HERE.

Everybody driving into work the next morning would have to pass below the banner. The arriving employees were most of the permanent staffers at HQ, seven floors worth of civilians, sworn police officers, detectives, sergeants, lieutenants, captains, assistant chiefs and, of course *the* Chief. Only our unit friends knew who the culprits were.

With SED, those days were almost over.

CHAPTER 57:

MORE PRANKS

On weekends at HQ, the building was sparsely occupied. Most of the detectives and civilian staffers enjoyed Saturdays and Sundays off. WECAN/SEU still slugged it out with the mean streets. An afternoon constitutional was much more relaxing on the unoccupied, upper floors when the building was ninety percent vacant. I chose the highest floor for the solitude of an empty and quiet bathroom. My mistake was my team knew which floor and which bathroom I intended to use.

The seventh floor hosted the big wigs. All the chiefs' offices were up there. This austere floor also includes the inner sanctum of Internal Affairs. This enclave of secrets and hot seats was well-protected from outside and inside forces interested in cracking open its mysteries. The rooms behind that door were so shielded that the entry was alarmed. One good tug on the locked door handle and an alarm would go off downstairs at the Watch Commander's Office, the nights and weekends' boss of bosses. All hell would break loose if that electronically guarded portal was crashed.

I was finished in the bathroom when I tugged on its door and found it wouldn't open. I gripped it tighter and tugged again. The heavy door would budge a little, but the resistance apparently came from the other side. Ahh, a prank. I shouted through the door to open it up. I knew somebody was out there messing with me. I used more force to shake the door free and knew something my captors probably didn't.

I figured the culprits had tied the doorknob to something and the only object in proximity to tie it off to the doorknob to Internal Affairs. The voices that materialized on the other side of the door were Roger, John, and Chuck. They had their good laughs while I exerted a little more force. That got them laughing louder. Then I stopped, and announced, "You guys know the doors to IA are alarmed, right?"

Somebody blurted out, "Shit!" That was when the three jokesters panicked and went into rescue mode. Now I had THEM right where I wanted them. I gave the door handle more forceful yanks and really shook the hell out of the door. I wanted that alarm to go off and nail the clowns. They worked feverishly with the various utility knives they wore with their gear. Their plan to loop a string of plastic flex-cuffs together in a chain, backfired. The high tensile strength nylon was tough to cut through quickly. The three stooges were in a race to see how fast they could save me before I set the alarm off and brought the cavalry in. I jerked on that door with rabid exertion, to the point where I broke into a sweat. I could hear those guys straining to cut through the super-resilient nylon as they cursed and yelled at me to knock it off. I gritted my teeth and pulled on the door to set the alarm off. I'd watch the fun and those maniacs would get chewed out.

The boys got lucky and cut me free before I could exact vengeance. They were tense and perspiring, one of them gave me the bird. No harm had been done and the alarm remained undisturbed. There'd be no more screwing with Jamie during a workday relief break.

Roger and I were paired up prowling for black gangs on either side of Freeway 15 for the day. We left line-up and decided to leave HQ through the doorway into the sally port. The DL's Office was across the hall from a bulletin board filled with wanted posters. Some of the printouts were quite accurate and the photos were easily identifiable. Others looked like copies of copies of copies, the photos indistinguishable from ink blots. One such picture was of a black male gang member wanted for armed robbery of a bank downtown. The description was bland and could have applied to anyone. The photo was just a black blob with no details to the image. Yet, Drone 7 from Sector C did their duty and pinned the legal pad-sized paper to the wall. My partner and I packed our car with our gear and set out for WCC territory.

We got as far as 31st and Imperial when the dulcet sounds of "Fuck You, Offay," rang out in the stillness. I was the passenger and saw the gentleman, a Crip, was mad-dogging me while he held up his sagging pants with his left hand. His right hand was busy extending his middle finger at us. Roger jerked the car to the right and jammed it against the curb. I pushed open my door and swung out onto the sidewalk to confront the guy. Rage at the cops from Crips was met with business by said police.

Roger flanked the man as I faced him head-on. "What's the problem, man? Neither one of us said anything to you," I declared. Free speech is a given in this instance. But neither of us were going to take it from the very thugs we were there to suppress.

"Y'all got nothin' better to do than jack up a black man. That's why I said what I said. To hell with y'all."

Roger slid in closer to him and asked him his name. "I don't gotta tell you nothin'. You pigs are harassin' me for no reason."

We didn't have anything on the guy. Shouting obscenities at cops is not a crime. Shouting obscenities at gang cops by a gangster was likely to be a bad move. We didn't have his name and he didn't seem to carry a wallet when I patted him down. If this cat had a weapon the least that I could do was find it before it found us. He was just angry enough to try to hurt us if he felt pushed hard enough. I sensed the heat coming of him. What to do?

"Hey Roger, remember that wanted poster in the DL's Office? The one for armed robbery downtown?" Roger looked at me quizzically. "You know. The one we were laughing about because of the detailed photo?"

"Yeah, now that you mention it."

"I think this might be our guy."

"You're right. Turn around, pal. We're detaining you as the suspect in a robbery."

"What kind of bullshit is this? You motherfuckers got no crime against me. Y'all is fucking with me. See, you fucking po-lice always be makin' shit up to mess with me!" He was angry, but smart enough after all not to take this confrontation to the next level. That was fine. I didn't want to fight him. We cuffed him and had him crouch to slink into the back seat.

"Now what?" asked Roger. "We detain him and run some computer time on him?"

"Yeah, I'm thinking we park him in the sally port and bring the flyer out for him to see. He'll get more pissed off, but he'll also learn a lesson about words likely to incite a police officer."

"It is what we're out here to do." The detention guaranteed a full search of his clothing before we stuck him in our car. Still nothing. We headed back to the barn.

By now, Marcus had given us his name. He was still riled, but I sensed he knew how this game was played and would wait it out under some level of self-control. We parked behind the gates in the sally port and stood outside the car to talk. "If we can't find anything on him in the computers the wanted poster won't help," I offered. But he'd be inconvenienced by the tiring seventeen-block walk back home.

"Suits me fine. Fuck this guy. Let me show him the picture." Roger held it up to Marcus' face and asked, "Is that you?"

"What kind of cracker bullshit is this? That ain't me. It ain't anyone. That picture look like any brother. I knew you motherfuckers were gonna mess with me!"

"Yeah, but is this you?"

"Fuck no, motherfucker. That ain't me and you know it!"

Roger delighted in giving the guy a hard time. "You wouldn't be here if you hadn't opened your mouth."

"Marcus, you yelled at gang cops who weren't even interested in you. You know our white car. Go yell shit at the cops in black and white. We never even disrespected you until you advertised that you're an asshole," I drilled into his eyes with mine with that sort of body language and facial expression vibe that gets down to the truth. "You keep calling us fuckers, but you're the one that fucked up, pal."

"Oh, fuck, man. I know. I'm just pissed off, you know what I'm sayin'?"

"Yeah, I get your drift, but take it out on someone else. Why bring this kind of attention on yourself?" I figured we were reaching an accord.

"Marcus. You're being cool right now. We got no hard feelings. I'll make you an offer," Roger suggested. "We can cut you loose here or we can give you a ride back. What'll it be?"

"Ohh, man, don't be dropping me back where I was. My homies will give me shit. Can you drop me off at the hospital? Nobody will notice there." He was referring to the old Physicians and Surgeons Hospital on 25th. Every cop and his mother knew that old landmark.

"It's a deal. Let me cut an FI and we're on our way." I had my FI pad ready and he answered all the prerequisite questions about his identity. As it turned out, he was on probation for drugs.

"You aint't gonna tell my P.O. about this, is you?"

"No. This wasn't really that bad. We're just fucking with you 'cause you started it. Remember, the next time you see a white police car, don't yell at the cops inside. Understood?"

"Yeah, I hears you." With that, we answered his wish and dropped him at P&S.

CHAPTER 58:
SHELLTOWN SWEEP

The new guys, Darby Darrow and Todd Sluss wanted to continue with some of their projects from Southeastern Division. Either Darrow and I, or four of us, Roger, Darby, Todd and I would tramp down to Southeast San Diego to attack gang and drug problems Darby and Todd considered unfinished business. One of those areas was an alley of 1000 Goodyear Street. The Shelltown gang named itself ages ago after an old Shell gas station sign that could be seen for miles. This street gang was yet another dangerous thorn in the department's backside. Their bangers' violent crimes made them a necessary police target.

Darby and Todd dealt with them more often than Central WECAN did since this was Southeast WECAN's turf. The two SWAT officers, mostly Darby, were anxious to add them to our list of Central WECAN objectives, at least one time. The two former Southeastern Patrol officers rarely had an army to back up the style of enforcement they desired and were constantly drawn away from the things they wanted to do to answer radio calls. The gang-hot, dead-end alley parallel to 1000 Goodyear was the spot to snare some gangsters when they least expected us.

Our plan was to conceal our cars and move into the neighborhood on foot without alerting anyone. The new guys knew the area better than Roger and I did. They took the lead and walked us into the spots optimal for a surprise takedown. None of us knew if the Shelltown thugs would cooperate or be there for us to snap the trap on them. The chance of success was either hit-and-miss, or strike it rich, when we operated this way with little intel beforehand.

Our approach was serene. Nobody was out in front of the gangster's homes on Goodyear. A couple of us slipped between the houses towards the alley. The other pair used the 8:30 evening darkness to creep along the edges of the gravel alley. If the approach went smoothly, our entry would box in anybody gathered at the alley's end. The attack worked like a charm, the gang members and associates were caught off-guard. We spread out so quickly in a pincer fashion that all chance of escape was cut-off. Nobody even bothered to run past us or fight. Maybe they thought uniformed cops were going to shake them down and then leave. That's what the patrol cops usually did. That would happen more often for the patrol officers who took the time to do gang sweeps like this one. The radio was the merciless mistress that interrupted most chances of patrol officers completing a raid on gangs. WECAN/SED operated with centric focus to lance the boil of gangs whenever we could. That was our mandate and our expertise.

The gang members, adults and juveniles, accommodated us quite well. About eight of them smoked pot and drank beer with the teens, some younger than sixteen. There were all sorts of crimes for adults who placed themselves in this situation. The teens' least worrisome problem was violation of curfew. In fact, almost all in the alley were witnessed committing some kind of violation. That made our jobs easier. We now had probable cause to either detain or arrest most of them for a milieu of crimes. We had them for the dope smoking inside and outside a couple of vehicles. That gave us legal permission to search those vehicles. We detained adults in proximity to the drinking teens for the contribution to their delinquency. Any alcohol seen through the windows of the gangster's cars we wanted to search provided us with just cause. The bad guys made no contingency for this run-in with police. They were totally taken by surprise and were resigned to their fate. Some were searched and arrested for drug possession.

We searched several cars the gang members were seated in. We found a nine–millimeter, semi-automatic pistol, a twenty-five caliber semi-automatic pistol and thirty-seven hundred dollars in cash. We tossed in a heavily taped lead pipe, which comprised a man-made billy club. One guy would go to jail for that weapon violation.

A neighboring law enforcement agency wanted two of the subjects for questioning in a homicide. This take-down was a good night's work and was punched up a bit when our sergeant, Bill Edwards wrote a commendation on our behalf. Bill elected to broadcast our endeavor to others within the department. The "Gangsters of Goodyear" got their asses handed to them, he announced.

The sergeants then running WECAN were good men. The three-stripers that ran Southeast WECAN tended to be the most assertive and respecting of their go-getter officers. Eastern began with a — how should I put this — a patrol sergeant used to less aggressive cops under him. He never left the office, so he had no feel for what his WECAN people were up to. He was also a weak communicator. Rather than talk to his people, he stuck Post-it notes on their lockers, on their timecards, on their reports and on their cars. I once worked out of the same building with the others, but our sergeant rarely had a need to provide us with the day's instructions. He knew who we were and what we were capable of. We knew our roles better than he did. The Eastern team supervisor was a product of F Troop. His officers had no idea why he was at WECAN. He got under their skin with his lack of leadership and his Post-It message. That sergeant's eventual replacement and the transition to SED made the lives of the Eastern team much more satisfying.

I'd seen the buffoonery one time when I walked into work at the Eastern WECAN trailer and saw a commotion around the sergeant's office. I peered in through the door and caught the reason for the buzz. Some despicable soul(s) had stuck Post-it notes on the walls. But it was more than just stickers on walls. The rascal(s) covered all four walls with little space in-between. The WECAN sergeant for the Eastern team had the sole desk in the tiny office. His desk was covered, top and sides with the blank, sticky notes. The bookcase was covered, and each book had its own separate stickered paper note. Each desk item was covered. Each pencil was wrapped in Post-it notes as well as the stapler, phone desk calendar, a potted plant and even the waste basket.

Witnesses saw the sergeant walk into the office, take stock of the neatly applied mess, and then walk out of the office and the building without a single word spoken. He transferred off the Unit not long after. His replacement was also a former F Trooper. John Wray was a good officer then and a great sergeant when Eastern lucked out and got him. He was also SWAT and part of the SED lieutenant's master plan. Against the wishes of the LT, this sergeant saw through the SWAT-evolution ruse and stood with his people, as did the Southeast sergeant. Those of us at Central went through a spate of purposeless supervision until we turned into SED and landed Sgt. Bill Edwards. We finally got a decent leader who understood us.

I continued my role as an acting sergeant whenever Edwards was off work. The role of an acting supervisor referred to lower ranked officers being temporarily promoted to supervisor with a commensurate raise in pay. I handled that role several times and welcomed the kick up in pay. WECAN was once ripe with opportunities for advancement. I wasn't so sure about SED.

CHAPTER 59:
SWAT-LESS

In the mid-1980s, LAPD saw a spike in shootings aimed at their officers. San Diego cops saw a spike in attacks on cops as well. To counter WECAN's vulnerability after it transitioned to SED our commanders decided we couldn't function safely on the streets without armed guards from SWAT to follow us around and back us on stops. The SWAT officers literally guarded us with machine guns as we went about the business of gang and thug contacts. This was not what we wanted. Neither the SWAT guys nor WECAN/SED folks felt it was necessary, or practical. A guy with a machine gun is no help in a fight to the ground with some thug in blue or red.

Roger Barrett and I stopped our car at West Coast Crip Central, 30th and Imperial, to snag a crack dealer. We got him because he'd been seen slinging crack all week and we wanted him to be dirty, so we could get him off the street. We rolled up with our SWAT babysitter behind us in his SWAT car. Paul Lennon, our SWAT bodyguard commented dryly on an earlier occasion that he saw no long-term point to his guardianship. He knew we were as aware of our surroundings as any SWAT officer. He was at the police gun range to watch WECAN/SED teammates train on the very same automatic weapons he carried in the field when he hovered over us. We were good with our own side arms, as well. Paul covered us from five yards away.

Paul stood guard with his MP5 rifle strapped over his shoulder and slung low across his chest. The coupling of WECAN/SED with SWAT spelled ill-conceived cross-pollination with a bunch of A-type personalities for a task ill-defined.

Our contact went well with the Crip crack dealer. He knew the score, wasn't holding and barely acknowledged us. Damn it. We'd purposefully left him untouched for days hoping to lull him into a false sense of security. Our timing stunk. He had no reason to fight or run. Paul behind us was not so lucky. An incensed, crazy drunk walked up to him and grabbed his rifle.

Paul was a big, tough guy, but when forced to protect his rifle he had no way to manhandle an attacker. His hands were full of a gun he couldn't shoot yet since the circumstances hadn't yet risen to a deadly threat. Instead, Paul had to shout at us for help.

We weren't even looking at Paul when the shit hit his personal fan. Roger and I let our man go and ran to help Paul. I grabbed a hunk of the drunk's clothing and tried to break his grip on Paul's weapon. Roger flanked all of us and tried to pull the drunk's left arm away from the gun barrel. The four of us engaged in a twisting dance of feet and wrestling grips to unclamp the feisty inebriate's fingers before he got one in the trigger guard. The guy was just a stupid drunk and his mumbled words were incoherent. Paul had managed to slip on the rifle's safety, so we were all safe anyway, unless the fool got lucky. Our savage jerking attempts finally broke the man's grasp and we turned him around with enough violence to wrench him to the sidewalk. Paul took two steps back and un-shouldered his weapon.

Paul examined the gun for scratches and scanned every screw and lever the attacker might have knocked askew. Roger and I cuffed the still thrashing rowdy. We took the drunk while Paul figured it was time to stow the weapon in his trunk. We conferred about this. Paul was embarrassed, but we all acknowledged this swat guard performance foisted on WECAN/SED cops was ill-conceived. Our feedback up the chain was immediate from both angles. SWAT was detached from guard duty and WECAN/SED returned to normal.

We knew not everybody was suited to be on our unit. I mentioned earlier that knowledge included supervisors. One of our sergeants was an import from F Troop. Although Sgt. Chuck Sleeper was a nice enough guy and understood the police system, maybe he wasn't built for our kind of training which included modified, shortened SWAT work.

Our unit commander wanted us somewhat experienced with SWAT tactics and weapons beyond what patrol officers were trained. This included shooting and tactical building entry exercises. San Diego and regional law enforcement trained at a site named Duffy Town after the almost mythical San Diego Sheriff John Duffy of earlier times. The site was located on U.S. Marine Corps property at the eastern end of Miramar Air Base where the movie, "Top Gun" was set. The land was dotted with training facilities for physical tests, range shooting, simulated building entry and attacker exercises and weapons tests. Bunkers built to train soldiers and Marines for duty in the Pacific in World War II lined a ravine south of Duffy Town. The WECAN-turned-SED officers went through a week of SWAT training, modified from the two weeks SWAT recruits go through to gain SWAT status.

One of the exercises placed two armed officers on either side of a closed door. Our task was to enter the door and cross one officer in front of another with their guns extended to sweep the room. Our sergeant was clearly unprepared for this exercise.

The first officer went in diagonally as the sergeant stepped in behind him with his gun pointed ahead. The clockwork movements were smooth and correct until the sergeant blew off a round from his handgun and scared the bejeezus out of the officer ahead of him. The whole training segment stopped immediately as we all triaged for bullet wounds. Fortunately, no one was hurt, except for one supervisor with a bruised ego who suffered through sour looks from our SWAT trainers.

WECAN/SED grew used to ignoring that sergeant. Moments were rare when he needed to speak to us. He wasn't a part of most of our operations. He wasn't really built for this forceful type of police work. He must have felt like more of a patrol sergeant than a special unit leader when he worked with us.

Rare was the occasion when Sergeant Chuck braved the night and drove into the Heights. If he did drive south of downtown, we presumed he was looking for his people. We never made contacting us easy for him. Central WECAN/SED always kept one radio tuned into a tactical frequency. That freq was radio-to-radio and didn't pass through Police Communications. Communications was hands off WECAN/SED and left us alone. On that night, one of us spotted the sergeant's car before he saw his desired officer or his partner. They let the others know that

Sgt. Chuck was on the prowl. We all decided to have a little sport with him and devised a game of hide-and-seek.

The sergeant saw the police car and turned down 28th Street to get behind it. The officers turned quickly into an alley and shut off all lights. Even the brake lights could be shut down with a special switch inside the car. Then, they escaped out the other end of the alley. All of us ran commentary over the radio to set up places to tease him and then disappear. As the sergeant roamed around, we could see the moon shine off the chrome frame of his overhead light bar. One of us crossed a street from one alley into another two blocks ahead of him. That car shut off its lights and ran out the other end just as the sergeant entered the alley. Another car passed down the street behind him with its overhead red and blue lights on. He caught it in his rearview and stopped. By the time he backed out of the alley, his people were out of sight. One distinct conversation went like this between Roger, John and me. John: said, "We got him at a red ball on Thirtieth. We're parked a couple of blocks up. He's turning, so he's all yours."

I had gone dark on Twenty-Eighth below Imperial. "We're repositioning," I said.

John: "We're behind him. Looks like he's going your way."

Roger replied, "I just crossed his path. He's gonna get stopped at a red ball if he goes after me. I'm monitoring Central's freq. He still hasn't come up on the air. This is really weird."

I replied, "Yeah, what the hell is he doing? I think he's afraid to look stupid and raise us on the air."

John responded with, "We're still behind him and he hasn't noticed. We're peeling off and going to the Burger King. Let's meet there."

"Yeah, we just saw him pass us at a stop sign on Clay. He must have seen us. We're taking the long way around to the Burger King."

Roger bellowed, "Baw-hahahaha!" as the cat and mouse game went on for ten minutes. He'd catch a glimpse and then that wisp of a sighting was gone. Finally, we all convened at a Burger King near Main Street. There was not one word from the sergeant over the radio. We guessed he was being clever, imagining he could surprise us. We had no idea why he looked for us in the first place. Maybe his boss, our lieutenant, kicked his ass out of the office. The sergeant wasn't a go-getter so maybe his boss gave him a mental shove. He left the unit shortly after. He was a nice guy, in over his head.

CHAPTER 60:
ABORTION RALLIES

Slowly, WECAN cops referred to ourselves as SED. WECAN was a badge of honor as an assignment, but the Kumbaya acronym lacked the machismo a bunch of male and female street fighters might have preferred. SED, or Special Enforcement Division, sounded more mysterious. SED rang out like FBI or CIU. The Criminal Intelligence Unit within the SDPD was a super-secret assignment that handled heavy-duty crime investigations like organized crime, political investigations, and criminal investigations coordinated with Mexico, and other "special" considerations. We sounded like more of special force than a neighborhood program. I liked it.

SED gathered a lot of attention from within the law enforcement community. The transition from WECAN bought us a new round of publicity. The press took notice of us again after losing interest in our second year. Before SED, WECAN was constantly drawn into other activities. We were a convenient manpower pool that didn't rob patrol divisions of officers and didn't force detectives back into uniform for a day. One of the least desirable assignments SED was thrown into was abortion rallies.

The abortion rallies were press-bait worldwide. Anti-abortionists played to the reporters to the hilt. Pro-abortionists mostly held smaller, sometimes silent vigils, in proximity to their opponents. Both sides of the argument set the stage for feuds and physical confrontations that required a large police presence at each rally. The anti-abortion clan was viewed as the aggressors at each of the rallies I was assigned to. The only unit with a staff large enough was SED. SDPD needed a mobile manpower pool and SED fit the bill.

The anti-abortionists offered passive resistance. Their motives forced confrontations with police officers required to remove them from the areas adjoining clinics that offered Planned Parenthood medical services, i.e. abortions. Their goal was to make abortion a universal disgrace and force the closure of legal abortion facilities. The cops would gather around and await orders to use non-violent extraction methods which included literally carrying the protestors away. That kind of lift-and-carry action tired a person out and added a potential source of injury. Police officers working the crowds were trained to use specific tools to make the obstinate protestors "come along" with a small amount of pain compliance. This involved manipulating a protestor's wrists with a hard, plastic form of the Japanese *nunchaku*, Americanized to nunchucks. This pain compliance tool worked even through protestors' duct-taped wrists that were designed to insulate against the agony. Whether they complied voluntarily or not, they would come to their feet and follow directions. The protestors that sat linked to each other with bound wrists offered even more of a physical challenge to police.

The earliest abortion protests began at clinics throughout San Diego. Word was given in advance by the protest organizers who sought to comply with city laws that governed mass assemblies in public. The gathering press, in ever increasing numbers, was the protests' primary goal. SED became involved only after the department calculated the number of bodies needed for crowd control. What began as groups numbering in the tens inflated to several hundred at congregations with the anti-side always outnumbering the pro-side. The police department was tested at the biggest of the rallies at a hospital in Point Loma.

Sharp Hospital, formerly Doctor's Hospital, in the Sports Arena area of San Diego was rarely ever a place to court controversy. Most times the only reasons officers were present was for trauma victims or to sit quietly and knock out paperwork. SED got word from above that we would be crowd control for, yet another rally scheduled for five days hence. Great, I thought, another Saturday ruined. Our superiors warned us that the expected crowd, on both sides of the zealotry, would number several hundred. Perhaps, this would be the largest gathering to date.

SED would arrive in force, supplemented by officers from other units. Our mobile offices would be put into action as prisoner process-ing stations. Officers were pre-assigned duties, with some as arresting officers and others working prisoner control. The majority of uniformed personnel compromised the thin line of uniforms that guarded the hospital entrance. The arresting officers were the poor bastards that had to do all the heavy lifting. Dozens of us formed one long human chain that separated groups with opposite opinions doggedly determined to challenge the other's ideology.

The hospital housed a clinic for pregnant patients. The clinic staffed at least one surgeon on duty to perform abortions. The women who entered the hospital for an appointment risked loud screams and shouts of ridicule. The police were not assigned to escort them through gauntlets of protestors, but they would step aside and break the line to let them in. The pro-abortionists were organized and even wore specific matching t-shirts that identified them as supporters of pro-choice. They approached the women that braved the circus and asked them if they were there for the specific clinic. If so, a cadre of two or three escorts, mostly women, would surround them. Their intent was to get them out of earshot of the anti-abortionists and guided them safely and quietly into the clinic. Sometimes the woman in the spotlight, there for pregnancy counseling or an abortion, was held by a friend or by the escort. Some women stood up to the crowd of agitated protestors that tried to call her out with cries of "Abortionist!" or "We can save your baby!" and walked on into the hospital without help. Those women defied the barrage of angry, nasty comments and braved the collage of fanatical faces all vying for their attention.

My chain of forty, or so, men and women in uniform went face-to-face with over a hundred anti-people. Many of them crowded the line and kept a minimal distance of two feet or less from our line. Another two hundred people stood en mass behind the opposing line, shouting and holding placards with words of protests, beliefs in God, and awful, graphic photos that they strained to get on camera. The press was allowed free range to roam throughout the crowds and the cops and snap photos by the score. News cameras ran miles of footage in the hopes they'd score some dramatic money-shot.

Our command and my fellow troops had been through this trial by fire several times. We were trained for the matter and experience helped keep us calm and determined. The presence of at least seventy officers instilled some level of civility. At least the protestors were no longer allowed to go nose-to-nose with the cops. I could see organizers mingling with the protestors. Most wore specific shirts that identified them as leaders. Others wore priest frocks or carried bullhorns to enhance their voices. They milled about for the first hour. Then, like clockwork, the protestors facing the officers sat down as if one life-form. I noticed that the line of anti-abortionists reacted to other commands I couldn't hear over the din of hundreds of voices. At first, I could discern no difference between them and the rest of that crowd. Then, I saw that each person wore particular clothing. Men and women alike wore baggy pants and thick, long-sleeved shirts. The reasons became clear shortly after when our arrest teams were ordered in to take out the sitters. The officers withdrew their nunchuks and wrapped them around the first few sitters. I saw the duct tape wrapped around the wrists of each of the seated people. They'd prepared ahead of time to take on their roles and gird for pain compliance.

The 'chuks work on the wrist bones. The two plastic handles connect with a nylon cord. The cord is wrapped around the wrists and the hard-plastic compresses against the wrist. The pain is excruciating when the pressure gets worse. Nobody can withstand the agony. The duct tape was considered a smart move, but an officer breaking up the line of seated protestors could apply more pressure than the tape could repel. The results were all seated protestors either got up on their own or were hauled to their feet in pain and trundled off to the prisoner control area marked off by cones and guards.

I watched my fellow officer sweat and grimace with fatigue and pain. Some of the protestors refused to stand. Two officers were required to lift them off the ground. Usually, the protestor didn't have the strength to hold their legs crossed when they in the air. They walked when walking became much easier than being dragged. A small handful held the lotus position all the way to prisoner control. The officers that carried those burdens had to come off the line to recover. We began to run out of cops.

My own back and feet felt the agony. I looked up and down the chain and saw my *compadres* were toiling to stay upright and comfortable.

Two and one-half hours in at an inflexible standing position took its toll. Supervisors took a few of the worst cases off the line to get water and a seated break. Our line slowly shrank.

Word circulated among the supervisors that an SDPD officer was spotted within the zone of anti-protestors. One of the officers in my line was temporarily assigned to this protest from Eastern Patrol. He nudged me and directed my view to a tall man buried deep in the crowd. "The guy's a cop out of Eastern."

"What the hell?"

"Yeah, right? I don't know how he can get away with that. The supervisors must know." Soon enough, I watched two sergeants move in closer to the anti-people and face down the Eastern cop with stares. I saw his face. He wore the determined expression of a man on a mission. The rumor mill later circulated that the officer quit his job not long after this protest.

This was my last abortion rally. Both sides had exhausted their press exposure. Anti-abortion people were no longer in vogue in the eyes of the press. Killings in the name of abortion prevention shocked the world. At least one doctor and a couple of staffers were murdered by the craziest of the anti-abortionists. News stories tried to run both sides of the debate with rival opinions over the killings. The press backed off a bit as public opinion began to detest the mass rallies and the violence they might have inspired. The press and their flammable pictures found other news topics that superseded the now-repetitive theater of the zealous.

A few officers could handle a few protestors. A few officers could not handle a massive crowd. We wore out quickly when we lifted and carried protestors. Their dead weight tore down our stamina, our backs and our knees. So, more officers were required as relief. The protests that SED worked involved all our teams. We all played our roles to quell any flare-up within the rallies and carried out resistant bodies. Backs strained while legs and arms weakened, and headaches brewed. There were never any provisions for food and water until after we mustered. Those necessities had to be picked up and brought to the protest. I worked until I was tired, thirsty, and hungry. Then I worked some more. Several of us hovered around a bag of sunflower seeds behind the SWAT van. This was the only nourishment we could squeeze into the day. The lieutenant in charge, Leslie Lord, saw us as she wandered purposefully up and down the line to gauge every cop's performance. She was angry at us, even though we were designated back-up at the time, and called our actions unprofessional. She was over-concerned that the press would see four of us over a pile of seed shells, as we nibbled like rabbits. Our sergeant got an earful.

The press, local, national, and international, remained for hours on end which increased the protestors' time on the ground. Both entities fed off each other. We didn't get fed. The abortion protestors and the television cameras wanted the police to misbehave and our actions to be filmed so that others would be convinced we acted brutally. SDPD never gave them any photo ops or misbehavior to hold against us. SED officers were consummate professionals. The presumed cases of police aggression made their way to court and were thrown out by one judge after another. The Unit looked good, but it was an awful experience to partake in. I hated those rallies.

The cameras were set loose throughout each event. Photographers darted around to find the next front-page newspaper shot for any news outlet that would pay. I watched a protestor dressed in a friar's frock move from officer to officer and stand toe-to-toe to pray for each officer's salvation. She caught a lot of attention for the holy get-up and the poster-board color photo of the lifeless, bloody body of an aborted fetus she carried. First her, and then others including children, held those ghastly poster-sized pictures within inches of each officer's eyes. Variations on that photo and others emboldened some of the anti-protestors to target cops with their frustration and their perceived righteous anger.

The Central SED officers were lined up as a human wall at one rally. We stood shoulder-to-shoulder and faced the anti-people, their ranks two and three people deep. The pro-abortionists were provided a path between us and the building. The antagonists jeered and screamed at them, but the loud voices, spittle and bad breath caught us full in our faces. Each rally lasted half a day. The slow-down only happened when the cameras and the reporters, mostly the cameras, packed up and shoved off.

We behaved honorably under the scrutiny of numerous news entities all waiting for million-dollar shots of us doing anything that put us in a bad light. SED came out clean at each of the weekly battles between opposing moralists.

The press and other agencies loved us again when they weren't trying to make us look like Nazi soldiers. Attorneys from the City and District Attorney's Offices came out for ride-alongs again. As with WECAN, SED generated a lot of well-written arrest reports. Those reports guaranteed uncontested conviction rates in the ninety-percentile. The prosecuting attorneys wanted to see us operate firsthand. We became somewhat of a learning tool for newer prosecutors. Our partnerships with the curious didn't just involve our side of the law. Defense attorneys requested SED rides and were routinely turned down. Our command was wise not to allow the "enemy" first-hand accounts of our performance in the field. Central SED worked four or five rallies. The only positive I got out of those ruined Saturdays and Sundays was an earlier work shift. I got to see my wife and son on several weekend evenings in a row for the first time in a couple of years.

Under the SED umbrella, we were again viewed with a fresh, favorable light. The team's inclusion with the tactical motorcycles and SWAT gave us a more public formidability. The Tac bikes raced up and down Crip Land and ran them off with the noisy engines. If we found a gangster we were interested in, the guy was up shit's creek if he ran. Me, he might outrun, but if a dirt bike pursued down any sidewalk or escape route, the fleeing crook was toast. The motorcycles came in handy until their unit was disbanded in a flurry of budget cuts. The helicopters and the airplanes were too expensive to waste on a bunch of gangsters.

Those gangsters began to recognize the change from to SED from WECAN. All the gangbangers knew WECAN from the streets we shared with them. Everybody knew everybody else. Our behaviors and tactics were recognized. Now, with SWAT and motorcycles, we played havoc with their expectations. Suddenly, it was a new ball game for everyone. Not only were we a novelty again, but we were potentially of greater alarm to the bad guys.

The SWAT guys had to figure out exactly where they fit in. Their operative style tended to come off as a little rigid in a business that had rougher, more fluid tendencies. If SED and SWAT wanted to hammer away at a problem, they wanted to study and plan the move first. SED drew up plans in their heads and caravanned to the target, with the appropriate safety protocols. One SWAT officer embodied the differences between us. Five of us and a couple of SWAT cops ventured to Memorial Park to remind the Logan gang that we were still threats. We had a couple of special cases we wanted to arrest for their prolific PCP marketing. The hope was we'd spill into the park from different angles and box them in. One of the targets was a piece of work with the moniker of Shooter. For obvious reasons, we were certain if Shooter was in the park, he might get shot.

Five cars drove in from several directions as we had done so many times before. The SWAT guys thought we were rash: "Don't you guys have a plan, like an approach that minimizes our risk?"

They were in our plan now. We'd swoop and trap them. Anyone that posed a threat went down. If they bolted, that was what the cars were for. We had no Tac bikes for this operation, so we'd wing it without them. We knew the park's exits and spider holes the gangs might flee to. If someone jumped a backyard fence or climbed over the tall, schoolyard fences, the cars would redeploy. We knew what we were doing. If possible, the guys that fled were pursued. Otherwise, we'd get the guy another day.

"And if there's a gun?" one of the SWAT guys asked.

"Shoot him if it's pointed at anyone," was our response.

The race to trap the Logans went off without a hitch. Shooter was with a couple of his homeboys near a eucalyptus tree. He was an OG and a little too old to run. He would look weak in front of his gang if he did. His profile among the other Logans remained strong when he stood his ground and appeared to be cool. One of the SWAT guys popped the trunk on his car and hauled out his H&K MP 5 automatic rifle.

"What are you doing?" I asked.

"This? For protection. Why?" was his answer.

"Put it away. Who are going to shoot? We're all bunched together. That gun's a liability if these guys get squirrely." The logic may have escaped him, but a couple of us smirked in that, "we gotta teach this soldier everything we do" way.

All that experience was its own reward. Our police reports were often commented on up the law enforcement chain. Our experience doing what we did lead to solid prosecutions and produced well-accepted accolades from the men and women destined to try our cases. Darby Darrow and I received a written example of the praise SED grew used to. The district attorney advanced a copy of a Complaint Request Evaluation to our unit.

Instead of a complaint, the report boasted. "This is a concise and well-written report. The facts of the case were used to summarily revoke the defendant's felony probation. Rather than file a new case, this case was strong enough to get a prison commit for the probation violations." The county saved money by not having to take him to trial. The strength of our report was enough to get him off the streets.

Another coefficient was also at work. WECAN/SED had a lot of its officers promoted to detectives. All that field experience moved into pro-active, specialized investigations units. Some would eventually gain rank and carry their respect for hard-working cops with them. For the time being, it didn't pay to be an impulsive, violent gang member. We would find you. That was proven through SED's inception with the massive reduction in gang shootings throughout San Diego's zip codes. Gang violence was at its lowest since the epidemic of crack first screamed through the city's inner neighborhoods. The District Attorney's Office released news about gang violence. Sure enough, the trend was downward for black and Hispanic gang shootings. But something aggressive emerged to re-engage gang cops, and in unexpected places.

CHAPTER 61:

NEW BLOOD

Cops had been chasing Philippine gangsters for years. Much of their activity was relegated to the Paradise Hills neighborhood shared by black Skyline Piru and several Hispanic rival gangs. The Philippine teenagers dueled with each other in that tough part of town. North of East San Diego, in much more affluent parts of town, Philippine families raised a generation of sons enraptured by gang imagery. Suddenly, Philippine gangsters that attended school regularly would gather up and bang on weekend evenings. They built alliances with Paradise Hills' gangs to bolster their images. These weekend warriors allied with either blue Crips or red-clad Pirus from SED's work zones.

San Diego was introduced to two new gangs: The blue-sworn Mira Mesa Crips from that part of town and the cross-town rival, PQ B-Down Boys of hilly Rancho Penasquitos, adorned in red. The two gangs were separated by a length of freeway and the public schools they attended. Both parts of town wore wealth well. The homes of Rancho Penasquitos were newer than Mira Mesa, somewhat larger and more exclusive than the southward Mira Mesa rivals. SED was surprised when we surveilled these kids and found they lived with up to two other generations of family members. Surely, these can't be real gang members? They had more stable homes than some cops I knew!

Let me back up a bit. SED took a lot of credit for a reduction in gang violence in the three divisions we were all assigned to. Shootings among black and Hispanic gangs dropped significantly. But, when the District Attorney's Office announced their office had recorded forty-two gang-related shootings to date, we were dumbfounded. How come we'd never heard about this? The answer was that gangs who produced the shootings were all Filipinos outside of our divisions.

Few of the wayward shootings made the news because no one was hurt. In fact, thirty-eight of the forty-two shootings involved Filipinos in target-rich areas within the northern confines of town. There were no SED divisions there. Out of the fired shots, thirty-seven missed their apparent targets and one target was wounded. Even odder, the shots were fired between Friday nights and Saturday nights. We interpreted this to mean a bunch of jacked-up teenagers played weekend chicken with each other. SED was detailed up north to cover both the identified, and the unknown gangsters.

Roger and I were still paired up when we set out to learn more about the higher-profile Philippine gangs. Right out of the barn on our first afternoon we zipped up to Mira Mesa to cover off on a search for a Philippine male in a dark four-door vehicle seen threatening another Philippine gangster with a handgun. Neither of us was familiar with the layout of that community. Mira Mesa Blvd. is the main east-west drag in a community that stretches out miles in each direction, so we chose to monitor one random intersection reported to be west of the villain's last known direction. Within five minutes we spotted the car.

Roger was the driver and cranked a left turn to catch up to the vehicle. We called for cover and initiated the stop just as the first patrol unit from Northeastern pulled up behind us. The driver steered off the boulevard onto a side-street and stopped. Our guns came out, pointed at the lone occupant. The driver gripped the top of his steering wheel. With his hands in view, we decided to approach rather than hot stop the guy. A hot stop refers to the method police officers implement to stop a vehicle with suspected armed occupants. In hot stops, cops stop a few yards behind the offending vehicle, with a slight offset on the driver's side so there's a protective corridor from traffic on the left side of the suspect. The officer(s) barricade behind their open car doors and point their weapons at the opposing vehicle. The occupants are ordered out of the vehicle under the strictest of instructions. If the occupants made a move other than instructed the officer(s) can construe that as a threat and shoot to kill. The suspects are met with a series of verbal directions over the PA or in a loud voice. When they are prone out on the street and handcuffed the threat is over.

Our detainee was nervous and cooperative. He had no attitude except for showing fear. The hands-on-the-steering-wheel thing was reflexive, like he'd been through this before. He was removed from the car at gunpoint and stretched out over the hood. I searched the vehicle beginning with his seat and found the gun concealed underneath. The twenty-something wanna-be gangster was now a prisoner, care of SED.

The cops and the gun seizure made him nervous. He was handcuffed for a curbstone line-up to allow the witness to see and match him up as our suspect. The victim was brought to the stop to give us a yes or no on the prisoner. We had the suspect stand on the sidewalk under street lighting so the victim could see him properly. The victim said we had the right guy and the rest was history. Interestingly, the victim was loosely affiliated with the Mira Mesa Crips and he was willing to talk about the gangs in his area.

The victim told us most of the guys in the Crips were Filipino. There were a couple of black guys and other Asians involved. Their gang culture was influenced by Crips from Central and Southeast Divisions. The Mira Mesa locals were enthralled with the real Crips and wanted to bang like them. I asked about the shootings that never seemed to hit anyone. He said the gunfire was mostly to scare each other. Nobody was intent on the kills. This was more of a weekend spree. Most of the gangs, the PQ B-Down Boys further north, and the Mira Mesa Crips, were school students. Some even held down jobs. All lived at home with parents, siblings, grandparents, aunts, and uncles. Sunday afternoons were for family, but weekend nights were for gang-banging. The Crip tribe felt brotherly pride when they wore the blue at school and away from their parents.

SED's indoctrination into this facet of the Asian gang scene was wildly different from Asian gangs in other parts of town. Eastern Division was a settlement for Vietnamese who escaped the Communists after 1975. Other Southeast Asian families also joined the exodus from their respective countries. Much of Southeast Asia was in conflict, which brought a diaspora of Laotians, South Vietnamese, and Cambodians to San Diego.

WECAN and then SED both faced off against angry and violent first and second-generation Vietnamese Americans. These kids held their adopted country in contempt. They didn't feel wanted here and rebelled against their parents, many poor, who thanked America for taking them in. What we got were squabbling teenagers who formed gangs to replace their families as the most important people in their lives. We met young thugs with gang names like the Oriental Killer Boys, Tiny Oriental Crips, and the Asian Insane Bloods. These gangs were mean, determined punks willing to steal and kill, punching outside of their weight class. The PQ Boys and Mira Mesa Crips were not ready for that level of thuggery.

After we'd spent a little time mixing it up with the Mira Mesa Crips through traffic stops and field interviews it was time to scout the Bloods-affiliated Penasquitos gang. Our timing was perfect. There'd been a recent shooting, a retaliatory attack from an earlier shooting that targeted the Mira Mesa Crips. The victim was winged by a shotgun pellet. There were two players in the getaway vehicle. Both were known to that victim. The names didn't register with us. That would change very soon.

One of the names provided, a kid named Navarro, unwittingly gifted us with his home address thanks to a search for his driver's license through the DMV. The Rancho Penasquitos neighborhoods were expanding with new housing tracts. Mansion-sized houses were built on tiered hillsides with four and five bedrooms, much larger than the sizes of the homes in my neighborhood when I was a kid. Navarro's parents bought a large, lovely house on a slope that overlooked a wide vista of development to the west. New house-building projects were finishing construction up above the Navarro home. This was a perfect place for SED to spy down on PQ gang activity at night.

The Saturday night we chose to put a team up the hill was party night at the Navarro's. We stood in the night concealed by one house under construction. The backyard and street outside overflowed with kids garbed in red. Backyard music blared and alcohol flowed freely from a keg. There didn't seem to be anyone concerned about who reached out and poured beer from the spout. Several dozen young people meshed happily with each other. I saw a few cliques of red stand off from the rest. Those guys looked like they were up to no good. A couple of them were young black men we'd later identify as documented members of the Skyline Piru Blood set who were frequent targets of Southeastern SED. Young Navarro was present, as well.

We decided to move in and talk to the young males when it looked like the party was breaking up. Before we could drag our forces into play, someone spotted Navarro getting into a small truck with a cab-high shell. He started it up and headed down the street before any of the other police units could tag him. Roger and I caught up to him in our marked unit.

We tailed Navarro from a distance until he entered the northbound lanes of Freeway 15. Nobody wants to make hazardous stops on the freeway. He was rumored to have a gun and the multi-lane freeway was no place for wild shots. We raced up and stopped him on the outside shoulder as soon as we could.

Carefully, we talked him out of the driver's seat. We got his license and found registration that identified the truck as his. We told him he was a suspect in a shooting and watched a relatively calm guy suddenly look less confident. We told him we aimed to search his truck for weapons, specifically a shotgun used in the earlier shotgun incident. Navarro was deflated. He volunteered the loaded gun's location, covered up in the bed of his truck. Roger climbed in to look and found it quickly enough.

Navarro was now under arrest. He gave us the name of the other guy we wanted and copped to being the driver but dimed off the other guy as the shooter. Everybody we contacted seemed to freely give up information. Nobody even needed to be admonished of their rights. Profoundly, all the Philippine gangsters we dealt with spoke freely to us, politely even. Navarro would make the Gangs detectives happy by giving them everything they wanted to know.

One of the other SED units met with Navarro's parents and grand-parents back at the house. We learned we couldn't walk up in uniform to speak to any Filipino parents without their elderly parents inserting themselves into the group. One officer broke the news of their son's arrest and the adults in the Navarro family listened to the facts. They claimed they had no idea of his gang involvement. The entirety of red clothing at the party meant no threat to them. With their kid headed to jail they knew better now. They also knew who the other kid was, the shotgun shooter we needed to find next. The Navarro father knew the shooter's family. He didn't hesitate to give us a number for that guy's parents. He wanted the boy taken into custody, so their son could possibly get a bit of a reprieve. The officers made no promises. The whole case was turned over to Gangs detectives.

Word was received through our command about the fate of the shooter within a week. That teen fled to the Philippines when he learned of his pal Navarro's arrest. He knew he'd be next. The Gangs detectives managed to wheedle a relative's number out of the shooter's family. That relative lived in the Philippines and his home was the shooter's destination to avoid U.S. Law Enforcement. The relative, his uncle, sent him back to San Diego with admonishment that what he'd done was wrong. His uncle made sure he was on the next flight. The shooter was met at the airport by Gangs detectives and taken into custody. I later learned the case was settled before court with Navarro and the shooter taking plea deals for their crimes.

Honestly, all of us were shocked at the level of cooperation from, not one, but two street gangs. Life wasn't like that in the low-income areas SED normally prowled. The honesty and respect we received astounded us. We all knew we couldn't make it last. As the vise grips of the law began to squeeze both gangs, their families took control and put a stop to their sons' gang activity. Colors were confiscated, rules for behavior were set and troublesome influences were banned from homes, work and schools. For SED, this was an unexpected victory through the complete closure of two gangs. At least for the time being.

CHAPTER 62:

RDF

SED made serious inroads into those two Filipino gangs, but the old neighborhoods summoned us back. One day, soon after the affair with the northern gangs, a jarring voice crashed into our radio frequency and told officers we were pigs. That brief clip set everyone to wondering who had access to a police radio. The voice surfaced a second time and told cops on another frequency to, "Fuck off and die."

What transpired after that was a lot of radio appearances by our mystery user of vulgarisms. He shouted, ranted, and insulted us constantly that early afternoon. He was so vocal he stepped all over the dispatchers and made transmissions difficult to follow. He posed a danger to us and the public by blocking radio talk. He had to be found.

Later that day, dispatch contacted SED units and told us to switch over to Central's frequency and identify ourselves as we logged on. Communications informed us that Southeastern Division's frequency was compromised by the unknown vocal vandal. I figured the message had something to do with the radio hacker. Once on Central's frequency, Roger and I were told to meet at an elementary school. All the SED units, joined by some patrol units, staged at the school. We were gathered into a group and told our job was to find the hacker.

We all worked in two-officer teams. The bad guy's transmissions gave off signals that already narrowed the electronic footprint to an area around 61st and Akins Streets. When a couple of officers asked how that was accomplished, a city Radio Shops worker made a short transmission over his hand-held radio. We all watched in awe as a peculiar truck rounded a corner and drove into the schoolyard. The truck was a simple utility truck with a shell large enough to stand in. The odd part was the metal loop on a pole mounted in the center of the roof of that shell.

The Radio Shops guy who called the truck in was a specialist for the city, trained and experienced at locating radio signals. The truck, straight out of a Nazi war movie, looked like the ones I'd seen driving around France in those World War II flicks. I'm recalling the stories where French resistance fighters hid in homes and called or listened on short wave radios to England. The loops or rings on the trucks pointed the Nazis towards the sources of the signals.

The Radio Shops man, a supervisor, explained that two trucks, called Radio Direction Finding, or RDF, vehicles were called in for this emergency. Our jobs were to saturate the blocks as the RDF trucks narrowed the perimeter. Twenty of us would walk the blocks and knock on doors to ask permission to search their places or find witnesses to the location of the hacker. For now, we didn't know what radio was being used. Was it one of ours, or some talented techno-neighbor good with radios?

The RDF trucks functioned by pointing the round antennas toward the strongest radio signal. Two RDF trucks worked from different coordinates and drew lines on maps. Where the lines crossed, detectors got proximate to the signal's transmission point.

A couple of sergeants drove around the target zone and handed out water to the officers on foot. As darkness began to creep in, the RDF trucks determined that the moron with the radio was running out of juice. They still had no identification on the type of radio we searched for. They speculated it was a hand-held like a police handi-talkie. Perhaps it was one of ours in the hands of a thief because the guy continued to transmit insults and obscenities. Communications shut off the repeater for all frequencies. The repeater was the system that allowed police to hear each other along with the dispatcher. Now, the vulgar ass wouldn't be able to hear anyone on his radio if it was one of ours. Only the dispatcher could hear the man. The supervisors with us met each pair of officers and told us to switch to the Tac 7 frequency, where calls would be dispatched in the interim.

While the RDF guys tried to triangulate the weakening signal, Roger and I continued to walk the blocks. We contact residents at each dwelling in the hopes we'd get somewhere door-to-door. One of the houses on Akins sat on a huge plot of land. The house was small and appeared to be early 20th Century. It looked forlorn and weathered with faded white paint and wood framing that was cracked and splitting in many places.

We didn't see anyone around and still had a lot of land to cover. Roger and I lazily walked up a gentle slope on the property and headed for a garage separate from the house and built way back up beyond the home. I peeked inside the old wooden doors and saw the most amazing site, a U.S. Army M3 halftrack.

Of all the things you might expect to find doing house-to-house searches, a military halftrack from World War II isn't one of them. I thought it was a remarkable coincidence that we were using World War II-era RDF truck designs while I stared at a World War II armored attack vehicle.

The owner of the truck was a cool old man from that war. He answered the door when we knocked. We were more interested in the Army vehicle than we were about the Mad Broadcaster. We assumed he wasn't our guy since intermittent transmissions still popped up after we met him. He'd purchased the vehicle ages ago and used it for parades and shows. The gun mount ring was still positioned over the cab. When asked, he gestured toward the ring and said he never owned the fifty-caliber machine gun that was once affixed to that truck. He said that item was kept by the Army. He chatted about the excitement he got from the kids in the neighborhood every time he cranked over the engine and rolled down his driveway into the street. Some lucky kids even got short rides around the blocks to the amusement of their folks. A few veterans from that war enjoyed the occasional ride, too.

The sergeants contacted all of us foot soldiers and told us to return to the staging area. Those of us with sore feet got rides. We had a meeting with the Radio Shops people on scene. They said the RDF trucks no longer picked up the signal. They asserted that the radio lost power. Time would have to pass if the guy had a radio charger before he could jam up the frequency again. If he did, we'd all be back on foot whenever he chewed us out next. He never did, so it was assumed his radio would remain dead. We no longer had a path to his location. This operation was over. Nobody came forward and claimed theirs was the radio that got flipped into that guy's hands.

The department lost radios on occasion. They got misplaced, stolen, forgotten by officers somewhere, or just faded from existence. There was no GPS chip, so the radios couldn't be located that way if it was one of ours.

I returned to Western Division two years after my transfer from SED. Randy Eichmann was an acting sergeant at Western and a friend of mine. We sat around the substation one early evening as I told stories about WECAN/SED. I happened to mention the half-track story in passing. Randy grew wide-eyed and stopped the conversation. "You found a half-track," half in alarm and half in wonder. I told him the complete origin tale.

"I want that vehicle!" Randy was a nut-job for militaria and suddenly fancied the addition of an Army all-terrain assault vehicle to his collections of rifles, pistols and one war-era jeep. "Do you know anything about it now?"

"I do not. I suppose if the guy still lives there the truck might still be around."

"Do you think you could find it again?" geez, Randy was hungry for that thing.

"I work tomorrow. You detail me out of the barn and I'll head down there to see if I can find the house again."

The next day I took my patrol car down to the scene of the original crime and drove around to try and identify the piece of property. I vaguely remembered. I cruised up and down Akins Street until I thought I might have passed the place. I made a U-turn and parked in front of the place that most reflected my memory. Finally, I just got out and stood at the foot of the driveway. Sure enough, that was the garage. The house looked in better shape than I recalled. A woman stepped onto the front porch, curious about a cop staring at her home. "Can I help you, officer?" she asked.

"This may sound odd to you, but is there a military vehicle in that garage?" Momentarily confused, she said she didn't understand the question. Then, some buried thought leaped to the front.

"Oh, you mean the old Army truck that belonged to the man that owned this place before me. He took it with him when we bought the house. Did you need something with that truck 'cause we have no way to find him."

"No, ma'am, I have a boss who wanted to talk to him about it. I happened to mention it to him and here I am."

Easy come, easy go, Randy, was my thought as I drove away.

CHAPTER 63:

DOUG COLLIER AND EASTERN SED

Doug Collier was happy with his assignment to the Eastern SED team. He was one of the newer guys from the WECAN days. In his mind, WECAN, and then SED, were elite units he wanted to be a part of. He wasn't disappointed when he joined the unit and showed as much energy and conviction as any of us. If I were to label anyone on WECAN/SED the "Happiest Guy at Work," it would be Doug.

Eastern Division was like policing a whole other county compared to the territory we Central SED guys patrolled. Central included downtown and wrapped around a couple of tightly boxed neighborhoods. Eastern encompassed a massive zone filled with many neighborhoods over a huge square mileage of town. North of the lower-middle class "war zone" and south of El Cajon Boulevard, or ECB, was the Eastern Division fraternity of gangs and crime. The north side of ECB began a series of blocks that blossomed into classical San Diego of bygone times that reached the rim of Mission Valley. From the valley north, Eastern was hills and canyons of middle-and upper-class San Diego living. Gangs of any note didn't exist north of ECB.

Eastern had a greater variety of gang members and a wider array of gang skin colors, compared to Central. The levels of violence written about in the news and witnessed daily by thousands of citizens made Eastern Division more violence prone than elsewhere. Eastern SED also had to deal with gangs that were not synonymous with other parts of town.

Asian gangs proliferated among the expatriates. Laotians, Vietnamese, Cambodians, and others resettled in the lower income neighborhoods inhabiting San Diego east of Freeway 805. They resided along the El Cajon Boulevard and University Avenue main drags. Inevitably, the sons and grandsons of those post-Vietnam War settlers produced children who were dissatisfied with their inability to connect to their environment. Some were more Americanized than their parents and grandparents and didn't identify with them either. The thinness of their connections to their forebears ran them into the hands of peers with the same feelings of alienation and anger.

Eastern Division suffered from one peculiar anomaly. Families from other divisions associated with gang problems brought their gangster children into Eastern to escape their old neighborhoods. They didn't flee far enough, and the gangs simply kept up their bad ways, but spread them around their new neighborhoods. Even worse, Los Angeles gang members began to show up in Eastern Division providing new headaches for the police.

There was a Crip gang set in Los Angeles called the Grape Street Crips. Based originally out of Watts, the Grape Street Crips chose purple over blue as their gang colors. This faction of black gang members flourished in a single housing project and ramped up their street cred with the introduction of crack sales. But like all L.A. gang members who slung dope, they were generally limited to specific neighborhoods. If they stepped outside their boundaries, that meant war with rival gangs.

Despite the proliferation of crack and the drug's high profile, most of the action remained relegated to lower class, minority communities south of Mission Valley. The Valley is generally viewed as the geographical Mason-Dixon Line for the City of San Diego. The Grape Street Crips' quandary was to find places in town to expand into so they could sell crack unopposed.

Eastern Division cops who patrolled around 50th Street and El Cajon Boulevard noticed a surge in crack sales. The same intrusion happened four blocks to the south on University Avenue. Eastern Division's SED noticed it, too. The team members also noticed purple-clothed black men hovering in the same spots along the two main drags. SDG&E's metal electrical boxes and AT&T's phone equipment boxes mounted onto the sidewalks became convenient seats for the encroaching gangsters. With a little surveillance, SED identified the actions of the men as they conformed to standard crack sales formations. Pretty soon, arrests were made, and the carpet would begin to roll up on these insurgent players.

SED pressured the L.A. gangsters to the point where they relocated several blocks away. Central SED came up to assist and brought more pressure on the Crips. All of us learned that the Grape Street gang members' move to San Diego was an extension of their drug sales business. A little field work taught them that Eastern San Diego wasn't well covered by black gangsters and crack. They assumed they could plant roots and business would thrive in a gap they'd fill with potential crack addict victims.

The other black gang members in town, some who lived in the same area now occupied by Grape Street, failed to challenge them. Perhaps parleys between gangs from L.A. and San Diego established a cooperative precedent. Whatever happened between them didn't include flotillas of drive-by shootings or rival operators who poached off each other's land. Another L.A.-area gang, the Denver Lanes Bloods out of Pasadena, tried to horn in on Grape Street's action. Between the pressures brought on by the police and shut-down moves by Grape Street and Crip allies, the Bloods failed to stake a claim and moved on.

Doug's team committed itself to the surveillance of an apartment rumored to be an outlet to users for small purchases of crack. Doug was joined by Frank Hoerman, Tim Fay, Cinda Jauregui and Mo Parga. They endeavored to catch a few buyers and gather enough arrests to validate a search warrant. The warrant was acquired simply enough. A meeting with a judge and the appropriate filed court paperwork provided the means to legally crash through the drug dealer's door.

The officers planned out their attack for the next day. The target was a small, ground floor apartment. There was no courtyard in front and no metal screen to protect the front door from violence like the kind SED would bring if they had to crash their way in.

Roles were assigned and proper positioning for the moment of attack insured they got through the door safely. None of the occupants escaped. The three people inside, coincidentally all Grape Street Crips, were taken down with little force. The fact they offered no resistance seemed a little pacifistic to Doug and his crew. They learned later that L.A. Crips tended not fight back against the police. The LAPD's decades of forceful offensive tactics taught the bad guys it was better to receive than give. They were habitually compliant in these circumstances because jail was a better alternative than the hospital, or the morgue.

The apartment was only two bedrooms, a living room, kitchen, and a bathroom, all scantily furnished. This place was not for living in, only for selling crack. Five cops made short work of the search while one stood guard. One of the SED officers found a large wad of cash in the bottom of a trash can in the kitchen. The count was about two-thousand dollars in fifties and twenties. The denominations made sense for narcotics experts. Crack is normally sold in twenty, and fifty-dollar rocks. Also, Crips don't make change. The Crips had tried to hide the money under the bag liner. SED cops were as good as any narcotics cops when it came to finding stashes and hidey-holes.

Doug searched one of the bedrooms and spotted an access utility panel in the closet's ceiling. With the assistance of a chair, Doug lifted the panel and lit up the confining interior. The only object up there was a dark plastic trash bag. There was some heft to it when he lifted it, so he brought it down to the floor to look inside. He was dazzled by one of the largest amounts of crack he'd ever seen outside of police impounds. There was at least a pound and a half of crystalline crack cocaine. Doug was as elated at the find as were the other officers the Crips, not so much. They tried to deflect the discovery and their imminent incarceration by getting mouthy to distract the cops. Personally, I wouldn't make the attempt in the face of six-foot seven-inch Tim Fay, but that's me.

"You planted that stuff. Hey Bro, the po-po be plantin' shit on us. That's messed up." The officers ignored their wayward accusations. The men were handcuffed and in no position to protest anything.

While the gangsters continued to babble, insult and whine, Doug knew the dope discovery was only half the battle, he still needed to tie it to the dealers. The surest way to do that was to find the dope on their persons. Since that didn't happen, Doug searched for paperwork that would identify these guys as tenants. That provenance would hold them accountable for the crack and crack sales. Neither man admitted to living in the apartment or being the renters. Conversely, Doug found utility bills in one guy's name. The key in his pocket fit the door and an address book in a drawer listed his name and this apartment as his address. He was sunk. When Doug presented the bag of crack to his partners, a resounding "Holy Fuck!" forever tattooed their responses.

Jeffrey Tolbert was one of the Crips in the apartment taken into custody. He'd been in the neighborhood awhile and knew the streets and the other players well. Since he was under eighteen, his initial time in custody was maddeningly short. Like most juvenile arrests, San Diego's Juvenile Criminal system wasn't built to store kids like him for long, unless the seriousness of the crime warranted it. In this case, apparently a sack of crack wasn't enough of a threat to society to keep the kid off the streets. His Grape Street Crip bosses left L.A. to meet him and his cronies in San Diego not long after he was arrested and released. They were unaware of the seizure and arrests, so they angered quickly when Tolbert revealed the police officers' actions the days before. Tolbert and his people blamed the police, but the L.A. contingent didn't believe them. "If you got busted, how come you're not in jail?" was the question posed one by one of the L.A. contingent.

"But I was. They let me go." Mistrust was salted into the gang.

Doug was surprised to see Tolbert on the streets again. Tolbert was wary of Doug and blurted out about the grilling he received from the L.A. bangers. They'd come to town to collect the cash from the crack sales by Tolbert's crew. The L.A. crew obviously dipped into other cities, maybe other states, to sell drugs. Tolbert said there were moments where he couldn't tell if his homie-superiors were going to disappear him and the others Doug busted that day.

At the time of this incident, San Diego's Criminal Justice system had porous laws on the books to enhance sentences, bail, or holds for gang members. With the augmentations in place, gang members could be held longer, with no bail, even if they were under eighteen. The L.A. contingent of "investigators" in purple only half-believed Tolbert. He was lucky they gave him half-credit because he and the others only took half-beatings. They'd be dead otherwise.

Doug and his wife went to the movies not long after the Grape Street Crips event. Jeffrey Tolbert was there, too. Fortunately for Doug, he spotted Tolbert in the theater before Tolbert spotted him. When Tolbert did see Doug, he made a cocky spectacle of himself by shouting out Doug's last name over the din of the crowd. Doug tried to ignore Tolbert as he and his Crip companions cat-called him. Tolbert bellowed, "Officer Collier. What you going do to me in here, Officer Collier. You can't touch me, Officer Collier!" The rest of the audience looked back at Tolbert as though this asshole was going to ruin the night. Nobody knew what to make of the "Officer Collier" call-out.

Nobody in the audience knew Doug was the target of the guy behaving all gangster-like. His tormenters were young, cocky and half-bright. Doug slipped his off-duty gun under one leg determined to watch the rest of the movie and display no fear. The Crips would draw pleasure from Doug's discomfort from their bully tactics if they sensed Doug was afraid. They might even go after Doug and his wife with aggression.

Doug hustled his wife out a side exit and made a beeline towards their car at the finish of the movie. The bad guys decided to make a sport of the couple's hasty exit. Doug and his wife rushed to their car and wound their way through the oblivious movie spectators from the theatre. Tolbert's crew raced to their car and drove after the worried couple. Doug watched them in his rearview mirror in disbelief. "Is this really happening?" He thought.

Doug was a sweet guy. He was a lean six-foot two with eyes that danced when he laughed. Doug would do anything for anyone and was always respectful to cops with more experience. He was a guy you never wanted to see endangered. The shattered wall between cop and crook with a simple trip to the movies was heart-shaking. Any police officer was vulnerable to the unnerving prospect of a confrontation with known criminals.

Doug had to let his wife in on the problem. He didn't want to frighten her, but the matter was too serious to try and wing it without her wondering why he was in the driver's seat and throttled through the movie theater lot like a madman. Tolbert and his pals seemed intent on hugging Doug's tail for maximum intimidation. Doug had to get his wife as far away from these ominous circumstances.

Doug made a sharp turn to the right to throw of his pursuers. The rapid change in direction caused Tolbert to get cut off by another car headed in his direction along the narrow parking lot driveway. Doug scrambled out onto University Avenue, punched it, and lost them in traffic. Doug was righteously pissed off and had major intentions to do something about Tolbert.

Doug was in court the next morning and caught up to his squad later in the day. Tim Fay eventually called a meet with him and asked for details on the previous night's events. The story was all over SED's Eastern team. People were steaming mad and wanted the details.

Tim Fay was the first fellow SED officer to speak with Doug after he got back to the station. Subsequently, a ferocious Officer Fay drove out into the field to hunt for Tolbert. Tim only had two speeds, wait until I get you, and now I have you. Tim didn't have to search long for Tolbert. He spotted the unsuspecting Crip on the street in his neighborhood. One moment cocky Tolbert was hanging out in a strip mall the next moment a giant stands over him with handcuffs in one hand and a rueful glare in his eyes. Once Tim found and arrested Tolbert, Doug made the field trip to Fay's location. Doug got out of his police cruiser and walked to Tim's car. He opened the back door to the prisoner cage and said, "If I ever see you around me or my family, I will just kill you 'cause I assume you'll try to kill me."

Tolbert was surrounded by two, tall and armed police officers. He'd already faced his near life termination with his gang set from Los Angeles. Now he was right back in trouble with two equally dangerous men.

Officer Fay took Tolbert to the Duty Lieutenant's office to book Tolbert for a charge loosely translated as Domestic Terrorism. He reasoned that Tolbert's actions were clear threats meant to frighten and antagonize Doug and his wife. This kind of confrontation between good guy and bad guy happened less frequently than television would have you think. The unfortunate coincidence spurred the unpredictable

Tolbert into the spontaneous act of stupidity and spiteful terror tactics. The concern Tolbert's actions invoked were tantamount to stalking for the purpose of instilling fear. Tolbert was a gangster. Who knows how far he'd have pushed the confrontation?

Surprisingly, the Duty Lieutenant didn't seem particularly interested in charging Tolbert for terrorizing the Colliers. The LT didn't consider Tolbert's actions of the night before worthy of the charge and refused to accept the booking. Fay's sergeant, John Wray, took a stab at the LT to book Tolbert. Sergeant Wray was a savvy and highly regarded leader. The booking LT would have been wise to take counsel with Wray. He too, failed to talk the man into it.

Former WECAN Lieutenant Bill Becker was in earshot of the DL's office and listened to the conversation. He knew and respected the officers involved and decided to help. He thought the booking LT was way off base when he tried to wash out the charge. The booking LT still declined to approve the charge based upon Tolbert's behavior at the movie theater. His lame retort; "Getting threatened is part of the job," incensed Lt. Becker even more.

Lt. Becker told the other lieutenant his attitude was bullshit. "These are my guys. They don't have to deal with this!" The Duty Lieutenant wasn't used to this much pressure to put a guy in jail. The arresting officers knew he was reluctant to pass a booking through that might get rejected at the District Attorney level. Lieutenant Becker suggested to the Duty Lieutenant he could look worse if the DA didn't see Tolbert in jail for threats to a cop and his wife. The DL let that thought roll around in his brain. With a neutral look on his face, he did something remarkable for him. He changed his mind and approved the booking.

By the next day, all of SED knew about this case. We really believed that kicking it upstairs to the DA would mean victory. The DA's Office had a Gang Suppression Unit staffed with a couple of ADAs willing to fight for SED. Instead, the case was thrown at the Issuing DA, not the gang guys.

The Issuing DA's job was to look over the arrests as they entered the State's domain. The job was to disperse cases for various hearings or reject them. The Issuing DA didn't consult with the Gang Suppression

ADAs and rejected the case. Doug and the rest of SED, myself included, chafed at the cold reality that we could receive legitimate threats to us, on-duty or off-duty, and no legal cog in the wheel of justice would protect us.

The Juvenile Criminal Justice system had formed a team around the same time as WECAN's formation. The attorneys, probation officers, and County Parole agents assigned to JUDGE, Juvenile Drug Gang Enforcement Task Force, was formed to fight the rise in teenage gang problems infesting San Diego County. JUDGE was run by the District Attorney's Office. A recent DA transfer to the unit was John Davidson. ADA Davidson was an experienced prosecutor who operated closely with WECAN/SED on many occasions. With his new assignment, he took the time to go through crime cases regular DA's wouldn't touch. When he spotted Doug's terrorism case, he got a hold of Doug by phone and asked if he could resurrect the case for prosecution. ADA Davidson had a polite, energetic conversation with an exuberant Doug who was happy that someone within the system knew the score and was ready to work. "They can't get away with this stuff," was Davidson's positive observation.

Tolbert would pay a price for that conversation. He was arrested for the terrorism charge days after the incident, brought to trial, and convicted after he took a plea deal. He would do some incarceration time.

As an interesting side note, Doug saw Tolbert on the streets again many months later. Tolbert had just been released from jail. Doug expected more of the same gangster attitude but was surprised when Tolbert apologized to him. His time in custody gave Tolbert time to reflect on his behavior and what consequences he was willing to pay as a criminal. Tolbert confessed to Doug that he believed if it had been any other cop that night outside the movie theater, he'd probably have been killed by that officer. Doug could read the man clearly and sensed the comment was heartfelt. They parted friendly and Doug never had to deal with Tolbert again.

CHAPTER 64:
COURT WRATH

As a police officer I was held to higher standards of responsibility than many of the citizens I policed. Above me, were the supervisors, commanders, and big bosses I was answerable too. Above them were the city officials, or at least equally powerful, were the prosecutors and then finally the judges. Police officers had a lot of bureaucrats in the legal system who expected us to manage our work and time. My job required following set policies and instructions, especially when it came to the court system. Step out of line there, and a police officer could face department discipline and even worse if prosecuting attorneys or bench judges were unhappy. Courtroom malfeasance by an officer was a serious thing.

Malfeasance is defined as the performance by a public official of an act that is legally unjustified, harmful, or contrary to law. Police wrongdoing in court is considered a violation of public trust. One example of the court system's operation considered an act of malfeasance is failure on a police officer's part to honor a subpoena and attend court.

In my day officers were expected to be in court for cases they were involved in. If they did get called up, the subpoena would show up at their duty station. The SDPD and the courts administration had a line of handlers charged with monitoring the subpoena flow from court to the police and back to court. There was never any disruption in the system and officers were expected to do as their subpoena ordered. An officer who failed to adhere to the subpoena's instructions had committed malfeasance and would be dealt with through our department, up to and including suspension. The wheels of justice couldn't turn if the police were not in court to testify. The department's policies outlined the fate of any subpoenaed cop that failed to make the court date. If the officer's malfeasance and betrayal of the public trust angered a judge, the officer could expect worse.

I've had to deal with the department's wrath at least once. I overslept on a court day. The court contacted the department's Court Liaison, who in turn, called my house and woke my ass up.

"Newbold?"

"Oh, shit!" The early morning ring in my ears was the phone, not a hangover.

"You're supposed to be in court," said the exasperated liaison. He was clearly long past being tired having to make these daily phone calls to SDPD officers.

"I am on my way," I told him. No shower, no teeth brushing, just a rumpled suit and a mad dash to downtown San Diego. If there was any safety valve in the tidiness of courtroom timing, it was that court always seems to start late, especially in the mornings. In the time it took me to get dressed and into court, nothing had happened in my court case. Everybody ordered to be in court was still seated on benches in the courthouse hallways.

I worked with plenty of SDPD officers who missed court by accident, not design. This was true of many officers who worked night shifts the evenings before. Long work hours and long commutes home could savage a cop's sleep time. Unless officers had a back-up wake-up plan, some were doomed to sleep past their court time.

I'd been at court when prosecutors searched the hallways and staging rooms for their police witnesses without success. The grim-faced prosecutors made calls upstairs to someone who called someone else and that someone was tasked with calling the recalcitrant officer. If the caller was the SDPD Court Liaison, at least it was an SDPD supervisor yelling in your ear to keep you from real trouble. The officer would hear about it at work from his supervisor and might have received some form of written discipline. A second failure to appear could result in time off without pay. Think suspension. In the worst-case scenario, a seated judge was perturbed by the absent officer and issued a bench warrant, a mandate directly from a seated judge to jail someone. As has happened in the past, cops had come within a hair's width of being jailed for not showing up in court. Do not piss off a judge. He or she could do damage that your bosses could not.

I endured countless court subpoenas as an SDPD officer. My three WECAN/SED years generated more of my subpoenas than the remaining sixteen years of my career combined. I'm proud to say I never missed a court appearance during those three years. I got lectured once for missing a traffic case and a written warning for missing a Municipal Court preliminary hearing, but those happened outside of WECAN/SED.

I'm proud of my court appearances. I'd become a narcotics expert which entitled me to testify for the prosecution on cases I was not directly involved with. One example of that maneuver was the day I was in court for my own arrest at a preliminary hearing. Most of the prelims were held in a series of adjacent courtrooms along one hallway in San Diego Municipal Court. The wall opposite all those doors to people's fates were lined with wooden benches so uncomfortable they seemed designed to prevent sleep. I was in uniform with gun belt and all the police ephemera and fidgeted to get comfy while a parade of people passed me by on the way to their destinations behind all those doors. This was my arrest and I would testify to the validity of a possession of heroin for sales case my own expert. My hearing was on hiatus because the defense attorney was tied up on another case. This problem cropped up all the time. Hearings had no clock.

Suddenly, a woman in a business suit plowed through the door of the courtroom adjacent to mine. "Are you a narcotics expert?" she asked almost plaintively. She doubled down on her search by scanning the aisles up and down the hall for another potential officer.

"I am. But I'm here on another case."

"Are you in Judge Clooney's court?"

"I am."

"Your case is delayed. I need you now or the judge is going to drop the prelim. Can you be my expert?"

"What's the charge?"

"Eleven-Three-Seventy-Seven A for PCP possession. Can you handle that?"

"How much dope?"

"About forty foil bindles."

"Marijuana laced with PCP?"

"Yes. Can you do this for me?"

"Yep, I'm your guy."

Of course, the defense objected to my entry. "Who is this officer? His name does not appear in this case?"

The judge engaged in some back-and-forth with both sides. The defense wanted me vetted before he'd agree to let me testify on behalf of the prosecution. I was in store for a voir dire motion.

Voir Dire, Latin for a special set of questions to test my expertise, meant the defense intended to ruin me out of the courtroom as a "put-up job" by the prosecution to try and squeak her case by the judge. The judge agreed and the pace of the hearing changed as I became a target.

I'd been through years of narcotics cases, went to narcotics classes, taught narcotics at the divisional level to fellow officers and most importantly, been certified in court as an expert. I was even certified in front of this judge, Napoleon Jones. The judge knew me but let the case ride on the defense attorney's request anyway.

The attorney asked all the prerequisite questions which extracted everything narcotics about Officer Newbold. The judge appeared to be engaged with something written in front of him and didn't seem to be paying attention to the rest of us. I spoke for about three minutes from mental cue cards I'd memorized from countless other testimonies. The trick was to have the two-page written form I carried with me that continued my resume of experience. By now, I'd recited from memory and rarely carried the paperwork with me anymore. The trick was to regurgitate what was written in chronological order. Sometimes, as in this case, I got a few lines out of order. The defense attorney raised his finger both times he interjected to compromise me. I realized I wasn't as prepared for this recital as I previously thought. The defense pounced and the judge sat him back down. Judge Jones knew this was a cake-walk the entire time. The judge interrupted me and told the defense he was satisfied with my expertise. The case continued.

I recited the elements of "possession for sale" for the prosecution. She asked the correct questions and I loaded the bases in the prosecution's favor with the right answers. The defense made a couple of interjections to try and contradict me, but the judge wiped them all away. All the talk boiled down to a guy who was arrested by a Central patrol officer with a paper bag filled with foil bindles of lovely. The officer nailed him, searched him and seized the dope. The arrest was cut-and dried. The officer's lack of narcotics education and experience in court precluded him from testimony as an expert. I got the case over the hump and the man was bound over for trial. The prosecution thanked me very being business-like and I was released to go back into the hallway and weigh the bench down to keep it from floating away.

I testified for so many hours over the years that court was an exercise in professional repetition. I was highly unlikely to be stumped by a defense attorney or have my confidence shaken. Almost all my cases resulted in some level of a criminal conviction. I could tell the prosecutor what the outcome of a case would be before we entered the courtroom. I know the statement sounds cocky. I flew through the system on the wings of repetitive narcotics arrests and the expertise to back up the charges.

The best WECAN/SED officers were the ones that stepped up in court and nailed down the prosecution's case. We all spent a lot of time in the DA's Office in pre-hearing consults. The results produced strong bonds with some prosecutors we teamed up with during generous quantities of court time.

I averaged one subpoena for court every two weeks in patrol before I joined WECAN. Most of those cases were traffic tickets. There was the occasional drunk driver or burglary caper where the only reason for my appearance was the police report I'd written. Pretty dry stuff. I went out of my way to pursue drug arrests because that was what I loved. My WECAN/SED tour quadrupled that number of subpoenas.

The attorneys on both sides of any case were better educated than I. I knew that going in, so I tempered my actions and the reports that followed with facts and observations that would stand up for the law and raise strong testimony against the opposing side. Most WECAN officers boasted the same aptitude. The earlier bridge camera arrests and court cases are great examples of WECAN members' planning and implementation. We knew how the justice system worked from both angles and functioned accordingly.

I can appreciate that clumsiness sometimes happens in courtroom testimony. I learned that after a few foul-ups early in my career. The mantra I adopted was, know the facts and the laws of arrest. Know your report exactly as stated and recall all the words written under oath. The prosecution couldn't do much to help if the officer stumbled on a defense attorney's question. The defense would turn officers into their playthings if statements showed gaps or weakness of memory.

Officers had the time to think before they spoke. No one was going to push for an immediate answer. The defense wanted to rush the officer's thoughts and gambled the answer would either be poorly conjured or misstated from the police report. The defense would work its darndest to trip up an officer with each answer. They ventured that the question would send the officer's mind into exploration for answers they couldn't correctly remember. This could be referred to as WAG, or wild ass guess. I suffered through that rare gaffe on few cases in court when I was on WECAN/SED. A good example was the testimony and rebuttal in Appellate court for that case where I moved a brick block to peer into a window back in Chapter thirty-seven. "Officer, your report states you saw my client flush drugs down a toilet. Is this accurate?"

"Yes."

"You mention you saw him through a small window. Were you standing outside that window?"

"Yes." Short, concise answers.

"Can you describe the height of the window from the ground and your relation to that height."

"The window was about five feet off the ground. It measured three feet in height and about two feet in width."

"How tall are you, officer?"

"Five feet, ten inches."

"Was the toilet mounted to the floor?"

"Yes."

"Could you see down into the toilet standing on the ground outside the window?"

"Uh, not really." Uh oh. "I had to stand on a large block I'd carried over to the spot."

"I see no mention of the block. You're saying you had to move a brick block to the window position to enhance your ability to see the toilet?" The attorney and I realized simultaneously that the report didn't cover the block, as if it was never there. The defense attorney pounced, and I apologized to the prosecutor with pleading eyes. The prosecutor knew the report as well as I and watched his case evaporate. I felt low because I was better than that.

"Your Honor. I move to dismiss this case due to a misstatement of facts. The officer has added a fact not in his report. The laws of search and seizure clearly state that the police cannot enhance their observations without probable cause to do so, or a court warrant." The defense attorney crucified me and ended the case.

The judge was matter of fact. He was left with little option and the Deputy DA envisioned an earlier lunch than planned. This ordeal became one of many lessons I learned from, and corrected, with an insight to detail. My WECAN/SED partners sat through similar errors and learned. We shared the details and pre-thought our actions before we engaged. Our triumphs came from unshakeable confidence and well-rehearsed responses in future court appearances.

We were all quite proud of the victories that came with match ups against sharp, practiced criminal defenders. WECAN/SED was effective on the streets and likewise in battle in court.

Court subpoenas will ruin a cop's social life. They come with dates scheduled into the future on the most inopportune days. If the subpoena dates to a Monday through Friday and the officer is at work those days, then life is okay. If the officer works weekends or evenings, then the date is often interruptive of time off from work and sleep. Days off become meaningless. All this came with the world I existed in, but those conditions included exemptions. Our traffic citations were an example. The bottom of the ticket contained blank boxes that required the signature officer's days off and provisions for vacation schedules. The officer hoped his vacation plans would be honored by the court's schedulers. The gist of those plans was that work breaks from court needed to be planned ages in advance. Vacations couldn't be spur of the moment decisions. Savvy officers were swayed to set up subpoena-free vacations by issuing fewer tickets in advance of the happy date. WECAN/SED wrote few tickets and rarely took advantage of playing the odds as traffic and patrol officers occasionally did.

I spent a lot of time-off in court, so I often missed my family on days off. I worked weekends too often to plan outings with my wife and son. Court had to matter to me, had to count for something to make the family sacrifice worth a damn. Unfortunately, nothing on the job was sacred when it came to court avoidance.

SED provided me with an opportunity to attend a three-day Gang Awareness school in Riverside, a couple of hours up the freeway from San Diego. Those educational events added luster to an officer's profile and helped make new law enforcement connections and increased street wisdom. We gained more ammo in the form of invaluable courtroom knowledge for stronger testimony. Those classes taught expertise to enhance our roles in the field. There were often changes in the behavior of criminals and the laws that govern crime. The schools provided updates and tactics to curtail the changes. Officers who sought career advancement used the special assignments to increase their chances, and the bullet-points on resumes boosted the chances for officers who sought promotions.

The department approved the Riverside school and cut me a check for travel expenses. Space was always limited for these schools and they didn't come around that often. I received a subpoena one week before my scheduled travel day to the Riverside class. The parolee defendant I arrested for being under the influence of a drug, a misdemeanor wanted his day in court. Usually, a week's notice would grant an officer a reprieve with the prosecutor's office. I completed the rarely contended Court Excusal Form and expected to make the school and deal with this court case another day. Instead, word came down through my command that the excusal was denied, and my Riverside class opportunity was cancelled. I was given instructions to contact a court supervisor by the name of Sherrell if I had any questions.

There was a response protocol with attorneys in both the District and City Attorney's Offices. If the caller was a concerned police officer; avoid calling them back. Prosecutors' non-communication skills were legendary and headache-generating obstructions for cops.

Sherrell took her sweet time getting back to me. I'd hoped for a quick rectification for my scheduling dilemma. Instead, Sherrell delivered a wry and dismissive message over the phone, "I get so many requests from officers attempting to salvage vacations and schools from court that I feel like a travel agent."

This was not encouraging news. She went on complaining "The city spent a lot of money to bring this defendant to court and neither I, nor the judge, will excuse you or continue this case."

The original arrest for this court case was six months in the past. Why it had to be dealt with now was never explained. Sherrell told me the only solution was to contact the defense attorney and strike a deal with them. Not only would that not happen, that concept is outside of accepted legal protocol. The parolee defendant and his attorney would dance all over my grave if I even tried to broker a deal as the arresting police officer. The inevitability of missing the upstate class painfully sunk in.

I knew I was screwed. The unsympathetic attorneys took more time off from full schedules than Santa Claus does between Christmases. I identified the prosecutor in the case but struck out there as well. I called Sherrell again and waited again for a call back. She said she could attempt a plea deal with the defense, but it would only happen the day before my school started. I reasoned I could make it to court and the school and miss only half a day of class. The plan would only work if she called me that morning with news of success.

I waited impatiently for her call on the day of the prelim. I sat around the house doing some pick-up work. My wife knew how glum I was. She detested court for its constant disruption of our lives. We'd long since stopped making plans greater than a few days in advance. Since I worked weekends, we had to figure out what to do with our boy who was in school and still enjoy ourselves anywhere but home. My packed suitcase was in the dining room just waiting to go on a road trip. My bundle of clothes stared at me constantly, urging, "Let's go!"

Sherrell never called. I ended up going to work that day instead of north on Interstate 15 headed for Riverside.

I headed to Police HQ to return the expense check to Fiscal Management nearer the afternoon of the day before that court hearing. I'd already cancelled my hotel reservation. Meanwhile, Sherrell left a message at my division that a deal had been made with the defendant. I didn't get the message until the end of watch late that evening. To recover the school opportunity, I'd need the next day to head back downtown to get a replacement check, make new hotel reservations and ask my command to please give me the days off again. Maybe I could get one thing accomplished, but not all of them. As a result of that mess, I told my wife when this was behind us that we'd leave Mike with his grandparents and take a night up the coast in beautiful Laguna Beach. We'd go on a Tuesday and come back when we felt like it on Wednesday. They aren't exactly hot party days in the Orange County beaches, but who would argue? She was amused I'd come on with this switch-up from our frustrating status quo. I told her if we didn't act spontaneously, we'd never get on the road.

A subpoena caught me at line-up the next day. Guess the date.

Life is so easy now with cell phones. The plots and stories on television and in the movies spin a whole new direction when all the characters have their own phones. When I wrote this story, I couldn't reconnect to the original anger I once harbored. Now the story reads like any golly gee, too bad aspect of life. Bad timing happens to all kinds. First responders get few breaks. Except for firefighters. Their lives are too easy.

CHAPTER 65:

GIANT

Day Watch on a Saturday was nice and quiet along the stretch of North Harbor Drive that separates the Harbor Island resort area from San Diego's main airport. That area was well-patrolled by Harbor Police and the SDPD. I liked to cruise the route as 614 John when I was in patrol at Western Division. I liked to sightsee and touch the perimeters of my far-flung beat. I favored the cruise past the USS Recruit at the southern edge of Naval Training Center. The Recruit was the only existent San Diego-based warship that had never been to sea, yet harbored tens of thousands of young sailors trained for ocean duty. The grey destroyer escort was a scaled down mock-up of the real deal, built to stand on solid ground. The old girl was a constant reminder of America's modern wars and brave ship-bound warriors. Unfortunately, my attention this morning, as I sped past the venerable old girl, was focused on the search for a thief on a bicycle.

A residential burglary victim called police about a theft he witnessed less than fifteen minutes prior. The caller happened to be cleaning dishes at his kitchen sink when he spotted a man walking out of his neighbor's garage. The caller was puzzled because his neighbor was out of town and nobody was supposed to be there. He realized he was watching a theft in progress when the suspicious man hopped on the yellow bicycle owned by the neighbor's little girl. The bike had a wire basket mounted to the handlebars. The man slung a pillowcase filled with who knows what into the basket and sped off. The caller had deduced he'd just witnessed a burglary and that the thief probably had stolen booty in the pillowcase.

The crime was close enough to my location that I reasoned I had a good chance of intercepting the thief if we crossed paths. Sure enough, as I passed the sea-less ship, I spotted the guy, a young Hispanic male pedaling for Kingdom Come along North Harbor Drive in the direction

of downtown. I saw him scurry down one of the footpaths at Spanish Landing, a stretch of bay-front recreational park along the major
thoroughfare. I skipped ahead of the bicyclist so I could head him off
in one of the narrow parking strips ahead of him.

The thief had little trouble seeing me since the park was relatively
empty. I jammed my car into a space and bounced out to cut off his
path on foot. I thought I had this. He had other intentions.

In a split second, cop met crook. The guy rammed his bike into
me as he slid off the seat. I almost had him and then I didn't. In that
moment I had a foot chase, a real ordeal carrying twenty-five pounds
of equipment on a weightlifter's frame. I wasn't the runner I once was.
The guy had the jump on me and raced as fast as his little thieving legs
could take him. All I had was marshaled adrenaline and a twenty-foot
gap to overcome.

I carried a Walther semi-automatic pistol on my right ankle. My
back-up gun's holster was untested in a footrace. The thief moved fast
on the sidewalk adjacent to the waterline. The hotels, marinas and yachts
were just across the inlet where the wealthy docked their yachts. What
a really great view, but not under pursuit conditions. At one point I lost
my balance and literally tripped over onto the shoreline boulders used
as water-breakers. I hopped from rock to rock for a few awkward steps
until I could regain my footing and veer back onto the sidewalk. My
target still moved at a fast clip and never looked back to see where I
was. I lost some yardage then, and when I called for help over my radio,
I had to hold it in one hand with both arms pumping.

The sidewalk entered the grounds of a Sheraton Hotel property. If the
guy took the right-hand split, we would run right past the wide eyes of
the hotel's restaurant guests. If he took the left fork, we'd pass the tennis
courts filling up with players. He chose to go left.

I couldn't gain on him no matter how hard I tried. I was fast once,
all heart, lungs, and legs. Not anymore. I was really frustrated that my
vaunted speed and distance prowess were dormant, maybe gone forever.

The speedster aimed for a service entrance into the hotel. He stopped
just long enough to tug one door open, an action I'd perform next when
I hit the doorway. He was still about twenty feet ahead of me when

we entered a long hallway. I was gassed. I had to believe he was tiring, too. The hallway ended ahead at a corridor. Two maintenance workers turned a corner and faced us completely unaware of what approached.

I managed to gasp out, "Stop Him!"

The hotel engineers were in uniforms and one was seven feet tall. The tall worker stretched his arms out to block my runner in reaction to my shout. The thief was startled enough by the immovable giant that he stopped and let himself be grabbed by the tall man. I pulled up to stop and quickly took the guy by the hands and spun him around to handcuff him. I radioed in that I had the guy in custody after I caught my breath. At that same moment, I realized my right leg seemed lighter by several ounces. Shit! My back-up gun was gone!

Other units arrived and parked by my patrol car. I switched over to the Tac radio frequency and asked one of them to check the path I took and search for the gun. Meanwhile, I asked the two maintenance workers their names for my report. I thanked them for their help. The tall guy, an engineer that changed out ceiling light bulbs without a ladder, seemed shy about his part. I repeated my thanks. His name was Chris Lewis.

I walked my prisoner back toward my car. He was resigned to his arrest, probably because he was too tired to do otherwise. I know I was. Those short bursts of expended energy take some time to recover from. The assisting officers found my wayward gun and returned it to me, a little scratched up. Thank the fates it hadn't ended up in the hands of somebody else, maybe even a child. I took my guy to jail, still dwelling on Chris Lewis and the brave thing he did.

Five years passed. Manny was about to break up our partnership for his upgrade to detective. WECAN was days away from transitioning into SED. We were going to use this day to goof around and do as little as possible in between meals. Naturally, we got flagged down by an energetic man standing on the curb-line at 22nd and Imperial.

"Officer Manny, I'm glad I saw you guys. You know you told me if I found anything going, I was supposed to tell you? Well, I have a place."

Manny sort of rolled his eyes. Sometimes you get what you asked for, but just not when you really wanted it. "What is it, Hector?" Hector was a part time snitch for Manny from his old patrol days in the Heights. His inopportune arrangement with Manny rarely paid off and most of his tips were worthless. Manny humored the infrequent crack user because he was harmless for the most part.

Hector was infatuated with Manny as a police officer because Manny treated him with respect and never taunted him. His spur of the moment decision to wave us down was his way of spending some "quality time" with his personal super-hero.

Hector told us of a crack house that operated on 27th Street around the corner from Imperial Avenue. Business flourished at this tiny yellow home with a white picket fence. Manny told him we'd check it out, to keep Hector happy. Maybe we'd get lucky and pry a buyer off the street from the house and generate a legal way inside.

We had nothing better to do and dinner was still three hours away. Why not check it out? Manny and I stuffed our police car in the alley somewhat concealed by a dumpster and walked down to Twenty-Seventh.

The house was right up front with a granny flat in the rear. Two black guys casually leaned against the yard's picket fence. One of the two smoked a joint, oblivious to two cops who approached from his right. When he saw us, he looked dumbfounded. I got to him and the joint before he could chuck it out of sight. The other guy froze as well. The guy with the joint was extremely tall and familiar, a slightly older and frazzled-looking Chris Lewis.

Lewis looked down at my face, but no lights went on in his head. I knew who he was immediately. My memory works that way naturally and from being a police officer for many years. I didn't tell him how we'd met before, not yet at least. I still had him hand me some identification while Manny and I prodded both guys about standing in front of a crack house.

I already had Lewis under arrest for the joint. The other guy turned out to be familiar to Manny. The man was another Lewis, Chris's older and shorter brother. He was on probation for drug use. Chris once seemed like a man who had his shit together. Now it looked like he'd followed his brother's path. I did a cursory search for more drugs on Chris and turned up a crack pipe. He had a pebble of rock in another pocket. Now everything fell into place. I felt bad about Chris and his obvious crack cocaine affinity. I told him who I was and asked if the memory reached the surface. I could read the shame pass across his face when my story dawned on him. His brother even remarked, "This is the cop?"

"Yeah," was the response as Chris hung his head, seemingly embarrassed. He'd lost his job at the hotel for, in his words, fucking around. I shook my head and looked up at him in pity. I asked him how he'd reached this point in his life. He shrugged and studied a blade of grass on the ground.

"For God's sake, man, you were an engineer." He looked like he was pouting, probably not happy his brother was part of this melodrama. I felt sorry for the guy. Crack addicts rarely switch on my pity mode. The pipe and crack in his pocket told me he was a frequent user, and this wasn't something new to him. I wanted to let him off on the joint. Just keep it and impound it later as found dope. But the crack raised the bar and forced my hand. The pipe was a lowly misdemeanor, but Chris had to be held accountable for the crack. I personally felt his best option was to make it through the system and wind up in drug court. With his work background, he might still have a chance at redemption. His brother, maybe not so much. Manny and I booked Chris into jail.

I saw Chris walk the same blocks months later, a tower among men. He hadn't cleaned up. These were the wrong streets to mope around on if he wanted to stay clean. If you were a crack addict and the Crips in the neighborhood could make a dime off you, rehab seemed like an impossible, if not unwanted goal.

CHAPTER 66:

OUR GIANT

In the beginning, WECAN fielded a few team members in the Mission and Pacific Beach areas. For WECAN purposes we were known as the Coastal Team. The Unit's goal was the same as the other teams to battle gang and narcotics crimes. Those two beaches were certainly drug-infested, but didn't feature a gang force, at least not in the daytime. The beaches and surrounding parks were attractive to gangs for the nighttime. That's when they coagulated into groups and staked out their various territories and challenged any comers to confrontations. The peak times for gangsters to hang out and get in trouble were Friday and Saturday nights. Their centers of association were within sight of the Big Dipper roller coaster at the foot of Ventura in Belmont Park. They were also within sight of rival gangs. Sometimes, these un-friendlies were too close to each other for comfort.

There was the always the constant background noise of the beach locals causing trouble. The summers were most egregious. Long, hot days turned into warm, busy nights for conflicts. Drugs, booze and fights often found their origins with local white males from their teens to their early thirties. They launched from low-rent beach apartments or prowled the boardwalk for buyers. Both Coastal WECAN and Northern Division's Beach Team had their hands full. Coastal WECAN spent much of their given shift attacking the problem where it was most aggressive day or night, the Boardwalk.

The Boardwalk was the familiar name given for the three-and-a-half-mile long stretch of concrete running north and south from South Mission Beach to northern Pacific Beach. It was an attraction I knew very well from my skateboard days. Boardwalks did exist nationwide when the Mission Beach Boardwalk was built during World War I, constructed with wood planks set parallel to each other on wooden framework for hundreds of yards. Concrete became more practical and replaced the rotted wood. But the newer iteration of the boardwalk was the place to see and be seen.

Want to meet girls? Sun-softened hair, tanned skin and a skateboard were your magnets. A low beach wall bordered the concrete pedestrian walkway and separated sand from pavement. The concrete boardwalk barrier ranged from six feet in width to as much as twelve feet. The crowds were thickest around the roller coaster and the shops built around the decade's old, wooden fun ride.

The Coastal Team members routinely took up points along the boardwalk to spot the problem people they wanted removed from sight. The bad guys made it easy on the cops by congregating at places along the boardwalk that had been gathering sites for the dirtbags and troublemakers for generations. One of those magnet locations was in front of a beach bar called Lahaina's.

Lahaina's was plopped down in a sandbox with a large, raised outdoor deck suitable for hours of tanning and cocktailing. The officers parked their vehicles on the sand or behind the bar and then watched humanity go by. When one of those humans gave off the symptoms associated with being high on other than booze, off to jail, he or she went.

WECAN Officer Tim Fay's teammates used a code system over a closed channel to talk to each other. If one officer saw somebody under the influence, the code was transmitted, and that derelict got pinched. Coastal was granted a prisoner van out of the WECAN budget. The van was parked close to wherever the pickings were heaviest. Lahaina's was in one of those zones the Coastal officers covered. They worked diligently to fill the van up before each day was done.

The Coastal Team was proficient, to say the least. They boasted a ninety-seven percent success rate for positive drug tests for those arrested for drugs. Those statistics didn't just mean they found a guy with dope in his system. The percentage meant they reached the threshold for prosecution ninety-seven out of one hundred times.

Tim was with the WECAN group that morphed into SED. He and I had some time to shoot the breeze one afternoon while my buddy Roger was getting a booking approved at HQ. Yet another gangster was nabbed on PCP. I kept the necessary eye on him in the back of our cage car. So far, he'd been sedate, even though he growled occasionally and had eyes that wouldn't blink. Tim's partner Cinda was likewise tied up with a Vietnamese gang member they picked up for a warrant near Menlo Street in Eastern's area. Neither of us had much to do, but chat.

Time grew a little maudlin and reminisced about the earlier WECAN days. He recalled an incident that took place at 700 Ventura Place, the road that dead-ended near the main lifeguard station and the most popular place to be seen by everybody on the beach. The short street is spotlighted by world famous Hamel's Beach Shop and a row of eateries on the north side of the street. The ancient Big Dipper roller coaster parking lot was across the street. The beach front dead-end street was always crowded with tourists, teens, beach bums, rowdies, and surfers. I think it was one of the best people-watching locations in San Diego. WECAN saw the parcel as the target-rich environment they could sink their teeth into.

Tim looked back in time and told me about the day his height, something he never exploited in conversation, became a real advantage. He and his fellow officers walked the sandy area of the beach off Ventura one afternoon when one of the Northern Division patrol units requested cover near Tim's location. The crowds were so thick Tim couldn't see the female officer who sent the call from a few dozen yards away. Several of the team members walked over to that officer's location from the beach side of the boardwalk. Tim saw a van decaled with San Diego County signs on the doors. The distressed officer was in the middle of a group of a dozen juveniles and one male adult. One of the juveniles stood on the sea wall and screamed, "Take the cop's gun and shoot her!"

He seemed to shout the threat for the benefit of the other kids as he waved his arms around wildly and gestured towards the officer. The loudmouth was attracting a crowd that included the types of beach people who turned into assholes with the slightest provocation. Tim had no idea what the female officer had gotten into, but the threatening teenager on the sea wall certainly made his intentions known.

Running through the soft sand is tough. Tim fought against the sand's resistance to reach the stranded officer. When Tim strained to reach the wall, he decided to take out the punk kid first. He braced one foot against the wall and propelled himself upward to get a good grip on the little shit. It was an athletic move that elevated his frame to a level the average man couldn't reach without stilts. With the back of the kid's shirt in his grip, he pulled the punk backwards and let him fall into the sand. That ought to knock some wind out of him, Tim planned. The teen twisted in the air and ended up face down in the sand.

The teen sputtered to clear out a mouthful of beach sand. He offered no resistance when Tim and fellow WECAN officer Brad Willis landed on him and cuffed his hands. The gathered crowd stood back. Nobody wanted to be the giant's next victim. The loudmouth had no idea what had happened to him. The two officers dropped him so fast all he saw was the sky and a huge body, before he was splayed out on the beach. A pair of huge black boots stood inches from his nose. None of his companions saw the grab either. One moment he hopped around on the wall playing it to the bone. The next minute he was a ghost.

Tim paraded the prisoner off the sand and onto the boardwalk. The female patrol officer was in an argument with the van's driver. The hostile crowd surrounding the officer turned as one in amazement to see their buddy in the hands of a giant cop walking decisively towards them. Tim took charge of the conversation. He glued his eyes on the van's driver and ordered him to either correct the attitudes of the other juveniles or see them arrested for interference with a police officer. The group of mostly young men lost its bravado when they saw the lone man in hooked up in handcuffs for the charge of 69 PC: Inciting or threatening to incite a riot. The female officer now had control and took over from there. The punk hit the pit.

Tim and the other officers learned later that the county van was some sort of community action transport for troubled youth. The program was called the Diversity Unit and was from Southeast San Diego. The group was supposed to be at the beach to perform civic duties by picking up trash. This was an attempt by a community outreach program to rehab troubled youth and interject a little wholesomeness into their lives. Before they even got started, the plans went off the rails. Some Brainiac within the group felt their presence would be better represented if they drove the van down the boardwalk in full view of walkers, runners, skaters, and bicyclists. They snickered between each other that this was the best way to ogle girls in bikinis.

No vehicles were allowed on the boardwalk. The idiots' van took up most of the width of the concrete pathway and forced people to clear out of the way or get crushed. The driver managed to rumble down the boardwalk for hundreds of yards without drawing any attention from law enforcement. Their leisurely cruise endangered dozens of people who didn't understand that the van was on the sidewalk illegally, or that it was filled with fools from Southeast just farting around. WECAN opted to leave the outcome in the capable hands of the patrol officer to decide the van's fate.

If WECAN hadn't been close, the kid on the seawall who agitated for a fight might have gotten his way. Things used to flare up real fast at the foot of Ventura. History records large groups formed into near-riotous mobs on several occasions. A cop in the middle of one of those melees was in serious danger.

The Coastal WECAN team's arrest accomplishments succeeded in putting them out of a job. Tim and the other assertive officers made a lot of beach contacts which infuriated some locals not used to aggressive police tactics. Because they were in Northern Division, that command began to collect countless complaints. All the grievances were directed to the Northern Beach Team sergeants because no one at the beach had heard of WECAN, and they dressed like beach cops. The WECAN exploits were kicked up to the Northern captain who pitched a bitch about the interloper officers.

The captain demanded that the Coastal Team be excommunicated from his division. WECAN bosses decided to comply and dropped the former sand fleas into Eastern Division where their talents were better suited, and the officers there could use a hand. Eastern got its own giant in the bargain. SED would see Tim get promoted to detective shortly after Tim closed the boardwalk story with a. "Gotta go, Bud. Cinda's ready to take our guy to jail and I need to use the head."

I watched Tim stretch vertically to a height that forced him to duck whenever he went through doorways.

CHAPTER 67:
SED AND OPERATION: RAGS

SED was focused on gang enforcement more than general narcotics arrests. The center of our attention was the crack epidemic and the African-American gangs that controlled the drug's sales. The City of San Diego implemented full attacks on those gangs through highly specialized units, with SED as a small, well-trained police force already in operation within the communities inundated with Crips and Bloods. We SED officers knew the players and had-so for years. When Operations Blue Rag and Red Rag kicked off, we were the highly mobile arrest teams.

Sgt. Ross led the SDPD task force hitched up to a litany of State and Federal law enforcement agencies instructed to use their resources to hurt the gangs. The first act, Operation Blue Rag, was a nine-month operation federally funded through the Urban Street Gang Drug Trafficking Enforcement Demonstration Project. The Task Force consisted of federal, state, and local law enforcers teamed together for San Diego. The Task Force utilized expertise and a crucial informant to document Crip crimes, identify the players and give federal and state prosecutors enough evidence to issue arrest warrants. SED assisted dozens of lawmen at the terminus of the operation when it was time to "hook 'em and book 'em."

SED teamed with a couple of SWAT officers and a gang detective for a hit on a place on Imperial Avenue. The wanted bad guy lived with his family in a downstairs apartment. Everything went down like clockwork. SWAT hit the fragile front door and stepped back for WECAN's entry. Four of us hustled in shouting, "Down!" repeatedly with our weapons in hand. When a cop screams that simple word, everyone we face is expected to hit the ground. Adults and children alike are petrified. The unfortunate innocents are caught up in the wrongs of their parents and everybody screams in fear. The presence of children sickened me. How could the parents profess love and allow their kids to be inserted into the middle of their chaotic lives?

Eight officers in raid gear stormed into the house while others guarded the perimeter against escapees. Armed cops rushed through the house and pointed their weapons at all the potential threats until quickly deciding if the person with his or her hands up was a hazard. These decisions were made in seconds.

I'd seen children of all ages stuck in the middle of way too many police raids. The kids panicked and screamed and cried. The officers only had enough time to go from room to room and sweep for the potentially armed occupants. They weaved through the children who were frozen in place. If there was any family consolation, the raids were often planned for the early morning hours to catch the residents in the target houses in bed and asleep. If the police were lucky, the kids were still tucked in bed and the raid occurred when so they had little time for their infant minds to process what had happened. I was amazed at the number of gang homes with children forced to live with the everyday dangers of the gangster life and all its facets of jeopardy.

I remember one home we'd stormed. Nobody responded to the initial announcement from the officer that shouted that we had a warrant and demanded entry. Maybe it was because the time was six o'clock in the morning and the occupants were still zonked out. One officer smashed the door in with the steel "door knocker" and a line of us rushed in with weapons pointed ahead. There were only two bedrooms. One held two small children in separate beds. The second bedroom was ground zero for the wanted man, Damone. He had a rap for armed robbery, a few battery charges, and the ubiquitous dope charges.

Damone was sluggish with crusty sleep in the corners of his eyes. He got a head full of "Police!" "Police!" shouted at both him and his female bedmate. Damone didn't bother to do more than slowly pull his hands out from underneath the blankets. Slowly, the woman, his girlfriend, also came to life and pulled her blankets aside so we could see the infant pressed in between the couple.

Damone the Crip was on parole and knew the score. The kids were an unexpected blow. None of us wanted to be the boogeymen the kids would have nightmares about for ages to come. I had the woman and baby leave the room to help settle down the other children. Damone and I were alone with just one other officer standing guard in the doorway. I wanted to shame him over the presence of his kids in his criminal and violent life. "Damone, how do you live with this, your children I mean?"

"I loves my kids, man. Where else am I gonna put 'em?"

"Look what they have to witness. Why would you live like this? I see that your girlfriend is pregnant. Doesn't she have a say in this?"

"My wife loves our kids. You po-lice come into our house and frighten my kids. This is my life and my kids!"

"And you're going to bring another child into your hell. Look at the way you live, man. This is a shitty apartment. You hardly have any furniture and the place isn't even clean. Why bring another hungry baby into this world?" I felt anger boiling up inside me. There was no room for agreement between us.

"Man, you don't know nuthin'. The county gives me three hundred and thirty dollars a month for each of my kids. We gonna get over thirteen hundred dollars a month when Laquisha has her baby, man."

I shut up. He iced the cake when he detached himself from my concept of family. This, then, is a facet of the perpetuation of the gang problem.

Another Blue Rag soldier wanted by police in one raid lived in an apartment with other Crip or Crip-related denizens. Everybody hit the floor when we burst in except for the one dude we wanted. Crip OG Paulsen was stuck in his wheelchair. Paulsen was a highlight of the gang life. He was once a formidable killer with a fierce reputation for swift violence. A rival's shotgun blast removed a lot of Paulsens's intimidation and replaced it with a colostomy bag. He now faced a task force of howling commandos who forced his kids to the floor, and all he could do was sit there in his wheelchair and wait for the madness to end. He was still a Crip and a player in the crack world. He had to go.

The same scenario played out all over San Diego. Thirty-plus locations were hit by police with equal ferocity. No shots were fired, and no one was seriously hurt. We did frazzle a lot of nerves, though. Some of the gangsters chose to retaliate by whining about the "Fucking Po-leece always be messing with me!" The rest stoically acknowledged their templated roles as the bad guys and went along with the program.

There was one injury that I was aware of. The raids and searches continued into the early evening. SWAT was called in to make entry into a lower level apartment in the 6400 block of Imperial. SED took up positions behind SWAT to replace them after they got inside. SWAT was involved because the informant that led us to this man Lawrence swore he'd seen guns in the place on one visit two weeks prior. Swat decided some shock and awe in the form of "flash-bangs" would soften up the occupants just before the door was smashed and SAT swarmed in. I was part of the SED arrest team and waited for the lights and noise to kick-off.

A flash-bang, or stun grenade, produces both a blinding light and a frightful burst of sound. Together, the person targeted loses his visual ability to aim a weapon, while the fury of the sound upon detonation renders the victim temporarily deaf. The goal of the explosive is to take the fight out of the recipient.

SWAT tossed a couple of flash-bangs through the front and rear windows. They timed their entry with the explosions and then smashed their way in through the only door. Immediately, I heard people screaming and SWAT on the radio calling for paramedics. Holy Cow! What went wrong?

SED entered behind SWAT when all the weapons were shouldered or holstered. I went in with three other teammates to see the most horrific, blood-curdling sight. There was blood everywhere. Lawrence and four other people were covered in blood and frightened to death. One woman hyperventilated from the terror of the moment. I couldn't tell who to triage first among all the carnage. One of my partners tried to discern what a SWAT supervisor was saying over the din of screams and tears. "The flash-bang through the rear window landed in a bowl of spaghetti," he calmly explained. "None of that, well, almost none of that is blood."

"Is somebody injured?"

"Well, yeah. That woman on the floor holding her head got spiked by a grenade fragment. A piece of metal hit her in the head, and she got a cut. We called the ambulance for her. Everybody else in this place got covered with sauce when the grenade blew pasta every which-way. I already put out Code Four except for the ambulance." That was it. The bloody caper turned out to be a ruined meal.

The Blue Rag operation included help from the District Attorney's Office, the state Justice Department's Bureau of Narcotics Enforcement, the Federal Bureau of Alcohol, Tobacco and Firearms, the U.S. Attorney General's Office, and San Diego County Probation Department.

The first day of warrant service led to a raucous morning with a rainbow coalition of cops and investigators hitting homes, apartments, businesses and even schools, all in search of targeted gangsters. Seventy-seven violent, or potentially violent, gang members were taken off the streets when the last guy was found. Some did real prison time. Some did six months or less, others walked free. From SDPD's point of view, we made a statement that we controlled the behavior and freedom of these gang members, not the other way around. The press and the good guys were welcomed by many as taking the kind of offensive action the public wished to see.

Blue Rag led to Operation Red Rag, targeting the Pirus, also known as the Bloods, and nailed ninety-six documented gangbangers. This time, prosecutors wanted audio, along with videotaped locations where both Bloods and Crips were observed selling drugs to a confidential informant. The CI's resilience, savvy and cleverness kept him alive where others might have been uncovered and killed.

I had a bad guy under arrest one night when Central SED was deep in Eastern's turf to apply some more pressure to the gangs in one particularly heinous neighborhood. My partner and I stopped him in a car with no plates. The car wasn't stolen, but it wasn't currently registered either. "Scott," as he called himself had no identification. I knew the name he gave me was a lie but there was no way to refute Scott as his name, yet.

The types of tats he had were inked with hints at a gang affiliation. There just wasn't enough information with those tattoos tied to any criminal computer system. The ink didn't even hint at a specific gang set. I had to take him downtown for the misdemeanor driving without a license anyway, so I would figure out who he was down at the police station.

I tried once again to pressure some truth from the guy once I parked in the sally port for prisoners. No dice. He just smiled at me with that kind of smirk a bad guy wears when he relishes a cop's frustration. I floated the idea of checking to see if Detective Dean was working that night. Dean had helped me out in the past with biker gang identification and interviews, as well as with other hard-core thugs. I checked with the Watch Commander and learned that Police Communications showed Dean in the field. I had Radio Dispatch call around the city for Dean. My prisoner was within earshot while I awaited a response from Dean. I watched my guy's face for any reaction. Some of the crooks in town were wary of Mike Dean. He put a lot of hoodlums in jail over the expanse of his career. He remembered them all. This cat, Scott, played it cool and probably gambled he'd get out of this soon enough. Dean answered up on the air. I had him switch to a tactical radio frequency and told him what I needed.

Dean rolled on into the sally port and parked his undercover car within fifteen minutes of my inquiry. My prisoner wasn't looking that direction. I flagged Dean over and he approached the driver's side of my car. From the prisoner cage in my car, Scott could only see Mike Dean from the chest down. I opened the door for Mike so he could crouch down and peer in. I watched my guy turn toward the open door with a neutral expression. As soon as the two men were face-to-face, my prisoner's expression began to sink at the eyes and mouth. Dean greeted him with his true name and the man's chin sagged to his chest. Out-done by Dean. Outstanding! So was the felony warrant for narcotics the guy had been hiding from.

A second confidential informant agreed to work for our department in the ongoing Operation Red Rag. This venture was intended for equal opportunity criminal enforcement. "As goest the Crips, so goest the Bloods," was the phrase we used. His was a courageous undertaking and took him back into in the most dangerous turf in San Diego. He was more than ready to deal crippling blows to the bangers he used to run with.

For Operation Red Rag, community parks were often selected as the traps. The tactic was to film and record the drug deals the CI made as the buyer, locked down any concerns about defense attorney arguments. The villains would simply lose in court.

Public parks are wide open spaces that can be observed from cover. With buildings in an urban area, there are too many corners to run around and hide, or attack from, and too many places to hide. The detectives chose community parks for several of their "buy, walk," or buy the dope now and get arrested later, actions. The spotters could watch the affairs from any angle. The detectives had specific Bloods in mind with the goal of nailing the most violent in the drug. The law enforcers running the Red Rag operation had cameras and microphones at the ready as their CI made drug deals. Those eventual arrests would be made with the teams I was a part of.

The two initial Rag Operations were touted by local law enforcement with great fanfare. An oversight was pointed out, however. While the black gangs were hit hard, the equally violent and deadly *Latino* gangs were untouched. That was rectified with another months-long task force working the *Latino* gangs in San Diego. "Operation Bandana," was born with the consideration that San Diego Law Enforcement was an equal opportunity gangster jailer. Six local, state, and federal agencies, along with SED, were set for the sweeps that would take most of the wanted people off the streets at once.

Operation Bandana was run much like the first two outings. Controlled buys, video and audio recordings, informants and multiple agencies were all mixed into a soup together. For my part, I had already returned to Patrol at Western when my command was asked to attach me to the task force for couple of days. My job was to begin as a member of one of the arrest teams and traverse the city with a list of arrest warrants to be served. One of those warrants brought us to the suburbs of Clairemont above Mission Bay. My assigned team aimed for Clairemont High School to snatch one kid out of his class.

This arrest felt contrary to me. I knew he was a gang member. I knew he sold dope, but it didn't equate to this studious kid with a high grade point average. We did find his class and took him out with the least amount of disruption and drama. I thought this boy's misguided life was a waste. He was trying to live in two worlds. The banger choice would likely ruin him, while the scholastic choice laid the groundwork for a better future.

All three Operations scored quantities of the usual drugs that users seek in the lower-income, ethnic neighborhoods, heroin, marijuana, crack cocaine, powdered cocaine, methamphetamine, and PCP. There were ninety arrests for this operation. Between the three Operations almost two hundred and fifty bonafide criminal gang-types were put out of commission for a while.

My chores on Operation Bandana were split between morning arrests and afternoon paperwork. Roger Barrett was another ex-pat SED guy temporarily brought back from the minors to work in the task force. Neither of us was prepared to spend most of the day doing other people's paperwork after we completed ours. But that's what we were told to do. The SED Command had finally succeeded in replacing us with more SWAT guys. Contrary to the Unit boss's dreams, SED needed a few of the old WECAN officers back in the fold to figure things out. How about that? I was irreplaceable.

The command post for Operation Bandana was a meeting and dance hall in a serene portion of Balboa Park near the Aerospace museum, a city gymnasium, a car museum, and various venues for social activities. This was a rather strange setting to process some of San Diego's worst people. The building we occupied was large enough to contain several hundred law enforcers and their prey but was also the stage for weekly square dancers. What a paradox.

I'm sure Roger would agree that we'd have been better off not attached to this arrangement since it was mostly to process paperwork. We did enough of that in patrol. Doing it here was not what we signed on for. We were now temporarily teamed up with the guys that replaced us on

SED. Many of those guys were SWAT cops who I thought were not suited for SED's design. They certainly didn't want the paperwork which was probably the genesis for the scribing grind I now found myself in. I was losing my good mood.

For one reason or another, I needed to cross through the mass of good guys and bad guys to deliver some reports to some guy at the other end of the big room. On the return walk I passed by a table full of SWAT officers doing more lounging than writing. One of them, Frank, had a little history with me. Frank was one of the F Troop rookies some of us used to mess with. Now that he was SWAT, his penis had apparently grown longer. Frank saw me and decided to put the veteran in his place when he told me to get him a bottle of correction fluid for him. Demonstrably, I stopped, with a neutral expression and channeled the legendary and snide SDPD veteran RD Brown. "SURE FRANK," I said to all two hundred people in the room with my loud voice spewing volume like a foghorn. I turned to the general audience and shouted, *"Frank needs Wite-Out! Does anyone have a bottle of Wite-Out for Frank!?"*

From somewhere, somebody tossed a bottle to Frank who almost missed it while he tried to stare me down. Good luck with that, pal. I had F Troop blood in my veins and three years of WECAN/SED in my soul. He'd have better luck holding a red flag up to an angry bull.

When WECAN first hit the beach back when there were only twelve officers, RD Brown was a dominant character at Western Division. He was an investigator and still maintained his sharp, sarcastic timing. He loved to rag on people just to get reactions, but he rarely meant harm. Few of us really wanted to be selected out for special "acid bath" treatment. If you were unlucky enough to be in his line of sight and he was hungry for a little mordant heckling, you were on your own.

Roger Barrett and Bill Woods were fledgling WECAN beach cops for Western and were directed to wear beach cop attire. That uniform was comprised of Class B khakis with knee-length shorts and white tennis shoes. Patrol officers wore the standard poly-blend pants material that would literally melt if too close to a lit flare. Beach cops could change-out the shorts for loose-fitting bloused pants for the colder months. Neither officer wanted the bloused pants and preferred the exotic feeling of shorts when every patrol cop was stuck in slacks. Neither Woods nor Barrett was tanned for the job.

Nobody outside of the unit was certain of its function in the beginning. Woody and Roger worked Ocean Beach, which seemed a lot like working the OB Beach Team. They even wore the same khaki shorts and bright white Reeboks matching the OB Beach Team. Of course, Woody and Roger needed to catch more sun and re-color their skins with deeper tans, so they didn't glow on the beach with white legs. The two beach officers looked fit and relaxed in their specialized uniforms.

One day the two partners happened to be in the hallways at Western when they came face-to-face with RD Brown. RD sort of stopped them by blocking their path and stood silently looking the two officers over. He was unavoidable and there was no way to go around him gracefully. His face was neutral as his eyes looked down, then looked up, and then looked down again. No one spoke. He looked straight ahead at the guys not saying a word. He slowly looked down, again, and back up for the final time. He studied their white Reeboks, light tan beach uniforms and their lily-white skin. There was a dramatic pause. Both Woody and Roger knew he was setting them up for a wise crack, but there was no way out of it when you're in RD Brown's sights. Leave it to RD to drop a zinger worthy of the best, "What are you guys, nurses, or something?"

The comment was so non sequitur that the two trapped cops couldn't help but burst into embarrassed laughter. RD's dry, acerbic wit was always timed perfectly. His comedy was not reserved for just his friends, everyone was a grateful target. To be gaffed by the Big Man himself meant you were one of his people. If you weren't, you already knew it.

I wonder what WECAN would have been like with a squad of RD Browns. I know the SED lieutenant's head would have exploded.

CHAPTER 68:

ENDING

Doug Collier was one of the last officers on SED before it folded. Combined, the entities known as WECAN and SED lasted about four years. Doug recalls that the unexpected end came when SED's lieutenant came to line-up to announce that SED was being disbanded. They all wanted an explanation. The LT's quizzical answer amounted to, "You folks worked yourselves out of a job."

The statistics were studied by the department's upper echelon and it was decided that violent gang crimes had lessened SED's need to be apart from Patrol. Divisions all over the city needed patrol officers, SED had the redundant manpower, so the troops were tasked with going that way.

The city and the SDPD had a good thing with WECAN/SED. There were lots of uniformed cops tasked with the destabilization the city's gang structures. We put some fear into their criminal lives. The public had reassurance that their general concerns were addressed in the toughest neighborhoods. But at the end of the four-year run, the whole scheme was gone. Manpower had to be shuffled so Patrol could handle a general increase in radio calls for help. The department "robbed Peter to pay Paul" and SED was no more. Soon enough, gang crime went back up in the statistics, as predicted by the former SED members. Homicides were up and beat the annual record that existed before WECAN/SED's weighted presence really took effect. Someone within the department did the math. Before WECAN/SED there were plenty of homicides. During WECAN/SED, homicides reduced. Ergo, WECAN/SED's gang enforcement approach reduced homicides.

The police department had no choice, but to find a novel approach to attack the epidemic of gang violence, but with restricted manpower. Times were tough for SDPD and the department was policing a city with fewer officers than necessary. Staffing was down by too many percentage points. Radio calls were going unanswered or Patrol's response times were stretched beyond the public's tolerance. The gangs felt free to test their wings and return to business as it was before the lean years of WECAN/SED.

The new variant on WECAN's gang sweeps, "Directed Runs," abbreviated as D-Runs, was concocted to attack selected problems. The process required specific supervisors to identify areas where surging problems led to rampant crime. At pre-arranged times, several two-man units from one area made D-Runs to other areas to bolster the patrol forces already in the area. The theory was that the visibility of a larger number of police officers in marked cars would suppress the problem-makers. D-Runs typically lasted about twenty minutes.

Police officers not supportive of D-Runs pointed out they lessened staffing in response to higher volumes of radio calls for service. D-Runs elsewhere stretched the force too thin within the areas vacated for D-Runs. The efforts to beat back sudden flare-ups of crime without any real consequences were a waste of time. One division formed their own special tactics operatives with STOP, Selective Tactics in Policing. When they endured the same constant realities, not enough patrol officers for STOP, STOP stopped.

The city was faced with the same problem WECAN was constructed to end. Homicides were up, gang violence was up, narcotics-related crime was up, and cross-border criminality from the Mexican side was on the increase. The city needed a solution to at least target the gangs. The answer for the future of gang enforcement lay in the past. The formation of a "flying squad" of uniformed police officers tightly bound to the street gang world took over. They would be assigned to work the gang-infested neighborhoods and operate in almost the same manner as SED and WECAN before. The birthing of the Gang Suppression Unit will be somebody else's story to tell.

Overall, the years I spent on both WECAN and SED were the most rewarding of my career. I loved the tasks. I loved the fellow team members, at least the ones who were savvy enough to belong in the unit. Not everybody was a fit. Even the long work hours punctuated by the toilsome time in court while off-duty was rewarding.

The adrenaline flow with WECAN/SED was measured. We controlled the streets; they didn't control us. We worked without radio calls, which is where the real stress comes from. I could spot the danger from a gangster quicker than an irate husband or wife likely to turn on me at a domestic violence call. I got great satisfaction out of arresting bad people. I was good as a hunter of bad men and that's all I ever wanted to do on the Job.

I knew I had reached the burnout stage with SED during my phase with my last partner, Dan Blake. Dan was the most laidback SWAT guy a non-SWAT guy could ask to be partnered with. We performed our duties and chased bad guys around as directed. Dan was with me the night SED filtered through Mission Beach looking for gang colors. A bunch of partying Logan members were in a parking lot a block inland from the shore. They'd started the summer with bayside turf they claimed as theirs for the weekends. The guests of the Bahia Hotel across the parking lot entrance and the evening fishermen that trolled the calm bay waters had to put up with mad-dog stares and the aggressive behavior that came with the gangs. Booze was banned in every beach and bay parking lot, but the gangs feared no repercussions. The beach cops of Northern Division were so understaffed they couldn't manage the additional antagonist squatters spoiling for trouble every weekend.

The Mission Beach topography was a fingerling of sand bisected with one main drag. Homes, businesses, and apartments lined the isthmus on either side of the street. The ocean lapped the western edges of the land-strip, while the bay rested comfortably against the sandy edges of the eastern shore.

Dan and I rolled up and confronted the ones with the beers in the restricted parking lot near the Bahia Hotel. I knew one of the turds was from Memorial Rec Center area, a guy named Ayala. He was one of the ones always around the PCP sellers, one of the bangers I hadn't yet caught on the wrong side of the law. He and his cronies were clustered around two vehicles with a couple of twelve-packs of Budweiser in cans. Dan and I were accompanied by another SED vehicle. We rolled up on the group.

Ayala gave me lip when I told him to toss his beer away. That was enough for me. I hit him in the face with my fist and knocked him down. Not only was he shocked, so was I. I was normally not a hitter. I lost my temper at that moment. Ayala plopped onto his ass and stared at me with a stunned look that broadcasted, "What the hell just happened?"

His homies were equally baffled. What happened? Cops never slugged them. Two of the men balled up their fists, but there were four of us. My *compadres* cordoned off the other five gangsters. The rules had swiftly changed. They were uncertain about what to do next. One complained that it was police brutality, but he never made a formal complaint about that. That wasn't gangster-style.

I picked Ayala up and arrested him for getting in my face. I surprised myself and not in a good way. He'd have to go to jail to cover my ass. I'd write a report with no heart in it for the arrest, to cover my impulsive reaction to a thug's words, something I'd walked off so many times before.

The day finally came when I knew I was doomed if I didn't get a change of pace. Danny and I were bored. We finished dinner at Furr's Cafeteria, another defiant supporter of police officers with discounted meals. Mid-evening was upon us and I was our driver. We wanted something else to do besides futzing around with gang members who would slither into the shadows when they saw a looming SED car on the horizon.

We discussed plans for the night in the Furr's parking lot not far from San Diego State University. The beach was currently a hot bed of gangsters who gathered in large, segregated groups, and our Command suggested we move a couple of units down there on Friday and Saturday nights. Despite the dust-up with Ayala, I was still in the company of gang cops and the gangs that flew their flags at the beach. Besides the Bahia lot, the gangs collected in the roller coaster parking lot, the most desirable place to be seen at the beach. There was a nightclub at one end of the lot that had THE reputation as the trendy place to hang out. The gangs wouldn't be allowed inside the Red Onion. The dress code and cover charge were in place to keep those clowns out. But there was no deterrent to multiple opposing gangsters loitering around parked cars. The stink-eye looks they gave each other could erupt into violence. Weak security paid for by the property owners couldn't stop an inferno from kicking off.

"Before we head down to Mission, let's cruise SDSU and look at chicks," I suggested. I held the notion that SED was at low ebb of function. Too many WECAN vets were gone and the SNACK Team, Collier's goofy tag for SWAT's eating capacity, lacked interest to pursue the gang problem with the same interest WECAN/SED officers tried to continue to self-impose. The lack of drive, the loss of the motivation we once had as a team, was infectious. Too many of us chose to drive aimlessly, instead of mapping out ventures to corral the target gangs as we once had. Our zones no longer had borders. The Teams found their worlds expanded beyond the boundaries that were ours. We had an entire city to probe for gang issues and a coalition of forces that lacked cohesion. We were just there to roam at will and look for something to do.

"Why not? Nobody gives a shit what we do anymore. After that, we can do some more cruisin' down at the Red Onion," Danny added. Danny always liked to stylize the vernacular "cruising" as though he had a Mexican accent. The plans seemed reasonable enough, and hey, we deserved a break. SED had no plans for its cops anymore.

The short drive to the SDSU campus was spiked with pedestrian traffic on a Friday night. Dan rested an arm through the open passenger window while I drove with my left arm propped on the door's armrest. SDSU is a spread-out campus, with between little and no gang issues. Oh, the gangs did menace students. There are occasional muggings and harassed coeds, but there was no reason for us to be there.

We rode around the dorm housing and took in the sights of the student life. I never ventured beyond junior college, by choice. I maintained an 'A' average through junior high school, high school and into college, but I wanted to work. Money was always tight for my family. So much of my money came from my labor which began at the age of thirteen. I never got to experience university life, fraternities, professors, or beer bongs. I just worked.

I took a left turn behind a student gaming parlor, near 70th Street and across from the main campus. The parking lot was empty behind several college-age pizza joints. I drove through a parking lot completely devoid of cars and listened to Dan tell a story when, for reasons I still don't know, I drove us right into a light pole. Maybe I'd nodded off. Maybe I had my head up my ass. Whatever. We had to call our sergeant to come take a report and start the On-Duty Traffic Incident paperwork. Dan asked me what happened. I sincerely did not know. I just zoned-out and hit a light pole for no God-damned good reason. I knew it was growing close to the day I'd have to go. My lieutenant surely knew it.

Only months prior, Lieutenant Welter had been keyed over on the police radio. "Keyed over" meant that other cops deliberately blocked his transmissions by simultaneously keying their microphones. And this was not the first time. Team discipline had broken down and the troops who disliked the LT reduced their behavior to pranks and vitriol. Someone on Central's frequency keyed over him with greater frequency than the rest of us. He assumed the culprit, or culprits, worked under him. That meant my team. I don't know why he picked me out as the perpetrator, but he was wrong. He called me into his office and warned me of the consequences of my actions. I sat and listened while a wailing sound pounded in my brain. Finally, he leaned over his desk with both hands steepled on the desktop and accused me of abusive radio use. I lost it and raised my voice, "Don't accuse me of doing something I didn't do," which was true. "Even if I did know I wouldn't tell you." That was a half-truth.

I knew who did it. At least, I knew of some of the people who keyed him. There were others who expressed their extraordinary displeasure with this boss. That was the last straw. My sanity and career were in jeopardy. He was a consummate politician and sat back into his chair. The calm attitude he'd regained told me I'd get chopped to pieces if I stayed and he'd do it from a distance. I made the decision to put in for a transfer before he forced one on me.

I put in for any other command, but Western Division, when comments from Sgt. Edwards made it clear the LT wanted me out of the teams. I told my sergeant I was aware my time there was done. I had only one low-cost request. Don't send me back to F Troop. A week later, my sergeant informed me I was indeed headed back to patrol and back to the career dead-end known as F troop. The LT didn't like me and told me in his unique way with a transfer back to promotion hell.

Roger Barrett was in the same boat. He got his travel papers the same day I did. He wanted to go anywhere but Northern Division. I wanted to go to Northern. I lived close to that facility. Roger lived too far away to make the twice-a-day drive comfortable. Instead of me, it was Roger they sent to Northern. Neither of us got what we wanted. Both of us found ways to be happy at our drop-off points within the first year.

EPILOGUE

I wrote this book for the public. I figured they'd get a thrill from my stories and learn something about the police culture. Some of the tales have angered early reviewers, or made them laugh. Some saw and appreciated a theme of constant irony while they contemplated my more thoughtful memories. I gave San Diego center stage because I lived the life there. I want to thank all the people who contributed to this book. I toiled for months to dredge up stories I'd repressed or forgotten. I estimate I've forgotten or can't reach about ninety-seven percent of the memories of my cop life.

WECAN was the highlight of my career. I had more fun, more suspense and more adventure in three years than the other seventeen combined. I melded into the team concept like the men and women on the teams were my extended family of brothers and sisters. That level of camaraderie among so many was impossible to achieve in any other aspect of my career. Thirty-six men and women in uniform are nearly impossible to hone into a family in police work as tight knit as WECAN became. I'd join the ranks of a WECAN or an SED in any department in any city if I could turn back time.

San Diego had a Gang Suppression Unit at the time I wrote this segment. That unit suffered a painful loss when one of its members was gunned down by a hateful gang member. I never met Jonathan "JD" De Guzman. His GSU duties were my duties decades past. He stood with the thinnest of the thin blue line, posted at the wall to keep the hordes of street bastards at bay. I salute you.

About the Author

JAMIE NEWBOLD is the son of Retha and James Newbold, both passed away. As an only child, his parents indulged him and his whims. Jamie was an A student in high school and junior college where he chose to major in life sciences, specifically anthropology and paleontology. He left college after two and a half years to pursue carpentry. He loved working with his hands and trained to build everything from furniture to houses. A former roommate suggested he "cut your hair and get a real job," so he took a look at police work for yet another direction to his life. Jamie hired onto the San Diego Police Department in 1980 and found the anchor in his life he needed. He took a full medical retirement in 2000.

Jamie went into business for himself with ownership of a collectibles store, yet another reinvention of his life. He is the author of the *Forensic Comicologist,* a book about his business. Jamie is married to Kim Newbold, also SDPD retired. His son Michael is a campus police officer at Duke University. Mike blessed Jamie with a granddaughter, Elise.

Jamie and Kim live in San Diego, where it all started.

WWW.COPWORLDPRESS.COM

CPSIA information can be obtained
at www.ICGtesting.com
Printed in the USA
FSHW022156010820
72065FS